The Whiz Kids

The Whiz Kids

HOW THE 1950 PHILLIES TOOK THE PENNANT, LOST THE WORLD SERIES, AND CHANGED PHILADELPHIA BASEBALL FOREVER

DENNIS SNELLING

UNIVERSITY OF NEBRASKA PRESS

Lincoln

The University of Nebraska Press is part of a land-grant institution with campuses and programs on the past, present, and future homelands of the Pawnee, Ponca, Otoe-Missouria, Omaha, Dakota, Lakota, Kaw, Cheyenne, and Arapaho Peoples, as well as those of the relocated Ho-Chunk, Sac and Fox, and Iowa Peoples.

LIBRARY OF CONGRESS CATALOGING-IN-PUBLICATION DATA
Names: Snelling, Dennis, 1958– author.
Title: The whiz kids: how the 1950 Phillies took the pennant, lost the World Series, and changed Philadelphia baseball forever / Dennis Snelling.
Description: Lincoln: University of Nebraska Press, [2025] | Includes bibliographical references and index.
Identifiers: LCCN 2024034041
ISBN 9781496242686 (hardback)
ISBN 9781496243546 (epub)
ISBN 9781496243553 (pdf)
Subjects: LCSH: Philadelphia Phillies (Baseball team)—History—20th century. | New York Yankees (Baseball team)—History—20th century. | World Series (Baseball)—History—20th century. | Baseball—United States—History—20th century.
Classification: LCC gv875.p45 s64 2025 | DDC 796.357/640974811—dc23/eng/20240812
LC record available at https://lccn.loc.gov/2024034041

Designed and set in Guyot Text by Katrina Noble.

For my youngest grandchildren, Isla Diane Snelling,
Cora Mae Snelling, and Liam Dean Snelling.

May you pass a love of reading to your children and theirs.

CONTENTS

ILLUSTRATIONS

ACKNOWLEDGMENTS

BOOKS ARE NEVER written in a vacuum. Myriad people assist the process in myriad ways, and this project was no exception.

C. Paul Rogers read several chapters and offered corrections and suggestions, while also providing audio files of several players he had interviewed for the book he coauthored with Robin Roberts, *The Whiz Kids and the 1950 Pennant*. Every baseball historian should be grateful to those two for contacting and interviewing so many members of the "Whiz Kids."

Noted Philadelphia baseball writer Robert Warrington reviewed in detail the first chapter of the book and offered corrections, clarifications, and suggestions, while also providing a wonderful photo of Connie Mack and his sons on the day of a pivotal vote regarding the Athletics' eventual sale.

I am also indebted to the Society for American Baseball Research for its rich treasure trove of newspapers, especially *The Sporting News* and Black newspapers, provided through ProQuest. In addition, the SABR Oral History Project, which is continually growing, was an excellent source for several player interviews.

I want to say a special thanks to friends who have supported me over the years. As he has with all of my previous books, Jim Norby read the entire manuscript and gave valuable feedback. My great friend Frank Belcher was a constant source of encouragement as I advanced through this project. Dan Harris generously provided another author photo for me and somehow made me seem presentable.

Other friends and family who have read chapters in the past or provided encouragement impactful to me in ways they will never really understand include Gary Baker; Jim Beggs; Lark Downs; Rob Fitts; Jon Leonoudakis; Alan O'Connor; Pat O'Doul; Tom O'Doul; Rick Peterson; Mike Shannon; Burt Vasche; Marlene Vogelsang; Kris Walley; Ken White; my daughter Andrea; sons Tyler, Garrett, and Connor; sisters-in law Julianna Snelling and Melanie Snelling; and my grandchildren.

John Horne, rights and reproduction coordinator at the National Baseball Hall of Fame in Cooperstown, not only helped locate several photos in the library's collection but also shared anecdotes from an event he organized in 2010 around the Whiz Kids, featuring the family of Jim Konstanty and Konstanty's friend Andy Skinner.

Zachary Fisher was very helpful in tracking down a photo of Robin Roberts at Michigan State, connecting me with Randy Coole in securing licensing for the image.

Josue Hurtado was extremely helpful in navigating the Robert McDowell Photograph Collection at Temple University. Leslie Willis-Lowery was likewise helpful in securing rights to photos from the John W. Moseley Collection housed at the same institution.

Steve Gietschier was helpful in providing background on photographs published in *The Sporting News* and on the state of its archives. Mitchell Nathanson provided some sound advice regarding the marketing of this project.

Drew Cuthbertson of Gannett was helpful in tracking down the rights to a photo of Curt Simmons in Wilmington in 1947. Staff of the Lehigh Valley Historical Society and the Oneida County Historical Society were friendly and eager to help with my inquiries.

Jeff Warren, councilman for Whitehall Township in the Lehigh Valley region of Pennsylvania, provided background on the rededication of the ballpark in Egypt in honor of Curt Simmons and put me in touch with Joe Robinson, who generously provided a wonderful photo of Simmons for use in this book, which he had taken at that event.

Rob Taylor, Taylor Martin, Ryan Masteller, and Tish Fobben at University of Nebraska Press were always supportive and quick to answer my questions, put up with my pushback, and keep me on the straight and narrow. Special thanks goes to copyeditor Joseph Webb, who straightened out my syntax and cleaned up a few errors along the way.

Above all, I am grateful to my wife, Linda, without whose love and support I would not be completing another book.

The Whiz Kids

1

A Not Always Concise but Nonetheless Relatively Brief History of Philadelphia Baseball from Its Beginnings, with a Particular Emphasis on the Trials and Tribulations of the Philadelphia Phillies up to and through 1942

IT IS, OF COURSE, not unusual for baseball teams to gain lasting fame following a successful World Series. Noteworthy examples include the 1927 Yankees, the "Gashouse Gang" Cardinals of 1934, and the "Miracle Mets" of 1969. There are also teams remembered less fondly after a World Series loss—the 1919 "Black Sox" being the most infamous example. Then a select few—three really—that *lost* the World Series are remembered in a manner usually reserved for champions. Despite lacking a Series title, these teams are accorded a certain reverence, especially among their home fans—although most if not all of the players are gone, and that reverence is observed almost exclusively among those with hair that, if it exists, lacks any discernable hint of natural color.

The three World Series losers that bucked the trend include Bill Veeck's 1959 "Go-Go" Chicago White Sox, the 1967 "Impossible Dream" Boston Red Sox, and the subject of this book, the 1950 Philadelphia Phillies—most famously remembered as the "Whiz Kids." What was it that made the Whiz Kids memorable? And why did the Phillies fail to become a perennial contender? Many baseball experts were surprised in 1950 by the team's success and equally surprised by its subsequent lack of same. How are dynasties made—and opportunities for them lost?

Before we tackle the subject at hand, some history is necessary to provide context for the team's achievement and resulting fame. Appreciating the endurance of Phillies fans is key to understanding the impact that Robin Roberts, Jim Konstanty, Richie Ashburn, and the others had on the city of Philadelphia and why they earned a place among the city's sports legends. Although the history of Philadelphia baseball features long periods of failure and frustration, the game has some important and significant roots in the City of Brotherly Love.

The origin of baseball in Philadelphia—as in the rest of America—remains elusive and subject to endless study and debate. The game was referenced in Philadelphia newspapers as early as 1826, when an editorial aside in the *United States Gazette* derided an effort to form a gymnastic school in Boston.

"If a boy wants to play," wrote an unnamed editor, "let him play but do not spoil the fun by dictating the modus operandi—a game of base ball, or foot ball, is worth a dozen gymnassiums [*sic*], where the eye of surveillance is to check the flow of animal spirits."[1]

The Olympic Club of Philadelphia organized in 1833, and within five years it was governed by rules for "town ball," one of the game's variants that existed prior to the Knickerbockers developing rules in New York City for what evolved into the version of baseball we know today.[2]

Although recreational sports were frowned upon by Philadelphia's citizens, forcing most games to be played across the Delaware River in New Jersey, both baseball and cricket exploded in popularity during the 1840s and 1850s, with the city becoming an epicenter for both. In 1859 an All-Star cricket team from England made an overseas foray into the United States and Canada, including a heavily attended match in Philadelphia. Among the Americans providing the opposition was Harry Wright, who became one of the founders of modern professional baseball.[3]

In 1865, Philadelphia's best baseball team, the original Athletics, lured star Al Reach from the Brooklyn Eckfords by paying him "expense money."[4] He created a sensation a week into his tenure, accomplishing what was thought to be impossible by not once but twice hitting balls over the fence at the Union Grounds in Brooklyn, the first clearing a building at the ballpark entrance.[5] Despite the addition of Reach, the Athletics lost the mythical national championship to the Atlantics of Brooklyn later that year.[6] The team from Philadelphia sought a better result against the Atlantics in 1866.

The first contest, played in Philadelphia on October 1, lasted but an inning thanks to the crush of several thousand fans that crowded the players off the field.[7]

The second match of the intended three-game series was staged a fortnight later at the Capitoline Grounds in Brooklyn, with the Atlantics victorious, 27–17, before a crowd said to be upward of thirty thousand, the largest ever to attend a game there. Betting was "lively" according to the *Brooklyn Eagle*, "despite its positive prohibition."[8] Interest was such that *Harper's Weekly* carried a full-page illustration of the teams.[9]

The Athletics' loss received prominent coverage in the *Philadelphia Inquirer*, blared as it was from the middle of the front page.[10] The third and final contest—this time staged in Philadelphia without incident—drew four thousand fans paying one dollar each for admittance, plus another ten thousand or so peering in for free from outside the ballpark, all of them witnessing a 31–12 Athletics victory. Al Reach starred, scoring six times despite only seven innings being played due to rain.[11] But the Atlantics retained the championship, as the series ended in a dispute over gate receipts, each team having earned one victory.[12]

AFRICAN AMERICANS HAD a place in early Philadelphia baseball history. Octavius Catto, a prominent civil rights activist and teacher of mathematics and English literature, helped establish Philadelphia as a major force in what eventually became Negro League baseball before his murder on October 10, 1871, amid Election Day violence.[13] Catto's club, the Pythians, was founded in 1866—the same year as the city's first such aggregation, the Excelsior Club—and comprised educated professionals. It quickly became a regional force. But within a year, Black players were formally banned by the National Association of Professional Baseball Players, as Catto discovered when the Pythians were pointedly "requested" to withdraw an application to join the white leagues, despite support from the Athletics.[14] Two years later, he and his Pythians challenged the Olympic Club at the Jefferson Street Grounds. With Catto at second base, the Pythians lost that interracial contest, 44–23, in what the local press termed "Perhaps the first base ball game of the kind."[15]

An editorial published in a number of eastern newspapers noted the event: "But while we have been slowly brought to concede that a black man should have all the rights of a white man, we have most of us tacitly con-cluded that the *social* line would never be passed. Here however, we see the ice broken in the most fastidious city of the Union. The Olympics (white) play the Pythians (black) in the presence of the greatest crowd that probably ever assembled in the Quaker City to see 'our national game.'" The editorial concluded, quite prematurely, "The distinctions of caste are rapidly passing away."[16]

THE ATHLETICS IN 1871 helped form baseball's first professional "league," the National Association, taking up residence at the Jefferson Street Grounds and capturing the first championship. Twenty-year-old third base-man Adrian "Cap" Anson arrived the next year from the Rockford Forest Citys, which had folded after finishing in last place, and he spent the next four seasons with the Athletics before joining the Chicago White Stock-ings and forging a legendary career. But he also has garnered an unfavorable reputation historically regarding his attitude about race, which allegedly contributed to his becoming a leader in the banning of Black people from organized baseball.

Anson was among the Athletics who traveled to Great Britain in the middle of the 1874 season for a series of games against Boston. One memo-rable contest was played on the cricket grounds at the Crystal Palace, with Al Spalding and the Red Stockings winning, 17–8.[17]

The English were not sure what to make of the game, which had become America's national sport: "The critics . . . have not yet made up their minds whether to sneer at [baseball] for its obvious inferiority to cricket or to accept it on those special merits of its own which it clearly possesses." It was noted that the umpire was "the great blot on the whole game."[18]

Additional National Association teams represented Philadelphia. The Whites or "Pearls," as they were alternatively known, joined in 1873 and finished second, while employing many of the Athletics players from the previous season. A third Philadelphia team, overoptimistically nicknamed the Centennials, appeared in 1875 but folded after only fourteen league games.[19] The Athletics compiled a record of 53-20 that year, with pitcher Dick McBride winning 44 times. But the team finished third, fifteen lengths behind Boston and its ridiculous 71-8 record, as the Red Stockings, man-aged by Harry Wright, captured a fourth-consecutive title.

The Athletics, still headquartered at the worn-out and unpopular Jefferson Street Grounds, joined the National League as a founding member in 1876, losing to Boston in the NL's first-ever contest and finishing a poor seventh with a 14-45 record despite featuring a number of players from the team's successful National Association run. However, sans Cap Anson, who joined Chicago, and Dick McBride, who signed with Boston, the team failed. Attendance was anemic. On July 4, the nation's centennial, the Athletics played in Cincinnati while a lacrosse tournament was staged at their home grounds.[20] The franchise was ultimately expelled from the National League, along with the New York Mutuals, after refusing to play a late-season road trip.[21]

The Athletics' moniker was revived in 1882, as Philadelphia gained entry for the maiden season of the American Association, a direct challenger of the National League. In their second year the Athletics captured the league championship.[22] Enthusiasm reached a fever pitch back home—upon the team's return from clinching the pennant, the players were greeted by ten thousand people who marched alongside their heroes in a six-mile-long parade through the city streets.[23] The team eventually failed, expelled by the league and replaced by Philadelphia's Players' League franchise in 1891, the year before the American Association's demise.

IN 1883, A YEAR AFTER the death of National League president William Hulbert—the man most responsible for banishing Philadelphia and New York six years earlier—the league matched the American Association's move into the two largest cities in the country by supplanting franchises in Worcester, Massachusetts, and Troy, New York. Al Reach, who had become a sporting goods magnate in competition with his old rival, Al Spalding, joined with John I. Rogers to take over the slot vacated by Worcester. They mitigated their financial risk by enlisting two men who would provide funding without wanting to run the franchise—John Pratt, a former pitcher whose family owned a local paint distributorship, and Stephen Farrelly, head of the Central News Company. Farrelly fronted for the actual money man, Chicago White Stockings shareholder John R. Walsh, who financed two-thirds of the total shares.[24]

The new team's core included three key players and the top two pitchers from a team sometimes called the Phillies, which had been backed by

Reach in 1882 as a member of the "minor" League Alliance, financed by the National League with only two entrants, New York and Philadelphia, the intention being the return of those cities to the National League.[25] The Phillies were no match for the National League that first season, winning only 17 games while losing 81. Their best pitcher, Hardie Henderson, was implicated in the death of a nineteen-year-old woman to whom he provided extract of ergot in what was likely an attempt to induce a miscarriage.[26] Henderson was released to Baltimore after pitching one game.[27] His replacement, John Coleman, set a still-standing Major League record with 48 losses.

Al Reach persuaded Harry Wright to take over as manager for the second campaign. The Phillies improved markedly, although what followed over the next century is best described as scattered islands of success surrounded by a sea of disappointment within an ocean of failure.

Reach and Rogers, the latter of whom eventually bought out the other partners, continued investing in the franchise. The team's fifth season, 1887, brought a brand-new ballpark. It was a hit. Located at Broad and Huntingdon Streets, people lined up two hours ahead of the opening that first day, standing in lines stretching four blocks to secure a seat or, failing that, simply an open patch of ground on which to stand. Eighteen thousand people were eventually shoehorned into a facility that seated some five thousand less—still double the capacity of the Phillies' first hastily built home—and those present were delightfully surprised. The outfield was enclosed in brick, and racks able to accommodate four hundred bicycles were installed. The park featured fanciful turrets some seventy-five feet tall at each end of the grandstand, and a central turret more than twice that height, giving one the sense that perhaps a knight on horseback, lance at the ready, would appear at any moment.[28]

The pitcher for the home opener, staged on April 30, 1887, was Charlie Ferguson, a rising star beginning his fourth year in the Majors. To this day, baseball historians consider him among the greatest players in Phillies history. In his second season Ferguson threw the franchise's first-ever no-hitter.[29] His third year brought 30 wins against only 9 losses.

Ferguson was also arguably the team's best hitter. Despite the death of his infant daughter during the summer of 1887, he led the team in batting at .337—sixty-eight points above the league average—and in runs batted in (an admittedly elusive statistic, not recorded at the time and difficult to reconstruct nearly 140 years after the fact), while leading Philadelphia to a

75-48 record and a second-place finish. When Ferguson was not pitching, Harry Wright stationed him at second base, at third base, or in the outfield. A couple of decades later, Brooklyn manager Wilbert Robinson listed him as one of the five greatest players he had ever seen. In 1925, long-time Phillies executive William Shettsline selected Ferguson ahead of Grover Cleveland Alexander as pitcher on his all-time Phillies team and then went even further, declaring, "He was the greatest ballplayer who ever lived." Shettsline added, "That goes too, despite the fact that Ty Cobb is among those present."[30]

Ferguson's success was fleeting. A year later, on the first anniversary of the team's grand ballpark opening, fans scanning that day's edition of the *Philadelphia Inquirer* were jolted by the headline of a story involving the team's best player:

"Ferguson Is Dead."

The twenty-five-year-old had succumbed at the home of teammate Arthur Irwin, from whom Ferguson and his wife were renting a room, after suffering for close to three weeks with typhoid fever.[31] He had participated in several exhibition games that spring at both pitcher and second base, making his final appearance on April 11 at the keystone sack against the American Association Athletics.[32] Excepting one trip to the ballpark a few days after taking sick, Ferguson was confined to bed until his death on the evening of April 29.[33] A funeral was held at Irwin's home, with both the Philadelphia and Washington teams attending. The Washington contingent marched around the casket in full uniform, among their number catcher Connie Mack, as Ferguson's body was borne by his Phillies teammates.[34] Charlie Ferguson today is almost completely unknown despite a career that portended Hall of Fame credentials.

The team survived a major baseball insurrection, the Players' League of 1890, which included a Philadelphia franchise that attracted several Phillies starters, most of whom did not return following the league's one-year existence. Despite this, and the loss of Charlie Ferguson, the Phillies of the 1890s were loaded with talent. Future Hall of Famers in uniform included pitcher Tim Keefe and infielders Roger Connor and Dan Brouthers. Left-handed catcher Jack Clements, whose big league baptism came in 1884 with the ill-fated Philadelphia entry in the equally ill-fated Union Association, was one of the best backstops in the game. Stars Billy Sunday, Kid Gleason, Lave Cross, Gus Weyhing, and Al Orth all suited up for the team.

During much of the decade, the Phillies boasted one of baseball's greatest-ever outfield trios: Billy Hamilton, Sam Thompson, and Ed Delahanty—each an eventual Hall of Famer. Yet Philadelphia failed to win, finishing no better than third during the decade. In 1892 the Phillies completed a stretch of 29 wins in 35 games—a streak that took 132 years for them to match. Yet they were never closer to first place than five games and eventually finished fourth. In 1894 each of their three star outfielders hit better than .400.[35] But the team's pitching was lacking, finishing eighth, tenth, and tenth in earned run average among the league's twelve entries, beginning in 1893. Youngsters, veterans—it did not matter. The pitching never measured up to the hitting, defining the 1890s Phillies as a good but not great team. Fans remained loyal—the team nearly always finished first or second in the league in attendance.

The same season that Hamilton, Delahanty, and Thompson each hit .400, the Phillies lost their ballpark to fire. The team was at morning practice when a finger of flame suddenly appeared above the roof of the pavilion and wrapped itself around one of the turrets. Pitchers Jack Taylor and Jack Fanning attempted to extinguish the fire but, fanned by a breeze, the blaze consumed the structure like the kindling it basically was, rendering it a heap of smoking ash.[36]

The Phillies played a few home games at the University of Pennsylvania, followed by a short road trip while a temporary ballpark was erected. The venue was rebuilt during the winter with brick and cement, and it featured a cantilevered upper deck, a swimming pool in the clubhouse, a forty-foot-tall right-field fence, and a distinctive hump in the outfield marking the subterranean path of the Philadelphia and Reading rail line. The Phillies also reached agreement for the electronic reproduction of road games to audiences at the Academy of Music, utilizing a large board that registered each pitch, relayed via telegraph within ten seconds of its occurrence.[37] Although interest soon waned, more than 2,500 attended the first such event, which displayed results relayed from a game played in Baltimore.[38]

For the 1896 season, the Phillies acquired a left-handed shortstop, Bill Hulen, who did not last, and twenty-one-year-old infielder Napoleon Lajoie, who did.[39] Four years later, Lajoie was an established star, but he learned that the team had lied to him about his being paid more than Ed Delahanty. As a result, Lajoie jumped to the newly formed American League, which had declared war on the baseball establishment. What made it worse was that he had jumped to its Philadelphia entry, operated by Connie Mack and longtime Philadelphia baseball entrepreneur Ben Shibe, a business partner of Al Reach. Within a year, Delahanty also jumped to the rival circuit, along with three of his teammates.[40]

Even when doing wrong, the Phillies couldn't get it right. During a September 1900 doubleheader, Cincinnati Reds captain Tommy Corcoran was absentmindedly kicking at the ground in the third base coach's box and uncovered a wire. He began digging, attracting the attention of the Phillies groundskeeper, who came on a dead run with police officers in tow. Before Corcoran could be stopped, he uncovered an underground box containing an electrical device connected to a location in the center-field stands, where reserve catcher Morgan Murphy sat peering through opera glasses. Murphy buzzed a code to the Phillies third base coach, signaling the coming pitch. Manager William Shettsline attempted to deny the subterfuge but was predictably ineffective doing so.[41]

In 1903 Colonel John I. Rogers, who had purchased controlling interest in the Phillies a few years earlier, grew weary of the war with the American League and the resulting to-and-fro of players. He and Al Reach sold the team to a syndicate headed by James Potter, a Philadelphia newspaper editor and squash enthusiast.[42] With the help of Cincinnati Reds owner Garry Herrmann, Potter convinced Rogers, as a concession in the peace process with the American League, to lend his support to the team dropping a lawsuit that was preventing Napoleon Lajoie and other ex-Phillies jumpers from playing in Pennsylvania.[43]

Five months into Potter's tenure, a balcony affixed to the outfield grandstand at the Phillies ballpark collapsed, killing a dozen people and injuring more than two hundred. Apparently, screams outside the stadium from several teenage girls who were teasing a couple of drunken men caught the attention of fans, who rushed to the uppermost back of the grandstand to witness what was transpiring twenty-five feet below. The shift in weight caused the balcony to separate from the wall to which it had been tenuously attached, resulting in a collapse that hurled a tangled mass of humanity onto the pavement below.[44]

Six years later, the rival Philadelphia Athletics opened baseball's first concrete and steel stadium, Shibe Park, with owners Ben Shibe and Connie Mack solidifying their newly minted dominance of Philadelphia baseball. The team had won two American League pennants with another four soon to follow—three resulting in World Series titles—while the Phillies struggled for attention. Despite four straight first-division finishes, James Potter had his fill of baseball.

Pennsylvania state senator Israel Durham led a group that purchased the Phillies. The team was reorganized with Durham as majority shareholder and his partners James P. McNichol and Clarence Wolf dividing the remainder of a 756-share block. The other 244 shares were owned by Phillies manager Billy Murray, team president William Shettsline, and a smattering of other individuals.[45] But Durham succumbed to a heart attack in late June, and his partners did not want to run the ball club.[46] Handicapped by an ownership group in disarray; an aging, subpar facility; and competition with Mack's perennial contender, the Phillies changed hands once again in November 1909. Sportswriter Horace Fogel, who had served two short stints as a National League manager, announced formation of a syndicate that purchased all but thirteen of the team's one thousand shares for $350,000, with another $35,000 reserved for player purchases.[47]

Publishing a revelation that recalled the founding of the franchise, the *Cincinnati Enquirer* claimed that, in reality, lawyer and newspaper editor Charles Taft and Chicago Cubs owner Charles Murphy had acquired the Phillies stock and that Fogel was an owner in name only.[48] Addressing the allegation, Fogel insisted that Murphy, who helped broker the deal, was *not* part owner, and declared that the other members of the syndicate, whom he did not name, were Philadelphians.[49] Few believed him—especially a month later when Taft, Murphy's financial backer and half brother of the president of the United States, announced his wife's acquisition of the Phillies stadium from Rogers and Reach.[50] The Phillies signed a ninety-nine-year lease with an option to purchase the park for $400,000. The option, which expired in 1929—other versions say 1921—was never exercised.[51]

According to F. C. Lane, editor of *Baseball Magazine*, Taft and Murphy had installed Fogel as head of the Phillies, with the three sharing equal ownership. Lane claimed Fogel received a salary and 10 percent of the profits the team generated and was to pay 7 percent interest to Taft on the funds lent him to purchase his shares.[52]

Fogel may have been a front man, but he was determined to make the team his own—including a laughable effort to change its nickname to the "Live Wires." He and manager Red Dooin did assemble the core of what would be the Phillies' first pennant winner. They acquired Fred Luderus,

Phillies first baseman for the next decade, from Chicago in July 1910 for pitcher Bill Foxen, who won a grand total of one game for the Cubs.[53] Two months later, Fogel drafted Grover Cleveland Alexander from Syracuse on the recommendation of Princeton baseball coach and former Baltimore Orioles catcher "Boileryard" Clarke—a deal that garnered scant attention at the time.[54] On consecutive days in August 1911, Fogel acquired catcher Bill Killefer and thirty-year-old outfielder Gavvy Cravath.[55] Killefer, who arrived during the final week of the 1911 season, became Grover Cleveland Alexander's favorite catcher, while Cravath, who debuted with the Phillies in 1912 after having failed trials with three Major League teams, became the most prolific home run hitter of the Deadball Era.[56] More was to come. Erskine Mayer, who would twice win 21 games for the Phillies, was purchased from Atlanta for $2,500.[57] He was joined by University of Virginia star Eppa Rixey, a 6-foot-5 multisport athlete who would go on to a Hall of Fame career.[58]

But Fogel would not enjoy the fruits of his effort. During the 1912 season, with the Phillies in the midst of a disappointing, injury-plagued campaign, Fogel, loose-lipped and never one to pass up a grievance—real or imagined—began blasting the league's umpires, declaring they were determined to see that the New York Giants won the pennant. His players took the cue and began baiting the arbiters. Fogel then leveled charges at the league office, insisting the entire Major League system was full of corruption, that it was an illegal trust, and that the reserve clause was also illegal. Fogel persisted to the point that the National League held a trial at the end of the season to decide whether he should be allowed to continue running the franchise. The other owners found him guilty of five counts.[59] Before an appeal could be mounted to challenge the league's authority, an irritated Charles Taft pulled the plug by calling his loan, thus formally exposing the arrangement everyone had suspected. When Fogel could not raise the necessary capital, he returned to the newspaper business, vowing revenge but never coming close to accomplishing his goal of destroying Major League baseball's ownership.[60]

Fogel's exit led Taft to divest himself of the Phillies. William Locke, secretary of the Pittsburgh Pirates, aggressively pursued the franchise, aided by his cousin, former New York City police chief William Baker.[61] On January 15, 1913, Locke closed the deal for an amount estimated at $300,000. Taft retained title to the stadium.[62]

But Locke was suffering from cancer. Not long after the season began, he underwent surgery to remove a large tumor from his back, and he died in mid-August. William Baker was named president and guided the team's fortunes for the next two decades. For better—and for worse.[63]

WILLIAM BAKER'S FIRST CHALLENGE was that of the outlaw Federal League—and his tight-fisted philosophy became quickly apparent. In a repeat of the Lajoie-Delahanty fiasco, the Phillies lost their double play combination as well as their second and third best pitchers, Tom Seaton and Ad Brennan. Only some fast negotiating and victory in a highly publicized lawsuit prevented catcher Bill Killefer's additional defection to the Chicago Federals.[64] The team fell from second to sixth.

Baker responded by hiring Pat Moran, who had no previous managerial experience, to replace thirty-six-year-old catcher-manager Red Dooin, who was traded to Cincinnati for second baseman Bert Niehoff to fill one of the infield holes caused by the players jumping to the Federal League.[65] To plug the gap at shortstop, Baker and Moran acquired a future Hall of Famer, Dave Bancroft, from Portland of the Pacific Coast League for utility infielder Milt Reed, who then jumped to the Feds.[66]

The unlikely result was a pennant that had eluded the Phillies for more than three decades, bringing the 1915 World Series to the twenty-year-old ballpark, now called Baker Bowl.

The Phillies roared out of the gate, winning their first eight games and eleven of their first twelve. After spending much of June and the first half of July in either second or third place, the Phillies compiled a 51-29 record during the second half of the season and won going away, by a margin of six-and-a-half games over the defending National League champion Boston Braves, which had made a second-half rush, going 50-26 after sitting in last place on July 13.

The Phillies were competitive and exciting and topped the league in attendance. Gavvy Cravath hit 24 home runs—his third straight season leading all of Major League baseball in that category—nearly double the number hit by runner-up Cy Williams of the Chicago Cubs. Fred Luderus was one of only five .300 hitters in the National League, finishing second with a .315 batting average. Grover Cleveland Alexander was magnificent, winning 31 games with a 1.22 earned run average. He pitched thirty-six complete games, twelve of them shutouts, and tossed a record four one-hitters. Erskine Mayer added 21 victories. Another pitcher, Al Demaree, who later became a prominent and prolific sports cartoonist, was acquired from New York and added 14 wins.

Alexander won the World Series opener against the Boston Red Sox 3–1, retiring pinch-hitter Babe Ruth on a grounder and outfielder Harry Hooper on a pop fly to end the game.[67] The Phillies followed that with four straight losses to Boston—all by one run—and did not win another World Series game for sixty-five years.

The Phillies finished second the next two seasons, with Alexander throwing a record sixteen shutouts in 1916 and reaching the thirty-win mark both years. Then Baker tossed aside all built-up reserve of goodwill in December 1917 when he essentially gave away Alexander and star catcher Bill Killefer to the Chicago Cubs. A year and a half earlier, William Baker had extolled Alexander as both a great player and a great man in a missive penned for *Baseball Magazine*.

"When times were turbulent with the Philadelphia National League club and prospects were clouded by the raids of the Federal League," wrote Baker, "Alexander refused to be swerved from what he considered his duty by any of the allurements which blinded other players. Some of our men deserted the club and of them or the reasons which actuated them in doing as they did I have nothing to say. But I will say of Alexander that he conducted himself throughout like a man who thoroughly understood the contractual obligations and refused, as others were doing, to pursue a course which he considered most dishonorable to his employers."[68]

Of course, when the contract ran out and Alexander wanted a raise, there came a shift in Baker's opinion when it came to the character of his star pitcher.

Philadelphia newspapers universally blasted the trade, which brought back-up catcher William "Pickles" Dillhoefer and pitcher Mike Prendergast, along with an amount of cash said to be somewhat north of $75,000, in exchange for two of baseball's biggest stars. The *Philadelphia Evening Public Ledger* bleated, "Sale Death Blow to Phils' Hopes."[69]

A pile of cash cannot take the mound and win 30 games for three straight seasons as had Alexander, and one of the game's best catchers cannot be replaced by someone who would only suit up eight times for the Phillies. The *Philadelphia Inquirer* called the deal the "most important in baseball since Connie Mack wrecked his champion Athletic team in 1915."[70]

Attempting to defend the transaction, Baker claimed Alexander would be drafted into the military and, while acknowledging that the right-hander had won 30 games, adamantly declared, "Alexander even then was not at his best, and there is no reason for believing he would be better next year."[71] A month later, Baker made another move, swapping center fielders with the Cubs—veteran Dode Paskert for Cy Williams, who was six years younger.[72] That deal would turn out in the Phillies favor, with Williams winning three NL home run titles during the 1920s. Meanwhile, Alexander—who did enlist—and Killefer were gone, and Phillies fans could only watch as the Cubs won the pennant in 1918 while their team dropped to sixth place.[73]

The Phillies never had another winning season under William Baker, who after trading Alexander remained in charge for another thirteen years. Thirty-three years passed before the Phillies boasted another *twenty*-game winner. Twenty-game losers would prove less scarce. The only postseason action at Baker Bowl came from outsiders, first in 1924 and 1925 when Hilldale, featuring Biz Mackey and Judy Johnson, played the first two Colored World Series against the Kansas City Monarchs, using the stadium instead of its normal home, Hilldale Park, located in the Philadelphia suburb of Darby. The Bacharach Giants, based in Atlantic City, also used the stadium for the fourth and fifth games of the 1926 Colored World Series.

Baker Bowl suffered another structural calamity in May 1927 when three sections of the lower-right-field stands collapsed during a game on May 14 against the St. Louis Cardinals. One man died of a heart attack, and more than fifty others were injured in the incident. The wooden structure first cracked loudly and moaned, dropping slightly before pausing, and then gave way as fans jumped to their feet and screamed in terror.[74]

The team's best post-Alexander season under Baker came in 1929, thanks to a trade for Lefty O'Doul, who set a National League record with 254 hits along with a .398 batting average, and the emergence of Chuck Klein, who set a new National League mark with 43 home runs. Klein later matched Ed Delahanty by hitting 4 home runs in a game for the Phillies.

Within a year, the Phillies traded away O'Doul after setting records for both prodigious offense and pitching futility. While Phillies batters collectively hit as high as .315 as a team, their hurlers compiled miserable earned run averages, nearing 7 runs per game. As a result, the Phillies returned to the bottom of the league standings.[75] By this time, Connie Mack had constructed another great Athletics roster, the team finishing second in both

1927 and 1928, followed by the capture of three straight pennants and two World Series between 1929 and 1931 while featuring the star power of Jimmie Foxx, Mickey Cochrane, Al Simmons, and Lefty Grove.

William Baker continued living in New York, commuting to Philadelphia when business called or the team was on a home stand. Otherwise, day-to-day operations were left to his secretary. Baker Bowl was no artistic edifice, as was Shibe Park. It was better known for its inadequacies—the short right field fence adorned with a forty-foot-high Lifebuoy sign (plus a twenty-foot-high screen atop it) and the outfield hump—and as a decaying structure that always threatened to maim its guests. The days of fanciful turrets were long past. The franchise was slowly falling apart while William Baker stubbornly held on.

On December 3, 1930, Baker was attending the Minor League Winter Meeting in Montreal. He had not felt well that afternoon, but he went to dinner with his wife; his secretary, Mae Nugent; and her husband, team business manager Gerald Nugent. After returning to his suite at the Ritz Carlton, Baker fell seriously ill, and a physician was summoned. At five-thirty the next morning, William Baker died, the victim of a heart attack.[76]

Immediately there was speculation that the Phillies would be sold. George M. Cohan was mentioned, as were Ty Cobb and Connie Mack protégé Tom Turner—all three having made previous efforts to convince Baker to sell. Cobb claimed that Baker was ready to relinquish control in 1929 but had changed his mind when Lefty O'Doul and Chuck Klein arrived and the team improved. After the 1930 World Series, Baker again signaled his reluctance to sell.[77]

William Baker left his ownership stake to his wife and to Mae Nugent. Lewis C. Ruch was named president, but he stepped down due to ill health after the 1932 season—the only year the franchise won more games than it lost between 1918 and 1948.[78] Gerald Nugent took over as president, with his wife serving as vice president and treasurer. Sunday baseball was finally legalized by Pennsylvania voters in November 1933, ending the ban for Pittsburgh and Philadelphia—the last Major League cities with such a prohibition.[79] But the Phillies still drew the fewest fans in the National League. Baker's widow died on February 5, 1936, and she bequeathed her shares to Mae Nugent, resulting in the Nugents holding the majority of Phillies stock.[80]

Gerald Nugent was both creative and an astute judge of talent, but with limited financial assets outside of the team, he struggled to keep the franchise afloat, primarily doing so by selling its best players. Two of them, pitcher Bucky Walters and infielder Dolph Camilli, became National League MVPs shortly after being jettisoned by Philadelphia. In 1933, a year after winning an MVP award, Chuck Klein took the NL Triple Crown with the seventh-place Phillies. He was traded to the Cubs after the season for three players and—of course—cash.

This era became the source of the Phillies' more derisive legends. Hugh Mulcahy lost 76 games in four seasons, twice dropping 20 or more. That "feat" earned him the nickname "Losing Pitcher," reflecting his most common designation in box scores. Pitcher Walter Beck earned the nickname "Boom-Boom" because of the sound made when batters swung at his pitches and lined them off the enormous soap advertisement in right field. That sign proudly proclaimed, "The Phillies Use Lifebuoy." An apocryphal tale has it that a fan snuck in and scrawled an additional message underneath the original one: "And They Still Stink."[81]

Baker Bowl was widely panned as an embarrassment. Fans arriving early had the pleasure of watching three sheep manicuring the grass.[82] Chicago sportswriter Edward Burns, in his series on Major League ballparks in 1937, joked that the only improvements at Baker Bowl were to the clubhouse, where rusty nails on which players hung their attire had been replaced by "shiny new ones."[83]

The Nugents tried cauterizing their red ink by renting out the stadium for other sporting events. It was not enough. After threatening legal action against the twelve heirs of Charles Murphy who controlled Baker Bowl's perpetual lease, backing was finally secured from enough of them to allow the Phillies to abandon the decrepit ballpark in the middle of 1938 and take up Connie Mack's standing offer to share his stadium.[84] On the evening of June 30, a fleet of moving trucks hauled the team's equipment a mile down West Lehigh Avenue to Shibe Park, where the Phillies began playing on July 4.[85] The added revenue enabled the Athletics to add lights for the 1939 season, making night games possible.

One could be excused for assuming the shift to a somewhat more pitcher-friendly Shibe Park would help the pitching staff. However, the Phillies earned run average during their last full season at Baker Bowl was 5.05, while it rose to 5.17 in the first year at Shibe Park. Meanwhile, the team's batting average declined twelve points over the same period.

The Nugents resumed their practice of selling players to make ends meet. After infamously shipping pitcher Kirby Higbe to Brooklyn after the 1940 season, Gerald Nugent promised to refrain from further sales.[86] However, by 1942 he was broke and openly shopping the team's three most valuable assets—outfielder Danny Litwhiler and pitchers Tommy Hughes and Rube Melton.[87]

At this point, twenty-year-old Philadelphia native Roy Campanella, a star catcher for the Negro National League Baltimore Elite Giants, struck up a conversation with Phillies manager Hans Lobert, suggesting he could help the club. Lobert encouraged Campanella to call Gerald Nugent, which he did, but was told by the Phillies owner that because of the unwritten rule against Black players in the Major Leagues, there was no point giving him a tryout.[88] As desperate as the Phillies were, some lines were still not to be crossed.

The National League took up the matter of Nugent's financial woes but decided against assuming control of the franchise, instead urging that he find a buyer for the team. Nugent responded by shipping Rube Melton to Brooklyn for thirty-seven-year-old reliever Johnny Allen and $30,000. "It was a question of cash to operate the Phils," explained Nugent. "That's why Melton was sold—to get the money to carry along."[89] Nugent made every attempt to hang on. But in February 1943, National League owners forced him to sell the team to them and then invited offers to avoid inheriting a reported $200,000 of debt, much of it owed to the league.[90] There were rumors that a syndicate led by New York Giants star Bill Terry was interested. Another group reportedly wanted to move the franchise to Baltimore. When Branch Rickey was squeezed out by the St. Louis Cardinals, he kicked the tires. Bill Veeck later made the dubious claim that he had intended to buy the Phillies from Nugent and stock it with the best players from the Negro Leagues but was blocked by Commissioner Kenesaw Mountain Landis.[91]

A local syndicate headed by former mayoral candidate John B. "Jack" Kelly, the father of future actress and princess of Monaco Grace Kelly, made a formal bid.[92] But the league chose the offer of a thirty-three-year-old New York lumber broker whose only previous professional sports experience was with the failed American Football League. That leads us to the saga of William D. Cox, whose turbulent one-year ownership resulted in the Carpenter family's acquisition of the Philadelphia Phillies.

2

The First Whiz Kids

ON FEBRUARY 20, 1943, the Philadelphia Phillies changed hands once more.[1] One of the stranger chapters in a strange Phillies history was about to unfold, thanks to the new owner.

William Drought Cox was an aggressive, driven man, a high school graduate at age fifteen who then attended both New York University and Yale, reportedly playing baseball and running track at one or the other. It was also said he spent a summer throwing batting practice for the Boston Braves.[2] Following college he was employed by an investment house, dabbled as a philatelist, edited a book on boxing, dealt in art, and was employed by a lumber firm, eventually taking control of the business, Piling Associates, at age twenty-seven. During the war, his company reinforced the pilings of the Panama Canal.

In 1941 Cox purchased the New York franchise in the American Football League and made a big splash by signing Heisman Trophy winner Tom Harmon.[3] Cox ultimately lost the football team when it, along with the league, ceased operations during the war and never returned.[4]

When Cox hired veteran American League manager Bucky Harris instead of former Phillies star Lefty O'Doul, whom Cox had previously named as a front-runner for the job (after receiving a slap on the wrist for also naming Yankees catcher Bill Dickey as a candidate), *San Francisco Examiner* columnist Prescott Sullivan congratulated O'Doul, explaining that he was too good a person to die the slow death that would have resulted from being Phillies manager.[5] Referencing a rumor that Connie Mack had recommended Harris, Sullivan wrote, "We don't know what Mr. Mack could have against Mr. Harris, but we thank him for giving our chum 'Lefty' a break. It was a kindly thing for him to do."[6] Prescott Sullivan's joke was right on the mark. By the end of the year, it would become clear O'Doul had indeed been fortunate in not landing the job.

Having participated in collegiate sports, William Cox fancied himself an athlete. During training camp in Hershey, Pennsylvania, Cox donned a jersey with PHILS spelled out in block letters across the chest—the team nickname had been shortened at the request of previous manager Hans Lobert—and jogged along with his players.[7] When the Phillies were short of infielders for a workout, Cox manned shortstop.[8]

He hired Olympic track coach Harold Anson Bruce for the newly created role of physical education director. Bruce explained his methods as a "combination of American, Swedish, Del Sar, German and other systems of calisthenics, some of which date back to Egyptian days."[9] Cox called it commando training.

Bruce preached a healthy diet, drinking hot water, and exercises designed to improve quickness. Training in weather conditions more conducive to throwing snowballs, it meant for long, unconventional workouts, unpopular among professional athletes with established routines.

After changing the team name back to Phillies, Cox addressed loose ends left over from the Nugent regime.[10] First baseman Nick Etten had been traded by Nugent to the Yankees for cash and a pair of Minor Leaguers who subsequently did not report to Philadelphia because of their draft status.[11] Cox appealed to Commissioner Landis, who ruled that the Yankees must replace the players—although canceling the deal altogether would have yielded a better result.[12] The Phillies ultimately received pitcher Al Gerheauser, who lost 19 games, and thirty-four-year-old catcher Tom Padden, who had not appeared in the Majors for six years. Etten drove in 309 runs over the next three years for New York. Another Nugent acquisition, Johnny Allen, was a holdout, and Cox sold him back to Brooklyn just before the season began.[13]

Bucky Harris, formerly nicknamed "Boy Wonder" and who two decades earlier had led the Washington Senators to a World Series title as a twenty-seven-year-old player-manager, sought to whip hope into reality by declaring himself excited to be working for the Phillies and William Cox: "I have a chance to build a ball club from the ground up under Mr. Cox, who is a hustling young executive. I'm having pretty much my way in how to put the team together and in tabbing players I'd like to have in trade." Harris went on to say, "Of course we still need a lot more than we have, but no one can say the Phils aren't improved."[14] Cox predicted a finish of no lower than sixth for the Phillies in 1943.

Cox and Harris began reshaping the team. Shortstop Bobby Bragan was sent to Brooklyn for pitcher Jack Kraus and cash, the latter of which was used to purchase pitcher Schoolboy Rowe from Montreal of the International League. "I'll still take him, and gladly," remarked Harris, who had managed Rowe a decade earlier when he broke in with the Detroit Tigers.[15]

Cox attempted, unsuccessfully, to persuade retired Cleveland Indians first baseman Hal Trosky to play for the Phillies, and the owner also set his sights, with an equal lack of success, on Jimmie Foxx, who had recently retired rather than catch for the Chicago Cubs.[16]

The new owner's most significant move was the acquisition of infielder Babe Dahlgren in exchange for thirty-seven-year-old outfielder Lloyd Waner—who subsequently took the year off to work in a defense plant—and twenty-eight-year-old second baseman Al Glossop, whose .223 lifetime batting average further deteriorated before his career ended.[17] Dahlgren played first base, third base, and shortstop for the Phillies—and even caught a couple of innings when the team ran out of catchers during a doubleheader against the Giants. He spent a significant portion of the season near the top of the league batting race and made the National League All-Star team. However, rumors of marijuana use, which Dahlgren unequivocally denied, were secretly spread behind the scenes, and he was traded to Pittsburgh after the season.[18]

The Phillies home opener on April 27 served as the tail end of a home-and-home series with Brooklyn, the teams splitting the first two games, which were played in the borough. The weather was unsettled and the footing tentative—the contest would twice include rain delays. Nevertheless, to mark his debut as owner Cox staged a pregame Australian pursuit race between Phillies and Dodgers players—All-Star outfielder Danny Litwhiler strained his hamstring during the event and was relegated to pinch-hitting duty for a week. Baseball clown Al Schacht unveiled a new act, featuring imitations of Walter Johnson, Bob Feller, and Carl Hubbell. Metropolitan Opera Company bass-baritone Norman Cordon rounded out the eclectic pregame lineup. Thanks to the bad weather, only four thousand were on hand to see Schoolboy Rowe make his Phillies debut, which ended after four innings and also ended in a 4–2 loss for the Phillies.[19]

Having missed out on Foxx and Trosky, Cox and Harris convinced thirty-eight-year-old Chuck Klein to take the field for a couple of games. In the second of those contests—his first regular season appearances in the outfield in nearly two years—Klein's singular fielding opportunity was on a ball hit by Billy Herman that bounced through his legs. It was scored as a double and an error, Herman ending up on third.[20] Klein returned to pinch hitting exclusively.

Nevertheless, the Phillies seemed to have improved, winning five of six in early May to reach the .500 mark. Fans responded. Nearly twenty-five thousand attended a doubleheader on Mother's Day against the New York Giants, and thirty thousand came out the next weekend for a twin bill versus the Cardinals. The first night game of the season, on May 18, drew twenty thousand, and on May 23 a club record 37,176 witnessed a double-header against the Pittsburgh Pirates.[21] During all of 1942, the Phillies had only twice boasted crowds exceeding twenty thousand.

The roster continued evolving, including a trade of Danny Litwhiler and Earl Naylor to St. Louis for outfielders Buster Adams, Dain Clay, and Coaker Triplett.[22] On June 25, against Brooklyn, Triplett drove in 5 runs with, appropriately, a pair of triples, and Schoolboy Rowe picked up his fourth straight win, moving the Phillies into fourth place with a record of 30-28.[23] Everything seemed to be clicking.

It was a mirage. Within a month the team had fallen apart in spectacular fashion after dropping twenty-five of thirty-four and falling to seventh.

Cox, the model stereotype of a young, impatient, ambitious owner lacking familiarity with failure, began demonstrating his penchant for misplaced resolve, fueled by unrealistic expectations. He blasted National League president Ford Frick for a pair of decisions made regarding protests. Although he later apologized, in a statement that recalled the days of Horace Fogel, Cox declared that the Phillies had "no confidence whatever in any decision coming from the league office."[24]

Cox began entering the clubhouse and instructing players, in some cases contradicting Harris's directives. Sportswriter Stan Baumgartner reported that the Phillies owner had strongly advocated fining the team's best player, Ron Northey, for not scoring from second on a single. Cox was said to be openly second-guessing Harris, and it was no secret they were clashing.

In July, a friend of Harris gave him a heads-up that he and coach Earl Whitehill were going to be replaced. When confronted, Cox told Harris to assure the players that no changes were forthcoming, while admitting that the board of directors—of which Harris was a member—was concerned about the team. Cox later met his manager in Pittsburgh during a road trip and sent him on a quick scouting assignment. Upon rejoining the team in St. Louis, Harris was inundated with calls from reporters, breaking the news that he had been fired and Fred Fitzsimmons was the new manager.[25]

"I don't know a thing about it," snapped Harris, who quickly added, "I may have plenty to say tomorrow."[26] The players erupted, demanding that their manager be reinstated, or at the very least allowed the opportunity to resign. Harris calmed them down, and the demand became one of apology to Harris from Cox, who sat outside the locker room, penning amends for his atrocious handling of Harris' dismissal. Cox signed and presented it to Harris, averting an outright rebellion. The ex-manager proudly said of his players, "The stand they have taken flatters me no little."[27]

Harris then complained publicly that during a board of directors meeting six weeks earlier, he had been responsible for Cox receiving a $20,000 raise as Phillies president—a 400 percent increase.[28]

An outraged Cox, who reportedly had been assured Harris would remain silent, responded with a statement, in concert with the board of directors, asserting that his now former manager had been told of the board's dissatisfaction during a July 12 meeting. It was claimed that Harris responded by labeling the team a seventh-place club and the players "jerks." The press release quoted Harris as telling the directors that if they were unhappy, they "could get a new manager." Cox also complained that Harris would not work on baseball "after hours," resulting in missed trade opportunities, and had curiously "defended" coach Earl Whitehill as "dumb" but "loyal."[29] Cox did confirm rumors that Fred Fitzsimmons had been hired after being recommended by Branch Rickey but angrily denied that Rickey had any financial interest in the Phillies.[30]

Harris exploded. "It has taken Cox three days to get together a complete set of lies for his own defense." He called Cox "an All-American jerk."

The exchange further devolved into the equivalent of one normally heard on an elementary school playground, with Cox retorting that Harris "must have been looking in the mirror when he made that statement."[31]

Behind the scenes Harris began furnishing evidence to Commissioner Landis that Cox was betting on baseball, and specifically on the Phillies. He claimed that Cox's secretary maintained a running ledger of his wagers.[32]

Landis launched an investigation. Cox initially denied the allegations, then admitted to making "15 to 20" bets of $25 to $100 on the Phillies to win. He claimed to have stopped doing so upon learning it was prohibited.[33]

The team at first played well for Fred Fitzsimmons, winning eleven of fourteen contests and reaching fifth place before skidding to thirty-four losses in forty-eight games and ending the year in seventh with a record of 64-90.

Of the attempted big-name reclamation projects, only Schoolboy Rowe proved successful. He compiled his most innings pitched since 1936 while winning 14 games with a 2.94 earned run average. Rowe pulled double duty as the team's best pinch-hitter, successful on fifteen occasions to lead the National League. Two of his four home runs came in that role, including a grand slam against Boston.[34] For the year, he hit .300 in 120 at bats.

Some younger talent was secured. Near the end of the season, Cox purchased Andy Seminick from the Milwaukee Brewers of the American Association, whose owner, Bill Veeck, had acquired the catcher's contract from Knoxville the previous day.[35] Three days later, the Phillies promoted outfielder Del Ennis, who had completed a spectacular first season at Trenton. But he enlisted in the Navy and did not play for Philadelphia until after the war.[36]

The investigation into Cox's betting ground on. Unfortunately, the testimony being gathered was not working in his favor. On November 23 Commissioner Landis announced that William Cox was banned from baseball for life.[37]

"I made some small and sentimental bets before I learned of the rule against this," Cox told a radio audience the night of Landis's announcement. "I leave it to the public and my friends to decide if I was wrong."[38] But the public and his friends were not the decision-makers.

Cox attempted to backtrack his confession, highlighted by an unconvincing claim to have made an intentionally false admission about placing bets in a sting operation of sorts, meant to test the loyalty of one the Phillies directors.[39] It didn't matter. The Phillies were sold to retired DuPont executive Robert Carpenter Sr., who lived in nearby Wilmington, Delaware, and had married into the du Pont family.[40]

William Cox continued his involvement in sports, returning to football as an owner in the All-American Football Conference, which later merged with the National Football League.[41] He helped promote professional soccer in the United States during the 1960s and was involved in the birth of the North American Soccer League. He also created a program that allowed foreign countries to sell stamps depicting Disney characters. But when he died in 1989, William Cox remained banned from baseball.[42]

Despite his obvious shortcomings, Cox could boast of several accomplishments. He had abandoned the franchise's quarter-century strategy of selling off its best talent, and the Phillies had improved by 22 wins to finish ahead of the New York Giants, ending a five-year streak of last-place finishes. The team's earned run average, which had ranked last in the National League all but once between 1918 and 1942, was sixth-best in 1943. And Cox had brought to an end eleven consecutive seasons of the franchise drawing the league's fewest fans. Phillies attendance was the highest for the team since 1916, and the team outdrew the Athletics for the first time in nearly a quarter century.

But these facts soon entered the realm of trivia. Cox was out and Robert Carpenter Sr. was in. His personal interests dominated by big-game hunting, Carpenter named his twenty-eight-year-old son—stationed at Camp Grant, Illinois, for army boot camp—as team president.[43] Robert Jr., known as Bob, would run things. In the process, he arguably became the first Whiz Kid.

BOB CARPENTER JR. had played varsity baseball for Tower High School in Wilmington; he was a wild right-hander who sometimes reached double figures in both strikeouts and bases on balls. Former Yankees great and incumbent Boston Red Sox Minor League director Herb Pennock, who convinced Robert Carpenter Sr. to buy the Phillies, was a longtime family friend. He had even once worked out young Bob as a favor to the elder Carpenter, who subsequently suffered a badly fractured finger when Pennock had him catch during curveball instruction.[44] Nicknamed "The Squire of Kennett Square" for his hometown in Pennsylvania, located only twelve miles from where the Carpenters resided, Pennock spent twenty-two years as a left-handed pitcher in the Major Leagues with the Athletics, Red Sox, and Yankees, winning 241 games, plus a 5-0 World Series record and five Series championships to his credit. During his more than two decades in the Majors, he never allowed a grand slam.[45]

The younger Carpenter had attended Duke University and played end on the football team, including the 1936 squad that featured future football Hall of Famer Ace Parker during a 9-1 season. The next year he scored 3 touchdowns while starting several games in place of injured Blue Devils star Herb Hudgins for a team that finished 7-2-1.[46] Carpenter dropped out of college prior to his senior year to marry and therefore missed out on Duke's Rose Bowl appearance the next season.[47]

Completely uninterested in a career at DuPont, the married father of two had immersed himself in sports. He owned half interest in the Minor League Wilmington Blue Rocks, with Connie Mack as partner.[48] He also managed a pair of prize fighters and ran the Wilmington Bombers of the American Basketball League, while also financially supporting the University of Delaware football team.[49]

During Bob Carpenter's first press conference, he vowed to never lie to reporters. He explained that if asked a question he did not want to answer publicly, he would declare himself off the record and trust newsmen until they gave him reason not to.

He also announced the Phillies would be building a farm system from scratch—no small feat when few Minor Leagues were in operation during the war. Carpenter's first outreach, to negotiate a working agreement with the Pacific Coast League Hollywood Stars, was rebuffed. Stars business manager Oscar Reichow explained, "We need young player talent, and the Phillies have none of that to offer."[50]

Freddie Fitzsimmons continued as manager, and the team's three full-time scouts were retained. Later, five more, Eddie Krajnik, Bob Coltrin, Chuck Ward, Steve Yerkes, and Bill Laval, were hired to join holdovers Cy Morgan, Ted McGrew, and Jocko Collins.[51]

Rumors swirled about Herb Pennock becoming general manager. Despite the speculation, Carpenter was coy at first, revealing only that his preferred candidate was under contract with another organization.[52] On November 30 Carpenter met with Pennock, who before committing to the job wanted to meet face-to-face to inform his boss, Red Sox owner Tom Yawkey, of his decision.[53] The next day, Pennock agreed to a five-year contract to become general manager of the Phillies.[54]

Pennock immediately went to work. He hired Joe Reardon, general manager of the Boston Red Sox Minor League affiliate in Scranton and said to have an "encyclopedic" knowledge of baseball, to run the Phillies farm system.[55] Two weeks later, Reardon announced the Phillies would be establishing a chain of baseball schools in Philadelphia and in cities where the Phillies operated their farm teams.[56] Utica was retained, and the Carpenters bought out their partner, Connie Mack, in order to shift Wilmington's Interstate

League franchise from the Athletics, replacing Trenton.[57] A Minor League affiliate, in the PONY League (Pennsylvania–Ohio–New York), was added in Bradford, Pennsylvania.[58]

One of Carpenter's immediate goals was to improve the brand. In that spirit, he announced a contest to select a new team nickname. Contestants were to submit suggestions along with an explanation of no more than one hundred words. The top three entrants would win season tickets, with the one deemed best also earning a one hundred dollar war bond.[59]

More than five thousand contestants submitted letters suggesting 634 different names. The winning entry was submitted by Elizabeth Crooks, one of seven fans who suggested "Blue Jays." Crooks, who along with her husband served as caretaker at the Odd Fellows Grand Lodge in Philadelphia, insisted, "The Blue Jay will reflect a new team spirit. The Blue Jay is colorful in personality and plumage. This bird's fighting, aggressive spirit never admits defeat."[60]

Mrs. Crooks posed for a photo with the team's new emblem, a blue jay perched on the double *l* in the old Phillies logo. But the new moniker was not universally hailed. A group of students from Johns Hopkins University in Baltimore alleged that the Phillies had stolen their school mascot and further argued that the team would sully its use in light of its constant failures, listing in great detail Phillies futility over the previous half century.[61] The fuss was good-natured for the most part, but Bob Carpenter did release a disclaimer with the announcement of the new nickname, declaring that Blue Jays would serve as an additional sobriquet, not a replacement for the long-standing use of Phillies.[62]

The blue theme eventually filtered down to the team's Minor League affiliates. Wilmington was the "Blue Rocks," Bradford the "Blue Wings," and, in late May, Utica became the "Blue Sox." Joe Reardon announced that Utica players were being fitted with new home and road uniforms.[63]

Like Cox before them, Carpenter and Pennock overhauled the roster in 1944, some of it by design, some by necessity thanks to military inductions, including that of Schoolboy Rowe. In late May, Carpenter visited Philadelphia while on furlough from the army and looked over his team. He was asked whether he was happy with the way things were going for the Phillies. He laughed and said, "Some days I am, and other days I'm not."[64]

That first season was far from an artistic success. A streetcar strike caused cancellation of several games in August.[65] War-time travel restrictions resulted in monthlong road trips and an incredible number of doubleheaders—seventeen of them during the final six weeks of the season—putting a major strain on a pitching staff light on talent and limited in depth. There were only fourteen home dates between June 22 and September 1, a span of seventy-one days. Dick Barrett, three days past his thirty-eighth birthday, won the season finale to run his record to 12-18, and the team's to 61-92.[66] It was the twelfth straight season the Phillies had finished last or next-to-last.

Three months later, the team's best hitter, outfielder Ron Northey, was inducted into the army after the War Department ordered a review of all professional athletes classified as 4-F—the Battle of the Bulge in December 1944 tested public attitudes about athletes playing ball instead of serving their country. Northey, who drove in 104 runs in 1944 (forty more than team runner-up Buster Adams), boasted one of the strongest throwing arms in the Major Leagues. He had previously undergone four days of physical examinations and been classified draft exempt. A few weeks later, without explanation, he was ordered to report for duty.[67]

There was a bright spot to 1944—near the end of the season the Phillies netted a future Whiz Kid, Granville Hamner, a seventeen-year-old high school junior from Virginia who had spent the summer playing local semipro baseball and working as a camp counselor in Maine.[68] Granville's older brother, Garvin, was already playing professional baseball with his hometown Richmond Colts in the Piedmont League.

It was Hamner's mother who fostered the love of sports in her sons—she had made older brother Garvin's first uniform and bought Granville his first mitt. Their father's interest in baseball was limited to deliveries from his ice wagon to the Richmond ballpark.[69] Hamner was an outstanding high school athlete and captain in three sports, but he had never seen a Major League game before his debut on September 14 as a defensive replacement against the Giants at the Polo Grounds. He turned a 4–6–3 double play and handled 3 chances without an error. Alongside him at third base for the final two innings was Ralph "Putsy" Caballero, six months younger than Hamner.[70] Caballero hailed from the same New Orleans high school that later produced Rusty Staub and Will Clark. A high school graduate at age sixteen, he had signed five days earlier with the Phillies for an $8,000 bonus. Putsy's father drove the two of them from Louisiana to sign the contract.[71] Like Hamner, Caballero was a three-sport star for his high school and was making his debut as a professional ballplayer.

Hamner made his first start the next night, at Shibe Park, handling 5 chances without an error while drawing a walk and scoring a run in 4 plate appearances.[72] His placement in the lineup coincided with the beginning of a six-game winning streak that vaulted the Phillies from last to sixth, with Hamner drawing some of the credit. But the Phillies then lost nine in a row, returning to the cellar where they remained as the season drew to a close.

Hamner was the Phillies starting shortstop for the season's final twenty games, hitting a creditable .247. Defensively he was aggressive, committing 9 errors but also participating in 17 double plays. As expected, his fielding was ahead of his hitting, but Freddie Fitzsimmons said, "That will come, and I don't want him to worry about it."[73]

Meanwhile, Granville's brother Garvin became a free agent shortly after the 1944 season ended when their mother questioned the fact that his Richmond contract lacked either parent's signature, making it void since Garvin was a minor. Garvin Hamner immediately accepted an offer from Herb Pennock to join brother Granville with the Phillies.[74]

THE PHILLIES FOUND ANOTHER gem in February 1945, signing a young catcher from Nebraska named Richie Ashburn.[75] His hometown, Tilden, in the eastern part of the state, boasted a population of barely one thousand and did not field an American Legion team, so Ashburn played in Neligh, about fifteen miles away. Ashburn's father, Neil, owned a blacksmith and machine shop in Tilden, and his older brother Bob was an excellent athlete with a promising future until an automobile accident ended his athletic dreams.[76] Ashburn, whose first name was actually Don, had a twin sister named Donna. The towheaded Ashburn, who would earn the nickname "Whitey," was brash and quick with wisecracks.

Neil Ashburn bought his son a catcher's mitt and turned him into a left-handed batter, feeling the combination would prove the fastest route to the Major Leagues. The teenager remained behind the plate in high school despite 10.2 one-hundred-yard speed. Ashburn had already been signed once, illegally while in high school by Cleveland and assigned to Wilkes-Barre, but Commissioner Landis voided the deal and fined the Indians.[77] In July 1943 Ashburn attended a tryout camp in Omaha sponsored by the St. Louis Cardinals but did not sign.[78]

The next summer, Floyd Olds, editor of the *Omaha Herald*, was asked to designate a player for the inaugural 1944 Esquire East-West game in New York City. After canvassing American Legion coaches in his area, he selected Ashburn as Omaha's representative.[79]

A week before the Esquire contest, Ashburn attended his first Major League game, at the Polo Grounds, and witnessed a slugfest between the Giants and Reds. Watching war-time replacements in big league uniforms, the teenager casually remarked, "It certainly didn't look like the Major leagues to me." When asked if he could step into the Majors, he replied, "No, I don't think I'm that good. But I certainly wouldn't be scared to try."[80]

Virgil Jester, who later pitched for the Boston Braves, took the mound for Ashburn's West team against Billy Pierce, a future seven-time All-Star for the Chicago White Sox. West manager Mel Ott inserted Ashburn about halfway through the game, with the teenager failing to get a hit in his 2 at bats. Pierce dominated the contest, striking out 6 in an equal number of innings while allowing only 3 hits to beat Ashburn and his West teammates, 6–0.[81]

Ashburn signed another contract, this one with the Chicago Cubs; the team was to send him to Nashville, but the deal included a bonus clause and was nullified by National Association president William Bramham.[82] At this point, Ashburn's father soured on scouts and sent his son to Norfolk Junior College to play basketball.

While digesting Cy Morgan's Esquire scouting reports, Herb Pennock became intrigued with Ashburn. When told the Nebraskan was indeed as good as the report claimed he was, Pennock dispatched scout Eddie Krajnik to meet with the young athlete and his father.

"I doubt if any other man could have done the job," said Ashburn. "Dad didn't like scouts. We had two unfortunate experiences with them earlier. But he and Krajnik sort of took to each other and the proposition the Phillies gave us was so clean-cut that he accepted right away."[83]

THE 1945 SEASON SEEMED a step backward for the Phillies. Granville Hamner got off to a rough start both in the field and at the plate, and his performance deteriorated from there. After beginning the season 4-16 and sitting solidly in last place, the Phillies could not afford to let Hamner learn on the job. Despite his promising debut the previous September, the teenager was not ready for the Major Leagues. Things finally came to a head on May

5 when "Granny" made 2 errors in the first inning, opening the floodgates for 5 Brooklyn runs. After Hamner committed another error in the third and the home crowd exhibited its vehement disapproval, Freddie Fitzsimmons pinch-hit for the teenager in the bottom of the inning and moved his brother from second to short to take his place.[84] Hamner was said to be in tears while sitting alongside Freddie Fitzsimmons on the bench—Hamner disputed that, allowing that while he was emotional about his performance, he had not cried.[85] A week later, Granville Hamner was optioned to Utica.[86] While Herb Pennock still believed in Hamner, he lamented, "I brought him up too early, even in a war year," adding, "[The fans] riding him as they did was one of the cruelest things I have ever witnessed."[87] Outside of annual cameo appearances, Hamner remained in the Minors until 1948. Meanwhile, Garvin Hamner did not play again in the Majors after the 1945 season, although he remained active through 1953, mostly in the high Minors.

The ravages of the draft and enlistment of ballplayers during the war put a crimp in the Phillies rebuilding plans. As a result, the team employed several players with name recognition but little else to offer. Thirty-nine-year-old catcher Gus Mancuso was picked up after his release by the New York Giants and hit .199. Hard-drinking Dick Barrett, still popular due to an incredible semipro stint in Philadelphia more than a decade earlier, became the ninth 20-game loser for the Phillies since the infamous Alexander trade after the 1917 season.[88]

Thirty-seven-year-old Whitlow Wyatt, an All-Star only three years earlier, was purchased from Brooklyn and went 0-7. Jimmie Foxx came out of retirement and was a bright spot, hitting the final 7 home runs of his career in a part-time role. He also pitched on occasion, compiling a 1.59 earned run average in nine appearances, including two starts.[89]

But, unlike in past years, these ancients donning Phillies uniforms did not signal a lack of commitment to developing home-grown talent and keeping it. These already-faded athletes were a symptom of the time, placeholders until other, younger men returned from the battlefield.

At the end of June 1945, Fred Fitzsimmons resigned as manager—only four players remained from the team he had taken charge of two years earlier. Pitcher-outfielder Ben Chapman, who had been acquired from Brooklyn two weeks prior but had yet to appear in a game because of a sore arm, became a playing-manager.[90] During his first week, the Phillies began a ten-game losing streak. Their final record was a dismal 46-108.

The Phillies promoted another key Whiz Kid in 1946, Del Ennis, a local boy out of Olney High School and one of the last amateur signings of the Nugent regime.[91] As a child, Ennis regularly attended games at Baker Bowl with his father and idolized Chuck Klein—he said the first Major League game he ever attended was as an eleven-year-old on the day Klein hit 4 home runs.[92] Ennis began his career with Class B Trenton at age seventeen, winning the Interstate League batting title and leading the circuit in total bases. During the war he honed his skills at Guam against the likes of Schoolboy Rowe, Johnny Vander Meer, and Billy Herman.

Discharged in April 1946, Ennis reported to the Phillies just before Opening Day.[93] Even though he had not played after being called up by Philadelphia in September 1943, the team was required to keep him around for fifteen days and provide him an opportunity to maintain his "prewar job." Ben Chapman decided to put Ennis in the lineup, and on May 5, he slammed 2 home runs in the nightcap of a doubleheader against the Cubs at Wrigley Field.[94] On his twenty-first birthday, Ennis's eighth-inning single broke up St. Louis Cardinals right-hander Red Barrett's quest for the National League's first perfect game in sixty-six years.[95] Chapman worked with Ennis, having him stand closer to the plate and choke up while using a heavier bat in an effort to help him more consistently pull the ball.[96] By midsummer, Herb Pennock was saying he would not take $100,000 for Ennis.[97] He was one of three Phillies on the 1946 National League All-Star team and was named NL Rookie of the Year by *The Sporting News.*[98]

The Phillies still lacked on-field success, but fans were becoming interested in the team, topping one million in attendance for the first time in 1946. Philadelphia managed a fifth-place finish despite a lackluster 69-85 record. Schoolboy Rowe returned after two years of military service with an 11-4 mark and a 2.12 earned run average, Del Ennis was a coming player of note, and Andy Seminick was starting catcher. When it came to Ennis, Bob Carpenter said he had inquiries from the Braves, Cubs, and Giants and raised his price to "$750,000 or a Triple A franchise."[99] Carpenter and Pennock signaled the Phillies were now buyers instead of sellers. News leaked from the 1946 Winter Meetings in Los Angeles that the team was aggressively pursuing Enos Slaughter, thirty-year-old star outfielder of the St. Louis Cardinals. It was reported that they were offering $150,000 in cash or a combination of cash and outfielder Ron Northey.[100] Cardinals' president Sam Breadon quashed speculation by publicly declaring his disdain for the proposal.[101] The Phillies eventually made a deal with the Cardinals shortly after the 1947 season started, sending Northey to St. Louis in exchange for outfielder Harry Walker.[102]

THE 1947 SEASON MARKED the arrival of Jackie Robinson in the Major Leagues, and his first visit to Philadelphia was historic, although not for the right reasons. Ben Chapman was no fan of integrating the Major Leagues, and no team in the National League fired more vile epithets from the dugout than did he and his close friend, trainer-coach Dusty Cooke, along with several of the players. Howie Schultz, a first baseman who came over from Brooklyn early in the season, called it embarrassing and characterized Chapman as among those still fighting the Civil War.[103] Andy Seminick said, "Everybody knew how Chapman felt about Robinson. He was anti-black. He was against them coming into the league, and he showed it."[104]

When Robinson and the Dodgers prepared to make their first visit to Shibe Park, Branch Rickey was contacted by either Herb Pennock or Bob Carpenter—there are differing claims as to the caller's identity—and warned in shocking but, for the time, sadly crude language that Robinson should not come to Philadelphia.[105] Rickey ignored the "advice," and by the time the Dodgers arrived in the City of Brotherly Love, reaction of the press and public had turned against the Phillies—and also the St. Louis Cardinals, whose players had been rumored to threaten a strike rather than take the field against Robinson. The blowback was such that Chapman was forced to pose for a photo, sharing a bat with the Brooklyn star, while unconvincingly portraying the racial bench jockeying as a harmless baseball tradition.[106] For years, the Phillies treatment of Jackie Robinson shadowed the franchise—and the perception of players and public alike when it came to the organization's racial attitudes.

Although controversy hung over the team's 1947 season, that year saw the Phillies Minor League system beginning to bear fruit. It was true that the Phillies slipped to seventh place, and their biggest contributors tended to be anything but young. Twenty-nine-year-old Harry Walker won the batting title, and thirty-eight-year-old knuckleballer Dutch Leonard teamed with thirty-seven-year-old Schoolboy Rowe to win half of the team's games.

But 1947 was also the year that the Phillies signed two future pitching stars who would play a major role in transforming the fortunes of one of baseball's least successful franchises.

3

Signing Up 479 Wins in Four Months

HERB PENNOCK'S MASTER PLAN continued in 1947. With Bob Carpenter willing to open the checkbook, the Phillies farm system had more than doubled in size during the previous two years. The organization now boasted eleven Minor League affiliates, with five of those franchises owned by the Phillies outright, giving Pennock the freedom to sign and develop a surplus of young talent.

Despite coming off their best finish in fourteen years and taking advantage of the postwar economic boom to top one million in attendance, by late summer 1947 the Phillies had settled into their accustomed role at the rear of the National League—by a significant margin. Nevertheless, fans sensed a difference this time, and indeed the team's long-range fortunes were about to change dramatically with a pair of signings that would cost them nearly $100,000 but net them many times that.

Within a four-month span, Philadelphia made two significant acquisitions, future Hall of Fame right-hander Robin Roberts and star left-hander Curt Simmons. Between them they would win close to 500 Major League games—nearly three-fourths of them while wearing Phillies uniforms.

Simmons, whom the Phillies had been watching for more than two years, was the more prized prospect, tracked closely even as a high school sophomore in the tiny Lehigh Valley community of Egypt, Pennsylvania, near Allentown, where he lived with his parents and sister. His father, Lawrence, worked in a nearby cement mill and took an early and active interest in his son's athletic accomplishments.

A shy but friendly five-foot-eleven Pennsylvania Dutch boy, Simmons never wanted to do anything except play baseball, and he showed an imme-

diate talent for it—the best athlete Whitehall High School had ever produced, and that included Andy Tomasic, the "Hokendauqua Hurricane," a
college football and baseball star for Temple University and a member of the
Pittsburgh Steelers in the National Football League, immediately preceding
and following the Second World War.[1]

Simmons, who was also an excellent student, got his start in the local
Cement Borough League for players eighteen and younger. "We used to
load into milk trucks," he remembered, "and play teams from Nazareth,
Cementon, Northampton and a few others."[2]

He began playing American Legion baseball at fifteen years of age under
the tutelage of Sammy Balliet, who managed Coplay. Simmons was an
instant star and chosen for the first Pennsylvania American Legion All-Star
Game at Shibe Park that July, belting a single and a triple while playing left-
field for his team, dubbed the Athletics.[3]

Even more dominating in his second year, Simmons was a repeat choice
for the state Legion All-Star Game in 1945, again scheduled for Shibe Park.[4]

Despite heavy rain, the forty-three competitors gathered at the Loyal
Order of Moose Lodge on Broad Street in Philadelphia to await pregame
instructions. Instead, they received the disappointing news that due to the
weather, the game was being postponed for five days. Eighty-two-year-
old legend Connie Mack tried to temper the collective disappointment by
encouraging the young athletes to keep up their work for the rest of the
week, reminding them that it was quite possible a future Major League star
was among them.[5]

Simmons took Connie Mack's words to heart, pitching for Coplay
against Bethlehem in the opener of the local Legion playoffs. That he was
dominating was an understatement, striking out 23 batters while surrendering only 1 hit in a 4–0 win.[6]

Three days later, as the Big Four Allies received a Japanese offer of surrender, Curt Simmons took command of the All-Star contest. Scouts representing a half-dozen franchises were at Shibe Park, watching players divided into
competing squads representing Philadelphia's pair of Major League teams. It
was a hard-fought battle, ending in a 1–0 win for Herb Pennock's "Phillies,"
despite the fact that the sixteen-year-old Simmons struck out 7 in three no-
hit innings for the Athletics. Nevertheless, the effort earned Simmons honors
as the All-American Boy, a trip to New York to play in the Esquire East-West
All-Star Game, and undoubtedly the attention of Herb Pennock.[7]

A crowd said to number twenty-five thousand gathered at the
Grounds on August 28, along with two teams consisting of the nati
premiere teenage ballplayers. The West squad was managed by Ty Cc
The East, including Simmons, was managed by Babe Ruth, who effusi
praised the whipsaw left-hander. "He could give big league teams trou
right now," Ruth crowed to Brooklyn columnist Tommy Holmes. Privat
the baseball legend advised Simmons to extend his career by becoming
he had, a full-time outfielder.[8]

Simmons was starting pitcher for the East and struck out 4 in an eq
number of innings but surrendered 4 runs in the third thanks in part t
errors—one of them his. Ruth then moved him to right field for the res
the game.

The East rallied in the ninth to win, Simmons driving in the first i
with a triple and later scoring. Following the postgame dinner, a comm
tee that included Cobb, Ruth, and Carl Hubbell, voted Simmons the gam
outstanding player.[9] Cobb took Simmons aside and echoed Ruth's admo
tion, telling him, "Anybody who can hit a low, inside pitch the way you
has no business wasting his time trying to be a pitcher."[10]

Simmons traveled to Pittsburgh to pitch the opening game of the Per
sylvania American Legion finals on August 31. He tossed the first five innii
of a 19–3 slaughter, striking out 12 before moving to the outfield. On top
that, he hit for the cycle.[11] With Simmons playing first base the next d
Coplay won the state championship with a come-from-behind 9–8 win.[

Simmons repeated his dominating accomplishments in 1946. He led
high school to another league championship in May.[13] Three months la
he played a key role in a doubleheader sweep that secured Coplay's sec
consecutive state title, and then he pitched and batted Egypt to the l
Twilight League pennant, an overflow crowd spilling onto the field to
him play.[14]

The calendar shifted to 1947 and another season of high school do
nance. Simmons kicked off his senior year with a no-hitter against Qu
ertown High, striking out 20 in a seven-inning contest.[15] Two weeks l;
he struck out 11 in five innings of a 15–0 win.[16] A week after that, he ha
strikeouts in an 8–0 win over Allentown High.[17] A couple of days before
eighteenth birthday, it was announced that Simmons would pitch in Eg
against the Philadelphia Phillies, who wanted to see what the left-har
could do, as the bidding war for his services was ready to begin.[18]

ON JUNE 2, 1947, more than five thousand people ringed Egypt Memorial Park, considered overflow at one-third that number. The electric atmosphere resulted from the presence of the Philadelphia Phillies, whose front office brass wanted to test Curt Simmons, pitching for the local town team, against Major League competition. Midseason exhibitions by big league teams visiting small towns were not out of the ordinary, but most often they were promotional vehicles played in the hometown of one its players. They were not generally staged as a tryout.

One can only imagine the mood of Phillies players, in the midst of a losing streak and only three days removed from a sixteen-day road trip, disembarking from an hour-and-a-half, exhaust-choking bus ride to battle a group of high school kids on a local diamond in the middle of nowhere.

It was a diamond Simmons knew well. Located only a few blocks from his home, he and his friends regularly used their father's push mowers to cut the outfield grass—a task made all the more difficult thanks to a center field that rose uphill toward the fence and, illogically, a left field that sloped *downward* to meet the same barrier.[19]

Wide-eyed Egypt baseball fans watched Del Ennis, Johnny Wyrostek, and Andy Seminick take practice swings. A dozen Major League scouts were on hand, as were Phillies president Bob Carpenter, scout Cy Morgan—who lived in nearby Allentown—and general manager Herb Pennock.

Grumbling as they tightened their shoelaces and hitched up their belts, Phillies players took measure of the task before them. Warming up on the mound was a nondescript 160-pound, left-handed teenager—nondescript, that is, until he threw. The kid pitcher's windup began with his right foot pointed toward first base. Then he contorted himself as if a pretzel, violently twisting his hips and then throwing across his body. Not only did he throw hard, but his curveball also had a late, nasty break. The Phillies managed to score twice in the second inning, thanks in no small measure to a pair of Egypt errors, but Simmons and his teammates scored four times in the third.

The Phillies cut the lead to one in the fourth, but there was no further scoring until the top of the eighth, when Del Ennis led off with a high fly ball to left-center field that two Egypt outfielders pursued full-out on the uneven turf—right up to the moment of their violent collision. The ball fell safely, and Ennis made his way to third with a triple. After several minutes spent reviving one of the teenage outfielders, a Buster Adams double tied the game.

A couple of ground ball outs moved Adams to third, bringing up School-boy Rowe to pinch-hit. Simmons bore down and struck out Rowe on three pitches, bringing the locals to their feet as one with a roar.[20]

At the end of the ninth, with score still knotted, 4–4, the game was called due to darkness. Simmons posed for a photo, wearing his Esquire wind-breaker and a wide grin while kneeling among a group of hero-worshipping elementary school kids. He had struck out eleven Phillies, including Joe Albright and Johnny Wyrostek twice each. Simmons even fanned Emil Ver-ban, the All-Star second baseman who struck out only 8 times in 540 official at bats for the Phillies that year.

"I noticed Del Ennis was a low ball hitter," Simmons told Herb Pennock after the game. "Jim Tabor went for high ones, and Andy Seminick missed several low ones. So I tried to feed them the same type of pitch."[21]

"That kind of observation from an eighteen-year-old kid who never pitched better than high school and sandlot ball is what sold us," said Pennock, who had broken into the Majors at Simmons's age with the Philadelphia Athletics in 1912.[22]

There wasn't anything left for the Phillies to ponder, except to make sure they outbid everyone else. On June 16 Curt Simmons signed a contract—dated the next day so he could pitch one last time for Egypt in a Twilight League game. As his father explained, "We told them he would be there to pitch, and when we make promises, we try to keep them."[23]

Joining Simmons in Philadelphia's Packard Building for his signing were his mother, father, and sister, as well as Herb Pennock and Cy Morgan—with the unprecedented amount being given to the teenager, the occasion was photographed for posterity. Curt was assigned to the Wilmington Blue Rocks—located in the backyard of the Carpenter family—with his bonus hinted only as being more than $40,000. Pennock refused to be specific, admitting only, "It's one of the biggest prices ever offered a player to sign a contract with a major league club."[24] Bob Carpenter simply called it "a considerable sum."[25]

Simmons's pro debut three days later was spectacular—a 7–1 complete-game victory against the Lancaster Red Roses before more than seven thousand spectators, including George Earnshaw and Phillies scouts Cy Morgan and Joe Labate.[26]

Wilmington manager Jack Saltzgaver was grinning from ear to ear when met by reporters after the game. "What do I think of him?" he retorted. "I like him very much. He'll win me about twelve games between now and the end of the season. That's what I think of him."

For Simmons's part, he admitted, "I was a little nervous at first, but I knew my stuff was there after I got to working. Then everything was all right." Catcher Jim Turner called him the best pitcher he had ever caught and raved about the movement on his fastball. "Man, that ball either jumps or it sinks," Turner said. "You never know which it's going to do."[27] Neither did the hitters.

Not everyone was sold on Simmons being a can't-miss star. Teenager Dallas Green, who would grow up to manage the Phillies to their first World Series title, saw him pitch in Wilmington and told his uncle that because of his "herky-jerky" delivery, Simmons was not "worth a nickel."[28]

As word spread that Simmons's bonus was actually $65,000, Yankees scout Bill McCorry blasted the Phillies for paying large amounts to players before they had appeared in a game.[29]

Bob Carpenter gave a pointed response, noting that times had changed since McCorry had first signed a contract, that baseball was a business, and that the Phillies intended on succeeding in that business. The Phillies president produced a chart, comparing Phillies and Yankees farm teams, showing all of Philadelphia's affiliates higher in the standings. Wilmington sports editor Al Cartwright, reporting on the dust up, speculated that the Phillies might be settling the argument with the Yankees in a World Series sometime soon.

Carpenter's final retort to McCorry was "I would like to know what his boss was doing in the Simmons home on the evening of June 15, two days before Curt's signing with the Phillies. As I recall, the figures jumped a dollar or two the following morning."[30]

Simmons revitalized the Blue Rocks, which went from seventh place when he signed to second at the end of the season. He started eighteen games, completing seventeen and lasting eight and one-third innings in the other, and then added a pair of complete-game wins to help Wilmington clinch the postseason playoff title against Allentown. He struck out 16 in a game three times and registered 11 or more strikeouts in eleven of his starts, including in seven of his first eight. He fanned 197 batters in 147 innings during his ten weeks with Wilmington.

Because of his herky-jerky motion, control *was* a problem at times. On July 16 at Hagerstown, Simmons struggled the entire game, but led, 4–3, going to the bottom of the ninth, at which point he completely lost the plate.

A double, a walk, a single, a walk, and a single led to defeat. He stranded 17 base runners and struck out 11 but had also walked 13.[31]

On another occasion, Simmons carried a 4–1 lead against Sunbury into the bottom of the ninth, having allowed only 1 unearned run, when he again suddenly could not find the plate, surrendering 3 hits and 4 bases on balls to lose, 5–4.[32]

Often, his control problems disappeared as quickly as they had surfaced. In a game against York, he walked 6 batters in one inning—4 of them with the bases loaded—but only 1 otherwise, and he struck out 16 in cruising to a 12–6 victory.[33]

One of Simmons's strengths was that he did not let control lapses shake his confidence—he saw them as an opportunity to grow. His maturity, only weeks after graduating from high school, was impressive. Asked about his performance against York, he explained, "I was going good . . . when all of a sudden my control slipped and bingo, I gave a lot of free rides." He added, "I've got a lot to learn, but as I said, I'm learning it with each game."[34]

George Earnshaw was dispatched to work with Simmons, tasked with changing the across-the-body delivery that led not only to control problems but also to potential arm injury. "I get my feet all twisted up after a pitch." Simmons explained. "I never finish my follow-through with my feet in the same position twice in succession. I end up different every time."[35]

Contrary to Jack Saltzgaver's prediction, Curt Simmons did not win 12 games in his half season in Wilmington. He won 13—plus 2 more in the playoffs. And because of the bonus rule dictating he had to be on a Major League roster before season's end, Simmons was called up to Philadelphia.

ON SEPTEMBER 26, 1947, the Philadelphia Phillies placed an ad in the *Philadelphia Inquirer* that said,

NO!
You won't have to wait 'til next year to see Curt Simmons pitch. Come out and watch the phenomenal fire-baller throw his high, hard one at the home-run-happy Giants.[36]

Herb Pennock had picked an intimidating opponent—the New York Giants were in the midst of setting a Major League record for home runs in a season with 221, 40 more than any team had ever hit before. With their swing-for-the-fences lineup, the Giants were a good test, Pennock felt, for a wild eighteen-year-old who threw hard and had a curveball that rolled off the table.

A crowd of 14,004, including a contingent bused in from the Lehigh Valley, witnessed a season-ending doubleheader on September 28. After the Giants won the opener, 4–1, defeating another young Phillies pitcher, Dick Koecher, thanks to 7 Phillies errors, New York moved Johnny Mize to leadoff for the nightcap in order to get him an extra at bat; he and Pittsburgh's Ralph Kiner were tied for the National League lead in home runs with 51.

"I was a bit nervous, always am just before I start a game," admitted Simmons. "But once the game started I just kept telling myself that it was just like Wilmington—just another ballgame."

Stan Baumgartner described the rookie's curveball as breaking "like a jug handle." Simmons's fastball was also dancing that day—several squirted from Andy Seminick's glove. "He seemed to know just what to call," Simmons said of Seminick, "and three times when I broke my curve ball in front of the plate with men on, he made great pickups."[37]

Simmons, who also stroked a single and laid down a sacrifice bunt, surrendered only 4 hits through the first eight and two-thirds innings. Then his control problems surfaced. He walked a pair and surrendered a run-scoring single that narrowed the lead to 3–1. That brought Johnny Mize to the plate as the potential lead run. But Mize, who had managed only a squib single to left field against Simmons, grounded weakly to second baseman Emil Verban, who threw him out to end the game. Hundreds of kids instantly streamed out of the stands, engulfing their newest hero, who signed scorecards while being pushed along in the rush.[38]

Philadelphia's win gave the team a final record of 62-92, securing a tie with the Pirates for seventh place. Less than four months after graduating from high school, Curt Simmons had won his Major League debut, holding a record-setting offensive team to a single run while striking out 9.

Despite that success, Herb Pennock was not secretive about his desire to leave Simmons in the Minors for another season rather than have him forced onto a Major League roster for the next two years because of regulations surrounding so-called bonus babies.

"The present rule not only is a drawback to the clubs, but it does not work to the advantage of the player," complained Pennock, who confirmed his intention to pursue a change in the rule at the Winter Meetings.[39]

THE OTHER FRANCHISE-ALTERING acquisition by the Phillies in 1947 was that of Robin Roberts, best known at the time as a college basketball star for Michigan State University. But his pitching for the Spartans against rival Michigan caught the eye of opposing head coach Ray Fisher, an ex–Major League pitcher who had taken the mound for Cincinnati against the "Black Sox" in the 1919 World Series and who eventually led Wolverines baseball for thirty-eight years. Impressed with Roberts's determination, Fisher talked the strapping six-foot-one pitcher into joining the summer league team he managed in Vermont. Fisher had coached Charlie Gehringer in college; he was about to develop his second Hall of Famer.

THE ROBERTS FAMILY EMIGRATED from the coal fields of Wales in the early 1920s. Robin's father, Tom, had served with the British Army during the First World War and then returned to the coal mines until a strike curtailed his employment prospects. He heard of work in the United States and made the journey with his wife and two sons, purchasing a plot of land in Springfield, Illinois. He found employment in the local mines but later took a job with Sangamo Electric as a night watchman.[40]

More children came, including Robin, the fifth child, who grew up in the "Land of Lincoln" in a two-room house that was soon expanded on a two-acre lot. The family became self-sufficient, raising chickens, rabbits, and pigs, as well as peach and cherry trees.[41] Robin's middle name, Evan, honored an uncle killed in action during the First World War. Ironically, Roberts was called Evan by everyone in Springfield except his father, who could not bring himself to use his late brother's name in connection with his young son, always addressing him as Robin.

Roberts demonstrated an early affinity for mathematics, winning citywide contests three years running while attending East Pleasant Elementary School.[42] Chores—not so much. "He was always too busy playing," recalled his father. "When I finally did get him to do something, like hoeing the garden, the hoe was always breaking and he would be off to play with the rest of the boys."[43]

When he could not find any of his friends or brothers to throw a ball to, Roberts propped an old mattress against the garage and threw a baseball at a hole that had been cut out of the middle.[44]

A week before his eleventh birthday, Robin made the front page of the local paper, one of three boys who happened upon a discarded pistol that had been wielded during an attempted murder. After hearing that it was suspected the gun had been dumped in a field near their school, the boys decided to find it and were successful. Robin was photographed handing the weapon to the chief of detectives.[45]

Robin's mother was a big sports fan, especially enamored with the Chicago Cubs, and Robin followed suit, pursuing his love of baseball and plastering his bedroom wall with photos of his hero, Lou Gehrig.[46] Robin would play outside while listening to a Cubs game on a radio, mimicking the players as he imagined them performing in the game.[47] Roberts met Bob Feller when the Indians star came to Springfield in 1937 as guest of honor for the opening game of the Illinois State amateur tournament.[48] Despite rain falling throughout, nearly one thousand fans were on hand, and Roberts managed to snag Feller's autograph, although he lost it without getting it home.[49]

That same year, Grover Cleveland Alexander, down on his luck and living in a Springfield hotel, was asked to speak at a local sports banquet. Three decades later, Roberts recalled Alexander's remarks: "Boys, baseball has been good to me, but don't ever drink. Look what it has done to me." Roberts said that Alexander then sat down.[50]

After attending Springfield High School for two years, Roberts transferred to Lanphier High due to a school boundary change. He loved all sports, but his talents seemed most obvious in basketball and baseball. He was solid at football as well, named as an end on Springfield's 1942 All-City All-Star football team—among his teammates was future NFL player Billy Stone.[51] This happened a few months after Robin's brother was accidentally killed aboard the submarine USS *R-18* while patrolling the Atlantic.[52]

Although Robin played baseball, he pitched only in his senior year and was not a frontline hurler, instead playing mostly as a switch-hitting third baseman with some pop in his bat. The team was not well-funded; according to Roberts, players took the field in their blue jeans, although the school did provide caps.[53]

After high school graduation, New York Yankees superscout Bill Essick offered Robin a $4,000 bonus, but he had already signed up for the Army Reserve with plans to become a fighter pilot.[54] The reserves sent him to a six-month training program at Michigan State, which ended a couple months prior to his required reporting date. During that time in limbo, he decided to play basketball for the university, serving as team captain and leading scorer.[55]

The war ended not long after, and he was given the option to be discharged rather than become a fighter pilot; he chose civilian life. That resulted in his return to Michigan State, where he again starred in basketball.

Roberts also decided to try out for the Spartans baseball team, hoping to play first base. Coach John Kobs was unimpressed after watching him as a hitter, so Robin asked for a second audition, as a pitcher.

"I was very skeptical," remembered Kobs, "but I told him to go ahead and try."[56]

After the team returned from a road trip, Kobs put Roberts through the motions and quickly recognized his talent. Roberts earned a spot on the team and, despite pitching infrequently, winning 4 and losing 2, he continually improved, striking out 49 and walking only 15 in forty-six innings. For good measure he threw a no-hitter against the Great Lakes Naval Training Station.[57] Joining Ray Fisher in Vermont that summer, Roberts pitched a no-hitter against Keene despite losing, 1–0, thanks to a second inning that featured a lead-off walk, a stolen base, and two groundouts that resulted in the game's only tally.[58]

After compiling a 5-4 record with a 2.88 earned run average and 86 strikeouts in 91 innings for Michigan State as a junior, Roberts spent his second summer with Ray Fisher and everything clicked. He found an effortless delivery that created perfect rhythm, a deceptively easy motion from which his fastball was effective. He was not overpowering, but his fastball had excellent movement, and he could put it exactly where he wanted. Roberts also loved playing the game beyond just pitching—he was a decent switch hitter and an aggressive baserunner, unafraid to make a headfirst slide or take the extra base. The young right-hander was dominating that summer, compiling a record of 18-3.

Phillies scout Chuck Ward was impressed and arranged a three-day tryout for Roberts at Wrigley Field in September—he reportedly became convinced of Roberts's moxie after Robin was hit in the back of the head in

Vermont by his catcher on an attempt to throw out a baserunner. Despite being nearly knocked out cold, Roberts completed the game and won in impressive fashion.[59]

Ward also discovered Roberts had a huge appetite. On the train from Springfield to Chicago he and Roberts had dinner, the scout treating him to steak with all the trimmings. After the pitcher had happily devoured the meal, Ward asked Roberts if he'd like another. The pitcher readily agreed, quickly devouring a second helping. After Robin cleaned his plate yet again, Ward confessed he had been joking about the second meal.[60]

The tryout was a success, and on October 21, 1947, Robin Roberts signed a contract with the Philadelphia Phillies. It had been planned for the contract signing to remain secret so Robin could maintain his eligibility for basketball at Michigan State, but word leaked, and he was not able to play his senior year.[61] Roberts and Spartans teammate Marty Hansen ultimately announced they were to join the Phillies, with Roberts receiving a $25,000 bonus, and Hansen half that much.[62]

When asked what a young man collecting that kind of bonus would do with it, Roberts quipped, "He spends it." He quickly added that he was having a house built in Springfield for his parents—he had always promised his mother that if he signed a pro contract he would do as his idol Lou Gehrig had done for his mother. When asked if he was going to purchase an automobile, he shook his head and said, "No, I don't need a car. Gotta stay in shape."[63]

Joking aside, Robin did buy a car, but in his naïveté regarding such matters he failed to set aside money out of his bonus to pay his income taxes and had to borrow from his father to do so. He finally repaid him from his 1950 World Series share.[64]

Roberts spent the winter working out at Michigan State's Jenison Fieldhouse while he waited for spring and an anticipated assignment to Wilmington in 1948, where he was expected to follow in the footsteps of Curt Simmons. During spring training he was having problems with pulled leg muscles and was unable to take the mound in the early going.

One day Roberts was walking behind Bob Carpenter, who was unaware of the young pitcher's presence, and the right-hander heard Carpenter remark to another Phillies official, "Well it looks like I blew another $25,000." A crushed Roberts was consoled by Coach Cy Perkins who told him, "Wait till they see you pitch."[65]

Perkins was right. When Roberts did finally start pitching, he nearly made the opening day roster. Ultimately, he was one of the last cuts, as the Phillies decided not to rush him. Unlike Curt Simmons, who had a violent, cross-body motion, Roberts was built for durability, thanks to a solid physique, powerful legs, and a delivery that minimized strain on his arm. And Bob Carpenter had come around, predicting Roberts would win 20 games for Wilmington. Roving Minor League pitching instructor Lew Krausse opined that Roberts was ready to pitch in the Majors but agreed a season in the Minors would benefit him.[66]

Roberts did not hide his disappointment, which due to his competitive nature bordered on anger. "I'd rather stay in Philadelphia—and take my regular turn," he told Al Cartwright before turning diplomatic. "But, seriously, I realize that this season in the minors is going to help me. Look at Curt [Simmons]. One year at Wilmington and he's on top of the world right now. I want to get up there and pitch with him as quickly as possible, and if joining the Blue Rocks is the quickest way to accomplish it, that's that."[67]

Twenty-one-year-old Robin Roberts's professional debut on April 29, 1948, made the front page of the *Wilmington Morning News*, and he picked up right where Curt Simmons had left off, with a 19–1 win over the Harrisburg Senators in which he struck out 17 batters, including eight of the first ten men he faced. Roberts allowed only 5 hits and walked 1 batter in a performance that might have resulted in a new league strikeout record had he not been staked to such a large lead. Only a ninth-inning, run-scoring single by Ed Musial, younger brother of Stan, prevented Roberts from pitching a shutout.[68]

Roberts's second start was arguably even better, a four-hit shutout against Trenton, with 14 strikeouts against only 1 walk. He had a much smaller margin for error in his second effort, with Wilmington only able to scratch together 2 runs of support in the bottom of the eighth. The only baserunner to reach third came on a two-out, ninth-inning triple. Roberts responded with a strikeout to end the game.[69] Among his biggest fans in Wilmington were Bob Carpenter's parents, who sat behind the Blue Rocks dugout for most home games.[70]

Early on, Roberts showed his ultracompetitive nature—just as he had as a child, Robin hated to lose more than almost anything in life. In the Majors, he would often walk back to the hotel by himself after a loss, even if that meant a trek of several miles. Phillies coach Maje McDonnell would later say of Roberts, "A fierce competitor. There's one or two times in a game you got to get a certain guy out. When it came to these situations, Robby said, 'Hey let's go. It's you and me.' And he'd give it his best shot. And more often than not he was successful."[71]

Roberts exhibited great poise from the outset; Major League umpire Al Barlick later described the right-hander as possessing the outward disposition of an oyster. Nothing seemed to faze him—crowd noise, catcalls from opposing players, not even Leo Durocher.[72]

His pitching motion was easy on his arm, with a follow-through later baseball fans would recognize as similar to that of Tom Seaver, his right knee touching the ground as he released the ball. He worked fast, sometimes too fast—coach Benny Bengough instructed him to devise a routine to keep him from rushing his pace.[73] After each delivery, Roberts would stretch while reaching down to adjust his pant leg, tug on his cap and, ritual complete, prepare for the next pitch. His was a simple but effective mix of fastballs and curves, but mostly fastballs that he could consistently place where he wanted.

After an impressive fifteen-inning, 2–2 tie against York, *The Sporting News* published a cartoon depicting Roberts dragging a ball and chain labeled "Class B League" as an argument against the bonus rule that was impeding his ability to go to the Majors—even Commissioner Ford Frick began to admit the rule deserved criticism.[74] At that point, Roberts had won 4 games without a defeat and struck out 70 batters in fifty-one innings. Interstate League hitters were batting .129 against him, and his earned run average stood at 0.71. Absent a bad pitch in the ninth inning against Lancaster that resulted in a three-run home run, Roberts's earned run average at that point would have been 0.18.

Roberts lost only once with Wilmington—a game on May 27 in which he clearly was not himself, walking 7 and allowing 9 runs to Sunbury in five and two-thirds innings. It was the first time Roberts failed to pitch a complete game and also marked manager Jack Sanford's first ejection of the season, for arguing about a check swing after which the opposing batter slammed a bases-loaded double. Sanford's ejection coincided with his taking Roberts out of the game.[75]

Wilmington was averaging in excess of two thousand fans per home game, a more than 30 percent increase over 1947's record attendance. On

June 5 Roberts thrilled the more than 3,600 on hand by tying the league record with eighteen strikeouts in a 4–1 win over Trenton.[76]

As with Curt Simmons the year before, there was not much left for Robin Roberts to prove. After he ran his record to 9-1, the Phillies decided it was time to move him up to the Major Leagues. Jack Sanford's reaction was "I knew it was coming, but I had hoped to be able to pitch him one more time. I wish him all the luck in the world with the Phils. He deserves it."

For his part, Roberts admitted, "Naturally, I'm nervous, but I'm sure glad of the chance to pitch in the big time."[77]

The anchors of the "Whiz Kids" starting rotation were in place.

4

Moving On without the Squire

WITH CURT SIMMONS and Robin Roberts on the scene, here is a good time to take stock of Herb Pennock's efforts to change the course of Phillies history, through a wider view of his revamped farm system. The 1947 season had been a watershed year for Phillies Minor League teams—the resources committed to finding young talent was paying off. Of Philadelphia's eleven Minor League affiliates, five won titles—including three Class C entries—and three more had finished second.[1]

Richie Ashburn, Stan Lopata, Granny Hamner, and Bill Glynn had spent the year in Utica. Third baseman Willie Jones was in Terre Haute, driving in 107 runs. Curt Simmons had been spectacular in Wilmington, where outfielder Ed Sanicki led the Interstate League in home runs with 37. After spending spring training in 1948 with Philadelphia, Robin Roberts began his pro career in Wilmington, taking Simmons's place.

Emory "Bubba" Church won 21 games in Salina while striking out 219 batters and completing 27 games. He also hit .280 and drove in 39 runs, playing some in the outfield before switching to the mound full-time in his first season as a professional.[2] Church's teammate Art Hartley won 22 games, while a third pitcher, Paul Stuffel, struck out 205 batters in 181 innings.

Eighteen-year-old pitcher Steve Ridzik won 9 and lost 3 for Schenectady, while infielder Mike Goliat played for Vandergrift, where Alex Garbowski won the Middle Atlantic League batting title with a mark of .393. Raymond Burnett struck out 262 batters in 253 innings, winning 21 games for Americus—although he also walked 179.

Some of these players would make it, some becoming stars. Others would not. But there was no arguing that the Phillies had invested heavily in young talent as never before.[3]

The scouting department had expanded as well. Thirteen full-time talent hunters were on the payroll in 1947, among them Edith Houghton, the first full-time female scout in baseball history. She had secured employment a year earlier after boldly walking into Bob Carpenter's office and refusing to leave until he hired her. An impressed Herb Pennock said, "I am convinced she knows baseball. She should help us a lot in our scouting semi-pro and sandlot players in and around Philadelphia."[4] She was paid on a percentage basis, the amount depending on the time a player remained in the Phillies system.[5]

Pennock was buoyant as the calendar turned to the New Year. Following a two-week vacation at Bob Carpenter's South Carolina plantation, the Phillies general manager returned to his office at the Packard Building and began planning contract talks for 1948. He declared that batting champ Harry "The Hat" Walker and 17-game winner Dutch Leonard were in for big raises.[6] Curt Simmons signed his contract during the third week of January and announced he was anxious to get to spring training. "I realize I have a lot to learn about the big leagues," he explained. Pennock warned fans that Simmons might start slowly in the coming season but thought it possible he would win 10 games.[7] The war had impacted the timetable, but now everything seemed to be proceeding as planned.

On January 30, 1948, Herb Pennock was in New York City with Bob Carpenter for the annual Major League meetings. The two men left the Commodore Hotel that morning to begin the seven-block walk to the Waldorf-Astoria, where the event was being held. Along the way, Pennock complained about a nagging headache that had suddenly worsened.

Upon reaching the doorway of the Waldorf-Astoria, the fifty-three-year-old Pennock collapsed, unconscious. Carpenter shouted for the hotel doctor, and Pennock was removed to a gift shop while awaiting an ambulance. During the interval, the doctor examined Pennock and determined that he had suffered a catastrophic cerebral hemorrhage. There was nothing to be done. Pennock was pronounced dead on arrival at the hospital.[8]

Carpenter was stunned. After breaking the news to Pennock's wife, Esther, he told the press, "I just can't believe it. . . . We had not only been friends but business associates. I had known Herb since I was twelve years old. And our families were very close."[9]

Two days later, those wishing to pay their respects gathered at the American Legion Hall in Kennett Square for the public viewing. Among those filing past the Squire's bier were Bob Carpenter, Del Ennis, Curt Simmons, Harry Walker, Rube Walberg, Delaware governor Walter Bacon, and Byrum Saam, announcer for both the Phillies and Athletics.[10] A private graveside service was held later, with Carpenter and Ben Chapman, along with a handful of Phillies front office personnel and Pennock's old teammate, Hall of Famer Eddie Collins, among those invited.[11]

Bob Carpenter announced he would be assuming Pennock's duties and confirmed that Ben Chapman would remain as manager, with full authority (and responsibility) for everything that happened on the field. "Chapman's job is to win with the material he has. If he wants to run the bases backwards, that's okay with me." Carpenter insisted he never considered bringing in someone from the outside. "We spent four years building our organization, setting our policy, making our plans for victory in the future," he said.[12]

At the time of Herb Pennock's death, a grieving Carpenter had said, "It was too bad that Herb couldn't see the fruits of his labors, because they are inevitable."[13] Now he declared, "I want the Pennock system, based on the strong and sound farm system set up, to continue."[14] To that end, Carpenter promoted Cy Morgan to the role of Joe Reardon's assistant, and hired Lew Krausse and George Earnshaw to formally tutor Minor League pitchers.[15]

Addressing the fact that he had not played professional baseball, Carpenter confirmed that he would be leaning heavily on Ben Chapman, George Earnshaw, and Joe Reardon when it came to player evaluation. At the same time, he said he had learned from Herb Pennock and added, "A man does not have to have played baseball or been in baseball from the time he was a kid to handle such a job as this. How many of your men who own major league teams or direct their destinies have played organized ball?"[16]

At the end of February, it was announced that Herb Pennock had been elected posthumously to the National Baseball Hall of Fame at Cooperstown.[17]

BOB CARPENTER MADE his first major trade a week and a half after Pennock's death, sending outfielder Johnny Wyrostek to the Cincinnati Reds for fiery thirty-one-year-old shortstop Eddie Miller.[18] A seven-time National League All-Star, Miller was extremely smart, extremely outspoken, and extremely unconventional. Not much of a hitter, he had shocked everyone by knocking 19 home runs and batting .268 in 1947 but was unhappy in Cincinnati and unapologetic about letting everyone know. The trade of Wyrostek opened a potential outfield slot for Richie Ashburn, who had been shifted from catcher to take advantage of his speed and to end his bad habit of arguing with his own pitchers during games.

On April 7, 1948, Bob Carpenter made one of the most significant trades of his tenure, acquiring Dick Sisler from the St. Louis Cardinals for shortstop Ralph LaPointe and cash.[19] Looking back, Sisler said, "I didn't like it at first," then laughed, "but the way it turned out, it was the biggest break I ever had."[20] Sisler may have been hesitant upon joining the Phillies, but the Phillies were anything but.

On Opening Day in 1948, several of the eventual Whiz Kids had arrived. Dick Sisler was at first base. Putsy Caballero was playing third. Del Ennis was in right field, and Andy Seminick was behind the plate. Granny Hamner had returned after three years spent almost entirely in the Minor Leagues—incredibly, he was still a month shy of his twenty-first birthday—slotted to back up Emil Verban at second and Eddie Miller at short. When Miller was sidelined with a foot injury during the second game of the season, Hamner took his place and won a game with a sacrifice fly in the thirteenth inning.[21] He spent the next two weeks at shortstop and was involved in 9 double plays, while also committing 6 errors. On Memorial Day, with Emil Verban hitting only .224, Hamner took over at second base and stayed there. Verban, an All-Star the previous two seasons, was sold to the Chicago Cubs in August.[22]

Defending National League batting champion Harry Walker returned as center fielder but started slowly after holding out for most of spring training. In his absence, Richie Ashburn had capitalized on the opportunity with a spectacular spring. As Ashburn remembered, Walker took an interest in him, saying, "We hit a lot alike and I'll help you all I can." During the season, Walker went over pitchers before each game with Ashburn, even after Walker lost his center-field job to him.[23]

The Phillies continued uncovering prospects. Bob Carpenter had a well-known predilection for hard-throwing pitchers, so it came as no surprise that the most prominent signees plied their trade on the mound—Bob Miller from the University of Detroit and Hugh Radcliffe, a high school phenomenon out of Thomaston, Georgia.

Radcliffe was in greater demand, a right-hander boasting two curveballs plus a sinker and an intimidating fastball. He attracted attention after striking out 28 batters in a high school game in April 1948.[24] Within a month, a dozen scouts were hounding his every move, even during his high school graduation. "They have talked to me unofficially," Radcliffe remarked, "but no money has been mentioned. I'll probably sign with the club that offers the most money and the best contract."[25] On the day of his commencement, the Phillies were among four teams considered to have the inside track—the Red Sox, Tigers, and Reds being the others.[26] Two days later, Radcliffe signed with the Phillies for a $40,000 bonus and was assigned to Wilmington, where he replaced Robin Roberts in the Blue Rocks starting rotation and won 7 of 10 decisions, despite walking 82 batters in 96 innings.[27] He also acquired a wife, marrying high school sweetheart Margie Carraway a month after signing his contract.[28] They remained together for seventy-one years until his death in 2019.[29]

Originally, the Phillies told Radcliffe he would join them once the Interstate League season was over, but, recognizing he had not yet harnessed control of his pitching repertoire, it was decided to assign him to Toronto instead, gambling that no Major League team would draft him.[30] None did, and the Phillies essentially hid him in Toronto during the entire 1949 campaign. He made only 2 starts, two months apart, the second against Rochester in September the same day it was announced the Major Leagues had again rejected any changes to the bonus rule. With Joe Reardon on hand, Radcliffe picked up the victory despite walking 6 and allowing 5 runs in six innings.[31] Radcliffe was not listed in the league's final statistics because he pitched fewer than forty-five innings, but the attempt to hide him failed. After the 1949 season, the New York Yankees claimed the pitcher, another example of Carpenter's disdain for the bonus rule. It was not beneficial for Radcliffe either. Buried in the Yankees organization, he never reached the Major Leagues.[32]

ON THE DAY ROBIN ROBERTS learned he was going to the big leagues, the Phillies were rained out. At that point they had a record of 26-26 and were in fifth place—an encouraging pace at the one-third pole of the 1948 season. They had been consistent—only one day as many as three games above break-even, and only one day as many as three games below the .500 mark.

Richie Ashburn was hitting .347. But Curt Simmons was struggling, walking 20 batters in his first fifteen innings before settling down for an easy 14–2 complete-game win against Cincinnati, as Schoolboy Rowe sat in the dugout in street clothes, nursing a broken thumb and chatting with legendary trick-shot bowler Andy Varipapa.[33]

Simmons threw four complete games in a row in late May and early June, shortly after his nineteenth birthday, but was then cuffed around in five consecutive starts as the Phillies attempted changing his corkscrew delivery to improve his control. The bonus rule being as it was, Simmons had to learn in the big leagues with the Phillies. For the first time in his life, he was not dominating the competition, and his confidence suffered.

On June 18, 1948, Robin Roberts made his Major League debut, at Shibe Park against Pittsburgh. He pitched well but lost, 2–0, the runs scoring on a force out and a Wally Westlake home run.[34] Five days later, Roberts dominated the Cincinnati Reds during an impressive 3–2 victory, striking out 9 to earn the first of three straight wins. Foreshadowing a career-long tendency, the 2 runs scored on solo home runs, by Hank Sauer and Danny Litwhiler, who each struck out twice against the young right-hander. Richie Ashburn stole his 18th base that day, already the most by a Phillies player in seven years.[35] The winning runs were manufactured by Ashburn, Hamner, and Seminick. It was a preview of the team's future and came the day that the late Herb Pennock's daughter, married to Eddie Collins Jr., gave birth to a baby boy.

The Phillies entered the 1948 All-Star break in seventh place with a 36-42 record, thanks to a seven-game losing streak. But they were only two-and-a-half games out of fourth. The young players—especially Roberts and Ashburn—were drawing raves. If Roberts was impressive, Ashburn was a revelation, maintaining his batting average above .300 virtually all season, although some detractors dismissed him as a slap hitter who legged out infield hits that padded his batting average. Ashburn was the lone Phillies player participating in the National League All-Star Game, staged at Sportsman's Park in St. Louis. Placed at the top of the batting order by National League manager Leo Durocher, Ashburn started in center field. He stole a base, collected 2 hits in 4 at bats, and scored a run on Stan Musial's home run onto the right-field roof. Musial's blast accounted for the only runs the National League scored, as the American League won for the eleventh time out of fifteen contests played.[36]

The Phillies were rapidly gaining a reputation as a team of the future. However, that future did not include Ben Chapman, who had not been Herb Pennock's choice to move the team to the next level. Pennock had recruited Eddie Sawyer for that purpose. Bob Carpenter was determined to stick to Pennock's plan.

On July 16, the day after the team returned from the All-Star break and ended a seven-game losing streak, Chapman was fired and coach Dusty Cooke named interim manager. The move was a surprise, as most observers had thought Chapman's position secure. Chapman and Cooke posed for newspaper photographers, Chapman smoking a pipe and "reading" about his dismissal—an unmistakable call back to the Bucky Harris debacle. But, unlike that mess presided over by William Cox, Chapman had been told of his firing before it reached the press. Although shaken, Chapman declared at a press conference, "There is no animosity," while adding, "but this move by Mr. Carpenter came as quite a shock. I wish that Mr. Carpenter would tell the public his real reason for my dismissal." Carpenter termed it "concluding business" with Chapman, rather than firing him, insisting, "We are parting good friends."[37] The Phillies front office, including Carpenter, then awkwardly gathered for a party celebrating the ninth birthday of Chapman's son.[38]

Ten days later, Eddie Sawyer became manager of the Philadelphia Phillies, signed through the 1949 season.[39] A former outfielder who had made it as high as the Pacific Coast League before a shoulder injury curtailed his Major League dreams, Sawyer had a reputation for handling young talent—he had already managed many of Philadelphia's top prospects in Utica and Toronto. Carpenter felt he was perfect to advance the team's youth movement. Where Ben Chapman was fiery and volatile, Sawyer was calm, never chewing out players when they made mistakes. At heart he was a teacher—he held a master's degree in physiology and biology from Cornell and taught biology at Ithaca College in the off-season. "He was the same every day," remembered Maje McDonnell, "whether we won or lost."[40]

The Phillies lost Sawyer's debut to the Cubs, 3–2, in eleven innings, and afterward the players awaited a tongue-lashing tirade.[41] Instead, Sawyer quietly entered the clubhouse, looked around, and said, "Well, this game isn't much fun when you lose, is it?"[42] The team responded with a five-game winning streak that brought the Phillies within a game of break-even for the season. The energy soon faded as reality set in, the team staggering through seventeen losses in their first twenty-one games in August. But Sawyer had won over the clubhouse.

On August 28, the Phillies ended a ten-game slide with a 9–2 win behind Schoolboy Rowe in the first game of a doubleheader in Pittsburgh, but it was a costly victory. First, Johnny Blatnik was removed from the field on a stretcher in the third inning after suffering heat exhaustion. An inning later, Richie Ashburn injured his left hand on a headfirst slide while securing his 31st stolen base of the season. Saying nothing, Ashburn remained in the game until the eighth, stealing another base before having to admit to the injury when he could not catch Johnny Hopp's triple. Before exiting, he collected 4 hits and raised his batting average to .333. He had fractured his ring finger and would miss the season's final thirty-five games.[43]

A couple weeks later, the Phillies celebrated Old-Timer's Day with a cornucopia of Philadelphia legends on hand, including Jimmie Foxx, Home Run Baker, Chief Bender, Howard Ehmke, Harry Coveleski, Bill Killefer, Hans Lobert, Max Bishop, and four-time National League home run champ Cy Williams.[44]

At the same time the past was celebrated, so was the Phillies future during an 8–0 loss that dropped the team's record on the season to 58-80. Two more Whiz Kids made their 1948 debut. One was third baseman Willie Jones, who struck out twice against Cardinals left-hander Harry Brecheen but also handled four chances flawlessly.

Jones was originally signed by Johnny Nee in 1947 while playing semipro ball in South Carolina, and he reached the big leagues before the end of his first year as a professional. The story goes that Bob Carpenter received a letter from the manager of his estate in the Carolinas, extolling the virtues of a local semipro infielder and recommending a scout be dispatched, posthaste. The Phillies owner delegated the task to Nee, who was suitably impressed and met Jones's demand for $16,000 to sign.[45] He played shortstop his first year at Terre Haute and then was shifted to third upon being promoted to Philadelphia. After exhibiting shaky defense and a .226 batting average in his September 1947 audition, Jones spent 1948 with Toronto and Eddie Sawyer. In his second September chance, Jones hit .333 with 2 home runs and was in the Majors to stay, despite chronic foot problems that plagued him his entire career. Stan Lopata recalled Jones soaking them between games in a bucket of ice water. When asked about his feet bothering him, Jones supposedly replied, "They only hurt when they touch the ground."[46]

The other Phillies addition was no kid, but became a whiz nonetheless. Jim Konstanty took the mound in the eighth inning, a thirty-one-year-old bespectacled right-hander with previous big league experience for the Reds and Braves. Twenty-seven months after his most recent appearance in the Majors, Konstanty threw a scoreless inning of relief against St. Louis.[47]

Konstanty had graduated from Syracuse University, earning letters in baseball, basketball, football, and boxing. After graduation, he became a high school physical education instructor. While playing semipro ball in 1940, Konstanty attracted the attention of the International League Syracuse Chiefs, who sent the twenty-four-year-old to Springfield in the Eastern League, where he went 4-19 under manager Rabbit Maranville and roomed with twenty-one-year-old future Hall of Famer Early Wynn.

The right-hander joined Syracuse the next year and, lacking an effective fastball, learned to change speeds with pinpoint control to hold hitters at bay. By 1944 Konstanty was pitching for Cincinnati, winning 6 games with a solid 2.80 earned run average before entering the navy. On his return from military service in 1946, he was traded to the Boston Braves, for which he struggled. In midseason he was sent to the Minors and continued to struggle in Toronto, winning 4 and losing 9.[48] In the off-season, his career hanging by a thread, Konstanty became friends with his neighbor, an undertaker named Andy Skinner. Although Skinner had never played baseball, he was an excellent bowler and began teaching Konstanty angles and spins he could apply to his palm ball, which served as his changeup, and to his slider. Skinner would continue to advise Konstanty for the rest of his career.

Jim Konstanty won 13 games for Toronto in 1947, and the next year the team became a Phillies affiliate with Eddie Sawyer as manager. After Sawyer moved up to the Phillies, he made room for Konstanty in Philadelphia's bullpen.

FOR THE SECOND STRAIGHT season, Curt Simmons won Philadelphia's season finale, defeating Brooklyn, 4–2, with help from Jim Konstanty, who took over after Simmons walked two straight batters in the ninth with one out. Konstanty struck out Pete Reiser and Jackie Robinson to end the game and the season, notching a save.[49] As was the case the previous year, Simmons was a bit wild, walking 7. But the win was less celebrated than his first had been, as it was only his 7th of the year against 13 defeats. It had been just Simmons's second start in nearly a month, after spending most of September in the bullpen. Despite his struggles, no one was giving up on Curt Simmons—he was only nineteen years old.

A day earlier, Robin Roberts failed to get out of the first inning of his final start of the year, thanks to 3 hits and 3 errors—one of them his.[50] But at age twenty-two, he was beginning to be regarded as a potentially better prospect than Simmons. Roberts finished the year with a 7-9 record, walked 2 batters fewer per nine innings than Simmons, and finished 1948 with a solid earned run average of 3.13. The next spring, Roberts was signed to a contract calling for a reported $12,000, the same amount being paid to Schoolboy Rowe.[51]

Overall, the Phillies had a record of 13-22 after Ashburn's injury, and the team went 23-40 under Eddie Sawyer after a 43-48 record for Ben Chapman and Dusty Cooke. But they had placed sixth—their best finish in well over a decade. There was still work to do, especially with the fans. After a brief postwar boom, the Phillies were back to trailing the National League in attendance in 1948, outdrawing only the woeful St. Louis Browns among all Major League teams.[52] But Bob Carpenter could see progress.

WHEN THE PHILLIES GATHERED for spring training in 1949, there were some new faces, courtesy of three off-season deals made with the Chicago Cubs, which had become a favorite trading partner. The day after the season ended, the Phillies traded Harry Walker, whose average had dropped more than seventy points after winning the 1947 National League batting title, to Chicago for thirty-four-year-old slugger Bill Nicholson, a two-time NL home run champion.[53] A week later, the Cubs sent hot-tempered pitcher Russ Meyer to Philadelphia to complete the Emil Verban deal.[54]

Then in December the Phillies sent pitchers Dutch Leonard and Monk Dubiel to the Cubs for All-Star first baseman Eddie Waitkus and pitcher Hank Borowy.[55] Waitkus had become available because former Phillies pitcher Ken Raffensberger hit him with a pitch, injuring his wrist and opening first base in the Cubs lineup for Phil Cavarretta, whose subsequent success—and Chicago manager Charlie Grimm's superstitious nature— made Waitkus expendable.[56]

Bob Carpenter arrived in Florida brimming with optimism. "We're still a year or perhaps two away. But by 1950 or 1951 we're going to be the ones to beat for the National League flag," he said. "This is a young ball club with great potentialities. While we're still building for the future, there is no telling how far it can go."[57] Nineteen of the thirty-one players in camp had never been with any organization other than the Phillies. Eddie Sawyer, while refusing to make any predictions for his first full year as a Major League manager, proudly pointed out that nearly half of the team's players were under twenty-five years old.

Richie Ashburn had recovered from the injury that ended his 1948 season, and Eddie Sawyer was certain his young outfielder would avoid the dreaded sophomore jinx. When Grantland Rice asked about Ashburn, Sawyer responded, "Don't worry about Richie. He is one of the naturals . . . a natural competitor."[58] The young star, who had led the National League in stolen bases in 1948 despite his early exit, heeded Sawyer's suggestion to take infield before games to improve his defense on outfield ground balls.

But Ashburn's second year got off to a rough start when he was drilled in the face by a thrown ball during an intrasquad game. It came on a play at home plate and Ashburn was knocked unconscious. After being revived by a doctor called from the stands, he was carried from the field. Luckily, while he needed stitches, nothing was broken.[59] Ashburn returned for an intrasquad game three days later, slamming 4 hits, including a pair of doubles and a triple.[60] A week after his injury, Ashburn slammed a pair of home runs against the Detroit Tigers in an exhibition game.[61]

Happy to escape the exhibition season without further damage, the Phillies began the 1949 season with a record of 2-6 before jolting their fans with an electrifying, come-from-behind, 12–11 home win against the New York Giants in eleven innings.

The Giants had scored twice in the top the eleventh off Schoolboy Rowe, opening up an 11–9 lead in what had already been a wild contest. With two out and Ashburn at first, Eddie Waitkus smashed a line drive that scooted through New York outfielder Willard Marshall's legs, allowing Ashburn to score. Del Ennis then hit the first pitch from Andy Hansen into the upper deck in left field; Hansen reacted by slamming his cap and glove to the ground in anger as Ennis circled the bases.[62]

Everyone could feel the Phillies were different. During an off day in May, Cy Perkins and Maje McDonnell were watching the team work out when Perkins turned to McDonnell and said, "Maje, these kids are going to win it next year."[63] On June 2 the team tied a Major League mark, hitting 5 home runs in one inning, scoring 10 runs in the eighth off three Cincinnati Reds pitchers. Two of the blasts were struck by Andy Seminick—who had also homered earlier, giving him 3 on the day. Del Ennis, Willie Jones, and Schoolboy Rowe, who picked up the win in relief, added circuit blasts as the Phillies turned a 3–2 deficit into a 12–3 win. Seminick became the eleventh Major Leaguer to homer twice in one inning and the first Phillies player to turn the trick. A triumphant Bob Carpenter visited the clubhouse afterward and gave each of the players a hearty handshake while declaring, "That was the best game I've ever seen!"[64]

Each of Schoolboy Rowe's credited victories in 1949 was dramatic. His third and final win of the season, and the 158th of his career, came on June 7, with Eddie Waitkus and Andy Seminick slapping run-scoring singles after Pittsburgh had taken a 5–4 lead in the top of the ninth. Curt Simmons had allowed only 1 hit through the first seven innings before falling apart in the eighth, allowing 3 hits and committing an error, leading to Sawyer summoning Jim Konstanty. After Konstanty was pinch-hit for in the bottom of the eighth, Rowe came in but allowed a run. Waitkus and Seminick then rescued the thirty-nine-year-old Rowe in the bottom of the ninth for the 6–5 win.[65]

The 1949 Phillies kept bumping up against the .500 mark and falling back. They reached 8-8 and lost. After winning the next day, they lost. On May 22 Robin Roberts, with help from Jim Konstanty, beat Pittsburgh to bring them even at 15-15. Then they lost two in a row before reversing the trend and again reaching the .500 mark at 17-17. Three consecutive losses followed.

Once again, they clawed back to a mark of 22-22 going into a double-header against the Cubs on June 5 and won the first game before dropping the second, leaving them at break-even at the end of the day. Then came the crazy game on June 7 that the Phillies almost blew, but ended up winning for Schoolboy Rowe. That put them at 24-23, and anticipation grew that the team had a chance to finish the season in the first division.

But yet another tragedy was to bedevil the Phillies before they could take their next big step forward.

5

I'm Unpredictable

THERE WAS NOTHING in the life of Phillies first baseman Eddie Waitkus that foreshadowed the tragic event that was to befall him in the summer of 1949. He had no idea—indeed could not have—of his being in mortal danger. There had been a time when he was all too keenly aware of his mortality, at places such as Morotai and Lingayen Gulf during the war. But in his mind, those brushes with danger had passed leaving him unscathed, at least physically. But fate had a surprise in store for Eddie Waitkus, in the form of a total stranger with a fatal fixation.

Waitkus was born in East Cambridge, Massachusetts, to Lithuanian immigrants who met on a ship crossing the Atlantic for America. Eddie's father was industrious, variously making his livelihood as a butcher, truck driver, baker, crane operator, and clerk at Faneuil Market.[1] The family was devout Catholic, and the young Waitkus served as an altar boy at his church.

He grew up loving sports and joined other boys who habitually wandered to the nearby park to shag flies for neighborhood hero Jack Burns, a first baseman for the St. Louis Browns. Waitkus was a right-handed pitcher in those early pickup games. His father, who knew little about sports, gave Eddie his first glove, and family tradition has it being a left-handed first baseman's mitt. Instead of expressing disappointment, Waitkus taught himself to throw left-handed and play the position manned by Jack Burns.

Waitkus's mother died in 1933, just as he was entering high school.[2] He was an excellent student-athlete, playing first base for Cambridge Latin, located blocks from Harvard University, hitting .600 his senior year and named his team's Most Valuable Player, earning him a trophy presented by Jimmie Foxx.[3] He also earned a spot on the 1937 *Boston Globe* All-Scholastic

Baseball team.[4] Among Waitkus's high school feats was slamming a home run over the right-field fence at Russell Field that landed on the third floor of an apartment building across the street, a blast matched only by Ike Boone, who had done so during an exhibition game for the Boston Red Sox.[5] After playing for Frisoli in the Boston Suburban Twilight League, Waitkus was recruited to spend the summer in Maine as cleanup hitter and first baseman for the semipro Worumbo Indians, managed by an old Minor League catcher and college baseball coach, Wilkie Clark, and sponsored by a wool mill in Lisbon Falls.[6] The team earned a trip to the National Baseball Congress Tournament in Wichita and won its first two games but fell short of making the finals.[7] Waitkus and the team returned the next year—this time reaching the finals, finishing eighth, with Waitkus named to the 1938 All-Tournament team.[8]

Waitkus was then signed by the Chicago Cubs and hit .326 in his first professional season at Moline.[9] He spent the 1940 season in Tulsa, during which he cemented his reputation as an outstanding defensive first baseman and solid line drive hitter effective against all kinds of pitching—and spent a memorable summer rooming with Dizzy Dean. Waitkus was the Cubs Opening Day first baseman in 1941, singling off Ken Heintzelman in his third Major League at bat.[10] But the twenty-one-year-old was not yet ready for Major League competition and was returned to Tulsa. Following a brief end-of-season call-up to the Cubs and an outstanding year in 1942 with Los Angeles in the Pacific Coast League, Waitkus entered military service, where he served with distinction in the Pacific Theater, earning four Bronze Stars.

Despite not playing baseball for nearly the entirety of his three years of military service, he made the Cubs out of spring training in 1946 and in the process displaced reigning National League Most Valuable Player Phil Cavarretta from his preferred spot to the outfield. That summer, Waitkus and teammate Marv Rickert had the distinction of being the first post-1900 duo to hit back-to-back inside-the-park home runs, at the Polo Grounds.[11] Waitkus developed into a superior first baseman and excellent hitter, batting .304, .292, and .295 in his first three postwar years, and was named to the National League All-Star team in 1948.

Always dressed impeccably in tailored suits, usually brown, Waitkus was considered the epitome of class—erudite, well-read, witty, and popular, especially with women, who saw him as someone who treated them with respect. He delighted in the symphony and read poetry but did not put on airs. While neither riotous nor reckless, he *was* a bachelor and partook in Chicago nightlife; he was often found at the 5100 Club with teammates Russ Meyer and Marv Rickert, sitting at a ringside table courtesy of resident comic Danny Thomas, a rabid Cubs fan.[12]

In late 1948 the Cubs tinkered with their lineup, moving Waitkus to left field after his recovery from injury, and kept the thirty-two-year-old Cavarretta at first. Meanwhile, Eddie Sawyer wanted to upgrade from Dick Sisler at first base. During the off-season, Sawyer approached the Cubs, with whom the Phillies had already completed a pair of deals, hoping to acquire Cavarretta.

But the conversation shifted quickly to acquiring Eddie Waitkus instead, and the third deal of the off-season between the teams was quickly consummated.[13] The Phillies were ecstatic about their acquisition, with team public relations director Babe Alexander boasting to the *Philadelphia Inquirer*, "Bob Carpenter had to put a gun at their backs to put it through."[14] Unfortunate metaphor aside, it was clearly a deal that strengthened Philadelphia.

While far from being a power hitter, Waitkus was exactly what the Phillies infield needed. He could catch anything, a handy talent in Philadelphia, quickly proving adept at handling third baseman Willie Jones's hard overhand throws, which had a tendency to pull first basemen off the bag. He was equally able to deal with Granny Hamner's sinker from short and, later, second baseman Mike Goliat's sidearm delivery that brought with it unpredictable and inconsistent results.[15] And you could almost never get a ball past Waitkus. He possessed great range and freakish reflexes.

Eddie Waitkus played every inning of every Phillies game through early June 1949. On June 7, the Phillies rallied to win on Andy Seminick's walk-off single that scored Waitkus, who slid in safely ahead of Pete Castiglione's throw.[16]

Two nights later, the Phillies had another walk-off win against Pittsburgh, this one in eighteen innings, as Waitkus collected 4 hits to raise his average to .300 and Jim Konstanty threw nine innings of shutout relief.[17]

On June 12 Robin Roberts took the nightcap of a doubleheader against St. Louis, the finale of a twenty-one-game homestand, and Philadelphia's record stood at 28-25. That victory put the Phillies in fourth place, a half game ahead of the New York Giants. Following a travel day, they began a two-week road trip with a series against the Chicago Cubs. It was the sec-

ond visit to Wrigley Field for Eddie Waitkus since being traded, the previ-
ous series having been truncated to a single contest due to bad weather.
His return was a red-letter day for his not insignificant, distaff-dominated,
Chicago-based fan club.

The fan clubs honoring various players were remarkable in both size and
enthusiasm. The crowd of teen and preteen girls, "bobby-soxers" as they
were called, was particularly rabid in the Windy City, said to outnumber
young boys by a margin of ten to one while lining the clubhouse runways
before and after White Sox and Cubs games.[18]

It was, appropriately enough, Ladies Day at Wrigley, a warm afternoon—
nearly eighty degrees at game time—with wind gusts up to twenty miles per
hour. The sky was clear, outside of a few clouds bouncing along overhead,
although the playing surface was not in great shape, morning rain having
muddied the outfield.

The game was an easy one for the Phillies, spoiling the debut of new
Chicago manager Frankie Frisch, who succeeded three-time pennant-
winning Cubs leader Charlie Grimm. The contest was essentially decided
in the third inning when Philadelphia scored 5 runs to break open a scoreless
game. Pitcher Russ Meyer opened the frame by smacking a double and then
scored despite slipping while rounding third on a Richie Ashburn single that
came to a dead stop in the outfield. Waitkus then singled Ashburn to third,
and Del Ennis in turn singled Ashburn home, with Waitkus going to third
and knocking Cubs third baseman Frankie Gustine out of the game with
a hard slide. An error and a two-run Willie Jones double rounded out the
inning. Andy Seminick later homered, his 9th in fourteen games, hitting the
ball so hard that the left fielder, former Phillie Harry Walker, stood dead in
his tracks as the ball sailed over the fence behind him. The Phillies won, 9-2,
dropping the Cubs into last place.[19]

Playing an afternoon game left the evening free, and Waitkus was not
about to let it go to waste. He joined Bill Nicholson and Russ Meyer for dinner and drinks before returning to the Edgewater Beach Hotel, the Phillies
headquarters when in Chicago. There, Waitkus found a note left in his box
at the front desk.[20]

The message was from a Ruth Anne Burns—a name that had a familiar ring to it. Waitkus searched his memory, thinking he knew someone by
that name from his old neighborhood, or at least someone with a name that
sounded similar. It was the kind of moment that left a nagging feeling of

familiarity regarding the person in question, where one seeks something to jog the memory so face and name will click into place. The note read in part, "We're not acquainted, but I have something of importance to speak to you about. I think it would be to your advantage to let me explain it to you."[21]

Waitkus made the fateful decision to respond to the request.

Among those on hand for Ladies Day at Wrigley Field was one particular lady who sat on the first base side, so as to be near the object of her compulsion, whom she had never met. She left during the seventh inning with plans that would alter Eddie Waitkus's season and his life. Her name was not Burns. She was a nineteen-year-old Chicagoan named Ruth Ann Steinhagen. Also a guest at the Edgewater Beach Hotel, Steinhagen returned from the ballpark and had a radio sent to her room, along with three drinks—a daiquiri and two whisky sours—and awaited the players' return.[22] She had penned two notes on hotel stationery, one to her parents and the other to Waitkus, slipping a bellhop five dollars to deliver the latter to the ballplayer. Waitkus was not in, so the bellboy left the note for Waitkus at the front-desk mailbox.

Ruth Steinhagen had previously harbored intense crushes for Cubs outfielder Peanuts Lowrey and actor Alan Ladd. But those infatuations were nothing in comparison. Steinhagen had been obsessed with Eddie Waitkus for two years, ever since first spying him from the right-field bleachers during a game at Wrigley Field, and had planned nearly the entire time to kill him. She had revealed her compulsion to a friend and also to her mother, neither of whom took the threat seriously, even as they recognized she had emotional problems. Waitkus's trade to the Phillies did nothing to dampen her ardor.

One version of Steinhagen's plan, hatched at least a month earlier when she reserved a room at the hotel to coincide with the Phillies' arrival, was to stab Waitkus using a five-inch paring knife secreted in her pocket and to then shoot herself. Originally, she had made plans to do so on May 21, during the Phillies' first visit, but the hotel was completely booked. So, she instead reserved a room for seven dollars and fifty cents per night during Philadelphia's next trip into town.[23]

Steinhagen claimed she had always wanted to be in the limelight and thought this her opportunity, explaining without a trace of emotion that when it came to Waitkus, "if she couldn't have him, no one would." She purchased a rifle at a pawn shop for twenty-one dollars—a friend with her at the time told police, "The bullets were extra, I think."[24] Steinhagen disassembled the weapon and snuck it into the hotel. After checking in, she reassembled the rifle and placed it in a closet.

Steinhagen's friend, Helen Farazis, visited Ruth the evening of the shooting until about eleven o'clock. She saw the note to Waitkus but did not think he would respond, claiming she would have warned the ballplayer if she thought something would happen. She added that she and Ruth saw ballplayers as "idols up in the sky and the thought of sex just never entered our minds."[25]

Steinhagen claimed she wavered that night about taking Waitkus's life and had fallen asleep. After reading the note, Waitkus called Ruth's room, waking her with the question "What's this all about?" Startled to her senses, Ruth told him it was important but that the matter could wait until the next day. When Waitkus replied he would not be available then, Steinhagen realized this was her chance and told him to come up, which he did.

When Steinhagen opened the door, Waitkus rushed across the room and plopped into a chair, insisting to know about the "issue of importance." He had moved so quickly, and she was so startled, that she neglected to stab him.

Recovering from the shock of seeing her target immediately in front of her, she stammered that she had a surprise and went to the closet. Producing the rifle, she ordered Waitkus to stand and move toward the window. She then told him, "For two years you have been bothering me. Now I've got a surprise for you. You're going to die."[26]

Confused and alarmed, Waitkus stammered, "I don't understand, what's going on here," at which point Steinhagen fired, the bullet entering Waitkus's chest and into his lung, just below the heart. Slumping to the floor, Waitkus moaned and asked Ruth why she had shot him.

Steinhagen later told police, "I really intended to commit suicide but Eddie was moaning on the floor and I couldn't find another bullet." She variously stated to police she was going to kill herself, turn herself in to Waitkus, and go to prison. She also stated that she just wanted to go back to being a typist and added, "I'm a good case for a psychiatrist."[27]

The moaning disturbed Steinhagen, and she ran down the hall but could still hear her victim repeatedly asking why she had shot him. She returned to the room and called the hotel operator, telling her, "Get a doctor, a man has been shot." If she had not done so, Waitkus likely would have died right there. The ballplayer was examined by the hotel doctor and taken to the Illinois Masonic Hospital, where at first it was felt his recovery was touch and go.[28] That evening, Steinhagen was brought to Waitkus's hospital room so he could make a positive identification. He asked her, "Why did you do it?"

She responded, "I don't know."[29]

Waitkus, who had a date with him earlier that evening, later told Maje McDonnell that he thought it was a joke, sure that Bill Nicholson or another teammate would be jumping out of the closet. He said, "Maje, I think I was still smiling when she shot me."[30]

By the next day, it was determined Waitkus would recover.[31]

After signing a pair of statements confessing to the attack, Steinhagen told police, "If I hadn't done it last night, I would have some other time. It depended on my mood. I'm unpredictable."[32]

RUTH ANN STEINHAGEN'S MOTHER told police that Ruth had talked of murdering Waitkus and had hundreds of photos of the ballplayer that she would spread all over the floor, spending countless hours staring at them.

Steinhagen prepared a twelve-page autobiography at the request of a court psychologist, in which she recounted her nagging worries about possible insanity and always being unhappy. Then she saw Waitkus. She collected photos of him and began fantasizing that he was with her in her room or when she ate out at restaurants. When taking walks at night, she pretended Waitkus was alongside her, and she carried on conversations with him in her head.

"I started getting ready to go after him," Steinhagen explained. "Then, no matter what happened, I knew I would see him and I didn't worry too much over other things."[33]

Steinhagen posed willingly for photographers at her arraignment, seeming to enjoy the attention. Her parents and her sister Rita spoke to her, as bail was set at $50,000. At one point she briefly covered her face, and a bailiff tried to console her, telling her not to cry. Steinhagen reportedly replied, "I'm not crying, I'm laughing."[34]

Two weeks later, Steinhagen was declared insane and committed to Kankakee State Hospital. The doctor in charge of Steinhagen's examination testified that she was suffering from schizophrenia. Waitkus appeared in court, sitting in a wheelchair less than three feet from his assailant. He did not look at her, and the two did not speak to each other.

Afterward, Steinhagen was asked whether she would shoot Waitkus again if she saw him. She replied, "No, I tried once and failed; I wouldn't do it again." When asked whether she expected to ever see him again, she said, "Yes, when we are both dead."[35]

Waitkus underwent a second surgery the next day on his lung, which had partially collapsed. It was decided not to remove the bullet, which had lodged near his spine, since it posed no immediate danger.[36] He was up and around in the hospital within a week.[37] He underwent a third operation, on his lung in early July.[38] Because of a low-grade infection that was difficult to control, the bullet was finally removed during a fourth procedure on July 9.[39]

A week after that, Waitkus was released from the hospital and flew to Philadelphia to continue his recovery. Five hundred fans were on hand to greet Waitkus at the airport. He expressed thanks for the support and told the crowd, "I'm raring to go, and Dr. Adams, in Chicago, says I will be able to play ball again sometime before the season ends. About what happened, I still don't believe it. Sometimes I think it was all a dream."[40]

Athletes the age of Eddie Waitkus, indeed, most human beings that age, tend to feel immortal, oblivious to dangers around them. Waitkus knew the truth of mortality firsthand, through the war, a danger he expected and understood—and now through celebrity, a danger that he had neither expected nor even entertained. The first experience had left emotional scars he had largely hidden from public view. The second carried physical scars as well, ones that would prove a constant reminder of a momentary encounter with an irrational psychotic. Although he would recover physically, these scars sowed doubts and suspicion that would haunt Waitkus for the rest of his life. Three years later, Bernard Malamud published one of the most famous sports novels of all time, *The Natural*. While Malamud, who rarely discussed the inspiration for his work, never claimed the Waitkus shooting as a basis for the tale, the timing of the book's release forever fostered such speculation.[41]

LOSING IS A BAD HABIT. One of the most difficult things in sports is to convert a losing culture to a winning one. Eddie Sawyer soon confronted that reality.

The Phillies initially played well after Waitkus was shot, winning four in a row and eight of eleven. Dick Sisler, whom Sawyer had benched after the acquisition of Waitkus, appeared only in pinch-hitting roles during the first two months of the season. After reclaiming his old position at first base, Sisler promptly lined 3 hits and went 14 for 33 in his first seven games.

The Phillies were 20-11 in June, but stalled a bit toward the end of that month. July brought a mediocre record of 12-15, and that was only after closing with three straight wins. Sawyer, anxious for more punch in his lineup, requested that Toronto move third baseman Mike Goliat to second base, which he had never before played. After a few days at his new position, Goliat was told during a game in Rochester that he was going to be called up to Philadelphia.[42] But he suffered a knee injury that day turning a game-ending double play.[43] Goliat was sidelined for three weeks while Eddie Miller continued playing second base for the Phillies.[44]

When Goliat finally arrived, he moved into a three-story home being rented by Richie Ashburn's parents, who moved to Philadelphia for the baseball season to be near their son while leasing their home in Tilden to the local high school principal.[45] Neil Ashburn had sold his machine shop and delighted in following his son's career. The home was spacious enough to serve as a boarding house for other young, single players, including Robin Roberts, Curt Simmons, and Charlie Bicknell. Ashburn's mother was the big draw, thanks to her culinary talents. The Ashburn's lodging was on the Main Line in Philadelphia during the first year. After the address was leaked to the press, they rented a home the next season in Bryn Mawr, where Goliat took up residence.[46]

FEW PLAYERS WERE more competitive than the right-hander from Arkansas, Lynwood "Schoolboy" Rowe. He had an uncanny ability to identify when an opposing pitcher was about to throw a curve. Del Ennis remembered being at bat and hearing Rowe signal him. "He'd sit at the corner of the bench and whistle," said Ennis, "and I knew it was a curveball."[47] In 1948 Rowe pitched three games with his broken left thumb in a cast, and went 3 for 5 as a hitter despite having to swing his bat one-handed.[48] Having battled injuries much of his career, he hated to lose, as demonstrated in a game against Pittsburgh.

After a sluggish July, the Phillies began August with five straight defeats, the last 1–0 in the aforementioned contest against the Pirates. Philadelphia had lost a golden chance to score in the eighth when Andy Seminick bunted foul three straight times attempting to sacrifice and Rowe struck out swinging with such force that he fell atop home plate on his follow-through. The Phillies were defeated on a walk-off heartbreaker due to a Granny Hamner throwing error with two out in the ninth, spoiling a heroic performance by Rowe, who had shut out the Pirates on 5 hits to that point. While Hamner was charged with the miscue, popular opinion held that Sisler should have handled the throw—and that Waitkus would have.[49]

Rowe was so disturbed by the outcome that he threw his glove high into the air, and then kicked it when it was returned to him. Umpire Babe Pinelli finally walked over to console the fiery veteran. After the game, an upset Hamner confronted the pitcher, accusing Rowe of "pulling a bush league trick."[50] Composing himself, Rowe approached Hamner, put his hand on the shortstop's shoulder and apologized, one Southerner to another, saying, "Don't feel bad about that Granny. . . . It is all part of the game. . . . You have saved me many times."[51]

On August 4, Russ Meyer, another hot-tempered pitcher, was knocked out of a game against Cincinnati in the first inning and erupted, punting a chair in the dugout high into the air.[52] Earlier that season, Meyer had reacted after a rough outing in New York by kicking the pitcher's rubber and spiking the baseball before stalking off. Sawyer had said nothing to him. This time, the right-hander's foot swelled, putting him on crutches and his foot in a cast. Meyer's self-inflicted injury came at a particularly bad time, as the pitching staff was already missing Curt Simmons and Charlie Bicknell, who were serving two weeks training in the National Guard.[53]

Meyer told Sawyer, "I'm going home to rest," to which Sawyer replied, "Oh no, you aren't. I think you better stay with the club."[54]

A couple of days later, Meyer realized he could move his toes, and X-rays confirmed that his foot was not broken—previous images taken immediately after the injury had instead revealed an old injury.[55] Meyer returned to the mound and ultimately had his best season.

"Sawyer's a great guy," said Meyer. "He's the only manager who ever made an attempt to understand me. I'd go to hell for him."[56]

Meyer was straightened out, but the Phillies were two games below .500, and Sawyer was growing frustrated. He benched Dick Sisler and moved Mike Goliat to first base, even though the rookie had only 1 hit in his first 15 Major League at bats. The next day, Sawyer was ejected for the first time in his career, disputing balls and strikes, and Sisler smacked a two-out ninth-inning pinch-hit single to win the game.[57] Twenty-four hours later, Sisler clinched the nightcap of a doubleheader with a ninth-inning pinch-hit home run. He was returned to the starting lineup.[58]

Philadelphia subsequently dropped five of six, and Sawyer had enough. He had been hired because of his calm demeanor and ability to handle young athletes. But the players needed to grow up. He was not much older than they were, not to turn thirty-nine until September 10, but he recognized their immaturity and knew the team had too much talent to be where it was in the standings. Usually unflappable to the point of silence, he was annoyed that even while losing, the players seemed unaffected, satisfied with fifth place. Sawyer wasn't. He fumed as he witnessed players joking around and ordering room service, some running tabs of up to ten dollars per meal. Del Ennis and Willie Jones often had food sent to their room or slipped out on clandestine midnight runs for bags of hamburgers.[59]

After the team was swept by the Giants in an August 14 doubleheader, Sawyer read his players the riot act. He set down several rules, including a ban on signing for meals at the hotel and limiting per diem to six dollars per day, which they were to collect each morning from trainer Frank Wiechec. Wives were banned from road trips, fines were established for lack of hustle, and a curfew was set for both going to and rising from bed.

Making it clear the malaise was not the fault of only one or two players, Sawyer emphasized that no one was safe, adding a pointed warning to the team's bonus babies. He made it clear that, despite the investment, if they did not produce, they would be placed on waivers. At this point Curt Simmons, who walked 9 in relief during an 8–1 loss to New York in his return from National Guard duty, had a record of 3-10 with a 4.82 earned run average. Fellow bonus baby Charlie Bicknell's ERA was 6.33. Sawyer declared that Bob Carpenter was prepared to take the financial loss. "The club has been more than generous to you both in your style of traveling and the liberties you have been allotted," he scolded. "I know, however, that you are not hustling as you were earlier in the year." He then added, "I feel that if everyone gets down to business we can finish in the first division. We have the men to do it. . . . It is up to you. . . . If you don't hustle and finish there it will be your loss and your headache."[60]

Some forty years later, Sawyer explained, "Some of the guys were taking advantage of just signing for their meals and were overeating, sometimes before games. They were young and some of them just didn't have much discipline yet," adding that he felt the press blew the incident out of proportion to some degree.[61]

Sawyer's downplaying aside, at the time it was an astonishing tongue-lashing from a manager whose words were few, much less raised in tone. The Phillies responded with a twelve-inning, 2–1 win over Brooklyn, Ken Heintzelman earning his 14th win of the year, with Richie Ashburn's triple driving in the winning run off Don Newcombe.[62] They won five more in a row—and the fans were as fired up as the players, perhaps even more so. Perhaps a bit too much.

The Phillies and New York Giants had a curiously raucous history, with many examples going back to Horace Fogel and indeed nearly to the beginning of John McGraw's tenure as Giants manager. More than three decades earlier, Philadelphia pitcher Ad Brennan kayoed McGraw with a left hook after the Phillies lost a wild extra-inning game. When the Giants returned to Philadelphia later in the year, a riot ensued involving Giants players, umpires, and Phillies fans that spread outside the ballpark.[63] Another crazy chapter was about to unfold.

On August 21 the Phillies were trying for their seventh straight win in the nightcap of a doubleheader against New York. They trailed in the top of the ninth, 3–2, when Giants first baseman Joe Lafata stroked a low line drive to center field. Richie Ashburn made a tumbling shoestring catch and then threw the ball to second base. But umpire George Barr ruled that the ball had hit the ground before Ashburn gloved it, enabling a run to score that gave the Giants a 4–2 lead.

Ashburn exploded, charging toward the infield to register his protest. He was immediately joined by Del Ennis, Granny Hamner, Willie Jones, and Eddie Sawyer. Barr defiantly stood by his decision.[64] The fans in the left- and center-field bleachers erupted, hurling bottles and trash. Several leapt over the fence and onto the playing field. They were cleared away, and the Phillies, having lost the argument, began to return to their positions. This reignited the fans, who resumed launching projectiles that narrowly missed Ennis and Ashburn. The players were pulled from the field for their safety, and the umpires warned the Phillies that their patience was wearing thin.

"What can I do?" pleaded Sawyer, as the crowd drowned out the public-address announcer at each mention of the game being forfeited if demonstrations continued. The situation finally calmed, and Schoolboy Rowe threw some warmup pitches before facing Bill Rigney.

Then fans behind home plate began to boo. Third base umpire Lee Ballanfant was struck by a bottle. Home plate umpire Al Barlick was pelted with a tomato. The game was declared a forfeit to New York—the first in the Major Leagues in seven years—and the umpires left the field.

Afterward, Eddie Sawyer labeled Barr's decision on Ashburn's play as "stupid," but added he was helpless to challenge it. "We can't protest that decision to anybody," he complained. Ashburn argued he caught the ball eight inches off the ground, while Barr insisted, "Ashburn never caught that ball."[65] It was just another pleasant Sunday at the ballpark.

IN MID-AUGUST, Eddie Waitkus was given a day in his honor at Shibe Park. It had been two months since the shooting, and on the surface, he seemed to be recovering, although several teammates were shocked at his gaunt appearance. Waitkus visited the team several times and even joked about the incident. While at dinner one evening in Philadelphia with Babe Alexander and press agent Arnold Stark, a woman sent over a menu that she wanted autographed. Waitkus told his dinner companions, "You guys go over and frisk her first."[66]

Of course, jokes often hide emotions, and Waitkus was struggling. On August 19 he put on his Phillies uniform for the first time since the shooting and appeared in front of fans at Shibe Park. One can only imagine the thoughts running through his mind as he scanned the faces in the crowd. During the pregame ceremony, Dick Sisler handed Waitkus a first baseman's mitt, bronzed and mounted onto a plaque bearing the signatures of his teammates. He was given an automobile, a television set, two radios, luggage, wristwatches, a $500 savings bond, a lifetime membership in the Veterans of Foreign Wars (VFW), and a set of golf clubs.

Obviously emotional, he received a rousing ovation as he stepped to the microphone and said he hoped to play again that season but that the final decision was up to the doctors. At the same time he betrayed his uncertainty about recovering. "I don't know what the future holds for me," he told the crowd, "but you have given me something I will never forget."[67]

That night Robin Roberts beat the Giants to move the Phillies into a virtual tie for fourth place. Eddie Waitkus still had a long road to recovery. But he would be diligent in working to come back in time for the 1950 season.

AS SEPTEMBER BEGAN, Philadelphia baseball fans could hardly believe their eyes. The Phillies were in fourth place with a 64-62 record, only two games behind Boston for third. The Athletics were in fifth in the American League, but with a solid 67-59 mark. No one was printing World Series tickets, but it was clear baseball was on the upswing in Philadelphia.

After losing on September 1, the Phillies reeled off seven wins in a row and moved into third place, where they remained for the rest of the season.

The team won nineteen of its last thirty, with several highlights along the way. On September 4 Willie Jones hit a walk-off home run to spark a doubleheader sweep of Boston.[68] Although Ken Heintzelman struggled down the stretch, losing seven of eleven to end the season, Russ Meyer won eight in a row between August 28 and the end of the year to match Heintzelman for team high in victories with 17. That included three straight wins on only two days of rest. On September 8 Meyer surrendered a lead-off walk and a run-scoring double in the first inning against Boston and then completed the game without allowing another hit in a 3–1 win—a performance Eddie Sawyer called the finest by a Phillies pitcher that year.[69]

Curt Simmons continued to struggle, but Robin Roberts won 15 games despite barely pitching the final two weeks of the season after showing signs of fatigue. There were other highlights—twenty-four-year-old Del Ennis topped 100 runs batted in for the first time and hit .302. Catchers Andy Seminick and Stan Lopata combined for 32 home runs. Jim Konstanty was a first-rate closer out of the bullpen. Willie Jones and Granny Hamner had solidified the left side of the infield—Hamner was still highly regarded despite his fielding lapses on simple plays, offset by spectacular diving stops beyond the ken of other National League infielders. Hamner also had a temper, as exhibited by his run-in on the season's penultimate day, shoving a photographer from a Black newspaper to the ground shortly after letting a ball get past him at shortstop.[70]

Meyer's 17th win came on a 2–0 shutout of the New York Giants, the winning blows coming on homers by Del Ennis and rookie Ed Sanicki—for Sanicki it was his 3rd hit since being recalled from Toronto in early September, all of which were home runs, including in his first Major League at bat against Rip Sewell in Pittsburgh.[71] The win was the eightieth of eighty-one for Philadelphia that season, the most registered by the Phillies since 1917, and their third-place finish netted the players $24,542.79, which they spilt into thirty-two full shares of $721.85 each.[72]

The Phillies also nearly played spoiler when they hosted the Brooklyn Dodgers for the final game of the season. The Dodgers needed a win to avoid a playoff with the St. Louis Cardinals and jumped out to a 5–0 lead in the third off Russ Meyer. The Phillies answered back with 4 runs in the fourth off Don Newcombe and tied the game at 7–7 in the sixth, which it remained until the tenth inning. The Dodgers then plated 2 runs, and the Phillies could not answer, earning Brooklyn the pennant.[73]

It was easily the best finish for a Phillies team in more than three decades. But Eddie Sawyer remained uneasy. He made it clear that players would have to earn their jobs in 1950. He listed only four men as untouchable in the trade market—Robin Roberts, Willie Jones, Granny Hamner, and Ken Heintzelman.[74] Bob Carpenter Jr. put price tags of $125,000 on Hamner and $100,000 on Jones.[75] Three days before Eddie Waitkus was shot, Bob Carpenter Sr., who had been battling cancer, succumbed to a heart attack.[76] With both Herb Pennock and his father gone, Bob Carpenter Jr. was in total control. And he was intent on winning, having just lent the franchise $465,000 out of his own pocket, a five-year note due October 31, 1954.[77]

Eddie Sawyer recognized Carpenter's determination and thought that he might become impatient. Despite the team's strong finish in 1949, as far as the Phillies manager was concerned, everyone was on notice.

Sawyer's parting message to his players was, "We are going to win it all in 1950. Come back next year ready to win."[78]

6

I'm Glad to Be!

IN RECOGNITION OF the Phillies' best finish in decades, Bob Carpenter was named Major League Executive of the Year for 1949 by *The Sporting News*.[1] Upon learning of the award, Carpenter wisecracked, "I appreciate the honor, but I'd be willing to trade it for a pitcher who could win 20 games for the Phillies this year."[2]

During the winter, Carpenter took stock of the Phillies farm system and terminated three of the working agreements. At the same time, he assured fans that the team's considerable investment in the Minors, which he revealed as approaching a half million dollars per year, would continue apace, at least for the time being. Insisting that he intended someday to turn the franchise over to his children, Carpenter added a warning: "This is a business, and we expect a return on it. We're willing to spend money to build a pennant-winning team. At the same time, we want to realize a profit."[3]

Carpenter was a regular presence at Minor League parks, keeping tabs on the lifeblood of the franchise. The five Minor League teams owned by the Phillies had lost a combined $108,000 in 1949, somewhat improved from the $144,000 shortfall accumulated the year before, but a substantial financial deficit nonetheless.[4] These were not insignificant sums—especially when considering Minor League baseball had set attendance records four years running, reaching a pinnacle of more than forty-one million.

And clouds were looming on the horizon. Some of baseball's Minor League attendance gains could be attributed to the postwar explosion in the number of teams, especially in rural, less populated areas. But there were signs the novelty was wearing off. In addition, Major League attendance had declined 3 percent in 1949—from a record level, but concerning none-theless.[5] Those paying attention understood that the ever-increasing reach of broadcasting, especially television, and a prosperous economy fostering a more mobile, entertainment-craving society dominated by young families, meant that the public had options and would seek to exercise them. Base-ball would have to fight harder for patrons.

Despite these economic pressures, Carpenter retained his faith in Herb Pennock's plan for the franchise to develop its own talent. He assured every-one, "The farm system will cost just the same with 11 clubs."[6]

He continued his full-throated criticism of the bonus rule, which forced inexperienced players onto big league rosters. Indeed, most Major League teams disliked it. But there was no consensus on what changes to make. So once again the National Association, the Minor League's governing body—whose votes were controlled for the most part by Major League teams—voted down a proposed repeal and retained the rule for 1950 as written.[7]

EDDIE WAITKUS ARRIVED in Clearwater, Florida, in December 1949 to begin his comeback in earnest, exclaiming, "I'm not only glad to be here, I'm glad to be!"[8] Able to quip about his misfortune of five months earlier, he faced a long road ahead—working to regain thirty pounds he had lost while neither throwing a ball nor swinging a bat since the shooting.[9] Waitkus had confided to *Sporting News* publisher Taylor Spink that he had gone through some tough, fearful moments in the wake of the shooting, but for the most part he kept his deepest fears and doubts to himself.[10]

One-liners aside, the ghastly scars running down his back were testa-ment to the magnitude of effort required for his return to the Phillies start-ing lineup. Waitkus had to adjust to musculature that was altered—he had to relearn how to use hands controlled via back muscles torn asunder by a bul-let and by surgeons attempting to save not only his career but also his life.

Both Bob Carpenter and Eddie Sawyer considered the first baseman a major key to the Phillies moving higher in the standings, and Carpenter sought and received special permission from Commissioner Happy Chan-dler to make an exception for Waitkus by waiving the prohibition against players reporting for spring training prior to March 1.[11] The Phillies paid trainer Frank Wiechec to round Waitkus back into shape, and Waitkus's roommate and best friend, Bill Nicholson, along with newlywed Russ

Meyer, joined the workout sessions. Meyer threw batting practice to Waitkus until Happy Chandler found out and declared he had to stop doing
so immediately.[12] Chandler had bent the rules for Waitkus. He was not
going to allow the Phillies to get a further jump on the rest of the National
League.

Wiechec, who joined the Phillies in 1948, was an excellent choice as
architect of Waitkus's successful return. Among the most advanced trainers
of the time, Wiechec boasted a strong background in anatomy and physiology and had helped establish the physical therapy department at the Mayo
Clinic where he treated, among others, Lou Gehrig.[13] He began the sessions
by having the Phillies first baseman take long walks and then work in some
jogging. Resistance exercises were introduced, followed by outings in a
rowboat placed at Waitkus's disposal by the generous citizens of Clearwater, the spring training home of the Phillies, who had invited him to recover
there. Wiechec also looked after Waitkus's psychological well-being, recognizing attention to mental health as an equally important factor in the
player's recovery.[14]

The entire country was interested, and news traveled fast. The press
carried photos of Waitkus working out under Wiechec's guidance.[15] It was
not long before nationally syndicated gossip columnist Walter Winchell
reported that the Philadelphia first baseman was making progress—and
going steady with one of his nurses.[16] Waitkus gave up smoking and limited
his alcohol intake to beer.[17]

At the end of January, Russ Meyer was in Miami serving as umpire for a
charity baseball game benefitting the March of Dimes and was asked about
Waitkus. Meyer declared that his friend was on his way to a full recovery. He
also forecast the Phillies to be in the middle of a four-way race for the 1950
National League pennant.[18]

BOB CARPENTER TURNED his attention to the marketing side of the business and caved to the inevitable in January 1950, officially dropping the
team's alternate nickname Blue Jays, which had never caught on.[19] He told
Stan Baumgartner, "Blue Jays is not our type. We are rather 'Fighting Phillies' or 'Whizz Kids.' Those nicknames seem to fit us better."[20] Eddie Sawyer chimed in, telling Grantland Rice what he wanted in a team: "A ball club
is about as good as its spirit is—its willingness to hustle, to train, to work—a

club that won't do this isn't going to be much good."[21] The term Whiz Kids caught on quickly, used by the *Philadelphia Inquirer* first during the City Series against the Athletics.[22]

The Phillies owner also approved a change in home uniforms to togs featuring red pin-stripes, created by Eddie Sawyer. Reserve outfielder Jackie Mayo modeled the new design. When Bob Carpenter's wife was asked her opinion she retorted, "This really isn't fair. Jack Mayo would look good in anything."[23]

Mrs. Carpenter's blushing assessment aside, her husband and his manager wanted a new look for the team, reflecting its new, bright future. The pinstripes were accompanied by red stockings, red undershirts, and red caps with a white insignia. Baseball uniforms of the era were drab—players donned home whites and wore their grays, drearily gray, on the road. Outside of the St. Louis Cardinals and their iconic pair of birds perched upon a baseball bat splayed across the chest, the classic Yankees pinstripes, and the Braves with their tomahawk, uniforms circa 1950 were generally understated and unspectacular. When questioned about the new, colorful garb, gaining a reputation as the most startling in baseball, Carpenter retorted, "This is going to be a red-letter year for the Phillies. So why not make their uniforms with a touch of red?"[24]

Carpenter also announced that six Saturdays during the season would be designated as Children's Days, allowing a parent to take two children to the game for free, all three being admitted for the price of one adult admission.[25]

The Phillies projected starting lineup was the youngest in the National League—Eddie Waitkus the sole starter to have attained thirty years of age, and he having only recently done so. Eddie Sawyer had hoped the Phillies could acquire a couple of pitchers and a good-hitting outfielder during the off-season to bolster the team's fortunes, but nothing had materialized. Only two members of the spring training roster, Dick Whitman and Milo Candini, were new to the team.

"Our increased strength has to come from within, from experience," sighed a resigned Sawyer. He then added a shot aimed at the team's young bonus babies, remarking, "If some of our young pitchers don't come through, we are going to have to put up a scrap to finish third. If Curt Simmons comes through this season, or if Bob Miller, Bubba Church or John Thompson prove real major leaguers, we can surely finish second. We'll give the Dodgers a fight, maybe upset 'em."[26]

The pitching staff did not have a reputation for being overpowering—the Phillies finished last in the National League in strikeouts in 1949 and also issued the fewest walks. Only Curt Simmons averaged more than 4 strikeouts per nine innings.

In contrast to the everyday lineup, the pitching staff that reported to spring training was not all that young.

Jim Konstanty, a favorite of coach Cy Perkins because of his ability to come out of the bullpen after only nine or ten warm-up tosses, was the ace reliever on the strength of his 1949 performance, which included 9 wins and 7 saves in fifty-three appearances.[27] Konstanty kept a black book filled with notes about every batter he faced. He never seemed under pressure.[28] When Casey Stengel managed Konstanty later in his career, he observed, "He's a cool one. Comes in from the bullpen like a guy walkin' to the corner to buy a newspaper, throws a couple of warm-ups and goes to work."[29]

Konstanty responded, "It's just a day's work to me. I don't think about pressure. If somebody has to worry, let it be the batter."[30]

The right-hander fastidiously watched his diet and was a strict teetotaler, unafraid to confront teammates who partied all night. He was considered a loner, although Ashburn would often converse with him. "We never agreed on much," Ashburn remembered, "but we talked a lot."[31]

Konstanty, who always carried a well-worn YMCA bag with him, maintained a strict regimen at the ballpark, running its perimeter seven times every day. If he had not pitched in two or more days, Konstanty would throw five to ten minutes of batting practice. Then he changed his shirt and went to the bullpen, where he sat during the game alongside Cy Perkins and Ken Silvestri, waiting to be called.[32] While he could seem aloof to teammates, Konstanty's daughter always remembered her father at the ballpark, picking her up and hugging her before shifting his attention to autograph seekers.[33]

Blix Donnelly, who had labored in the Minor Leagues for nine years before finally reaching the Majors at age thirty in 1944 with the World Champion St. Louis Cardinals—striking out 9 while pitching six scoreless innings in two World Series appearances, including a win in relief—was another non-Kid among the Whizzes. He was thirty-six. Konstanty was thirty-three. Hank Borowy was turning thirty-four. Ken Heintzelman already was. Ex-paratrooper John "Jocko" Thompson was thirty-three. Thirty-two-year-old Milo Candini had been drafted from Oakland in the

Pacific Coast League, where he won 15 games after being cast adrift by the Washington Senators.[34] He was acquired during the same winter draft in which the Phillies lost Hugh Radcliffe to the Yankees.

One missing veteran was Schoolboy Rowe. The right-hander and pinch-hitter par excellence had received his release near the end of the 1949 season and opted to pursue his own deal in the Pacific Coast League.[35] During the Winter Meetings in Baltimore, Rowe signed with the San Diego Padres, whose highly respected manager, Del Baker, had been a coach for the Detroit Tigers during Rowe's dominant seasons there.[36] Rowe's Major League career ended with 158 wins against only 101 losses, plus three World Series appearances, including one Series title. Fifty-two of his wins had come in Phillies livery, as had 9 of his 18 career home runs.

There was some young talent of course, including Robin Roberts, Curt Simmons, and Russ Meyer, plus several untried hopefuls. But unless more pitchers developed quickly, the staff with which Sawyer intended to start the season was decidedly more wizened than whiz.

ALWAYS SEEKING TALENT, Carpenter was among the owners flirting with the idea of signing ex-Army football star Glenn Davis, who was also an accomplished baseball player. Davis, who had won the Heisman Trophy in 1945 and remains among the greatest all-around athletes to ever enroll at West Point, was about to complete his military obligation in Korea.[37] However, he decided not to play baseball in 1950 despite interest on the part of several Major League teams, choosing instead to sign a two-year contract with the Los Angeles Rams of the National Football League, which had acquired his rights from the Detroit Lions, the team that had originally drafted him second overall in 1947.[38]

Carpenter turned his attention to securing his own players under contract. The first priority was Del Ennis, who had prepared for the upcoming season by following the advice of coach Benny Bengough, soaking one dozen of his bats in linseed oil during the winter to harden them. Ennis became the highest paid player in team history, at a reported $35,000, and arrived at training camp a dozen pounds lighter than in 1949.[39] The dapper if sometimes daft Russ Meyer, one of baseball's consistently best-dressed men, was offered $11,000, plus another $3,000 on top of that in attendance-related bonuses, but was holding firm at wanting $17,000, even after receiving a couple of hefty salary advances during his time in Clearwater.[40] He agreed to report while continuing to negotiate.

Jim Konstanty had threated to hold out but relented after meeting with Carpenter.[41] Granny Hamner received a 33 percent raise to $10,000.[42] Andy Seminick proved the most recalcitrant, seeking $15,000, $5,000 more than the Phillies were offering.[43] At one point, he left camp for his home in Tennessee, stubbornly refusing to accept a deal he deemed inadequate.[44] Contract negotiations remained at an impasse until after the exhibition season began, Seminick eventually signing for a 30 percent raise over his All-Star season.[45]

While various negotiations dragged on, so did the annual ritual of trade rumors connected to those negotiations. One had Seminick going to the Brooklyn Dodgers, and another claimed the Giants had interest in Dick Sisler.[46] Nothing came of them.

Meanwhile, faced with the increasing realization that the aging Bill Nicholson was unable to play every day, and with the sophomore slump of Richie Ashburn—whose attitude had declined in 1949 along with his statistics—Sawyer sought outfield reinforcements.

In addition to acquiring Dick Whitman from the Brooklyn Dodgers, the Phillies announced the signing of outfielders Johnny Blatnik and Ed Sanicki to Major League contracts for 1950.[47] Blatnik had debuted in 1948 as a twenty-seven-year-old rookie with a spectacular stretch, batting .384 with sixteen extra base hits and a .636 slugging percentage during the month of May. He was batting a solid .277 near the end of August when he suffered heat stroke during the same game in which Richie Ashburn broke his finger.[48] Blatnik faded a bit over the season's final month and in 1949 lost his job to Bill Nicholson, spending most of that year in the Minors. Now he was getting another chance.

Another outfielder, twenty-four-year-old bonus baby Stan Hollmig, who hit .255 in eighty-one games for the Phillies in 1949, drew Carpenter's ire when he blew off a workout. An irritated Carpenter fumed, "Hollmig is a smart youngster, but lazy mentally. He knows he needs to be a step faster. This winter, we made all arrangements with a track coach to teach him sprinting, but he never showed up. That didn't exactly make me happy."[49] Hollmig eventually joined others in working with Frank Wiechec but would ride the bench the entire season, rarely appearing in box scores.

IN MID-FEBRUARY, Eddie Sawyer and Hank Borowy joined several others for a jaunt to Europe to conduct baseball clinics for troops stationed there. Other instructors included George Sisler, New York Yankees infielder Snuffy Stirnweiss, recently retired Washington outfielder Buddy Lewis, White Sox manager Jack Onslow, and umpires Art Gore and Bill Summers.[50]

Before leaving on the trip, Sawyer decided to spark Eddie Waitkus's competitive nature by announcing that Dick Sisler was still the team's first baseman. Sawyer declared, "Waitkus has to win his job back. He knows it and so do I." He then revealed the challenge he had made. "Before the [1949] season closed, I made a wager with Waitkus that Sisler would be in the lineup opening day. It was for a dinner."[51]

Waitkus assured columnist John Webster that he would be in great physical condition for the start of the season, saying, "It never used to be hard for me to get in shape in the spring." Waitkus acknowledged the value of his time in Florida with Wiechec by adding, "But I'd never have done it this year if it hadn't been for this three month stretch." He then admitted, "So I'm glad I've been working this way, but I never want to do it again."[52]

Waitkus was out some $4,000 in hospital bills and appealed to the State Workmen's Compensation Bureau to allow him to pursue payment from the team's insurance company, arguing that he was acting in a "public relations capacity" for the Phillies when he encountered Steinhagen.[53] Waitkus was ultimately awarded a judgement of $3,500.[54] He also welcomed a new fan club, headed up by Audrey Barry, who had no plans to harm her hero.[55]

Among those Eddie Sawyer had in mind when he had told reporters that the Phillies would have to improve from within were pitchers Bubba Church, Bob Miller, and Paul Stuffel; first baseman Bill Glynn; and Ed Sanicki.[56] Church was the most anticipated prospect, having won 15 while losing only 8 during his second year in Toronto, with a league-best 2.35 earned run average. Sanicki hit 33 home runs and drove in 104, plus the 3 home runs for the Phillies after his September recall. Glynn slugged 23 round-trippers with 98 runs batted in for Toronto and was called up for 10 at bats in September with the Phillies.

Sanicki was a squat power-hitting outfielder with outstanding range and a superior throwing arm. He had originally caught the eye of Larry MacPhail, who paid Sanicki's way through Seton Hall with an eye toward bringing him to the Brooklyn Dodgers. However, after Sanicki entered military service and MacPhail went to the New York Yankees, Branch Rickey took control of the Dodgers and had a less enthusiastic view of the outfielder. When Rickey countered Sanicki's request for a $2,500 bonus with a retort that he would offer zero because he had not picked up a glove or bat during his four years in the military, the outfielder signed with the Phillies.[57]

Sanicki was seen as a direct challenge to Ashburn, who had gotten a little too big for his britches even as his batting average dropped forty-nine points compared to his rookie year and his stolen bases declined from a Major League–leading 32 (despite missing the last six weeks of the season) to 9. Ashburn was also one of the poster boys for the change in policy to a straight per diem for players rather than allowing them to sign for their meals.

During the 1949 season Schoolboy Rowe had attempted to offer Ashburn advice, and the Nebraskan retorted, "When are you going to win a game, old folks?"[58] Eddie Sawyer had been aware of the exchange but waited for the right opportunity to send a strong message. Prior to spring training, he announced that Sanicki was getting a shot at center field, pointing to Ashburn's lack of power and less than intimidating throwing arm. Ashburn would likely move to left field or the bench.[59]

The outfielder, whose off-season marriage had been front-page news in Tilden, Nebraska, admitted he had become, as he put it, "swell-headed."[60] "I got the idea it was easy, that you didn't have to put out all the time. I didn't work as hard in '49 . . . and I found out. When you're not particularly big or strong, you have to work every minute in this business."[61] He watched nervously in Clearwater, muttering in the strongest language he ever used, "Darn it. Double darn it," as Sanicki swatted the ball during batting practice.[62]

Meanwhile, Eddie Waitkus demonstrated his comeback was serious during the first intrasquad game, slapping out 3 hits in 3 at bats, including a double, and turning a 3–6–3 double play. Dick Sisler, in the opposing lineup, had 2 hits but committed an error, dropping a throw from Willie Jones, and could have been charged with another on a pop-up that fell safely in foul territory. Ed Sanicki drove in a pair of runs.[63]

Sisler, upset about potentially losing his job again to Waitkus and riding the bench, began working on improving his speed under the tutelage of Frank Wiechec, who had coached track at Temple University. Sisler was popular among his teammates, ribbed about the stammer he did not try to hide, which did not hamper his ability to lead frequent team sing-alongs. He was also respected for his ability as a clutch hitter. Sisler rarely spoke about his famous father, George, against whom he knew he would always be measured and come up short. "I love my Dad," Sisler told Stan Baumgartner, "I admire his baseball ability. But I got fed up with having his name thrown at me everywhere I went."[64]

Recognizing that Waitkus had the edge at first base, Sisler had asked Eddie Sawyer for a shot playing outfield, and the veteran, who had been a first baseman exclusively for the Phillies but had played the position in the Minors and occasionally with the Cardinals, was working hard at it.[65]

Ashburn realized that if Sisler was moved to the outfield, only one spot was open, since he would not displace Del Ennis. And now Dick Whitman and Ed Sanicki were in competition with him for that spot. "I know I have to win that job back," Ashburn told reporter Jack Hand. "I'm giving everything I've got because I want that job."[66]

Eddie Sawyer was also determined to get Curt Simmons on the right track. He felt that Simmons's confidence had been hurt in the 1949 opener when he carried a 3–0 lead into the ninth, only to lose, 4–3. He had stopped throwing his magnificent curveball, and attempting to radically change his pitching motion had proven counterproductive. The coaching staff still strongly believed in Simmons's talent, with Cy Perkins urging patience and insisting that the twenty-year-old left-hander had grown during his stint in the bullpen the previous year.

"The great danger in handling a young pitcher is to complicate things for him," Perkins argued, "or to attempt to change his style."[67] Perkins recalled Connie Mack's advice against tinkering with a pitcher's mechanics from the waist down, arguing that pitchers were comfortable with the way they threw and would never successfully change.

Sawyer asked coaches Benny Bengough and Ken Silvestri to work with Simmons. They utilized a Yankees drill, having the left-hander throw at four types of targets—high, low, inside, and outside—in order to improve confidence and reduce the number of full counts that forced payoff pitches thrown over the heart of the plate. They returned the curve to his repertoire and allowed Simmons to retain his jerky pitching motion, while removing some of the more "violent spasms" that impacted his control and caused him to tire during the game.[68] Instead of corkscrewing, he twisted his hips quickly and then stretched out his left leg in front of him before following through.

From the beginning of spring training, Eddie Sawyer continually reinforced his message that players needed to be prepared and serious about what lay ahead, challenging them by insisting that the team could contend but was likely to finish third because they weren't yet ready to win.

Bob Miller, who had been an American Legion teammate of Stan Lopata in Detroit, was impressive in the early days of camp and earned the praise of Cy Perkins. "He's got an active fast ball that really does something," gushed the veteran coach.[69] Perkins added, "He's ready for the big leagues right now." Declaring that the young right-hander who had won 19 games at Terre Haute in 1949 reminded him of former Cleveland 30-game winner Jim Bagby Sr., Perkins said, "He has the poise of a 10-year man. He hasn't got as much speed as some, but his fast ball is active. It does things. He's got a good curve and a nice change."[70]

Later that season, umpire Frank Dascoli said of Miller, "I have never seen such poise in a young pitcher. And on top of that he is unbelievably fast. His quick one takes off about 10 or 15 feet from the plate and shoots off like a bullet."[71]

Perkins continued working with the team's other young pitchers, including Roberts, Church, and Simmons, admonishing them, "Have an object in your work, know what you can do and do it." His other commandment was to "learn mental control—without it no pitcher ever will have control on the mound."[72] Otherwise, Perkins was largely hands-off. Robin Roberts would swear by Perkins's advice the remainder of his career and made it his goal to become the Phillies first 20-game winner in more than three decades. He was said to be working on his changeup and curveball to supplement his fastball. Sawyer remarked, "The boy is smart in realizing he needs more than a high, hard one."[73]

Perkins, who caught Lefty Grove when he played behind the plate for the Athletics, saw a future Hall of Famer. That spring he told Roberts, "I've been in baseball 35 years and the best five pitchers I've ever seen are Walter Johnson, Lefty Grove, Herb Pennock, Grover Cleveland Alexander, and you. I'm not kidding you." He told Roberts, "You've got the best delivery I've ever seen. You're our next 300 game winner."[74]

THE PHILLIES DEFEATED Detroit in their exhibition opener, 9–8, in Clearwater, before a crowd of more than four thousand, thanks to Granny Hamner's tenth-inning, bases-loaded sacrifice fly. Ed Sanicki started in center field and had 2 hits in 5 at bats—Eddie Sawyer forced Richie Ashburn to watch his rival from the bench, using him only as a pinch-hitter, for Curt Simmons in the sixth inning. Also significant was that Eddie Waitkus was in the lineup at first base.[75] Afterward Waitkus proclaimed, "This will be a happy season, at that. After all, for a good while I didn't know if I'd stay alive, let alone play ball."[76] By the end of spring training, Bob Carpenter admitted, "I was afraid Waitkus wouldn't make it, but he certainly has. He's just as good as he ever was."[77]

But there was concern about Russ Meyer, who was hit hard by Detroit and then cuffed around again in a 23–6 loss to the New York Yankees four days later, allowing 2 grand slams in three innings.[78] Complaining of a sore elbow, he was sent to Johns Hopkins in Baltimore for further tests after a preliminary examination revealed a potential ulna bone fracture that could sideline him for two months.[79] In a repeat of the "broken toe" incident the year before, further tests showed it to be an old injury—a floating bone chip—that would eventually require surgery but was not something that needed to be addressed immediately.[80] Meyer soldiered on, vowing to pitch every day if Eddie Sawyer asked him to. "He is the only fellow I ever worked for who patted me on the back when everyone else gave me a kick in the pants," Meyer explained.[81]

Meyer's elbow continued hurting as he tried rounding into shape. After decent starts against the Senators and the Cardinals, he was pounded for 7 hits and 6 runs in three innings by the Shreveport Sports, which would finish in seventh place in the Texas League that year.[82] Sawyer's concern about Meyer was compounded by the extended loss of Steve Ridzik, whose kneecap was fractured during an intrasquad game, leaving the pitching staff thinner than had been hoped.[83]

As the final roster began taking shape, Eddie Sawyer decided on Putsy Caballero as utility infielder and released Eddie Miller, who subsequently signed with the St. Louis Cardinals.[84] Philadelphia was unquestionably solid at the other infield positions: Waitkus at first, Hamner at short, and Jones at third—one of the best defensive infields in baseball. Second base was the question mark. But Mike Goliat, the converted third baseman, was a star during spring training, driving in 27 runs in his first eighteen spring training games.[85] He had improved defensively as well, thanks to extra work with Toronto manager Jack Sanford, who had been brought in by Sawyer to help Goliat learn the proper method of playing the second sack.[86] Stan Baumgartner called Goliat the best second baseman in Florida that spring, ahead of St. Louis Cardinals star Red Schoendienst.[87]

The battle between Ed Sanicki and Richie Ashburn lasted about a week. After starting the first two exhibition games with 3 hits in 9 at bats, Sanicki then failed to connect safely in five straight appearances. Meanwhile, Ashburn went 9 for 17 during the week. On March 21 Ashburn added to his hot streak by going 2 for 4 against Cincinnati. Sanicki took over for Ashburn in the eighth inning and hit his first home run of the spring, capping off a game that featured encouraging pitching performances from Curt Simmons and Bob Miller, and a 5-for-5 day at the plate by Mike Goliat.[88]

Sanicki's home run earned him a start the next day against Detroit, a game that saw Sawyer flanking him in the outfield with Dick Sisler in left—a sure sign that Eddie Waitkus had won back the first base job—and Dick Whitman in right. Sisler played well, even as Sawyer cringed at his unconscious habit of occasionally catching fly balls one-handed as if he were still playing first base.[89] Many observers thought the Sisler experiment would lead to him being a reserve at both first and the outfield, but then he slammed out 3 more hits, including his 3rd home run of the spring, and made a great throw to discourage a runner thinking about scoring, instead forcing a retreat to third base.[90] The day after that it was 3 more hits, including another home run, running his batting average to .461 for the exhibition season. Sisler had won the left-field job.[91]

It became apparent Ed Sanicki was losing his opportunity to be the center fielder. During the March 22 game, he doubled in 3 at bats and then did not play in the next three games.[92] By the end of spring, the notoriously slow-starting Sanicki had hit .229 with 1 home run. Meanwhile, Ashburn batted .417 with 4 stolen bases and 7 runs batted in. A disappointed Sanicki was demoted to Toronto.

As training camp neared its end, Sawyer was pleased with the attitude of his charges. He listened to "whooping and singing" taking place within shouting distance of his office in Clearwater and told *Miami Herald* sportswriter Jimmy Burns, "That's a peppery gang. I'm glad of it because we've got a position to maintain."[93] Upon returning to Philadelphia, as the team prepared for the City Series against the Athletics, Sawyer wrote himself a note that said, "We can win the pennant," and placed it in his desk drawer to serve as a daily reminder.[94]

The Phillies received a scare when Robin Roberts was smacked in the calf by Johnny Blatnik's line drive during batting practice, putting his availability for the City Series against the Athletics—and for Opening Day against Brooklyn—in doubt.[95] Dealing with inclement weather all spring, Sawyer was concerned that he had to chop up outings of his hurlers, with only Bubba Church completing a nine-inning stint.[96] He worried the staff would not be ready to go the distance once the bell rang.

Another injury of note was that of Bill Nicholson, who badly sprained his ankle against Washington on March 30.[97] It would be a month before he could even pinch-hit, and he did not play outfield until mid-June. But overall Sawyer had to be pleased with his offense, which had averaged nearly 11 runs per game over the previous nine contests, seven of them wins. It was a team featuring decent power, with excellent hitters up and down the lineup. Pitching was the question mark, along with second base, although Mike Goliat's progress was encouraging. Bob Carpenter remained chipper, even after Charlie Bicknell was claimed on waivers by the Boston Braves—the sixteenth bonus player the Phillies had lost because of the rules Carpenter so despised.[98]

THE OPENING OF the City Series in Philadelphia was postponed due to snow flurries, even as the *Philadelphia Inquirer* ran excerpts from Connie Mack's autobiography, *My Sixty-Six Years in the Big Leagues*, in honor of his golden anniversary as manager of the Athletics.[99]

The eighty-seven-year-old Mack, after three straight better than .500 seasons, had made it clear to everyone that he was not stepping down. During the winter, contacted at his off-season retreat in St. Petersburg, Florida, Baseball's Grand Old Man had testily knocked aside rumors of discord and an impending departure. He announced his intention to go on managing indefinitely, punctuating his irritation at the question by adding, "And so long as I have my faculties, I will run the club. . . . We are perfectly capable of running the ball club without outside assistance."[100]

The Athletics took the first game of what was reduced to a two-game set, in front of roughly four thousand shivering fans, 7–4, as the newly installed heating vents in the dugouts at Shibe Park got their first workout. Robin Roberts, ignoring pain from the nasty bruise on his calf, pitched the first four innings, starting strong before allowing a run in the third and two more in the fourth. Russ Meyer was tagged for a pair of runs in the fifth. Mike Goliat's three-run home run was one of the few bright spots for the Phillies.[101]

Curt Simmons took a big step forward in the finale of the City Series, allowing only 5 hits and 1 run in seven innings of an 11–2 win, although he did walk 7. The day started with Ed Sullivan serving as master of ceremonies, introducing Connie Mack for his fiftieth season at the helm of the Athletics. It ended in triumph for the Phillies. Simmons was impressive, escaping bases-loaded, one-out jams in the sixth and seventh innings, demonstrating poise that had deserted him the previous two years. At the plate, he banged out 2 hits, scored twice and drove in a run.[102]

With that, the exhibition season was complete. The coming regular season was eagerly anticipated in Philadelphia, a rarity for both fans and players. The Phillies were rated by oddsmaker James J. Carroll eight to one to win the 1950 National League pennant, placing them fourth behind the favored Brooklyn Dodgers, which were given odds of six to five.[103] It was up to the players to prove the prognosticators wrong.

7

You Guys Look like You Want to Win the Pennant

THERE WAS A GUARDED sense of excitement as the Phillies began the 1950 season in earnest on April 18. The team faced long odds—between 1947 and 1959, three National League teams, the Dodgers, Braves, and Giants, won every pennant, save one—this one. But it would take until extra innings on the final day of the season for the Phillies to be the only interruption in an otherwise thirteen-season streak.[1]

Stan Baumgartner was convinced the Phillies had finally arrived, gushing about the beginning of "what promises to be the greatest season for the Phillies since the pennant-winning days of 1915."[2] Two months earlier, the Phillies had paid the final bonus installment—$15,000—due Curt Simmons.[3] Columnist John Webster wrote approvingly that Simmons had shown with his performance against the A's in the City Series that, like the team, he had arrived as a force with which to be reckoned, thus justifying that $65,000 bonus.[4]

Others were not quite so convinced. Of the 194 members of the Baseball Writers Association (BBWA), only 9 picked the Phillies to cop the flag. Forty-eight thought they would finish in the second division, including 4 who thought Philadelphia would finish seventh, and another scribe who picked the team to bring up the rear of the pack.[5]

Bob Carpenter felt strongly that his team's chances depended on success at the center of the diamond, warning John Webster, "If our pitchers don't come through, we'll be like a fighter who's suddenly lost his punch."[6]

Twenty thousand tickets were sold ahead of Opening Day, with Robin Roberts slated to take on Don Newcombe and the Brooklyn Dodgers, the bbwa's odds-on favorites to take the pennant and the team the Phillies had nearly knocked into a playoff with St. Louis on the final day of the 1949 season. The Phillies took the field at Shibe Park, clad in their new pinstripe uniforms—which Dodgers players lampooned and New York *Daily News* reporter Dick Young derisively compared to peppermint sticks. Elliott Lawrence, future long-time music director for the Tony Awards and composer of the team's new anthem, "The Fightin' Phils," appeared with his orchestra and also joined the Police and Fireman's Band for pregame music.[7] Up in the press box, a young broadcaster named Vin Scully (introduced as "Vince") sat alongside Red Barber and Connie Desmond, making his regular-season debut as a Dodgers play-by-play announcer.[8]

Brooklyn manager Burt Shotton called out to Eddie Waitkus, and when the Phillies first baseman turned, Shotton pointed a bat at him and mimicked gun noises, all in good-natured albeit rather distasteful fun.[9] Later, a photographer asked Waitkus, "Can I take a shot of you?" Waitkus quipped, "Do you want a shot of me, or at me?"[10]

Mayor Bernard Samuel was on hand, as was Si Rappaport, a veteran of the First World War, who tossed the ceremonial first ball from his wheelchair, after which umpire Babe Pinelli bellowed, "Play ball!"

The Phillies set a franchise record for Opening Day attendance at 29,074. To the delight of the crowd, they made short work of the Dodgers by winning, 9–1.[11] Don Newcombe was taking a shower before the second inning ended, while Robin Roberts, pitching stellar baseball four days after it appeared he might not pitch at all thanks to a Johnny Blatnik line drive, went the route in earning his first career win against the Dodgers in six decisions. He even started a pair of double plays on balls hit back to the mound.

The Phillies were a confident group energized by the season's start. When Jackie Robinson came to the plate in the top of the second, after the Phillies had scored twice in the first, he remarked to catcher Andy Seminick, "You guys look like you want to win the pennant."

Seminick replied, "You're damn right we do."[12]

Granny Hamner was becoming a team leader at age twenty-three, with an attitude to match. "When he goes out there in that cocky walk, his chin out, arms swinging," said writer Frank O'Rourke, "you know what he's thinking—that Hamner can lick anybody and will prove it."[13] Hamner asked Eddie Sawyer permission to visit the mound when the pitchers got in jams. Sending a message through Coach Benny Bengough, Sawyer told Bengough to let him do so, remarking, "He does it anyway, doesn't he?"[14] Sawyer later praised Hamner's leadership, telling sportswriter Hugh Brown, "He is the oldest young man I have ever managed."[15]

It was a day of positives. Mike Goliat, who had hit .257 in his final forty-one games in 1949, continued his stellar play from spring training, with 4 hits, while Eddie Waitkus had 3 in his first Major League appearance since being shot. Every player in the starting lineup, excepting Roberts, collected at least 1 hit.[16] Dick Sisler was indeed on Sawyer's Opening Day lineup card, although he was in left field instead of at first base. It was the first of 137 games Sisler was to play in left field that season.

Russ Meyer and his achy elbow was pounded the next game, the right-hander surrendering 11 hits and a half-dozen runs before being lifted in the sixth inning.[17] Nevertheless, Sawyer praised Meyer, declaring that he was far from disappointed in the performance, pointing to the pitcher's slow start during a stellar 1949 season and the cold weather that limited everyone's work during the spring. "In fact," Sawyer insisted, "he was better than I thought he would be. He had more stuff on his fastball than I expected."[18]

But Sawyer had reason to be more concerned than he let on. He gave the right-hander three starts, the last resulting in Meyer's suspension because of his assaulting umpire Al Barlick after a close play at first base.[19] Meyer rested for two weeks and then failed to retire a batter in his next assignment, against the Giants.[20] He rested again for nine days. Meyer ultimately lost his first six decisions with a ghastly 8.67 earned run average.

After the opening series against Brooklyn, the Phillies struggled on their first road trip. They tied Boston in the Braves' home opener when the game was called after seven innings due to rain. Ken Heintzelman pitched well in the 2–2 contest but surrendered one of the runs in part to the new balk rule, when he did not come to a complete stop in his windup. A bright spot was Richie Ashburn throwing out speedy Sam Jethroe at second, even after bobbling the ball in center field.[21]

Curt Simmons made his season debut the next day and entered the bottom of the eighth leading the Braves, 2–1. With one out and one on, Simmons faced Bob Elliott, who was angry because his favorite bat went missing and he had to use another that was two ounces heavier. After working the count even, Elliott noticed Simmons shake off catcher Stan Lopata and was certain a fastball was coming his way. He was right.

Simmons threw the ball high and outside, and Elliott was on it, crushing it over the right-field wall to give Boston the lead.[22] As the Braves slugger rounded the bases, Simmons slammed his glove to the ground in frustration. Following a subsequent walk and a single, Eddie Sawyer replaced Simmons with Jim Konstanty. The young left-hander, who after his spectacular debut on the last day of the 1947 season had posted a record of 11-23, shook his head as he walked from the mound, angrily hurling his glove against the back wall upon reaching the dugout. Boston held on to win, 3–2.[23]

On the surface, it seemed a repeat of Simmons' 1949 debut, one that had impacted the twenty-year-old's confidence the entire season. Eddie Sawyer had a talk with Simmons after the game and later told reporters, "He used to get a little upset, but he took it all right. He's growing up now. . . . And what a sweet pitcher he is, too."[24]

Four days later, Philadelphia's record dropped to 2-5 after a ten-inning loss, during which the Phillies claimed fan interference on a long fly ball to left that Dick Sisler failed to glove. "I jumped and would have caught it," complained Sisler, "if a spectator hadn't knocked it out of my hands."[25]

Umpire Babe Pinelli disagreed, and a loud argument ensued, with all nine Phillies on the field, plus Sawyer and the bullpen catcher, surrounding the umpire. The Phillies finished the tenth inning under protest, and Pee Wee Reese hit a fly ball for a single that drove in the winning run for the Dodgers.[26]

At the end of April the team was back to breakeven, thanks to three straight complete game victories: by Robin Roberts over Brooklyn, Curt Simmons with a three-hitter over the Braves, and Bob Miller, making his first Major League start, also against Boston at Shibe Park on Children's Day.

The only run off Miller resulted from a failed pick-off attempt of Sam Jethroe at third base. Jethroe, who had raced from first to third on a ground-out, was hit in the back by Stan Lopata's throw and sped home for the run.

Nursing a 2–1 lead, Miller retired the first two batters in the ninth before surrendering a walk and a double, putting runners on second and third. He realized he was pressing, later admitting, "I had two outs but then I guess I started overthrowing." Sawyer called time and conferred with the pitcher, opting to leave him in. After the right-hander walked the next batter to load the bases, Sawyer again started for the mound but caught himself, deciding instead to give Miller the opportunity to work his way out of trouble.[27]

"His best pitch was a curveball," explained Sawyer. "He got more fellows out on a 3-2 curve than anybody I ever saw in my life. And of course I wanted to build up his confidence if he could get them out. So I decided to leave him in there."[28]

The next batter hit a line shot, directly to Del Ennis. Miller said, "Three or four feet either way and I would have been a losing pitcher." The rookie leapt off the mound, celebrating his first Major League win.[29]

In addition to Miller's stellar debut, Willie Jones, Eddie Waitkus, and Dick Sisler were all swinging the bat well. Jones especially was on fire, with 4 home runs and a batting average above .380. But Del Ennis hit only 1 home run in April. Andy Seminick, after missing most of spring training, was absent for nearly two weeks due to the illness and death of his mother. After a great Opening Day, Mike Goliat had only 2 hits in his next 35 at bats.

Overall, Sawyer expressed satisfaction with the team's start to the season, telling John Webster, "I don't think the Phillies were quite as ready as some of the teams we've played. That bad weather we got coming out of the South hurt a lot. Also, the Phillies are a young team. That means more problems, a slower start. But we'll be improving fast . . . and don't forget we've been playing the toughest teams in the National League."[30]

The Phillies manager strongly felt pitching and defense key to the team's success and was convinced of the pitching staff's depth, despite the struggles of Russ Meyer. Roberts was becoming a star, and Simmons had made tremendous strides. Sawyer reasoned that Meyer would sooner or later begin pitching effectively. Rookie Bob Miller's move into the rotation allowed Sawyer to use veteran Blix Donnelly as a reliever.

Sawyer tinkered with his everyday lineup at the end of April, benching Richie Ashburn, who was hitting .321 but without an extra-base hit, in favor of Dick Whitman, who he thought might provide more pop and a better arm in the outfield. In his first four starts Whitman collected 7 hits—all singles. After Whitman followed that with 13 straight at bats without a base hit against the Braves and Cubs, Sawyer returned Ashburn to the lineup for good.

IN ADDITION TO PLAYING, the Phillies made sure to pay attention to their fans. In early April, Del Ennis and Willie Jones visited Benjamin Franklin High, a largely Black school, and signed autographs for students after addressing them at a special assembly.[31] Bubba Church, Putsy Caballero, and Jones visited prisoners at Eastern State Penitentiary.[32]

They also visited the sick. Sixteen-year-old Larry Rosenthal had been paralyzed from the neck down in a January automobile accident. Originally given only twenty-four hours to live, Rosenthal had battled bravely against the odds, his fight for life publicized in a widely read *Philadelphia Inquirer* column.[33] Bob Miller, Curt Simmons, and Eddie Waitkus were moved by the teen's courage and visited him in the hospital in late April. An enthusiastic baseball fan, Rosenthal was thrilled when the Phillies were among those responding to his plight.

The three players were photographed with Rosenthal.[34] Later that night, the high schooler listened on the radio as Simmons threw a three-hitter, Waitkus banged out 4 hits, and Mike Goliat broke a 0 for 26 streak with an RBI double in the fifth.[35] Unfortunately, Rosenthal succumbed to his injuries a week later, but his family reported that those last days after the Phillies' visit were among the happiest of his life.[36]

And Phillies players fulfilled the role of Good Samaritan. After one game, a husband and wife returned to their car in the Shibe Park lot and discovered a flat tire. The husband began working on it but was having trouble with the jack when three men walked up and asked if they could help. They immediately set to work and got the tire changed before introducing themselves as Dick Sisler, Del Ennis, and Blix Donnelly.[37]

ON APRIL 27, the Phillies traded outfielder Johnny Blatnik, who had almost kayoed Robin Roberts two weeks earlier, to the St. Louis Cardinals for Ken Johnson, a left-handed pitcher.[38] Johnson, who was told by Sawyer he would primarily be used against teams with heavy left-handed-hitting lineups, had not pitched much for St. Louis the previous year—only thirty-three and two-thirds innings. He possessed a great curveball that he struggled to control, as evidenced by walking 73 batters in ninety-one Major League innings to that point. Sawyer instructed Johnson to abandon his breaking stuff and stick to fastballs.[39]

A week after his acquisition, Johnson won his first start, beating the Cubs, 5–2. With Andy Seminick absent from the team to attend his mother's funeral, Eddie Sawyer asked veteran third-stringer Ken Silvestri, who often worked on the sidelines with the team's young pitchers, to catch him.[40]

Sawyer told Silvestri, who was turning thirty-four years old that day, "Don't worry about pitching to spots. Just make him get the ball over the plate. As he goes to the mound each inning tell him to throw every ball through the center. We don't care if they make a hundred hits. What we don't want is 10 walks."[41]

It worked. Johnson yielded 12 hits but only 2 walks in eight-plus innings, while Willie Jones hit 2 home runs to give Johnson all the support he needed. Johnson later told Rochester columnist George Beahon, "You can say for me that Eddie Sawyer is a tremendous man to work for. Also that [St. Louis manager] Eddie Dyer did me a real favor when he let me go to the Phils."[42] Johnson's win sparked a stretch of eleven Phillies wins in thirteen games.

The series that featured Johnson's debut also marked the first trip to Wrigley Field for Eddie Waitkus since the shooting, and he told Bob Brumby in an article for Sport magazine of his being nervous returning to Chicago. "That's the Badlands of bobby-sox fans," said Waitkus. "Always has been. About 90 percent of the wildly enthusiastic autograph seekers are teen-age girls. They get to the park before the ball teams, which arrive around eleven in the morning. The ticket windows aren't open, but the bobby-soxers are there. And if you try to ignore them—wow! There is only one way to enter or leave the park for players."

"After the game it usually gets rougher," Waitkus warned. "Ignore them and they 'playfully' flick ink on the back of your suit. Tell 'em off and they become violent. . . .

"The girls know they have two strikes on you because of their sex and they take advantage of it. Nothing much you can do about it, either. Until what happened last Summer, I never thought too much about it, but now I'll admit I am sort of jittery about my first meeting with that bobby-sox crowd in Chicago."[43]

Waitkus overcame his apprehension, going 1 for 4 and scoring twice in a 10–8 loss to the Cubs, followed by 2 hits in 5 at bats during Ken Johnson's winning effort.

CURT SIMMONS CONTINUED showing signs of coming into his own. He picked up 2 wins in relief, threw a three-hitter against Boston to avenge the emotional loss of his season debut, and tossed another three-hitter against New York to run his record to 5-2.

Simmons was using his modified corkscrew delivery to great effect. Henry Aaron later declared the left-hander's pitching motion among the most difficult for him as a hitter, explaining, "He would turn his body, give me a view of his backside, then he would throw and I wouldn't see the ball until a split second before he would let it go."[44]

When asked what had turned things around for him, Simmons replied, "Just a lot o' luck, I guess. I'm older . . . stronger, too. And I've had a lot of help this spring." Ken Silvestri, who was assigned to be Simmons's roommate at this pivotal juncture in his career, said of the young left-hander, "We tell him what to do—but he's got to do it." Coach Benny Bengough added, "You can put ideas in the kid's head, but he's got to put 'em into practice. Well, it looks like Curt is doing that."[45]

On May 11 Robin Roberts picked up his 4th win, defeating the Pirates and moving the Phillies a game ahead of Brooklyn and St. Louis, which were tied for second place. Willie Jones hit a three-run first-inning home run, and Roberts held on for a complete-game 3–2 victory, surviving a ninth inning that saw the first two men reach base on singles and a third single bring the Pirates within a run. But Roberts responded by striking out the final two batters of the game.[46] Jones's home run was already his 7th of the year, Dick Sisler was batting .377, and Eddie Waitkus was at .326. Roberts had completed five of his first six starts. It was clear the Phillies were for real. "If this were October, it would be just dandy," gushed Bob Carpenter.[47]

The excitement in the team's offices was palpable. Public relations man Babe Alexander observed, "I think the Phillies have the fans of the town with them this year like they never were before."[48]

Equipped with a talented but young infield, Sawyer shored up his depth by purchasing thirty-two-year-old veteran Jimmy Bloodworth from the Cincinnati Reds. Bob Carpenter claimed that the amount paid to secure Bloodworth, who had a reputation for mentoring young players, was "above" the $10,000 waiver price.[49] It was the type of move contenders made—noticed by both players and fans.

On May 17 Ken Johnson picked up his third win in a row, thanks to a ninth-inning triple by Eddie Waitkus, a walk, and a Willie Jones walk-off single. Everything was clicking. Granny Hamner was playing despite a bad back and hip that set him up on Frank Wiechec's training table for thirty minutes before each game, just to get him loose enough to play. No one wanted to come out of the lineup when winning.[50]

The pennant race was shaping up as a three-team affair. As May begat June it was the Dodgers in first place with a mark of 23-13 and the Phillies in third, a game back, thanks to Brooklyn's sweep of Philadelphia in a double-header to end the month. More than fifty-three thousand fans attended the two games at Ebbets Field.

It had been a dramatic May for the Dodgers, with four painful walk-off defeats in six days to begin the month. But Brooklyn rebounded with 10 wins in 12 games, 6 of them in a row. Among them was an incredible come-from-behind win on May 18, when they defeated the Cardinals, 9–8, after trailing 8–0 going to the bottom of the eighth inning.

St. Louis was the other team in the immediate fight, like the Phillies a game back but ahead of them by percentage points. The Cardinals had won 17 and lost 9 in May, ending the month with a five-game winning streak.

DICK SISLER CONTINUED to make Eddie Sawyer's gamble of playing him in left field pay off. "He didn't look like Tris Speaker [in spring training], and still doesn't," commented John Webster. "But he's not a bad outfielder, and since he's trying like mischief at all times, he'll be improving as the summer sets in."[51]

While the Phillies lacked quality depth, it seemed as if every member of the bench came through with at least one big moment during the 1950 season. Jimmy Bloodworth was pressed into action after Mike Goliat injured his thumb on a ground ball in the opening game of a doubleheader against St. Louis on May 21, a couple of innings after Eddie Waitkus had somehow struck out into a triple play.[52] Bloodworth remained in the lineup, playing first base for three games after Eddie Waitkus was forced out of action with an injured finger—at the same time the durable Del Ennis missed a week with a groin pull.[53] Ennis was replaced by Dick Whitman, who had 10 hits in 25 at bats and 3 runs batted in while substituting for the Phillies slugger.

Bloodworth spent a week at second base in early June, giving the slumping Goliat a rest. That included a game on June 11 against Pittsburgh when the veteran utility man slammed a three-run double off Vern Law—who was making his Major League debut—during an eighth-inning rally that keyed a Phillies win.[54]

Less than three weeks later, Bloodworth was again the hero, with another eighth-inning three-run double—this time in a pinch-hitting role—that clinched a win, moving Philadelphia past Brooklyn and back into first place.[55]

Eddie Sawyer tinkered with the pitching staff. He had kept Hank Borowy around, but it was clear that the veteran was expendable thanks to the emergence of Bob Miller and Bubba Church—even as Church complained about his lack of work and Sawyer responded to him by counseling patience.[56] On June 12, as the Phillies prepared for a crucial series against St. Louis, Sawyer sold Borowy to the Pittsburgh Pirates for the standard waiver price of $10,000.[57] It was quite a comedown for the right-hander, who five years earlier had been sold to the Chicago Cubs by the New York Yankees for nearly ten times the amount Pittsburgh was paying. Even though he was said to be fine physically, Sawyer had only used Borowy three times, for six and one-third innings, explaining that because he needed twenty minutes to warm up, he was not a suitable choice for relief roles. And with the availability of Miller, Church, and Johnson, Borowy was not needed as a starter.

As Borowy left, Bill Nicholson returned from the injured list.[58] Nicholson had been counted on as a source of power in the outfield mix. But, sapped by weight loss later diagnosed as resulting from diabetes, it was becoming apparent his role would be more like Chuck Klein's during William Cox's year in charge, as a hopefully dangerous pinch hitter.

On June 20 Russ Meyer finally earned his first win of the season, a 7–3 complete game on a sloppy, rain-soaked field against Pittsburgh. When Wally Westlake grounded back to the mound with two out in the ninth, an exuberant Meyer sprinted to first to make the final putout himself.[59] When asked about the muddy conditions and what he would have done had he slipped during his mad dash, Meyer remarked, "I'd have swum to the damn bag."[60]

A pair of injuries to pitchers cropped up. First, Ken Johnson was unavailable for most of June after being hit on the back of his pitching hand by a line drive during batting practice.[61] Then Bob Miller hurt his back in late June. After defeating Pittsburgh on June 22, a game in which he started a triple play and ran his record to 6-0 with a 1.63 earned run average, Miller was handed a train ticket to Boston to prepare for his next start.[62] He tripped on the stairs at the North Philadelphia Station and felt a twinge that developed into a sharp pain upon boarding.[63]

"By the time I got to Boston," remembered Miller, "I couldn't even walk. I was tilting to my right side." Eddie Sawyer was alarmed when he met up with his pitcher, doubled-up in agony. Sawyer remarked, "He looked like he had slept in a bathtub."[64]

The injury was diagnosed as a pulled muscle, and Miller missed a start, returning on July 1 to defeat Brooklyn, driving in Philadelphia's first 2 runs with a bases loaded single. But he had to be replaced in the seventh inning.[65] He was not quite the same after that. Even while running his record to 8-0, Sawyer observed that Miller was "pushing" the ball more than throwing it.[66]

Meanwhile, Jim Konstanty, carrying a herculean workload that left much of the other bullpen members relatively idle, struggled in late June and early July. Upon blowing a save on July 4 after the Phillies had rallied from a 7–0 deficit against the Braves, Konstanty called his undertaker friend Andy Skinner to work with him.[67] Skinner, who had erected an antenna on the outskirts of his town so he could watch Konstanty pitch on television and correct any mistakes he noted, arrived at Shibe Park and recognized that his friend had altered his release point.[68] With that fine-tuning, the reliever was back on track.[69] From July 19 through August 29, Konstanty allowed only 3 runs, 2 earned, in forty-one innings pitched, winning 5 games without a loss and saving 10. He had a 0.44 ERA during this stretch, with hitters compiling a .148 batting average against him. "A lot had been written about me, but the influence of Andy Skinner hasn't been stressed enough," insisted Konstanty. "The big difference between my pitching at Toronto in 1946 and my pitching today is Andy Skinner."[70]

The Phillies entered the All-Star break on July 10 with a record of 44-29, one game ahead of St. Louis, two ahead of Boston, and four games in front of Brooklyn. They beat the Dodgers five times in a nine-day span, two of the victories thanks to a pair of Bill Nicholson late-inning pinch-hit home runs—a two-run shot on July 2, and a three-run long ball on July 8.[71] The latter, off Don Newcombe with two on and two out in the top of the ninth, cleared the scoreboard to give Philadelphia a 4-1 win.[72] Robin Roberts, who picked up the victory, later remembered the Dodgers having a major mound conference when Nicholson came to the plate to hit for Mike Goliat. Nicholson immediately crushed Newcombe's first pitch.

"I have often wondered," said Roberts, "what the Dodgers were talking about when they had that mound conference." Eddie Sawyer said, "We laughed and laughed and asked the Dodgers what they were meeting about."[73]

The season's first half ended with a wild loss to Brooklyn in which Andy Seminick homered twice and nearly brawled with Duke Snider, a defeat that ended a four-game winning streak for Philadelphia.

According to Stan Baumgartner's game account, the near fisticuffs came in the seventh inning after it appeared Seminick had thrown out Snider at third base on an attempted steal. When the home plate umpire overruled the call, saying Willie Jones had dropped the throw, a heated argument ensued. After things calmed down and play resumed, Jackie Robinson hit a grounder to Jimmy Bloodworth, who threw home to cut off Snider. Seminick blocked the plate and then sat on Snider to make the tag. The Dodgers star took exception and started after Seminick, at which point it appeared a fight was inevitable. But the ball remained in play. Seminick caught sight of Robinson tearing for second base and tried to throw him out. Unfortunately, Granny Hamner had abandoned his position—thinking his catcher might need help in a scrap with Snider—and the ball sailed into center field. Robinson kept on going.

Richie Ashburn finally got the ball back to the infield, with Hamner cutting off the throw and trapping Robinson off third. Robinson broke for home, but Willie Jones tossed the ball to Bubba Church, who tagged the Dodgers star out in the baseline—just your typical 4–2–8–6–5–1 double play.[74] The Phillies were definitely living up to the nickname Fightin' Phils.

AT THE SEASON'S HALFWAY point, Shibe Park hosted a marked contrast in baseball fortunes. The Athletics were stumbling badly in Connie Mack's fiftieth season, hit hard by pitcher injuries while mired in seventh place and on their way to eighth. They began surrendering the present and scouting players for 1951, including a serious look at the possibility of integrating the Major League roster. Conversely, Phillies fans were excited by their team.[75] Andy Seminick was hitting .316 with 9 home runs. After a slow start, Del Ennis hit 9 home runs in June and had 60 runs batted in at the All-Star break. Willie Jones led the team with 17 home runs—while striking out only 19 times—and was second in runs batted in with 54. Dick Sisler was hitting a team-leading .325 with 45 runs batted in and an on-base average of .425. The offense was firing on all cylinders, scoring 77 runs in the first eleven July games.

Among the pitchers, Robin Roberts was 10-3 with a 3.25 earned run average and was selected to start against Vic Raschi of the New York Yankees in the All-Star Game. Curt Simmons was 10-5, Bob Miller was undefeated, Russ Meyer had won four of his last six decisions, and Jim Konstanty had already appeared in thirty-six games, with 7 wins and 11 saves. The Philadelphia Phillies would be well-represented in the All-Star Game.

8

Don't Say I Am Predicting a Pennant

HAVING WON ONLY four of the previous sixteen contests, the National League was a nine-to-five underdog going into the seventeenth Major League Baseball All-Star Game, played at Comiskey Park in Chicago on July 11. Four Phillies, the most ever representing the franchise in the Midsummer Classic, made the final roster, each for the first time.[1] The Phillies could easily have had four more.

The All-Star Game circa 1950 was a different spectacle than it is today. There was no interleague play that counted—save for the World Series—and the American and National Leagues were separate entities, jealously vying for superiority. The contest was important to players, who tended to spend their entire careers in one league. Fans were also fervent in their support for one league versus the other—a sentiment that lasted into the 1980s.

One had only to go back one year to see an example of the partisanship's intensity. In July 1949, Phillies fans vented their frustration with Braves manager Billy Southworth, who had passed over Ken Heintzelman and Robin Roberts for the National League All-Star team. When the Braves visited Shibe Park shortly before the All-Star Game, fans repeatedly filled the stadium with a cacophony of vitriol aimed at Southworth every time he came into view.[2]

So it came as no surprise in 1950 when the National League manager, Brooklyn's Burt Shotton, created a bit of a controversy with his response to a fan vote that did not result in a true center fielder being chosen for the starting lineup. He replaced Cubs outfielder Hank Sauer with his own Dodgers centerfielder, Duke Snider, which did not sit well with the Wrigley Field faithful, especially since the game was being played in Chicago.

Shotton, likely all too mindful of the scorn heaped upon Southworth the previous year, swiftly reconsidered.[3]

More than forty-six thousand fans greeted the raising of the Stars and Stripes by the U.S. Marines, thousands of red, white and blue balloons were released, and Connie Mack, in recognition of his half century as leader of the Athletics, tossed the first ball to Vic Raschi. Hank Sauer received the biggest ovation when introduced, Burt Shotton the rudest. But Shotton disarmed his critics by smiling and waving his cap in response to the discord; with Sauer returned to the lineup, all was forgiven.[4]

Robin Roberts, his wife and parents on hand, allowed 1 run on 3 hits in his three innings of work as the National League's starting pitcher. Willie Jones served as the Senior Circuit's lead-off hitter and starting third baseman, playing the entire contest while collecting 1 hit in 7 at bats. Jim Konstanty pitched a scoreless sixth inning, striking out two, after Dick Sisler singled as a pinch hitter for Don Newcombe in the top of that inning. New York's Larry Jansen struck out 6 batters during his five innings of work, tying the All-Star Game record held jointly by Carl Hubbell and Johnny Vander Meer.

The game produced one serious injury, to Ted Williams, when he crashed into the left-field wall while catching a Ralph Kiner line drive. Although Williams played into the ninth inning, it was later revealed that he had fractured his elbow on the play. He was sidelined for two months.

The game was the first All-Star contest to go extra-innings, thanks to Ralph Kiner's ninth-inning home run; the sides traded goose eggs through the thirteenth.[5]

The crowd clapped impatiently and chanted, "Let's Go!" when Red Schoendienst took his place in the batter's box to lead off the fourteenth inning. The redheaded second baseman responded by lining a pitch off Detroit's Ted Gray that curled around the foul pole and into the first row of seats in the left field stands, giving the National League the lead. Afterward, Schoendienst said he could not recall what kind of pitch he hit. "It couldn't have been very fast though," the Cardinals star chuckled, "because I pulled it."[6]

Joe DiMaggio hit into a game-ending double play in the bottom of the fourteenth, clinching the National League's win. It was widely considered the best All-Star Game to that point and raised a record amount for the player's pension fund, more than $100,000.

DURING THE ALL-STAR BREAK, the Phillies played a pair of exhibition games against International League teams, the Rochester Red Wings and the Toronto Maple Leafs. On July 10, with Eddie Waitkus and Granny Hamner excused—along with the four All-Stars of course—the Phillies defeated Rochester, 8–7, in a game shortened by rain to six innings. Ken Johnson, making only his second appearance since his hand injury, used the game to reintroduce his curveball and walked 8 batters while allowing all 7 runs in going the distance. He also hit a home run in the sixth inning that was responsible for the winning margin. Eddie Sawyer, who earlier in the day was seen strolling downtown Rochester with his two young daughters in tow, left the game early to catch a train for Chicago.[7]

Johnson, a former Rochester pitcher whom local columnist George Beahon described as being "precise and correct as an English tutor" and also "still as easy to talk with, and as frank about everything," was asked about his new team. "We've got a marvelous opportunity," Johnson insisted. "They say pressure will hit the Phils because of their youth. Don't believe it. These lads don't know they are in first place. . . . They'll make the error that hurts here and there, but it won't be the result of pressure, just inexperience."[8]

The next day, the starless and Sawyer-less Phillies lost to their top farm team, the Toronto Maple Leafs, 5–3, while hitting into 4 double plays. Bubba Church, finally getting some work, took the loss. Ed Sanicki, enduring a disappointing season rooted in the disappointment of not making the Phillies out of spring training, stroked a pair of singles and drew a walk for Toronto.[9] With that, the focus turned to the season's second half.

MAJOR LEAGUE ATTENDANCE was continuing to crater during 1950, a decline that would finally make obvious the need to relocate franchises later in the decade—shifts that, among other things, handed the Phillies a Major League baseball monopoly in the city of Philadelphia for the first time since 1900. At the season's midpoint, headlines warned that eleven of the sixteen Major League franchises had declined in attendance compared to 1949, with the St. Louis Browns customer base plummeting more than 50 percent. Only the Philadelphia Phillies, with a 22 percent increase, were showing any significant gain.

The postwar attendance boom was fading fast, and overall Major League attendance was down nearly 1,700 per game—a pace of nearly two million for the year—with declines hitting 11 percent in the American League. Thanks to the Phillies, the National League loss was less, slightly more than 7 percent.[10] The decline worsened as the year continued, to a drop of more than 13 percent, and was even more pronounced in the Minor Leagues, plunging 17 percent, creating an alarming deficit of more than seven million customers compared to the previous year.[11]

AFTER WINNING THEIR first post–All-Star Game contest, the Phillies stumbled, losing five straight to the Cardinals and Cubs on the road. Robin Roberts lost twice, the first coming on a night held in his honor. Illinois governor Adlai Stevenson and Springfield Mayor Harry Eielson took part in the festivities, which included the presentation of a diamond wrist watch and U.S. Savings Bonds. Before that game, Milo Candini was hit in the eye by a Ken Silvestri line drive while throwing batting practice. Candini donned an eyepatch and resumed his duties.[12]

After Roberts was beaten by St. Louis, Jim Konstanty lost to the Cardinals after the Phillies had rallied from a 6–2 deficit to tie the game in the top of the seventh inning. With a runner on first, Konstanty pounced on a bunt, pirouetting and firing the ball to second. But the throw was off line and appeared to pull Granny Hamner off the bag. The runner was ruled safe by umpire Augie Donatelli, despite Hamner's protest of the call and its result. After a long delay for argument, a sacrifice bunt and a walk resulted in St. Louis sending up pinch hitter Rocky Nelson, hitless in his last 15 at bats, and he smashed a liner to left. Del Ennis misjudged the ball, breaking in before realizing it would carry. With Ennis's momentum leaning him in the wrong direction, the ball sailed over his outstretched glove, 2 runs scoring on Nelson's double. The Phillies lost.[13] The next day, Bob Miller and Russ Meyer both started well before collapsing in a doubleheader sweep by the Cubs, Miller absorbing his first loss of the year.[14]

The Phillies split another twin bill with the Cubs on July 18, the same day Boston walloped tail end Pittsburgh and the Cardinals topped the Dodgers.[15] The National League standings showed Philadelphia, Boston, and St. Louis all tied for first place with identical 46–34 records. Brooklyn was fourth, one game back, but tied in the loss column.

It was the doubleheader split with the Cubs that proved a catalyst for the Phillies. After losing the first game behind Robin Roberts, Sawyer rearranged the batting order for the nightcap, moving Eddie Waitkus from third to leadoff, Dick Sisler from sixth in the order to third, Granny Hamner from second to sixth, and Richie Ashburn from leadoff to second.[16] "I just wanted to shake things up a little," Sawyer later explained.[17] The change paid dividends, with the Phillies taking the nightcap, 8–3, and Sawyer stuck with the new batting order for the rest of the season. The reordering of the lineup especially benefitted Richie Ashburn, who raised his batting average from .279 to .311 by the end of August, including 11 doubles during that stretch.

For the first time in more than three decades the Phillies were in the midst of a pennant race. The hitting and defense were top-notch, and the rookie pitchers were contributing, including Bubba Church, who had picked up a pair of wins after the All-Star break. Jim Konstanty was providing an unprecedented performance out of the bullpen, and the two prize bonus babies of 1947, Robin Roberts and Curt Simmons, were approaching stardom.

There was however a cloud on the horizon. On July 22 the Associated Press reported that the Korean War was causing the government to reassess the draft status of young men, which of course included baseball players. Those unmarried and lacking previous military experience were at most risk. Among them was Simmons, soon required to report for two weeks of National Guard duty as he had in 1949. But now the concern was that Simmons's unit could be called to active service and the Phillies would lose him for the rest of the season.[18] And that would constitute a major loss—the left-hander paced the team with 12 wins.

ON JULY 23 the Phillies swept a doubleheader from the Reds, with Curt Simmons coasting to a 12–4 win in the opener to become the first pitcher in the National League to record 13 wins. In the nightcap, Eddie Waitkus went 5 for 5, and Russ Meyer bested Ewell Blackwell, 7–4, the fourth time the Phillies had beaten "The Whip" in 1950. Meyer had his sinker working, with Granny Hamner recording 11 assists and a putout at shortstop. Willie Jones, who had homered twice in the first game, was ejected after sliding hard into Reds infielder Connie Ryan, precipitating a fight that resulted in banishment for both.[19]

The Phillies lost a potential win the next day when Eddie Waitkus hit a two-run home run in the top of the seventh against Pittsburgh to give Philadelphia a 3–2 lead, only to see it wiped out after heavy rain began falling and the game was halted, the score reverting to the previous inning. This resulted in a 2–1 loss, dropping Philadelphia to second place, percentage points behind St. Louis.[20]

The Phillies regained their advantage with a doubleheader sweep of the Cubs—the Phillies first home date in nearly three weeks—Robin Roberts and Bubba Church each throwing shutouts. Church allowed only 3 hits in the opener, all singles, for his fourth win without a loss as a starter and third straight complete-game victory. Three of his four wins to that point had come at the expense of the Cubs.[21] Andy Seminick was growing in his appreciation of Church, saying, "He keeps his fastball below the batter's waist and inside, where it can do the least damage. He does the same thing with his curve. He doesn't seem to be putting much on the ball, yet every pitch does something."[22]

Robin Roberts matched Church's feat with a shutout in the nightcap, except his was a dramatic 1–0 win featuring a Richie Ashburn walk-off single, as opposed to Church, who had coasted to his victory by a score of 7–0.[23] Afterward, Church approached Roberts and jokingly complained it was unfair for Robin to have upstaged him and his three-hitter.[24]

A delighted Sawyer, who was marking his second anniversary as manager of the Phillies, was quoted as saying, "No, don't say I am predicting a pennant. Just say I see my dreams coming true."[25] He noted the anniversary by complimenting his players: "They're a great bunch of kids. They play to win and they never let down. No high school team ever had more enthusiasm. They're trying like hell all the time."[26]

Milo Candini picked up a win in relief the next day, after Russ Meyer struggled. Frustrated by a balk call, Meyer charged the umpire and was ejected. He was replaced by Candini in the fifth with the Phillies trailing, 4–0. Candini settled the ship while Cubs starter Monk Dubiel fell apart in the sixth, allowing 2 hits and 6 runs while walking 6 during the inning—including 5 in a row. Chicago manager Frankie Frisch remained rooted to the bench, raising eyebrows with his refusal to warm up a reliever to rescue his struggling pitcher.[27] Dubiel did not walk a batter before or after that inning, but the damage was done, and Philadelphia won, 6–4.

Frisch insisted his inaction was not a matter of discipline, while practically screaming at reporters, "I'm sick of watching some of my pitchers getting into jams, peeping out to the bull pen to see if a reliever is ready to take over his work for him.

"I may look bad for having kept such a pitcher in there against a contender but . . . I've got to find out what's going on when a pitcher can walk six men in one inning and none in seven other innings."[28]

After Bob Miller threw his first complete game in more than a month to defeat Pittsburgh, the Phillies swept a doubleheader from the Pirates to close out July, taking three out of four games in the series. July 30 was Andy Seminick Day, honoring the Phillies catcher whose fan club, run by sisters Anne and Betty Zeiser and their friends Dot Reilly and Kitty Kelley, arranged for local merchants to provide suitable gifts to their favorite player.[29] Del Ennis drove in 7 runs in the doubleheader, pushing him ahead of Ralph Kiner for the National League lead, and Robin Roberts threw his third straight shutout as the Phillies ended the month having won seven of eight to open a lead of three games over Boston, three and a half over St. Louis, and four over Brooklyn.[30]

WHILE THE PHILLIES were in the midst of a pennant race, their landlords were struggling. The disappointing Athletics were bringing up the rear of the American League. Attendance had dropped more than 50 percent and after the games of July 19, the A's win-loss mark was 29-56, slotting them a game behind the miserable St. Louis Browns. Connie Mack signaled his surrender, selling disgruntled third baseman Bob Dillinger, the reigning three-time American League stolen-base champ and batting .309 on the season, to Pittsburgh. Dillinger reacted by saying, "I'm not surprised. And not unhappy."[31] Seven months earlier, the A's had sent $100,000—plus four players—to the Browns for Dillinger and outfielder Paul Lehner.[32] The disposal of Dillinger came during a dramatic reorganization of the franchise, the announcement of which represented the culmination of a long family battle.

Connie Mack's first wife, the mother of his sons Earle and Roy, died young in 1892. Connie remarried in 1910, and his second wife, Katherine, gave birth to four daughters and one son, Connie Junior. The elder Mack wished for his three sons to eventually succeed him in running the franchise and to that end gave 163 of his shares to each of them, while leaving out his five daughters, including one from his first marriage. This decision resulted in estrangement between Connie Mack and his wife, and they separated for a few months in 1946–1947. Although they reconciled, Mack refused to change his mind regarding the split of shares.

Connie Jr. grew frustrated with his half brothers, who were not fond of him, or of each other for that matter, and wanted to continue running the team as it had been. He responded by forming an alliance, backed by his mother, with members of the Shibe family who still owned shares of the franchise. This gave Connie Jr. a controlling voting bloc.

At this point, Earle's role as A's manager-in-waiting ended, with Jimmy Dykes hired as a coach—essentially to assist Connie Sr., who was struggling physically and mentally in getting through his fiftieth season. Mickey Cochrane assumed the role of general manager. But Connie Jr., the only member of the family aware that his father had suffered a stroke two months earlier, soon came to the conclusion that the family lacked the resources to successfully run the franchise and urged its sale to a local group, headed by James P. Clark, a trucking executive and president of the Philadelphia Eagles.[33] Earle and Roy countered that they should be given first option to purchase the team, and they scrambled to patch together the necessary financing.[34]

On July 31, Earle joined with his brother Roy to formally exercise a thirty-day option to purchase the stock held by their stepmother, their half brother Connie Jr., and the heirs of the late Shibe brothers.[35]

The deal was completed near the end of August, with the older Mack brothers controlling 56 percent of the shares. Combined with their father, the three owned nearly 80 percent of the franchise.[36]

The consolidation of power was accomplished thanks in large part to a loan of $1.75 million taken against Shibe Park. The lender, the Connecticut General Life Insurance Company, also received control of income the A's received from the Phillies, other park rentals, and concessions—the last having supplemented the income of Connie Sr.[37] Earle Mack insisted that he would remain in the front office in his new role as the team's secretary-treasurer. The new board of directors consisted of Earle, Roy, and Connie Mack. Connie Junior was out. Roy Mack assured everyone, "Dad will remain manager as long as he wants."[38]

Connie Jr., tall and reed-thin like his father, took his windfall and moved to Florida, forming a land-development company and operating a fleet of shrimp trawlers out of Fort Myers. Connie Sr. visited each winter and delighted in taking a ride on his son's shrimp boats, one of which was named for him.[39]

Three days later, Mickey Cochrane resigned as general manager and hopped on a plane to his home near Detroit. The team insisted that Cochrane was not forced out, but he had already prepared a letter of resignation in anticipation of the new ownership structure. Only the timing of Cochrane's departure had been a surprise—it was thought he would finish out the season.[40]

While on the surface it seemed a new beginning, the reorganization merely delayed the inevitable. It actually represented the beginning of the end of both the A's in the east and of Connie Mack's involvement in baseball. Meanwhile, the Phillies clearly had the undivided attention of Philadelphia baseball fans.

THE PHILLIES BEGAN August with four wins in five games, and they streaked to sixteen wins in their first twenty-two games that month. Every one of those victories was to prove vitally important.

A highlight was Ken Johnson's first career shutout on August 7—the same day his wife gave birth to their daughter—against the team that had traded him away, the St. Louis Cardinals. A surprise choice making his first start in more than a month, Johnson allowed only 2 hits, although control remained a challenge—he issued 6 walks and threw 128 pitches. But 4 of those walks came in the first two innings, and he was in total command over the final seven frames, retiring the last eleven Cardinals in order. Such was Johnson's confidence that he did not even flinch when Enos Slaughter's bat flew toward the mound after a swing and miss and glanced off his shoulder.[41]

Curt Simmons returned safe and sound from his two-week National Guard stint, although potential assignment to active duty remained all too possible, despite front office assurances that the team was active behind the scenes attempting to avert that scenario. With Miller's balky back and resulting decline in reliability, Eddie Sawyer winced at the potential loss of Simmons.

On August 11, Simmons was beaten by New York's Sal Maglie in a pitcher's duel, 3–1.[42] Beyond the result, the game was notable for an incident that lit a fuse, leading to an explosion twenty-four hours later. As always, there was bad blood between the teams, with Eddie Sawyer charging that the Giants threw at Phillies hitters and New York manager Leo Durocher countering that the way Andy Seminick blocked home plate put his players in danger of suffering broken legs.[43]

The eventual explosion had its origins with Giants second baseman Eddie Stanky, who began gesturing from his defensive position, trying to distract Seminick at the plate. Stanky had originally come up with the stunt two days earlier against Boston, after Bob Elliott asked an umpire to move out of his line of sight. Stanky promptly slid into the same spot. Elliott promptly struck out.[44]

Seminick complained about Stanky waving his arms during each pitch, but the umpire indicated there was no rule against what the Giants second baseman was doing. Then Seminick was hit on the elbow by Sal Maglie.[45]

The next day was Kids Day, and the hot-tempered catcher, his throbbing elbow having turned black and blue, was in no great mood, even after Giants manager Leo Durocher agreed to have Stanky cease his arm-waving until a ruling could be made by league president Ford Frick.[46] It was not long before fans at Shibe Park had to be thinking about the riot a year earlier—also against the Giants—that resulted in a Phillies forfeit.

Trailing 1–0, with two out in the bottom of the second, Granny Hamner doubled and Seminick walked. The next batter, Mike Goliat, narrowly ducked a beanball thrown by Sheldon Jones. Starting toward the mound, Goliat thought better of it and instead let his bat do the talking, smacking a single that scored Hamner. At the crack of the bat Seminick rocketed from first base with an agenda, rounding second without hesitation. He approached third, intent on arriving safely by any means possible, and plowed into Henry Thompson, knocking the Giants infielder unconscious. As Thompson lay motionless, Seminick jumped to his feet and crossed the plate to give Philadelphia a 2–1 lead.[47]

When Seminick came to bat the next time, Stanky repeated his behavior from the day before, "stretching" his arms to distract the Phillies catcher. This resulted in Stanky's ejection, and the Giants immediately lodged a protest. Seminick swung and missed at the next pitch, allowing the bat to slip from his hands and sail in the direction of Giants pitcher Jack Kramer. After slowly walking toward the mound to retrieve his message, Seminick resumed his at bat and was safe on an error.[48]

The next hitter, Mike Goliat, slapped a grounder into a force play. Seminick ignored the fact that he was already out and slid hard into Giants second baseman Bill Rigney, who had moved over from third to replace the ejected Stanky after previously replacing Henry Thompson. All hell broke loose. Rigney began swinging his fists, and Seminick responded by pinning Rigney to the ground and pummeling him.

Players and coaches from both benches streamed onto the field. Bubba Church and Monte Irvin traded blows. Jimmy Bloodworth was throwing punches at anyone who moved. Stan Baumgartner claimed a Phillies player—whom he did not identify—took an unsuccessful swing at an umpire. Leo Durocher was in the middle of it all, mouthing off as usual. Police arrived in force and threatened to arrest Giants first baseman Tookie Gilbert, until one of the umpires talked them out of it.[49] Seminick was done for the day, but with Rigney's ejection he had taken three-fourths of the Giants infield with him.

As always, there was no love lost between the Phillies and Giants. "We didn't like Durocher," explained Del Ennis.[50]

Ford Frick fined Seminick and Rigney twenty-five dollars each, disallowed the Giants protest—the Phillies won the game, 5–4, in eleven innings—and declared that the arm-waving stunts that Stanky had employed were henceforth illegal.[51] That night, Andy Seminick kept his promise to attend the birthday party of the Zeisers' baby sister.[52]

ON AUGUST 16, after defeating the Boston Braves, 5–1, behind Robin Roberts, who pitched a complete game while throwing only seventy-nine pitches, fifty-four of them for strikes, the Phillies had their largest lead of the season—seven games.[53] Boston was in second, with Brooklyn a half game behind the Braves.

The team embarked on a two-and-a-half-week road trip on August 18 that began with a loss to the Giants and some rain, followed by a five-game winning streak, the last of which was a dramatic fifteen-inning victory against Pittsburgh. Jim Konstanty took over in the seventh inning of that game and pitched the final nine frames, while Cliff Chambers took the mound for the final eight and one-third innings for the Pirates. Dick Sisler made a leaping catch of a line drive in the bottom of the inning to close out the win. Konstanty allowed only 5 hits and 1 run, and also singled in a run in the fifteenth, to earn his eleventh victory of the year.[54]

Konstanty closed out the month with his third win in five days, a wild 9–8 win over St. Louis. The Phillies showed their fight, battling back from a 4–0 deficit to tie the game at 6–6 in the seventh. After Konstanty surren-dered a pair of runs in the eighth, Sawyer had Dick Whitman pinch-hit for him, and Whitman slammed a two-run double to once again knot the score, this time at 8–8. Jimmy Bloodworth followed with a sacrifice fly to put Phil-adelphia a run ahead.

Milo Candini walked the St. Louis lead-off hitter in the bottom of the ninth, so Sawyer summoned Curt Simmons from the bullpen to face Marty Marion, Stan Musial, and Enos Slaughter, and the lefty retired all three to clinch the win. It was Simmons's first save of the year, to go with 16 victories.[55]

It had been, as they say, a "phabulous" month for the Phillies—and sea-son. They had only been shut out four times in 128 games. Four pitchers, Roberts, Simmons, Miller, and Konstanty, had reached double figures in wins, and every member of the starting lineup—save for Mike Goliat—was hitting .279 or better. The Phillies were the youngest team in the league but boasted the senior circuit's lowest earned run average and its brightest young stars.

Philadelphia closed out the month with 9 wins and a tie in twelve games, and attendance already topped 900,000 for the year. With a month remain-ing, Phillies fans dared to dream about their team finally making it into the World Series after thirty-five years. But these are the Phillies after all, and they would not make it easy for their long-suffering fans.

9

The Fightin' Phils Fight Themselves in September

THERE ARE ALWAYS ebbs and flows during a long baseball season. As quickly as losing streaks start, they can end, and vice versa. After the Phillies went on a tear beginning in late July, winning thirty-five of their first forty-nine games after Sawyer's batting-order change, they had appeared to gain an insurmountable lead. Appearances can be deceiving, of course. There are always ebbs and flows during a long baseball season.

Perhaps an early omen that September would not prove easy for the Phillies was their plane trip from St. Louis to Boston on the last day of August. The same day the Braves were drubbed, 19–3, by the Dodgers as Gil Hodges hit 4 home runs—yet another omen—the team arrived on a four-hour flight that was initially delayed by mechanical problems and then banged around in a thunderstorm that had Frank Wiechec breaking out air-sickness pills. When the plane finally landed, everyone aboard gave the pilot a standing ovation.[1] The flight home was better, with thirty thousand fans waiting up to six hours to greet the team at the airport in Philadelphia. Eddie Sawyer addressed the crowd, reminding them, "We haven't won the pennant yet."[2]

Sawyer was not resting easy—he knew the Achilles' heel of the team was its depth and that the Phillies had been extremely fortunate regarding injuries. Despite their well-publicized aches and pains, Granny Hamner and Willie Jones ultimately played all 157 games of the 1950 season (including three ties). Hamner missed only two innings all season. Eddie Waitkus had exceeded everyone's expectations, playing in 154 games, while Del Ennis and Richie Ashburn also played in more than 150 contests.

Only two reserves, back-up catcher Stan Lopata and outfielder Dick Whitman, had more than 100 official at bats—and both barely, at that. Jimmy

Bloodworth had ninety-six. Outfielder Bill Nicholson, heavily counted on at the beginning of the season, was sidelined off and on, making only six appearances in the outfield after the All-Star break before his hospitalization for diabetes in early September, ending his season. Putsy Caballero appeared in forty-six games, all but ten of them as a pinch hitter or pinch runner. Outfielder Stan Hollmig, the player who angered Bob Carpenter in the spring by ignoring a workout, almost never got off the bench—he was with the team all season but played in only eleven games.

Ed Sanicki got off to a poor start in Toronto and then, when he was about to be recalled by the Phillies, tore a ligament in his knee—the first injury of his pro career.[3] So when the rosters expanded in September, another outfielder, Jackie Mayo, was recalled from Toronto. Mrs. Carpenter's favorite uniform model had hit .128 in 1949 in limited action for the Phillies before a broken ankle ended his season. A year later, he was now replacing Bill Nicholson to provide insurance behind Dick Sisler, who was hampered by a sprained wrist that limited his availability during the first half of September.[4]

Then the pitching staff began losing personnel—Curt Simmons became active military. On September 9, shortly after picking up a no-decision against Boston, leaving him with 17 wins on the season, Simmons shook hands with his teammates and left the clubhouse, bound for Camp Atterbury, Indiana, to train with the army's Twenty-Eighth Division. With Richie Ashburn having married and his parents no longer providing a rooming house for his teammates, Simmons was renting space at the Germantown Cricket Club with Bob Miller and Bubba Church, who drove the pitcher to meet his National Guard unit.[5]

All the players were sad, but Eddie Sawyer, who thought Simmons would have won at least 20 games to that point if not for his military commitments, was almost certainly saddest of all. "It's a shame about that kid," was Sawyer's reaction to the news, recognizing there were no guarantees that the left-hander, who had blossomed into a star, would return from his military duties as the same athlete.[6] While there was speculation about Simmons being allowed to pitch in the World Series should his team make it, which seemed a certainty at that point, he was definitely unavailable for the remainder of the regular season. Despite the loss of the talented left-hander, and being shut out three straight games, there was no alarm on the part of the Phillies. Russ Meyer had just defeated the Dodgers, 4–3, and it seemed, at least to him, that his luck had finally changed for the better.

Meyer's temper-plagued career had been cursed by injuries and misfortune, some admittedly of his own doing. But many episodes were just plain bad luck. While in military service in 1943 he suffered a ruptured appendix pitching for Ft. Leonard Wood and spent four months in the hospital.[7] His rookie season, with the Chicago Cubs, was cut short due to a broken ankle suffered in a collision while covering first base.[8] The next year it happened again on a slide into third base, ending his season a month early.[9] He had been hampered in 1949 by his kicking a chair in frustration and thinking he had broken his foot, and the 1950 season had begun with elbow problems and a six-game losing streak.

In part, Meyer credited his recent change in fortune to a good luck charm, a worn-out copper penny given to him by a Shibe Park security guard. "I guess it did some good at that," grinned Meyer, who had carried the penny to the mound in his back pocket, touching it when he felt the need.[10] The win over Brooklyn gave Philadelphia a five-and-a-half-game lead.

But there were signs in September that others would be less lucky. Reports surfaced that *Philadelphia Tribune* photographer Malcolm Poindexter had revived his $20,000 lawsuit against Granny Hamner, accusing him of assault during the incident at Shibe Park on the next to last day of the 1949 season, when Hamner allegedly shoved Poindexter to the ground for taking offense at slurs directed toward umpires regarding their allegedly preferential treatment of Jackie Robinson.[11] Hamner denied Poindexter's allegation and requested a jury trial.[12] The lawsuit was eventually settled out of court, but for a decade or more the incident colored the perception of Philadelphia's Black press when it came to racial attitudes of the Phillies organization.[13] And it was unwelcome news during a pennant race involving Jackie Robinson's Dodgers, adding fuel to the fire, no doubt.

On September 10, Eddie Sawyer's fortieth birthday, the Phillies for the second time were impacted by unfortunately timed rainfall. Philadelphia trailed Boston that day, 3–1, in part due to fielding lapses that led to a pair of Braves runs. In the sixth inning Jackie Mayo hit a home run, making the score 3–2. Granny Hamner followed with a single as it began to rain. A two-hour delay ensued before the game was called and the Braves given the win based on the score of the last previously completed inning.[14] The storm not only erased Mayo's first Major League home run, he did not hit another—his only official big league home run—until the 1952 season.[15] More than fourteen thousand fans had been on hand, pushing the Phillies to a new franchise attendance record, breaking the mark set in 1946. And they had nine home dates remaining.

Around this time, the sports editor of the *Brooklyn Daily Eagle* took note of the standings in the National and American leagues and observed, "The fateful 'final 20 days' began today in those pressure-cooker pennant races and if you think things are steaming now—stick around and see what happens as the leading Yankees and Phillies try to keep from getting par-boiled in the next three weeks."[16] Rarely had a truer sports prophecy been uttered.

PHILADELPHIA KEPT ROLLING, sweeping the Cincinnati Reds during a Friday-night doubleheader on September 15. But the victories proved costly, with major implications for the final weeks of the season. After losing Curt Simmons to military duty, the team lost another pitcher.

Bubba Church, who entered the opener with a record of 8-4, started for the Phillies and was leading, 1-0, in the top of the third when Ted Kluszewski smashed a fastball back through the box. Church had two strikes on Kluszewski, a power hitter known for cutting the sleeves off his jersey to expose his biceps, and tried to pitch him close in on his hands but got too much of the plate. "All I know is I saw the ball . . . it hit my glove and I didn't get it clean. I didn't know what happened."[17] The line shot caught the right-hander just below the bottom of his left eye, spinning him 360 degrees and knocking him to his knees, while his glove landed between the mound and second base. The ball continued on into right field, where it was retrieved by Del Ennis.[18] Because of the location of the injury and the amount of blood, several teammates thought they saw Church's eye hanging out of its socket. For a moment—before gathering his senses—Church was worried they were right.[19]

Still conscious, the pitcher was removed to the clubhouse, where he asked teammate Jimmy Bloodworth if they had retired Kluszewski on the play. Bloodworth said they had. Church responded, "You're lyin' to me, Bloodworth, I know we didn't."[20] Ken Heintzelman relieved Church and finished the game, a 2-1 win completed in an hour and forty-six minutes, including the delay caused by Church's injury.

The wound stitched, Church was transported to the hospital. It was announced that he would need plastic surgery and miss two weeks of action.[21] Ultimately the pitcher would miss only nine days, but he was understandably less effective in his last two pitching assignments of the season, allowing 12 runs, 10 earned, in fewer than six innings.

The nightcap of the doubleheader was a thriller, lasting nineteen innings. The Reds took a 5–0 lead against Robin Roberts, but the Phillies rallied to tie the game. Jim Konstanty pitched ten stellar innings of relief, shutting out Cincinnati for nine frames before tiring, allowing 2 runs in the top of the eighteenth by walking the bases loaded and then surrendering a single to Ted Kluszewski. The Phillies matched Cincinnati with a pair of runs in the bottom of the inning, thanks to a Granny Hamner sacrifice fly and a Stan Lopata triple. The Phillies won in the bottom of the nineteenth on Del Ennis's bases-loaded single just as the 1:00 a.m. curfew approached.[22] Meanwhile, Brooklyn lost, stretching the Phillies' lead to seven-and-a-half games, with Boston a half game behind the Dodgers.

The next day, another pitcher was injured. Bob Miller, who had continued to take the mound despite his back problems, was forced to leave the game against the Reds on September 16 while trailing, 2–0, after six innings. He had felt a twinge in his shoulder in the fourth inning, but pushed through. The pain escalated in the sixth, and Miller let Andy Seminick know. By the seventh he could not throw at all. Miller summoned Eddie Sawyer, who immediately took him out of the game.[23] A dejected Miller sighed, "I had more stuff than I'd had in a long time, and then—just like that—I couldn't throw anymore!"[24] He later recalled, "I think I may have tried to come back too soon [from the back injury]."[25] The Phillies went on to lose, shut out for the fourth time that month and held to 2 runs or less for the tenth time in the past fourteen games. On top of that, Bob Miller would miss ten days and, like Bubba Church, was not the same after his injury, making only two appearances and allowing 8 runs in eleven innings.

The Phillies were now without Bubba Church and Bob Miller, in addition to Curt Simmons, who had parlayed hitherto unknown musical talent into becoming the company bugler at Camp Atterbury.[26] And Eddie Sawyer seemed to have lost confidence in Ken Johnson, who was rarely called upon. He tried out Steve Ridzik in September, the right-hander having spent the season in the Minors after recovering from his broken kneecap. Ridzik made his big league debut against New York, surrendering 2 runs in three innings, and was not used again.[27]

Despite these setbacks, after defeating Pittsburgh behind Russ Meyer, who won for the fifth time in six decisions, the Phillies lead remained at seven-and-a-half games. It had been Gran Hamner Day, and during pre-game festivities, the Phillies shortstop was presented a refrigerator, golf clubs, a television set, a rifle, a set of tires, luggage, and a sterling silver set. Fans also gave his five-year-old daughter Patty a cocker spaniel puppy. Hamner hit a three-run homer, capping a satisfying day for both the short-stop and his admirers.

Stan Hollmig was satisfied as well, at least for one afternoon, making his first and only start of the season and singling in Philadelphia's second run before scoring on Hamner's home run. It was the twenty-four-year-old Hollmig's last appearance in a game that season, and he would have the opportunity to swing a bat in the Major Leagues only twice more in his career.

Jim Konstanty earned a save, after Russ Meyer surrendered a two-run home run to Wally Westlake with no one out in the ninth. Konstanty's performance was all the more impressive in light of his having pitched ten innings in relief only two days earlier.[28]

The first Phillies pennant in thirty-five years was within reach. Even with the loss of key pitchers, Philadelphia still had Roberts and Konstanty, with Russ Meyer taking the hill and pitching decently when his achy elbow was adequately rested.

THE PHILLIES BEGAN planning for a World Series appearance, with Bob Carpenter opting for single-game admissions rather than selling tickets for the full series in a package, as was customary. Box seats were to cost $8.75, reserved seats $6.50. Because of Shibe Park's limited seating capacity, Carpenter reasoned his plan would allow more people the opportunity to attend, which he thought important because of the multitude of long-suffering fans who had waited for a pennant. Anticipating extraordinary demand, Carpenter announced that applications would be accepted from within the city of Philadelphia and the surrounding area. If, as expected, demand exceeded supply after set-asides for season-ticket holders, players, and VIPs, remaining seats would be assigned through a drawing from those sending requests. "There should be 23,000 seats available for each game," explained Carpenter. "If it should be a seven-game Series, with four games in Philadelphia, we could thus give 92,000 persons the chance to see the Series—instead of merely 23,000. Fans who have supported us during the season are entitled to Series tickets. It isn't possible, of course, to take care of them all, but we're going to do the best we can."[29] More than one hundred thousand applications were received in the first few hours, with hundreds of people lining up at post offices by midnight in order to be among the first to enter the lottery.[30]

After the Phillies lost Bubba Church and Bob Miller, they were again shut out, by Frank Hiller, who pitched a two-hitter for the Chicago Cubs, a 1–0 win that denied Robin Roberts's second attempt to become the first Phillies 20-game winner since the Great Alexander. The only mistake made by Roberts was a pitch that Hank Sauer lofted into the seats, the right-hander losing despite allowing only 4 hits. Jackie Mayo and Granny Hamner collected the only safeties for the Phillies, and both were erased on the base paths, Mayo on a double play and Hamner on an attempted steal.[31]

The Phillies rebounded the next day, Mike Goliat slamming a pair of home runs to key a win over Chicago.[32] Philadelphia maintained its seven-and-a-half-game lead, with only eleven games to play. And, after his second time missing a week because of his injured wrist, Dick Sisler was ready to make his return to the lineup as the Phillies prepared to take on the Dodgers at Shibe Park for a short two-game weekend series. It was a golden opportunity for the Phillies to essentially end the pennant race.

ON SATURDAY, SEPTEMBER 23, Gil Hodges and Andy Seminick accounted for all the scoring by their teams with home runs, but Hodges's blast came with two on in the second off Robin Roberts, while only one runner was aboard when Seminick hit his in the seventh off Don Newcombe. The Dodgers cut Philadelphia's lead to a still healthy six games as Newcombe, whose uniform No. 36 matched Roberts, now also matched him with his 19 wins.[33]

Sunday was an 11–0 slaughter. Erv Palica shut out the Phillies on 2 hits and drove in 4 runs himself, on a grand slam during a six-run fifth inning that put the game away. Palica carried a no-hitter into the eighth; only Del Ennis, on a ninth inning double, reached as far as second base against him. Bubba Church, who had asked coach Maje McDonnell to hit balls at him to make sure he would not flinch, bravely made his first appearance the day after his release from an eight-day hospital stay. Unfortunately, he was the victim of the Brooklyn offensive onslaught—and 5 Phillies errors. Sawyer waved the white flag, using Paul Stuffel, Jack Brittin, and finally Ken

Johnson to close out the loss.[34] Nearly fifty-five thousand fans had passed through the Shibe Park turnstiles that weekend, the final home games of the regular season, hoping to see their team virtually clinch the pennant. But the Phillies had failed to shut the door on their closest pursuers.

The lead was down to five games.

The Dodgers had won six straight and had eleven games remaining, all at home. The Phillies had nine games left, all on the road. A few days earlier, Brooklyn had been nine games behind Philadelphia, in third place. Brooklyn manager Burt Shotton recognized that the Phillies had given his players a glimmer of hope and decided to take it a step further, declaring, "We're not worrying about the Phillies anymore. They'll come back to us."[35]

Following the losses to Brooklyn, Eddie Sawyer held a team meeting prior to the opening game of the series against Boston and gave his players a stern talk, pulling no punches about the way they had played against the Dodgers. The atmosphere was more frustration than panic. Dick Sisler came away declaring, "We'll get going—but fast. Sure, we missed Curt Simmons and Bubba Church and Bob Miller. But they've all got to catch us—and they won't."[36]

After splitting a doubleheader against the Braves, including a 12–4 win behind Ken Heintzelman, during which the Phillies pounded out 18 hits, Bob Miller made his return to the mound after being sidelined for ten days and gamely lasted into the seventh inning against Boston, allowing only 3 hits. But Jim Konstanty was unable to hold on to a 5–2 lead, and the Braves surged ahead, 7–5. The Phillies then rallied for 3 runs in the eighth, thanks in large part to shoddy Braves defense, as Del Ennis, who slammed 4 hits and drove in 4 runs, scored the game-winner on Hamner's single.[37]

The Phillies controlled their own destiny, the win over the Braves reducing their magic number to two. On September 27 they met the Giants for the first of back-to-back doubleheaders at the Polo Grounds, made necessary by rainouts during August. The schedule was not working to Philadelphia's advantage, the third doubleheader in four days taxing an exhausted pitching staff growing thinner by the day. The first game seemed to have gotten quickly out of hand, the Giants scoring twice in the second and thrice in the third to send Robin Roberts to the showers. The Phillies continued to trail going to the eighth inning, 7–2.

Then Del Ennis led off with an infield hit, followed by Dick Sisler and Granny Hamner singles, the latter making the score 7–3 and causing Leo

Durocher's summoning of Sal Maglie to rescue Monty Kennedy. Maglie promptly hit Andy Seminick in the ribs, loading the bases. Mike Goliat singled to make the score 7–4. Dick Whitman, pinch-hitting for reliever Milo Candini, followed by grounding a two-run single to right field.

Dave Koslo replaced Maglie. Eddie Waitkus hit a line drive sacrifice fly to tie the game, 7–7, but Koslo escaped further damage when Bobby Thomson made a shoestring catch of Richie Ashburn's soft line drive and turned it into a double play, taking advantage of Dick Whitman's aggressive base running.

Despite the desperate Phillies rally, the Giants won the game in the bottom of the tenth. Jim Konstanty walked Monte Irvin to lead off. Irvin took second on a sacrifice and raced past third on Alvin Dark's single to right, intent on scoring as Del Ennis fielded the ball and fired it to the plate. The play was close but Irvin came in hard, upending Andy Seminick, knocking him to the ground, face-down. Irvin was safe and the Giants had won.[38] Seminick was still holding the ball even as he suffered was what later diagnosed as a fractured bone in his ankle on the play.[39]

"The game is over," recalled Seminick. "And I'm laying there. My leg is killing me. I'm in agony. I thought, 'Oh my gosh, I really did it this time.'"[40]

Stan Lopata took Seminick's place in the nightcap. Bubba Church, struggling to regain the effectiveness he had displayed before taking a line drive to his face, surrendered 4 runs in the first, effectively handing the Giants a sweep.

The Phillies lead was four games.

Despite the undiagnosed ankle fracture, Seminick started the next day, catching both ends of the doubleheader, thanks to eight shots of Novocain and a special boot devised by Frank Wiechec to allow the catcher to function.[41] Maje McDonnell was amazed Seminick could play at all. "He could hardly walk," he remembered.[42] Seminick threw out two runners and made a great barehanded catch of a foul pop-up. But the Phillies again suffered double losses, both by a 3–1 score.

Sal Maglie defeated Ken Heintzelman in the first game, retiring the final fourteen Phillies in order. It was a game of missed opportunities for Philadelphia, loading the bases in the first inning with one out and failing to score, and having Richie Ashburn—who collected 3 of the team's 5 hits—on third with one out in the fifth and also failing to get him home. Bobby Thomson's pair of solo home runs was enough offense for the Giants.[43]

Recognizing the effort it took for Andy Seminick simply to be on the field, Leo Durocher visited the Phillies clubhouse between games of the doubleheader and saw the catcher being treated by Frank Wiechec. Pointing to Seminick, Durocher lauded his bitter opponent, announcing, "There's the greatest man in baseball. He gets hurt, but that doesn't stop him. He fights you all the time, doesn't give any quarter, or ask it, either. He's a great catcher and a fine asset to any ball club. He's my kind of player."[44] Seminick required more Novocain and did not emerge from the clubhouse until after the top of the first was already underway.

Robin Roberts started the nightcap and went the distance, after having pitched four innings only twenty-four hours earlier. Eddie Waitkus provided a great start for the Phillies, leading off the game with his second home run of the year. But that was the extent of Philadelphia's scoring. Eddie Stanky hit a home run in the sixth to tie the game, and Whitey Lockman's two-run single in the seventh gave New York a 3–1 lead.

The Phillies almost pulled the game out in the ninth. Del Ennis and Willie Jones, the latter suffering stomach pains that had initially been diagnosed as appendicitis, singled, giving Philadelphia runners at first and second with nobody out. Eddie Sawyer called for Granny Hamner to bunt, but he missed. He missed the ball again on his second attempt, but so did Giants catcher Wes Westrum. Del Ennis took third on the passed ball, while Jones held at first. Sawyer had Hamner swing away at the next pitch, and he hit a rocket headed down the right-field line. But Monte Irvin was playing near the first base bag to prevent Willie Jones from getting a good jump on a batted ball. Irvin made a spectacular leaping stab, stomping on the bag to double off Jones, while Ennis was forced to hold at third. The potential rally ended with Andy Seminick flying out to center, and the Phillies had lost— again.[45] Afterward, Seminick visited the Giants clubhouse and buried the hatchet with Eddie Stanky.[46]

The lead was three games.

Despite a heroic effort, Robin Roberts trudged dejectedly to the clubhouse, having failed in his fifth attempt for that elusive twentieth win. But the good news was that the Dodgers had split their doubleheader with Boston, so the Phillies magic number was reduced to one. They had clinched a tie for the pennant. The National League announced plans for a potential best two-of-three playoff between the Phillies and Dodgers, something that a week earlier had seemed impossible. If needed, the playoff would begin on Monday, October 2, with a coin toss determining home-field advantage.[47]

The Phillies were idle the next day, while the Dodgers swept Boston in a doubleheader.[48] Afterward, Dodgers players celebrated, shouting, "We're in! We're in!"[49] Brooklyn now had a realistic shot, albeit with one eye focused skyward—under the rules of the time a rainout this late in the season would not be made up, a scenario that would eliminate the Dodgers. But outside of intervention by Mother Nature, they controlled their own fate. Keep winning, and as the players had shouted, they were in.

Conversely, Phillies nerves were frayed. The team was idle, and several players witnessed the Dodgers sweeping Boston in person. Russ Meyer took a swing at a photographer attempting to record his reaction to Brooklyn's success against the Braves. The photographer got his photo, and an apology from Meyer, averting yet another court date involving a Phillies player and a cameraman.[50] The incident was an unmistakable sign that the pressure was taking its toll.

The lead was two games.

THE PHILLIES HAD TO play a pair of contests at Ebbets Field against Brooklyn—and a third there if the Phillies lost both. It was agreed that should the coin toss come up tails, which it did, the last two games of a playoff would be held at Shibe Park, with the first game staged at Ebbets Field.[51] Eddie Sawyer outwardly projected confidence, insisting, "We've just been having bad breaks. I'm pretty sure we'll win though. We've come too far to lose."[52] Privately, he was unsure how his players would respond. "The club was tired," he said. "It had been a long year and we had a young team which had never played under that kind of pressure."[53] Neither had Sawyer. No one knew what to expect.

Once again it was Erv Palica on the mound for the Dodgers. With few options, Sawyer started Bob Miller, who held firm for four innings, keeping Brooklyn scoreless. Palica did the same for the Dodgers.

Andy Seminick made a key defensive play in the bottom of the first, picking Duke Snider off third as Jackie Robinson tried unsuccessfully to draw a throw while stealing second base. Snider was thrown out again in the fourth inning attempting to score on a groundout.

Miller weakened in the fifth. With two out, Cal Abrams smacked a run-scoring single to center, and Pee Wee Reese followed with a triple to give Brooklyn a 2–0 lead. Eddie Sawyer brought in Jim Konstanty, whose second pitch resulted in a Duke Snider two-run homer.

Trailing 4–0, the Phillies rallied in the sixth, scoring 3 runs on a wild play. With Waitkus and Ashburn on base via singles and no one out, Dick Sisler lined a ball to center that caromed off Duke Snider's glove. While Snider frantically chased the ball, Waitkus and Ashburn scored. Palica cut off the relay to the infield and attempted to retire Sisler at third. But the pitcher's throw was errant and rolled toward the stands. A female fan reached over the railing to retrieve the ball, earning her an escort from the ballpark. The resulting interference call allowed Sisler to score, bringing Philadelphia within a run at 4–3.

Snider, who outside of his home run was having an indisputably rough day, said of his muffed play, "I was sure I could catch it when I started, or if I didn't that I could block it, but the thing sank fast and I missed both ways."[54]

Palica settled down and held the Phillies scoreless the rest of the way, while Roy Campanella hit a three-run home run off Konstanty in the eighth, stretching Brooklyn's lead to 7–3.[55] Snider made a stellar catch in the ninth inning, robbing Willie Jones of extra bases with a one-handed catch near the fence. A young Dodgers fan jumped from the stands in excitement to congratulate Snider before being ushered away.[56]

The lead was one game.

Eddie Sawyer's men were running on fumes, the team's lack of depth making it vulnerable at the worst possible time. The Phillies had dropped five straight, when winning any one of those games would have clinched the pennant. The team was in a major hitting slump. After being shut out only four times through the end of August, the Whiz Kids were blanked seven times in September, including one streak of thirty-three consecutive scoreless innings. Of their twenty-eight games that month, they scored two runs or less sixteen times. The Fightin' Phillies were fightin' themselves.

Despite a significant loss of pitching personnel, the runs allowed by the Phillies were nearly the same in September as in August. But after scoring 5.4 runs per game in July, and averaging 4.7 runs in August, Philadelphia's offensive output plummeted in September to 3.2 runs per game, contributing to the team's first losing month all season. A seven-and-a-half-game lead had all but vanished in ten days. Only one game remained for the Phillies to right the ship. Otherwise, they faced the possibility of playing two—or three—more, a daunting task with a dwindling number of able bodies. A loss in the next game would not end Philadelphia's hopes, but to everyone involved it seemed nothing less than a must-win.

Harold Burr of the *Brooklyn Eagle* wrote, "It's becoming the most gruesome fairy story a bunch of kids ever listened to, and the Whiz Kids from Philadelphia didn't sleep to [*sic*] soundly last night, stuffing the corners of their hotel pillow into their mouth to keep from screaming."[57]

"The last week was a nightmare," remembered Bubba Church. "It seemed like everyone was hurt. We were really depleted."[58]

10

Sisler, Hemingway, and a Date with the Yankees

WHILE BROOKLYN WAS making its frantic run at the Phillies, the Dodgers were in the process of undergoing a reorganization, with Walter O'Malley ultimately taking control. Previously the Dodgers had been owned by four partners—O'Malley, Branch Rickey, Dearie Mulvey (who had inherited her share upon her father's death in 1938), and John L. Smith, a prominent pharmaceutical executive with Charles Pfizer and Company—each possessing a one-quarter ownership stake. Following Smith's death in July 1950, O'Malley accelerated his effort to marginalize Rickey, whose contract as general manager was to expire at the end of the year. O'Malley wanted to run the Dodgers.

In late September, Rickey consummated a deal brokered by Pittsburgh Pirates owner John Galbreath to sell his stake to an outsider. O'Malley had the right to match the offer and teamed with John L. Smith's widow to do so, both of them coming away from the deal owning a three-eighths share of the team.[1] Galbreath then hired Rickey to run the Pirates.[2] None of this palace intrigue was impacting Dodgers players, who were one game shy of completing a miraculous comeback and forcing a playoff.

Absent a rainout, which would have ended the season with the Phillies in first place, Robin Roberts was the last hope to stave off an embarrassing, nearly unprecedented collapse. If the Phillies won the regular-season finale in Brooklyn, they would earn a place in the World Series against the defending World Champion New York Yankees. If they lost, a best-of-three playoff between the Fightin' Phils and the Dodgers would begin at Ebbets Field the next day.[3] A year earlier, the Phillies had failed to defeat Brooklyn to force a playoff between the Dodgers and Cardinals for the National League pennant. Now, the Phillies and Dodgers were meeting again on the season's last day, only this time it was the *Phillies* trying to avoid a playoff.

Tickets for the playoff series were printed and ready for sale once the final out was recorded, provided the Dodgers won.[4]

Maje McDonnell took a cab to the ballpark that day along with a couple of players, including Dick Sisler. While stopped at a light, another car pulled up beside them, and the driver motioned for Sisler to roll down his window. The man, a Phillies fan, was on his way to the game with his three sons. He took a rose he had removed from the altar at church that morning and handed it to Sisler, telling him to place it atop his locker for good luck.[5]

Eddie Sawyer held a team meeting in the clubhouse before the game, telling the players, "You know how to play good ball, just play; don't fool around. Go get 'em."[6]

The season finale was a rematch of Opening Day, Roberts versus Newcombe. Unlike that first game, Newcombe and his teammates were home this time, with all the momentum on their side. Both starting pitchers entered the contest with 19 wins on the season—Roberts was making his fourth start in eight days and attempting, for the sixth time, to win his twentieth game. Success would also make him the first pitcher to catapult the Phillies into the World Series in thirty-five years.

Both men were weary. Roberts admitted to being nervous before the game, until he looked over at Newcombe warming up and realized the Brooklyn right hander was in no better shape.[7] The Phillies had defeated Newcombe four times in 1950, but he had turned the tables and defeated them twice in September, including once in a heroic doubleheader effort on September 6, when he started both games, throwing a shutout in the first contest and allowing 2 runs in seven innings for a no-decision in the nightcap. The Dodgers were at the doorstep, the closest they had been to first place since the end of June. Conversely, the Phillies were buffeted by injuries and military commitments and seemed out of gas.

Among those attending the big game was George Sisler, employed as a Brooklyn scout and watching his son Dick play outfield for Philadelphia.[8] The game started out as an intense pitcher's duel. Newcombe and Roberts matched scoreless baseball through five stanzas, each successive inning ratcheting up the intensity.

The Phillies broke through in the sixth. After a pair of spectacular plays by Gil Hodges resulted in outs, Dick Sisler singled and advanced to third on

Del Ennis's looping liner that landed in short center field. Willie Jones then singled Sisler home. With runners on first and second, Granny Hamner hit a deep fly ball to the scoreboard in left, causing the heart of every Dodgers fan to skip a beat. But Carl Furillo had a bead on it, and the ball fell harmlessly into his glove for the third out.

The Dodgers struck back in the bottom of the inning, on a two-out Pee Wee Reese fly ball. It appeared that Del Ennis would be able to corral it, but the ball kept carrying and landed on a six-inch-wide ledge in front of the right-field protective screen and—incredibly—stayed there. In play.

Reese raced around the bases while Ennis and the rest of his teammates looked on helplessly.[9] "It had backspin on it and balanced on the ledge," remembered Ennis. "I kept waiting for the ball to come down but it spun and spun until it came to a dead stop on the ledge." Reflecting on the ground rules, Ennis lamented, "I should have thrown my glove at it because it would then have been a triple instead of a home run."[10]

The game was delayed between innings when a fan wandered onto the ledge to collect Reese's miracle as a souvenir. Order restored, Andy Seminick led off the seventh with a walk. But after Mike Goliat and Robin Roberts each bunted, moving Seminick to third, Eddie Waitkus grounded out to end the inning. For the Dodgers, three batters and three ground ball outs advanced the game to the eighth, tied, 1–1; the highlight of the otherwise uneventful inning was Andy Seminick's dive into the stands, sending hot dogs and beer flying in all directions as a result of his unsuccessful effort to snag a foul pop-up.

With one out in the Phillies half of the eighth, Dick Sisler banged out his third consecutive single to right field. But Don Newcombe escaped the inning without further damage. Roy Campanella led off Brooklyn's bottom of the eighth with a single, but Billy Cox lined a pitch to Roberts, who quickly fired the ball to first, doubling off Campanella.

With one out in the top of the ninth, Andy Seminick, who had been asked by Eddie Sawyer and Bob Carpenter to grind it out as long as possible on his injured ankle, lined a single. Recognizing the importance of a run, any run, in this game, Sawyer replaced Seminick on the base paths with Putsy Caballero. With Goliat and Roberts due up, Caballero attempted a stolen base but was thrown out. After Goliat lined out to Duke Snider, the game moved to the bottom of the ninth.

The most intense baseball game of 1950 continued, with Robin Roberts facing Cal Abrams, a Philadelphia native in Brooklyn's starting lineup for only the sixth time all season. After Abrams drew a walk on a full-count pitch that Roberts felt should have been called a third strike, every Phillies fan could be excused for internally mumbling, *Here we go*. If the Dodgers scored, the Phillies would lose and be forced into a playoff with Brooklyn. Abrams was indeed about to become a part of baseball history, but not in the way he wanted—or that Phillies fans feared.

The drumming of heartbeats in Philadelphia grew stronger when Pee Wee Reese, after failing twice to sacrifice, followed with a single, his third hit of the game, advancing Abrams to second. With two on and nobody out, Roberts prepared to face Duke Snider. Sawyer visited the mound but had no intention of taking his ace out of the game, explaining afterward that he only wanted to talk strategy and remind Roberts to take his time between pitches.[11]

Snider swung at the first pitch, and Dodgers fans jumped to their feet with a roar, realizing this could be the ending they were looking for. The ball fell safely in center field, just in front of Richie Ashburn, whose All-Star resume did not include an intimidating throwing arm. From his vantage point in the third base coach's box, Milt Stock saw an opportunity for a Dodgers win—without hesitating, he waved Abrams around third. But Stock failed to recognize three things that were to Philadelphia's advantage. First, Ashburn was playing shallowly, and the ball took a favorable bounce, allowing the center fielder to charge the ball as he fielded it. Second, the Phillies had positioned their defense against an unlikely but possible bunt, with Granny Hamner stationed near the second base bag, preventing Abrams from getting a big lead. Third, Stan Lopata was catching, not Andy Seminick with his bad ankle.[12]

Ashburn was somewhat insulted that Abrams was sent in that situation, especially with no outs: "He smoked it; it was a perfect ball for an outfielder to handle, right at you, you could charge the ball, it was hit sharply."[13] With the game on the line, Ashburn made the throw of his life.

Stan Lopata, who had been signed to a $15,000 bonus by Eddie Krajnik in 1946 after earning a Bronze Star in Europe, was a rock when it came to blocking the plate. It would not be necessary for him to do so—Abrams did not even slide, instead going in standing up while making a halfhearted attempt to jar the ball loose. When Lopata caught the ball, he knew he had

Abrams dead to rights. "Abrams could run pretty good, but not that good," Lopata remarked years later. "I had made up my mind that I was going to block home . . . and I don't think Abrams ever touched the plate. We should have sent Milt Stock a World Series share."[14] Stock, who ironically had been a third baseman for the 1915 Phillies, had made a decision that played a role in his former team heading to the Fall Classic a second time.

After the game, Burt Shotton moaned, "How could Ashburn dare play so close? He never threw a guy out before."[15] That was of course an exaggeration. And of course, whether he had previously thrown anyone out was no longer relevant.

Despite Ashburn's clutch defensive play, the Phillies were far from out of the woods. Snider and Reese advanced to second and third on the play, and there was still only one out. After intentionally walking Jackie Robinson to load the bases, Roberts retired Carl Furillo on a foul pop up to Eddie Waitkus for out number two. That brought Gil Hodges to the plate.

With the count one ball and one strike, Hodges flied to Del Ennis in right. At first it appeared to be a routine out, but Ennis sent a thrill through the crowd when he struggled to catch it. He ultimately secured the ball after causing himself and nearly every Phillies fan a heart attack.

"I knew it was coming right at me," Ennis explained. "I lost it in the sun. The line drive hit me in the chest and dropped right into my glove."[16] If Ennis had missed the ball, Ashburn's heroics would have been for naught, and the game would have been over. Instead, the score remained tied, 1–1.

ROBIN ROBERTS WAS DUE to lead off the tenth inning for the Phillies. Eddie Sawyer had no thought of pinch-hitting for him. Concerned that Brooklyn had seen too much of Jim Konstanty, Sawyer felt Roberts the better bet, even if that meant going to an eleventh inning. The gamble paid off when Roberts opened the tenth with a bouncer up the middle and advanced to second on Eddie Waitkus's base hit. Richie Ashburn followed with a sacrifice attempt, but Don Newcombe pounced on the bunt and fired to third to retire Roberts on a force play. Dick Sisler stepped to the plate, 3 hits already to his credit, with Del Ennis on deck.

If Newcombe had not made the play on Roberts, there would have been runners on second and third, and Sisler likely would have been walked intentionally. Instead, Newcombe pitched to the Phillies left fielder and quickly got ahead in the count at 0-2. After taking a pitch outside and then fouling a ball straight back into the stands, Sisler anticipated the right hander's next pitch and responded with arguably the most impactful swing in Phillies history.

"He tried to pitch me inside but he got one out over the plate a little too far," remembered Sisler. "I hit the ball to left, the opposite field, but I didn't know it was a home run at first."[17] Just a few minutes earlier, Cal Abrams had nearly been the hero of the game. Now he could only helplessly watch Sisler's fly ball sail over his head and into the left-field stands. Up in the press box, Phillies announcer Gene Kelly shared the news to those outside the ballpark:

"A fly ball . . . Very, very deep to left field . . . Moving back, Abrams . . . Way, way back . . . He can't get it . . . It—it's a home run . . . Wow! . . . A home run for Dick Sisler . . . The Phillies lead, 4-1."[18]

As the ball landed in the left-field stands at Ebbets Field, essentially knocking Brooklyn out of the pennant race, Dick Sisler's father felt a sense of pride even as his employer had been dealt a fatal blow. After the game George Sisler told reporters, "I felt awful and terrific at the same time. . . . You know, I have three sons. When each was 10, Dick looked like the worst ball player of the lot. I hoped one of my sons would follow my footsteps, but I never thought Dick would be the one."[19]

Newcombe retired Del Ennis and Willie Jones to close out the top of the tenth, but the Phillies had a three-run lead.

A half inning remained to be played. Jackie Mayo took over in left field for Sisler and caught a Roy Campanella line drive for the first out. A reinvigorated Roberts then struck out Jim Russell, a switch hitter batting for Billy Cox. Burt Shotton chose Tommy Brown, who had slugged 8 home runs in only 86 at bats on the year, to pinch-hit for Don Newcombe.

At 4:39 p.m. Eddie Waitkus caught Tommy Brown's foul pop-up to end the game.[20] The Phillies streamed out of the dugout and leapt on Robin Roberts, celebrating their triumph. Curt Simmons was at Camp Atterbury, spending Sunday afternoon playing touch football, unwilling to listen to what could have been the conclusion to an epic collapse. Simmons recalled years later, "Finally a guy hollers out, 'Hey, Sisler hit a home run! The Phillies won!' What a relief it was to hear that."[21]

Looking down on the scene from the press box, Harold Burr began typing his game account for the *Brooklyn Daily Eagle*, starting it with an Ernest

Hemingway reference. He wrote the opening sentence: "Death came in the afternoon for the Dodgers at Ebbets Field yesterday."[22] As some thirty-five thousand people filed out of the ballpark, the vast majority stunned by the turn of events, stadium organist Gladys Gooding mournfully played "Deep Purple." Here and there, dots of Phillies red were scattered among the crowd, emitting solitary shrieks of delight that echoed throughout the otherwise solemn Dodgers home. Brooklyn fans were stumbling about as if awakened from a nightmare only to realize it had not been a dream. Silence turned to anger as they blamed Burt Shotton, Milt Stock, Cal Abrams, or the baseball gods for their disappointment. At the clubhouse gate, knots of bobby-soxers sobbed to each other, inconsolable.[23] There was no mention of any passing ballplayers, just the familiar Brooklyn refrain "Wait Till Next Year"—not that next year would prove any less painful for Brooklyn baseball fans.

Milt Stock was adamant, saying he would send Abrams again, given the same situation, and Burt Shotton came to the defense of his coach, declaring, "Stock played it right. That's the sort of setup when you send in the big run. Even though they got Abrams we still had runners on second and third with one out and your big hitter coming up."[24]

Shotton insisted, "We have no regrets. We didn't cry all season and we won't cry now. It took a great team to beat us."[25]

Over in the Phillies clubhouse, a jubilant Eddie Sawyer told reporters, "This is the way the boys wanted to win it," before adding, "I would have been glad to win it any way."[26] The players tackled *Philadelphia Bulletin* sportswriter Frank Yuetter and held him to his promise to allow the shearing of his mustache if they won. During the chaos, Maje McDonnell glanced at the good-luck rose Sisler had placed above his locker, while beer and champagne flowed in celebration.[27] Bob Miller exclaimed, "Holy gee, what a day!"[28]

Despite his bitter history with the team, Jackie Robinson walked into the visitor's clubhouse and congratulated every Phillies player for winning the pennant. Robin Roberts was impressed, calling it, "a remarkable display of sportsmanship from a fierce competitor."[29]

In stark contrast to Brooklyn, the atmosphere in Philadelphia was of pure joy. It was an unseasonably warm Sunday, temperature in the eighties, and people were out and about. Factory whistles blasted shrill congratulations, greeted by replies from ship's foghorns on the Delaware River. Both battled for attention with car horns, blasting citywide in celebration. An impromptu confetti blizzard, the product of hastily shredded phone books, drifted out of downtown office windows, showering everyone celebrating below. *The Fightin' Phils* anthem was everywhere, blaring from radios and sound trucks all over the city. Scattered instances of joyful insanity were observed—men impulsively picking up checks for their dining companions, fans rushing outside to hang makeshift banners outside their homes, others setting off illegal fireworks. It was claimed that one automobile dealer, showing a used car to a woman on his lot when Sisler hit his home run, simply gave her the car.[30]

A few hours later, upward of thirty thousand fans were on hand to mob their heroes arriving at 30th Street Station on a fourteen-car train—the first such celebration for Philadelphia baseball fans of any stripe in nearly two decades, and a harkening to the American Association Athletics hoopla some sixty-seven years before, when ten thousand fans marched through the streets. An unfortunate bridal party arrived in the midst of the bedlam, the newly minted husband and wife attempting to depart for their honeymoon. They were quickly absorbed by the crowd.[31]

Another three thousand celebrating souls gathered at the Warwick, cheering the players arriving by bus for the team's official victory party. One of the heroes of the hour, an obviously drained Robin Roberts, was photographed on the bus beside his beaming wife, who was nine months pregnant.[32] At the party, the players presented a diamond ring to Eddie Sawyer. A phone call was placed to Curt Simmons at Camp Atterbury. First on the line was Bob Carpenter, who congratulated the left-hander and thanked him for his role in winning the pennant. Then every teammate took a turn congratulating Simmons.[33]

BURT SHOTTON, WHO had managed the Phillies during the last days of the Baker regime, was replaced in the off-season by Charlie Dressen.[34] Milt Stock did not survive the loss either. Three months after making the fateful decision to send Cal Abrams around third, Stock followed Branch Rickey to Pittsburgh, hired by manager Billy Meyer as third base coach for the Pirates.[35]

Meanwhile, inspired by Dick Sisler's home run, Ernest Hemingway pulled out one of his unfinished projects and completed it. *The Old Man and the Sea* became one of Hemingway's most famous works, capturing both the

Pulitzer and Nobel prizes. Set in September 1950, a Cuban fisherman and a boy talk about the pennant race between the Dodgers and Phillies, while also recalling Sisler's exploits in the country during the winter of 1945–46, when he came to the island to train for his return to the big leagues following the war and dominated the competition, slamming the longest home run ever hit at the ballpark in Havana and blasting 3 home runs in one game off Sal Maglie.[36]

After talking about the Yankees and his hero, the great Joe DiMaggio, the fisherman tells the boy,

> "In the other league between Brooklyn and Philadelphia, I must take Brooklyn. But then I think of Dick Sisler and those great drives in the old park. There was nothing ever like them. He hits the longest ball I have ever seen.
>
> "Do you remember he used to come to the Terrace? I wanted to take him fishing, but I was too timid to ask him. Then I asked you to ask him but you were too timid."
>
> "I know. He might have gone with us. Then we would have that for all our lives."[37]

The new National League champions had only two days to prepare for the New York Yankees and the 1950 World Series. They would be taking on the Yankees minus three starting pitchers and with a catcher playing on a fractured ankle. The city was also under pressure, thanks to a National Brewers Association convention coinciding with the event and a threatened strike of more than five thousand hotel workers. But these were minor problems when set against the backdrop of a World Series, the first Shibe Park had hosted in nineteen years.

Although not participating, Curt Simmons was allowed to attend the Series via a ten-day furlough and threw batting practice for the team's workout. Simmons could have been activated but opted not to be, concerned about the army's reaction should he pitch and not wanting to undercut Jocko Thompson's place on the roster. Bill Nicholson, discharged from the hospital but still not well enough to play, was also on hand.

Somehow, despite Bob Carpenter's announced intentions, some four thousand tickets were left unsold for each game at Shibe Park, undistributed due to some kind of mix-up in communication. Not only did fewer fans than possible attend the games, but the lack of sales also impacted the size of the player's bonus pool.[38]

JIM KONSTANTY'S FIRST starting assignment in a Phillies uniform came in the first game of the 1950 World Series. Having used Robin Roberts in an extra-inning, extra-human effort to win the National League pennant, and Bubba Church, Bob Miller, and Russ Meyer in various states of physical duress, Eddie Sawyer had limited options. Still, the choice of Konstanty was a surprise.

Sawyer explained, "I was looking for somebody different. Back in 1929 Connie Mack had started Howard Ehmke in the World Series opener against the Cubs. He couldn't throw hard and struck out like 13. So this was what I was thinking of. Konstanty would be something different for the Yankees to look at."[39] Starting Konstanty also allowed Sawyer to use Robin Roberts on his normal three days of rest.

"Sawyer told me I was going to pitch the day before," Konstanty revealed. "It was all right with me." Konstanty was preoccupied with guests he had invited to the Series, including Andy Skinner and his old high school coach, D. S. Collister. He said, "I was worried about whether I could get tickets and rooms for them, and I didn't even have time to think about the Yankees."[40]

Once the news sunk in, Konstanty was ecstatic. "The Skipper thinks I'm the pitcher to do it, so I guess that's it. I went 10 innings against Cincinnati and nine innings against Pittsburgh and didn't feel tired either time. . . . I'll be pitching my heart out in this one for the guy who was the only one who believed in me, who made me a big man as a reliefer [sic], the only fellow I would pitch for in relief—Eddie Sawyer."[41]

The Phillies were the public's sentimental choice, and the team was gaining national notoriety. Camel Cigarettes purchased full-page ads in newspapers around the country, coinciding with the opening of the World Series. The advertisements assured everyone that the company was "In first place with Pennant-Winning Phils" and that there was "Not one single case of throat irritation due to smoking Camels!" The ad featured a smiling Eddie Sawyer, whose large photo was accompanied by the caption "Camels score with me!" Andy Seminick, Bob Miller, Jim Konstanty, Dick Sisler, Willie Jones, Eddie Waitkus, Bubba Church, and Mike Goliat were also represented by photos and quotes about their favorite smoke. Miller claimed that Camels "suit me to a 'T,'" while "Puddin' Head" Jones was quoted, "I handle chances in every game . . . but I don't take chances with my throat. Camels are for me—they're mild."[42]

THE YANKEES WERE heavy favorites, with twelve World Series titles already in hand and a roster brimming with Fall Classic experience. Among the Phillies, only Dick Sisler, Dick Whitman, and Blix Donnelly had played in a World Series—Sisler and Whitman had appeared only as pinch hitters.[43]

Despite the unsold tickets, more than thirty thousand were on hand at Shibe Park, watching the Phillies and Yankees line up on opposite baselines, facing the stands. Then, at the request of Commissioner Happy Chandler, the crowd was instructed to observe thirty seconds of silence, during which everyone was asked to offer a silent prayer for universal peace and thanks for being an American. Following the National Anthem, Konstanty trudged to the mound from the bullpen rather than the dugout, in order to maintain his routine. After completing his warmups, Konstanty delivered the first pitch of the Series to Gene Woodling, who took it for a ball.[44]

Konstanty eventually walked Woodling and then allowed a single to Phil Rizzuto, putting runners at first and second with no one out and Yogi Berra, Joe DiMaggio, and Johnny Mize due up next. But Konstanty settled down and easily retired the middle of the Yankees lineup without incident.

Vic Raschi, a 21-game winner who had begun his career pitching for Eddie Sawyer in the Canadian-American League, started for the Yankees. After Gene Woodling suffered minor scrapes and bruises unsuccessfully pursuing an Eddie Waitkus foul pop-up, Raschi got the Phillies first baseman to foul out to Yogi Berra. He then successfully fielded a Richie Ashburn bunt and a Dick Sisler chopper back to the mound to complete a one-two-three first inning.

Raschi led off the third with the Yankees second hit of the game, and Woodling then walked for a second time, once again putting Konstanty in a two-on, no-out situation. After a sacrifice bunt, Konstanty got Yogi Berra to hit a pop fly to left, too shallow to score Raschi from third. Sawyer ordered Konstanty to walk Joe DiMaggio, loading the bases. The right-hander then retired Johnny Mize on a pop up to first base, ending the Yankees threat. While some questioned walking the right-handed hitting DiMaggio to face the left-handed Mize, Eddie Sawyer said, "Contrary to accepted theory,

Konstanty is more effective against left-handed hitters than he is against right-handed batters."[45]

Konstanty was again in hot water in the fourth inning, and this time did not escape unscathed, despite throwing only seven pitches. Bobby Brown led off with a double down the left-field line and moved to third on a fly ball, caught by Richie Ashburn in deep center field. After faking a squeeze play, Jerry Coleman hit another fly ball, to Dick Sisler, and Brown tagged up to score, giving the Yankees a 1–0 lead.

The Phils threatened in the fifth. With one out, Willie Jones hit a seeing-eye grounder for the team's first hit off Raschi. After Hamner flied out, Andy Seminick slapped a single to left, putting two runners on with two out. Mike Goliat hit a foul tip that nicked umpire Jocko Conlan, causing time to be called while Frank Wiechec tended to him. Repairs to Conlan complete, Goliat ran the count to 2-2 before Raschi struck him out swinging on an outside curveball.

Vic Raschi was in total control after that, allowing only one baserunner, Eddie Waitkus, who drew a walk in the sixth. Jim Konstanty was removed for pinch-hitter Dick Whitman after having pitched eight innings and allowing only 4 hits and 1 run, an incredible performance in his first starting assignment since May 1946. After Russ Meyer pitched a scoreless ninth for the Phillies, Raschi retired the Phillies in order in the bottom of the inning, striking out Dick Sisler to end the game and pinning Konstanty with a tough loss. The Yankees had won the first contest, 1–0.[46]

ROBIN ROBERTS STARTED the second game for the Phillies and declared, "The pressure is not so bad."[47] His mound opponent was Allie Reynolds, a 16-game winner for New York. The stocky right-hander from Oklahoma was a workhorse, coming off a brilliant 1949 World Series against Brooklyn, during which he pitched twelve and one-third scoreless innings.

The second game closely followed the pattern of the first, with Roberts, like Konstanty, in and out of trouble early but growing stronger as the game went on. Meanwhile, the Phillies continued struggling to generate offense.

The Yankees scored in the second inning when Jerry Coleman drew a two-out walk and took third on an Allie Reynolds single. Gene Woodling then hit a slow bounder that Willie Jones could not reach. Granny Hamner fielded it at deep short but had no play, as Coleman crossed the plate.

Hamner responded in the bottom of the inning with a one-out triple to right-center that bounced off the outfield wall. But he was left stranded at third.

The Phillies finally scored their first run of the World Series in the fifth. Jerry Coleman made a sensational stop on Mike Goliat's grounder to the right side of the infield, but in hurrying to gather himself threw the ball past first base. Yogi Berra alertly hustled down the baseline to back up the play, preventing Goliat from advancing. After Roberts fouled out attempting to sacrifice, Eddie Waitkus hit a ball that took a bad hop and bounded over Coleman's head. Goliat took third on the play and then scored on Richie Ashburn's fly ball to left, tying the game at 1–1.

Del Ennis was robbed of a triple in the sixth on a great back-to-the-diamond catch by Joe DiMaggio, and the Phillies had runners in scoring position in the seventh, eighth, and ninth but could not push across a run. Pressed later about not pinch-hitting for Mike Goliat, who subsequently grounded into a ninth-inning double play, Eddie Sawyer retorted, "You evidently don't know my bench."[48]

The Yankees best chance to win in regulation came in the eighth thanks to one-out singles by Hank Bauer and Bobby Brown. After a groundout moved the runners to second and third, Roberts shut the door, striking out Allie Reynolds looking to end the inning.

The score remained tied, 1–1, as the Yankees came to bat in the tenth. Joe DiMaggio, playing in his ninth Fall Classic and participating in his forty-third World Series game, led off for New York. Roberts started him off carefully, falling behind in the count, 2-1. But Roberts was not careful enough. DiMaggio swung at the fourth pitch, sending a bullet into the upper tier of the left-field stands, and a dagger into the hearts of Phillies fans, slowly twisting it as he loped around the bases, having given the Yankees a 2–1 lead with his first hit of the Series.[49]

Roberts and DiMaggio differed on the pitch that was thrown, the Yankee Clipper saying it was a slider and Roberts insisting it was a fastball. When a reporter asked Roberts if DiMaggio had hit a bad pitch, he retorted, "It was bad for me."[50] After the game, DiMaggio remarked, "It certainly wasn't a careless pitch. He just didn't get it where he intended, I guess."[51]

Roberts easily retired the three Yankees who batted after DiMaggio. It was up to the Phillies to see if they could extend the battle or go to New York down by two games.

Jackie Mayo pinch-hit for Roberts and drew a lead-off walk, giving Phillies fans a glimmer of hope. Eddie Waitkus sacrificed Mayo to second, and for the fourth straight inning Philadelphia had a runner in scoring position. But for the fourth straight time nothing came of it.

After Richie Ashburn fouled out to first base, Dick Sisler struck out to end the game for the second straight time, on a check swing.[52] It was a sad scene, a forlorn Sisler desperately arguing with home plate umpire Bill McGowan while the Yankees quietly congratulated each other on their win. Shibe Park would never again host a World Series game.

AS THE SERIES SHIFTED to New York without a day off, the Yankees had a key advantage—they played every year in Shibe Park against the Athletics, but the Phillies were unfamiliar with the House That Ruth Built. Meanwhile, Eddie Sawyer had real confidence in only two pitchers at this point, Robin Roberts and Jim Konstanty. With both unavailable for Game Three, he chose Ken Heintzelman to start against Eddie Lopat.

Although Heintzelman had won 17 games in 1949, his only full season with a winning record during his career, he had slipped to a 3-9 mark in 1950. But two of Heintzelman's wins came in September and, in his eleventh season, Sawyer felt him best equipped to face sixty thousand hostile fans in Yankee Stadium. Curt Simmons continued to impress during batting practice, leading several Phillies to question his not being activated. But Sawyer was adamant against forcing Simmons into what he felt was a no-win situation.

Casey Stengel held court for reporters before the game. When asked about the health of his players he said, "Oh just a few colds—up here in the shoulder muscles. Tightened up, you know. Their batting averages have tightened up, too." As fans began making their way into the stadium, tickets that had been stolen from Vic Raschi's hotel room while he was on the mound in Philadelphia during the first World Series game began appearing at the turnstiles. They had been sold to unsuspecting fans who, as innocent victims, were allowed to watch the game from areas marked for standing room.[53]

Guy Lombardo and Al Schacht entertained fans before the game. Operatic soprano Lucy Monroe sang the National Anthem.[54] Both teams got their lead-off men on in the first, but nothing came of either effort. The Phillies had runners at first and third with one out in the second but once again failed to produce a run. The Yankees threatened in the bottom of the third when Phil Rizzuto walked with two out and then stole second, advancing to third when Seminick's throw glanced off Mike Goliat's glove and into center field. Jerry Coleman, who Stengel had shifted from eighth to second in the batting order, singled to score Rizzuto but was thrown out trying to stretch his hit into a double. The inning was over and the Yankees led, 1–0.

The Phillies tied the game in the sixth, Del Ennis doubling into the right-field corner and Dick Sisler smacking a ball over Rizzuto's head into left, scoring Ennis. But Yogi Berra prevented further damage by picking Sisler off first.

Philadelphia took its first lead of the World Series the next inning. Hamner singled through the box to lead off and was sacrificed to second. Mike Goliat followed that with a run-scoring single, Hamner beating Joe DiMaggio's throw from center. Suddenly, the Phillies were ahead, 2–1. Heintzelman continued mowing down the Yankees with his "junk" pitches until the eighth, when he lost home plate after dispatching the first two batters of the inning.

Only four outs from victory, Heintzelman walked three straight Yankees to load the bases and was replaced by Jim Konstanty. Bobby Brown hit a routine grounder to Hamner, who gloved the ball but dropped it. Then it agonizingly squirted off his fingers when he tried picking it up with his bare hand. By that point, the tying run had scored. Johnny Mize fouled out to end the inning.

In the ninth, the Phillies faced reliever Tom Ferrick, a thirty-five-year-old right-hander who had spent most of his career with second division American League teams. Ferrick had been acquired by the Yankees from the St. Louis Browns in a seven-player deal at the June 15 trade deadline, winning 8 games for New York in 30 relief appearances.

Ferrick surrendered a lead-off double to Granny Hamner—Joe DiMaggio made a bare-handed cutoff in the gap to prevent it becoming a triple. Hamner advanced to third on Seminick's bunt.

After Mike Goliat was walked intentionally, Dick Whitman pinch-hit for Konstanty and grounded to first base. Joe Collins fielded the ball and fired home, catching Hamner trying to score. Waitkus flied out to end the ninth, the Phillies having one runner thrown out at the plate and two others left stranded.

With the score still tied, 2–2, Russ Meyer came on to pitch the bottom of the ninth for the Phillies and quickly retired the first two batters. Gene Woodling then hit a ball toward second that took a tricky hop and was awarded a single when Jimmy Bloodworth, who had replaced Mike Goliat at second base, hurried his throw and pulled Waitkus off the bag. Phil Rizzuto followed with a low screamer to Bloodworth's right. Bloodworth reached across his body, making a diving attempt, but could not hold on to the ball, as Woodling came sliding in and nearly kicked it away. Both Yankees runners were safe. Jerry Coleman then smacked a short fly ball into left-center between Jackie Mayo and Richie Ashburn. The ball fell safely, scoring Woodling with the winning run.[55] The Yankees now led the Series 3-0. The Phillies, dating back to 1915, had lost seven World Series games in a row, all by one run.

Hamner, despite having collected 3 hits, was distraught after the game, kicking himself for his eighth-inning miscue. "Oh what an error!" he exclaimed. "What an easy play! And I couldn't make it." Joe DiMaggio caught up with Hamner after the game and told him, "It was just a bad break for you. You are too good a ballplayer to let it get you down. Don't take it so hard. It happens to the best of us."[56]

THERE WAS A CELEBRITY visitor to Game Three. Grover Cleveland Alexander, the only pitcher to have won a World Series game for the Phillies, attended through the auspices of *The Tommy Bartlett Show*, a popular Chicago-based radio program.[57] "I was certainly impressed with the ability of the Whiz Kids today," Alexander told Stephen O. Grauley, a sportswriter who had seen Connie Mack as a *catcher* and was covering his forty-first World Series, including the one in 1915 in which Alexander pitched. "They look like a good, lively young team with a good future."[58]

At age sixty-three, Alexander remained the greatest Phillie of them all. His feats were the stuff of legend: 373 career wins—tied with Christy Mathewson for third-most all-time—including 28 as a rookie. Three straight 30-win seasons pitching in Baker Bowl, and 90 career shutouts, 16 of them in 1916 alone. (Through the 2024 season, Clayton Kershaw, the active Major League career leader, had pitched only 15 shutouts in seventeen *seasons*.) Six times Alex had pitched more than 350 innings—including four years in a row. During his more than five thousand innings pitched, he allowed only 1 grand slam.[59] And he was famous for striking out Tony Lazzeri with the bases loaded in the seventh game of the 1926 World Series, the day after pitching a complete-game victory. A motion picture about Alexander's life was soon to be in the works, although his ex-wife, the film's technical advisor, was portrayed as the hero of the story, and the pitcher's battles with his demons were dutifully sanitized.[60]

After baseball, Alex battled alcoholism, poverty, and declining health—a life spiraling out of control. Occasionally he was rescued and afforded an opportunity to improve his lot, such as in 1937 when a preteen Robin Roberts saw him speak in Springfield. More often, Alexander disappeared, surfacing occasionally with a House of David baseball team or at a race track or in a circus sideshow, attempting to make a buck off what was left of his fame. Or he would be discovered, passed out on a sidewalk in Evanston, Illinois, or New York City.

Alexander was being "rescued" one more time in 1950, after a story documenting his plight had been published in *Sport* magazine a few months earlier. A week after Robin Roberts won his 20th game, the Hall of Fame pitcher made his final public appearance.

S. O. Grauley claimed Alexander looked well, although considering the highly publicized story of his being found crumpled in a Hollywood alley the previous Christmas Eve, lacking money, sobriety, and one of his ear lobes, it was almost certainly a whitewash on the columnist's part.[61] Alexander went largely unnoticed until being invited into the press box, where he told a few old baseball tales. In truth, the pitcher had aged well beyond his years and was dying of congestive heart failure. He passed away four weeks later, alone in his rented room in Saint Paul, Nebraska, still the only Phillies pitcher to win a World Series game.[62] It was a distinction that would remain his for another three decades following his death.

THE FOURTH GAME of the 1950 World Series ended the cruel streak of one-run Series game losses for the Phillies but extended their overall losing streak in the Fall Classic to eight. The *Philadelphia Inquirer* failed to mention the game on its front page, so depressing was the outcome to Philadelphia baseball fans. It proved the easiest of the four not-so-easy wins for the Yankees, who captured their thirteenth World Series title, the sixth in a sweep.

The game featured rookie pitchers. Casey Stengel went with a twenty-one-year-old who first joined the team in July, Edward "Whitey" Ford, whose subsequent World Series exploits would rank among the greatest of all time. Ford had won 9 of 10 decisions following his arrival from the Minors.[63] With few options, Eddie Sawyer rolled the dice and chose Bob Miller, whose parents were to see their son pitch as a professional for the first time. If Miller faltered, Sawyer planned to call on Jim Konstanty.

The Phillies made some noise in the first inning. Eddie Waitkus drew a lead-off walk and moved to third with one out on Willie Jones's ground-rule double. Del Ennis followed with a grounder toward third. Standing in the coach's box with only an instant to make a decision, Eddie Sawyer sent Waitkus, but Bobby Brown threw him out at home while Jones held at second.[64] Dick Sisler struck out to end the inning.

In the bottom of the first, Gene Woodling was safe on an error and then took second on an infield grounder. Yogi Berra bounced a single to right, scoring Woodling. A shaken Bob Miller uncorked a wild pitch that caromed off the screen; alert to Andy Seminick's lack of mobility, Berra raced to third on the play. Joe DiMaggio then doubled in Berra, and Miller was done. Jim Konstanty took over, retiring Johnny Mize and Bobby Brown, but for the first time one of the teams had a two-run lead.

Philadelphia threatened in the fourth, but Del Ennis was thrown out at home by Johnny Mize on an inning-ending double play—to that point, the Phillies had scored 3 runs in the World Series, and an equal number had been erased at home plate. Leading, 2–0, the Yankees stretched their advantage in the sixth, finally solving Konstanty. After surrendering a lead-off home run to Berra on a full-count pitch, Konstanty hit DiMaggio with an errant delivery. The Yankees star took second on Johnny Mize's grounder that Eddie Waitkus uncharacteristically allowed to roll through his legs. Mike Goliat backed up the play and threw out Mize, but the Phillies had lost an opportunity to turn a double play. DiMaggio then scored on Bobby Brown's triple. The Yankees lead grew to 5–0 on Hank Bauer's liner to Sisler that scored Brown.

Meanwhile, Whitey Ford remained in command through the eighth inning, allowing only one base runner after Konstanty singled with one out in the fifth, on an error by Bobby Brown.

Konstanty was replaced in the eighth by Robin Roberts, who allowed an infield single to DiMaggio but nothing else. The Phillies were down to their last chance in the top of the ninth. Willie Jones led off with a single. Ford then hit Del Ennis with a pitch, but Dick Sisler forced Ennis at second and Hamner struck out. With two out, Andy Seminick lifted a high fly ball to Gene Woodling for what appeared to be the final out of the Series, but Woodling lost the ball in the sun and dropped it, allowing Jones and Ken Johnson, pinch-running for Dick Sisler, to cross the plate, making the score 5–2. Seminick, running best he could on his ankle, could advance no further than first base on the play, and Jackie Mayo came in to pinch-run for him.

Mike Goliat followed with a single, advancing Mayo to second. Casey Stengel had seen enough and replaced Ford with Allie Reynolds, the manager returning to the dugout amid a chorus of boos from Yankees fans, who wanted to see their rookie complete the game. But Stengel, anticipating that Ford would be throwing to a pinch hitter representing the tying run, was not about to take any chances. Stan Lopata batted for Robin Roberts, and Reynolds struck him out, ending the game and the World Series.

The Phillies had survived an excruciating final week of the regular season that had seemed to last forever. Without having a chance to exhale, the World Series was suddenly upon them. And then, in just over seventy-two hours, it was over.

Eddie Sawyer entered the Yankees clubhouse and shook hands with Casey Stengel, winner of his second straight world championship. "You have a fine ballclub Eddie," said Stengel, before adding a back-handed compliment. "I was surprised you gave us such a hard battle all the way. The way everybody was talking before the series, I thought we would beat you easier than we did."[65]

Sawyer returned to the Phillies locker room, lit a cigar and faced reporters. He said to no one in particular, "We don't have much to talk about, do we?"[66] He then stated that the Yankees were not that much better than his team and noted the number of lost opportunities, when a well-timed hit could have turned the tide. Dick Sisler left thirteen on base during the series, Del Ennis stranded seven. The two sluggers combined for 3 hits in 31 at bats. Not that they shouldered all of the offensive blame—only Granny Hamner, who batted .429, had more than 4 hits in the Series. The Phillies collected more extra-base hits than New York, 8 to the Yankees' 6—but no home runs.

During the Series, Jim Konstanty pitched nearly half of the Phillies innings. Overall, the staff allowed just 11 runs in four games, only 9 of which were earned. The Yankees pitching staff earned run average was 0.73, with only 3 earned runs surrendered. Joe DiMaggio had earned his eighth World

Series ring, with one more to come. It was also the last World Series in which neither team had a Black or Latin player on its roster.

Losing the Series, especially in four games, was a bitter pill for the Phillies to swallow. Philadelphia had played ten vitally important games at the end of the 1950 season and had lost nine of them. But there was nothing to be ashamed of. Eddie Sawyer's moves had been brilliant, the young players came through, and heroic efforts had been in abundance. The Phillies had given it their full measure, leaving it all on the field, as it were.

Eddie Waitkus was extremely glad the season was over. His comeback from near death was complete, and his had been one of several courageous performances for the exciting Whiz Kids. Waitkus admitted, "It's been a long, long year, and now I'm going to take it easy. If I never need the help of Frank Wiechec again, that will be o.k. with me. He's been a real buddy boy, but from now on I want to stay too healthy for him."[67]

Several of the Phillies had been hired to write columns during the World Series, detailing their experiences and providing fans an inside view of the games. Among them was Curt Simmons, who penned his frustration at having to sit in the stands after pitching batting practice, helpless to assist his team. But he remained philosophical. "My chance will come later," he said. "I'm sure the Phillies will be in other Series in the future."[68]

11

They'll Win the Pennant for the Next Six Years

ON TUESDAY, OCTOBER 10, the Phillies began the painful task of refunding nearly $250,000 to those that had been allotted tickets for the two home games of the World Series that were not played.[1] In addition, there was the usual postseason postmortem.

Stan Baumgartner published his conversation with a Yankees scout who, while remaining anonymous, explained New York's pitching strategy in the World Series.

"A free-swinging club like the Phils," explained the scout, "where every member, except Richie Ashburn, grabs his bat at the end and starts cutting, are usually a good low ball hitting club but can't hit the high ones. That is one of the fundamental rules of pitching.

"As a result we instructed our pitchers to throw high and keep going higher if they chased the high pitches. Dick Sisler was an outstanding example. We pitched him chest high. When he swung at that one we went up a few inches. Finally we had him swinging at pitches around his neck. The same was true in a smaller degree with Del Ennis and Mike Goliat.

"We told our men to throw curves to Seminick. With Ashburn we worked in opposite manner. Ashburn 'chokes' his bat. This ordinarily makes him a good high ball hitter so we tried to keep the ball low and, when we had lefthanders working, we threw sidearm curves."

The scout concluded, "Maybe we were lucky and the team was in a slump but it is also possible that in following the standard code for pitchers and hitters we helped keep them in their slump."[2]

To a man, the Phillies insisted there was not much of a talent gap between them and the legendary Yankees. They also felt certain of getting another chance in a World Series. Stan Baumgartner was of the opinion that the current Bronx Bombers could not be compared to their great predecessors and insisted that the Yankees had been ripe for the taking but the Phillies had failed to take advantage of the opportunity. It should be noted that this "less than great" Yankees aggregation was in the midst of becoming the only team in baseball history to win five straight World Series.

ON OCTOBER 18, 1950, during a luncheon at the Benjamin Franklin Hotel, a historic era in baseball ended. Connie Mack announced he was stepping aside as manager of the Athletics, ending his unprecedented run in the dugout. Jimmy Dykes was formally named his replacement, and Minor League director Arthur Ehlers took over as general manager.

"I am sorry I could not give Philadelphia all it expected," lamented Mack. "Thanks for keeping me 50 years as manager of the Athletics. I want to express my thanks too, to the Philadelphia public for their fine support."[3]

After three straight winning seasons raised expectations, the Athletics collapsed in 1950, losing 102 games while drawing a paltry 309,805 fans, a drop of more than a half million compared to 1949, and one-fourth that of the Phillies. Their financial loss of more than $300,000 came close to matching their payroll—which had been increased in anticipation of contending.[4] There had been whispers of Mack falling asleep in the dugout and losing track of himself during games. Baseball's Grand Old Man finally came to terms with the fact that his time had passed, as it eventually does for everyone.

Mack remained team president and said he planned to travel with the club—originally, he had intended to sit on the bench during games, next to Jimmy Dykes, but then wisely thought better of it. "I'll watch the game from the stands," he said.[5]

The next day, the eighty-seven-year-old legend held court in his famous "oval office," located within Shibe Park's distinctive cupolaed tower. The "Sage of Lehigh Avenue" remained the face of Philadelphia baseball, even against the backdrop of the Whiz Kids. During his run, the Athletics had won nine pennants and five World Series. His National League cotenants— the Phillies—achieved but one league title in their first sixty-seven seasons while finishing last eighteen times. Mack famously endured many down years as well, but regardless of their status, the Athletics historically outdrew the Phillies year after year—all but seven times between 1902 and 1948.[6]

There had been no doubt which was Philadelphia's dominant baseball team. But that began to change in the late 1940s, a change that accelerated in 1950. In capturing their second pennant and outdrawing the Athletics by a factor of four to one, the Phillies finally appeared to be the team of the present and of the future, while the Athletics had become a remnant of the past.

Connie Mack did not seem jealous of the way the baseball winds were blowing, which would buffet the franchise that he had been synonymous with for the entire century to that point and result in its sale and relocation to Kansas City within four years. No, he and the Athletics seemed genuinely happy for their National League counterparts.

Stan Baumgartner, who had pitched for the only other Phillies pennant winner, in 1915, and also hurled for the Athletics during the 1920s, recorded Mack's only regret about the Phillies success. "I'm just sorry Herb Pennock could not have seen it," he said. "Herb didn't expect they'd win so soon. Neither did I."

"Do you think the Phils will win the pennant again?" Mack was asked. "Are they going to be Whiz Kids or Was Kids?"

The Grand Old Man of Baseball leaned back in his red leather chair, rubbed his hands together, and with a smile enthusiastically declared, "They'll win the pennant for the next six years. They're wonderful."[7]

DESPITE THE PAIN of refunding World Series tickets, the season was a financial success for Bob Carpenter and the Phillies. They ended the year with a profit exceeding $300,000 on revenue of $1.8 million, including more than $27,000 collected from advertisers in World Series programs.[8] Ticket sales had totaled $1.125 million for the regular season.[9]

New media was changing the financial mix industry-wide. Players and owners continued haggling over $800,000 realized from television revenues for the World Series, with the players angling for the money to be distributed to World Series participants, and Commissioner Chandler pushing for the windfall to be deposited into the player's pension fund. The radio and television rights actually brought in slightly higher revenues for the 1950 Series than had ticket sales. It was widely predicted that television rights alone would fetch more than $1 million for the next World Series.

Later on, in the middle of the decade, Major League baseball signed a five-year deal for World Series radio and television rights, calling for more than $16 million.[10] Roy Mack, all too aware that the Athletics were dependent on the growing revenue stream coming from this new media, enthusiastically declared, "And I can see no end to this thing."[11]

The Phillies collected $117,500 in local television and radio revenue in 1950. After the season, they reached a $380,000, three-year agreement for those local rights. In 1952 they received another $25,000 from the Mutual Broadcasting System, which carried a national radio broadcast called *Game of the Day*.[12]

EVEN IN LOSING the World Series, Phillies players did well too, each full share worth $4,081.34.[13] Willie Jones didn't wait around for his check to be cut, receiving a $4,000 advance from the team three days after the last out and heading to his new house in Laurel Hill, North Carolina.[14] There, he planned to catch up with his parents, his younger brother, J.W.—who had just finished his first season of professional ball, hitting .293 as a catcher for Kilgore in the East Texas League—and play some American Legion basketball.[15]

Richie Ashburn returned to Tilden and persuaded fellow Nebraskan Johnny Hopp of the Yankees to join him and Cubs right-hander Doyle Lade for a week of exhibition games in the area.[16] The three played for Tilden against Oakdale on October 15, with Ashburn at shortstop in a game Tilden won, 11–2. Ashburn pitched the final two innings, while Hopp jumped over to the Oakdale side to pitch against him.[17] During the offseason, Ashburn also became an honorary member of the Kiwanis and traveled to Lincoln several times with his wife to attend University of Nebraska football games.[18]

Two days after the World Series, Granny Hamner was playing at Mooers Field in his hometown of Richmond, Virginia, helping Danny Litwhiler's barnstorming team defeat Luke Easter's All-Stars. Braves pitcher Vern Bickford offered a sympathetic ear to Hamner prior to the game, and Hamner confided, "The Yanks are a great team. They never make a mistake and they never let you [get away with] one." He added, "We'll get them next year. I think we'll win the National League pennant again."[19]

Hamner later revealed he would be moving to Philadelphia to live year-round, having bought a home in the suburbs, and had accepted a sales job at an automobile dealership while also planning some "television work."[20]

Andy Seminick returned to Elizabethton, Tennessee, and the town declared Andy Seminick Day, honoring him with a banquet at the Riverview Grill. Seminick had settled in Elizabethton after signing to play for the local team in 1941 and told his audience he thought it "the finest place in the United States." He added, "I want to thank every one who has helped me in my baseball career since I begun. You have all been extremely nice to me."[21] Seminick visited Philadelphia to have his ankle examined, with X-rays taken at Temple University Hospital confirming the injury.[22] After spending several weeks with his ankle in a cast, Seminick was allowed to resume normal activities at the end of November and began rehabbing with Frank Wiechec.[23]

In late October Eddie Waitkus was linked romantically to Carol Webel, a medical secretary from Albany, New York, the two having met during the ballplayer's recovery in Clearwater, Florida, the previous winter. Waitkus insisted the two were just good friends, although the diamond-studded wristwatch Carol received from him on her birthday seemingly signaled other intentions. Shaking his head, Waitkus declared, "Every time you date a girl the papers expect a wedding announcement. I just came over to deliver Carol's birthday present in person and spend the week-end with her."[24] But Waitkus had already told close pal Russ Meyer that Carol Webel was someone with whom he could spend the rest of his life.[25]

Waitkus won the Associated Press Comeback Player of the Year Award and, while pleased with the honor, expressed no pleasure regarding the circumstances that had resulted in his receiving it, including multiple surgeries and a painful rehabilitation.

He confessed, "Looking back now, they were the four most horrible months of my life. Worse than anything in the Army—worse than New Guinea or anything in the Philippines. The pain was so severe that more than once I found myself wishing that the girl had finished the job."[26]

Del Ennis did a little barnstorming in October and then returned home to Philadelphia for his usual off-season job at a brokerage house.[27] He also received an award as the Phillies outstanding player of 1950 from the Congregation Emanu-el Men's Club.[28]

After several weeks under the care of Phillies team physician Thomas McTear for his diabetes, Bill Nicholson declared himself fit again to play. It was McTear who, while sitting in the stands during an early September game, had observed Nicholson and told the Phillies something was physically wrong with him.[29] "I feel better than I have in the past 10 years," Nicholson declared. "I am strong, ready to go hunting and get myself in shape for the 1951 season. My eyes are clear for the first time in two years."[30]

Ken Johnson owned a producing oil well in Kansas and planned additional drilling in anticipation of generating $750 per month from his mineral rights. He declared, "When my income reaches $1,000 a month, I'm going to retire from baseball."[31]

Maje McDonnell, who had earned a Bronze Star at Omaha Beach and personified the heart and soul of Phillies spirit, was awarded a full World Series share.[32] Johnny Blatnik called him, "The best batting practice pitcher that ever lived."[33] McDonnell spent the off-season coaching the Villanova freshman basketball team until he had to leave for spring training, and he was a popular guest for numerous engagements, including one as the principal speaker at a young adults meeting of the Philadelphia Association of Settlement Houses, supported by the Community Chest.[34]

Frank Wiechec, whom Eddie Sawyer called the team's most valuable member, also received a full Series share. He then began his first season as trainer for the Philadelphia Eagles, dropping his past off-season endeavor, coaching soccer for La Salle College, to do so.[35]

Jimmy Bloodworth took his World Series share and built a house in Apalachicola, Florida. He called it, "The House That Sisler Built," telling his teammate, "Your homer, boy, bought every piece of lumber."[36]

Dick Sisler went home to St. Louis. At a hot-stove league banquet in November, honoring a local American Legion team, Sisler bemoaned the fact that the Phillies had no time to adjust from being National League pennant-winner to World Series participant. "We were so relieved to at last win the flag that the series just caught us as we were taking a deep breath." Sisler turned to fellow St. Louisan Yogi Berra and insisted he was not, of course, taking anything away from the Yankees. "They are a fine team," he continued, "but I think if we'd had a few days to recuperate from winning the pennant, we might have been a little better competitor."[37] Sisler also served his fourth year heading up the St. Louis Junior League, which supported local nonprofits such as the Forest Park Children's Center, which provided living space and counseling for emotionally troubled youth.[38]

Private First Class Curt Simmons received a trophy from Governor John Fine for Pennsylvania Athlete of the Year. The pitcher attended the ceremony and was photographed chatting with Cy Young during dinner.[39] By spring, Simmons was a corporal, heading the Twenty-Eighth Infantry Division baseball team at Camp Atterbury.[40] A few months later, he was shipped to Germany to continue his military stint.[41]

Robin Roberts became a first-time father on October 23, his wife giving birth to eight-pound Robin Jr.[42] The pitcher was also honored in his hometown, Springfield, Illinois, with two hundred on hand for a banquet held at the Hotel Leland in mid-December. George Earnshaw represented the Phillies, while others attending included umpire Al Barlick, pitcher Dutch Leonard of the Chicago Cubs, and Cubs infielder Emil Verban, who had briefly been a teammate of Roberts with the Phillies in 1948.[43] St. Louis Cardinals broadcaster Harry Caray was also on hand to make a few remarks.[44]

Jim Konstanty's amazing and historic season was properly recognized by his handily winning the National League Most Valuable Player Award. The selection caught him off guard. Upon being told the news at his home in Worcester, New York, he said, "It's something you always work for and never expect. I'm very excited and delighted." Konstanty added, "I never could have won it without help from the team. Without them, I could never even have been mentioned."[45]

The veteran right-hander had unquestionably given the team everything he had, appearing on the mound seventy-seven times in 1950, counting the World Series, and pitching 167 innings. He admitted, "I never was so tired in my life as on Sunday [the day after the World Series]."[46] At the beginning of the year, no one would have thought the thirty-three-year-old reliever anything resembling a contender for the honor, but here he was, garnering eighteen of a possible twenty-four first place votes to easily distance himself from second place finisher Stan Musial. He also received three second-place votes. Somehow, two writers failed to list him at all among their ten choices.[47] He became the first relief pitcher to win a Most Valuable Player Award.[48]

Eddie Sawyer praised Konstanty, saying, "I never have seen a player who takes care of himself better the year around. He is always in condition." He added, "I see no reason why Jim shouldn't be just as effective next year."[49] Four days after capturing the award, Konstanty was feted at a dinner attended by more than two hundred people at the Oneonta Hotel. Al Schacht served as keynote speaker, and Brooklyn Dodgers coach Jake Pitler also addressed the gathering, declaring ruefully about Konstanty, "If we'd had him, we'd have won the pennant by ten games."[50] These platitudes honored a pitcher whose college coach never thought he would make it because he did not know how to wind up. But Konstanty had confidence, telling the audience, "There is no such thing as a lucky hit. If a man makes a hit off you, it is because you pitch wrong to him. When I walk into a game, it is the hitter who is on the spot, not I."[51]

Konstanty returned to his annual winter practice of running the Oneonta sporting goods store he had opened in 1947 and officiating local basketball games. On New Year's Day 1951, he refereed a contest at Madison Square Garden between NYU and Cornell.[52] A week later Konstanty was named Associated Press Male Athlete of the Year, beating out Heisman Trophy winner Vic Janowicz, world heavyweight champion Ezzard Charles, and Yankees star Phil Rizzuto.[53]

Despite winning the pennant, no Phillies player made the AP All-Star team, not even Jim Konstanty. Two Phillies, Bob Miller and Bubba Church, were among twelve players named to the *Sporting News* Major League All-Rookie team.[54] Miller finished second to Sam Jethroe in balloting for National League Rookie of the Year, with Church finishing fourth.[55]

Eddie Sawyer was named National League Manager of the Year, picking up twenty of twenty-four possible votes, with Leo Durocher receiving the remainder. He then topped that by capturing the Associated Press nod as Major League Manager of the Year. Sawyer expressed surprise at the honor, insisting, "It was farthest from my thoughts. I knew we had a coming ball club, even though we finished a bad sixth in 1948, but as to myself being selected as No. 1 manager after so brief a period in major league baseball—well, I just never gave it a thought."[56]

Sawyer purchased a house in the Philadelphia suburb of Wayne and, outside of a trip to his parents in New York for Thanksgiving, spent the winter in his new home and worked on his 1951 plans for the Phillies.

BOB CARPENTER WAS understandably anxious to build on his team's success, wanting to seize an opportunity that does not come often and is almost always accompanied by a window that does not remain open for long. Recognizing this—and likely thanks to the development into stars of former bonus babies Robin Roberts and Curt Simmons—Carpenter reversed one of his formerly concrete pledges in his pursuit of building a long-term winning tradition.

Four days after the World Series ended, despite previous, public protestations that he would never again pay out large bonuses to amateur players, the Phillies beat out seven other Major League teams and spent $40,000 to sign twenty-year-old Fordham University pitcher-outfielder Tom Casagrande. Chuck Ward, the man credited with landing Robin Roberts, was the scout of record. Casagrande had apparently wowed the Phillies during a September workout at Shibe Park, during which he slammed five successive balls over the right field fence. Babe Alexander insisted that the Phillies did not outbid the other teams: "Casagrande signed with us because he liked the organization."[57]

With Curt Simmons lost for at least the 1951 season, Bob Carpenter openly fretted about the possibility of a universal military draft that would disproportionately impact his young roster. "Wait until this election is over (in November 1950) and you will see the greatest drafting of young kids in five years," he moaned.[58] "I had three great kids in our farm system, Joe Lonnett at Terre Haute, Charley Payls [*sic*], and Thornton Knipper [*sic*] who have already been called. Lonnett was the best young catcher in our organization."[59] Eddie Sawyer was equally concerned, noting that the Phillies Major League roster included only six men older than twenty-five years of age. If the draft expanded as feared, he joked, "I would have to put a club on the field made up of three newspapermen, two photographers and my four coaches."[60]

Despite the efforts of Carpenter and Sawyer, the Phillies made no major acquisitions in the off-season. Lacking confidence in Mike Goliat at second base and having only Putsy Caballero and Jimmy Bloodworth in reserve, the Phillies purchased Minor League infielder Buddy Hicks from the Brooklyn Dodgers for $10,000 a few days after signing Tom Casagrande.[61] And they acquired two veterans during the Rule 5 draft prior to the winter meetings, pitcher Andy Hansen from the New York Giants and catcher Del Wilber from the Cardinals.[62] But otherwise they remained silent, outside of the omnipresent off-season rumor mill.

BOB CARPENTER HEADED for the Winter Meetings, bound and determined to rid baseball of the rule that had infuriated him for so long. "I think we have it licked now," he told Stan Baumgartner.[63] On December 12, the

Major Leagues officially booted the bonus rule, along with the rule that prohibited contacting high school athletes prior to graduation.[64] The Major Leagues were far less sympathetic regarding a Minor League proposal to curtail broadcasting big league games into their territories.

During the meetings, Major League owners failed to renew Commissioner Happy Chandler's contract, a development that blindsided many, including Chandler. Apparently, he sided with players too often in the eyes of owners—Robin Roberts said that he later learned the owners wanted someone who would more reliably represent *their* interests.[65] Bob Carpenter had been rumored as among those in favor of ending Chandler's commissionership, although he denied that.[66] National League president Ford Frick was eventually selected to replace Chandler.

During the winter, Carpenter addressed the financial red ink in his farm system. He shifted the Phillies Eastern League franchise from Utica to Schenectady, writing off a $152,000 loss.[67] Carpenter also floated the possibility of moving the team's Interstate League franchise from his home base in Wilmington, saying he had been approached by interested parties from Reading, York, and Salisbury, and that he would need to see pledges for at least fifty thousand tickets to have him turn a deaf ear to those overtures. Community leaders in Wilmington mounted a drive to answer Carpenter's ultimatum, which would represent more than ten thousand in excess of the number of fans drawn in 1950 for a pennant and playoff-winning team. They topped that, with 62,659 tickets pledged, saving the franchise.[68]

AT A DECEMBER press conference marking his eighty-eighth birthday, Connie Mack maintained that he was adjusting to life after managing, although, he admitted, spring training was still a couple of months away, and he wondered about his future reactions to his team's fortunes. He continued reporting to his office five days a week and announced he and his wife were moving from Germantown to Fairmount Park. He also expanded on his lament about his final season.

After pointing to injuries as a major factor in the team's failure, Mack finally admitted, "It was my fault. I thought I could go on and on as manager, and I was determined to get through that 50th year, at least. I'm sorry now I didn't quit a year sooner. . . .

"A manager has to be able to talk to his players, and I noticed in 1949 that I couldn't do this anymore like I used to. I was a deterrant [*sic*] to the team."[69]

As Eddie Sawyer prepared for 1951, he did not realize that he was about to encounter the same problem Connie Mack said had been the case for him in 1949—losing touch with his players.

FIG. 1. Al Reach, one of the baseball's first star players, sporting goods magnate, and one of the founders of the Philadelphia Phillies in 1883. He owned the franchise along with John I. Rogers until 1903. The Miriam and Ira D. Wallach Division of Art, Prints and Photographs: Photography Collection, the New York Public Library.

FIG. 2. The Phillies built
a ballpark at Broad and
Huntingdon in 1887. It
burned down in 1894 and
was replaced by what later
became known as Baker
Bowl. *1943 Baseball Guide and
Record Book*, A. S. Barnes.
FIG. 3. Charlie Ferguson.
Longtime Phillies executive
William Shettsline called
him "the greatest player who
ever lived." The Miriam and
Ira D. Wallach Division of
Art, Prints and Photographs:
Photography Collection, the
New York Public Library.

FIG. 4. The 1915 Philadelphia Phillies, the franchise's only pennant-winner between its founding in 1883 and the Whiz Kids of 1950. Six-foot-five Eppa Rixey is easily spotted in the back row, as is a grumpy looking Grover Cleveland Alexander (*second row, second from left*), sitting next to manager Pat Moran. Star slugger Gavvy Cravath is seated in front of Rixey and next to Moran. Library of Congress, Prints and Photographs Division, LC-DIG-ggbain-22039.

FIG. 5. Grover Cleveland Alexander in 1913. Library of Congress Prints and Photographs Division, LC-DIG-ggbain-12276.

FIG. 6. Baker Bowl, with its iconic Lifebuoy sign, home of the Phillies from 1895 to 1938. Special Collections Research Center, Temple University Libraries, Philadelphia, Pennsylvania; George D. McDowell for the *Philadelphia Evening Bulletin*.

FIG. 7. *From left*: Owner William D. Cox, coach Earl Whitehill, manager Bucky Harris, and player-coach Chuck Klein at Phillies training camp at Hershey Pennsylvania in 1943. Author's collection.

FIG. 8. Robert Carpenter Jr. (*left*) and Herb Pennock. National Baseball Hall of Fame and Museum, Cooperstown, New York.

FIG. 9. After being signed by the Phillies, Curt Simmons was assigned to Wilmington in the Interstate League and dominated the competition. USA Today Network.
FIG. 10. Robin Roberts was signed by the Phillies after his junior year at Michigan State University. Michigan State University Athletic Department.

FIG. 11. Richie Ashburn became a Major League star in 1948, leading the Major Leagues in stolen bases and hitting .333 before a fractured finger ended his season in late August. National Baseball Hall of Fame and Museum, Cooperstown, New York.

FIG. 12. Cy Perkins. A former Major League catcher and mentor to Lefty Grove and Mickey Cochrane, Perkins told Robin Roberts he would become a 300-game winner. National Baseball Hall of Fame and Museum, Cooperstown, New York.

FIG. 13. Ruth Ann Steinhagen (*far left*) with her mother standing between her and Eddie Waitkus (*seated*) at Steinhagen's criminal arraignment in Chicago. Chicago Sun-Times Collection, Chicago History Museum, ST-17500605-E-1.

FIG. 14. Opening Day ceremonies at Shibe Park on April 18, 1950. Pictured from left to right are Granny Hamner, Richie Ashburn, bandleader Elliott Lawrence, Willie Jones, and Dick Sisler. Author's collection.

FIG. 15. Jackie Robinson is thrown out at first base by Robin Roberts on a bunt attempt in the eighth inning of the 1950 season opener. Mike Goliat, (#9) is covering first base. Earlier in the game Robinson had remarked to Phillies catcher Andy Seminick, "You guys look like you want to win the pennant." John W. Mosley Photograph Collection, Charles L. Blockson Afro-American Collection, Temple University Libraries, Philadelphia, Pennsylvania.

FIG. 16. Andy Seminick and Bill Rigney fight during a game on August 12, 1950, after Seminick slid in hard on a force out. Seminick had already knocked Giants third baseman Hank Thompson out of the game, and Eddie Stanky was ejected for waving his arms during Seminick's at bat. Author's collection.

FIG. 17. Russ Meyer apologizes to photographer Bert Brandt for punching him in response to being photographed while witnessing the Dodgers sweep the Boston Braves at Ebbets Field in late September 1950. The apology averted a potential lawsuit. Author's collection.

FIG. 18. Brooklyn's Cal Abrams is tagged out by Stan Lopata at home plate on a Richie Ashburn throw in the bottom of the ninth in the dramatic final game of the 1950 season against the Dodgers. Larry Goetz is the home plate umpire. Wearing number 10 for Brooklyn is Bruce Edwards. New York Daily News Archive.

FIG. 19. Dick Sisler is mobbed by his teammates after hitting a home run in the top of the tenth inning of the season's final game to give Philadelphia a 4–1 lead over the Dodgers, averting a monumental collapse. Bettman Archive.

FIG. 20. Dick Sisler (*left*) and Eddie Sawyer at the Phillies postgame party at the Warwick Hotel in Philadelphia, celebrating the team's clinching of the 1950 National League pennant. Author's collection.

FIG. 21. While on ten-day furlough from military service during the 1950 World Series, Curt Simmons could only pitch batting practice, wave to fans, and wish he was pitching. Special Collections Research Center, Temple University Libraries, Philadelphia, Pennsylvania; George D. McDowell for the *Philadelphia Evening Bulletin*.

FIG. 22. Dick Sisler strikes out on a check swing to end the second game of the 1950 World Series, a 2–1 loss to the Yankees. Author's collection.

FIG. 23. Granny Hamner slides in safely in the top of the seventh inning of the third game of the 1950 World Series, giving the Phillies their first and only lead of the Fall Classic. Special Collections Research Center, Temple University Libraries, Philadelphia, Pennsylvania; George D. McDowell for the *Philadelphia Evening Bulletin*.
FIG. 24. Jim Konstanty (*center*) with National League president Ford Frick (*left*) and Konstanty's wife, Mary, as he accepts the award as the National League's Most Valuable Player for 1950. National Baseball Hall of Fame and Museum, Cooperstown, New York.

FIG. 25. Coach Robert "Maje" McDonnell was in many ways the heart and spirit of the Phillies. After his coaching days, he spent nearly forty years as the team's goodwill ambassador. Awarded a Bronze Star for saving lives on Omaha Beach, he was also considered one of the game's great batting practice pitchers. Author's collection.

FIG. 26. After being suspended for jumping the Phillies in September 1953, Eddie Waitkus was sold to the Baltimore Orioles during spring training in 1954. National Baseball Hall of Fame and Museum, Cooperstown, New York.

FIG. 27. Jim Konstanty was considered by some teammates as difficult and a loner, but he was a dedicated family man with little patience for those on the team who partied. Like Waitkus, when Konstanty complained about his lack of playing time, he was jettisoned, sold to the New York Yankees in August 1954. National Baseball Hall of Fame and Museum, Cooperstown, New York.

FIG. 28. The Macks arrive for the American League owners meeting on October 28, 1954, at which Roy Mack secretly torpedoed the franchise's chances of remaining in Philadelphia. The Mack family (*left to right*): Roy Mack, Connie Mack, Earle Mack, and Roy's son, Connie Mack III. Courtesy of Robert Warrington.

FIG. 29. Del Ennis completes his home run trot on June 19, 1956, having hit his 244th home run with the Phillies, breaking the team record held by his idol, Chuck Klein. He is greeted by Phillies batboy George Strausser (*left*) and team mascot and little person Henry Rech. Special Collections Research Center, Temple University Libraries, Philadelphia, Pennsylvania; George D. McDowell for the *Philadelphia Evening Bulletin*.

FIG. 30. Bill Yancey (*left*) and John Kennedy. The Phillies finally signed their first Black player to the Major League roster in 1957. But John Kennedy was given little opportunity, appearing in only five games. John W. Mosley Photograph Collection, Charles L. Blockson Afro-American Collection, Temple University Libraries, Philadelphia, Pennsylvania.

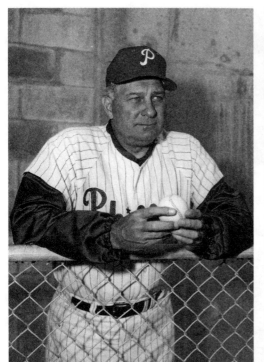

FIG. 31. Eddie Sawyer had a rougher time in his second stint as Phillies manager and resigned one game into the 1960 season. Author's collection.

FIG. 32. Robin Roberts during an exhibition game with the Phillies in March 1961. He started the exhibition schedule pitching twenty-four scoreless innings, but ultimately suffered through the worst season of his career, with a record of 1–10 for a team that at one point lost a modern Major League record 23 games in a row. Author's collection.

FIG. 33. After his release by the Phillies in 1960, Curt Simmons revitalized his career with the St. Louis Cardinals, won a World Series ring in 1964, and made a habit of defeating his former team. National Baseball Hall of Fame and Museum, Cooperstown, New York.

FIG. 34. Jim Konstanty arrived by helicopter during the Whiz Kids reunion game in June 1963. Author's collection and *The Sporting News*.

FIG. 35. The last game at Connie Mack Stadium on October 1, 1970, ended with the fans literally tearing the ballpark apart. Special Collections Research Center, Temple University Libraries, Philadelphia, Pennsylvania; George D. McDowell for the *Philadelphia Evening Bulletin*.

FIG. 36. Curt Simmons at the dedication of the Egypt Memorial Park baseball diamond in his honor. The ceremony took place on the sixty-fifth anniversary of the Phillies playing against him there, which led to the team signing him to a $65,000 bonus. Photo taken by and courtesy of Joe Robinson.

12

Will They Want Their Second as Much as the First?

ON FEBRUARY 4, 1951, Stan Baumgartner wrote a piece for the *Philadelphia Inquirer* entitled, "Are They Whiz Kids or Was Kids?" He interviewed Eddie Sawyer, who resisted characterizing the Phillies as favorites to repeat in 1951 but admitted he wanted to prove his team was not a one-shot wonder. "The only fun in winning a pennant is winning another one," he told Baumgartner.[1]

Sawyer knew that the Phillies had to find pitching they had lacked the previous September, when they skidded to the finish line without Curt Simmons and his 17 wins and carried injured young pitchers Bob Miller and Bubba Church. The latter two not only had to recover from their infirmities, but they also needed to improve on their 1950 showing to make up for the continued absence of Simmons. In winning the pennant, many of the Phillies had played the best seasons of their careers and, at that, it had been barely enough.

During his interview with Baumgartner, Sawyer revealed his intention to loosen the reins in spring training, allowing wives and families at training camp. "Leaving the wives at home won the pennant for us last year," explained Sawyer. "We'll see what happens this spring."[2] In the article, Baumgartner posed the question "A year ago, the Whiz Kids were 'hungry' for World Series money. Now they have had their first piece of cake. Will they want their second as much as they did the first?"[3]

THE CITY OF CLEARWATER rolled out the red carpet for the reigning National League champs, the mayor welcoming the Phillies to spring training with a high school band and a motorcade from the train station to their hotel.[4] Contract negotiations went smoothly for the most part—it helped that Bob Carpenter had increased the payroll by a reported 30 percent.[5] Jim Konstanty signed for what was estimated at more than double his previous salary.[6]

One player who had not yet signed was Bubba Church. Upon arriving at spring training, he was informed by Eddie Sawyer that he could not don the red pinstripes without affixing his signature to a contract. Church responded that while the sides were not far apart, he thought the difference enough to merit awaiting Bob Carpenter's arrival in Florida.[7]

Eddie Sawyer almost immediately detected a change in the team's attitude. The players did not seem as energized as they had been the year before. Looking back, he observed, "I knew there was something wrong at spring training. The men went through the motions of training but they didn't put their hearts and heads into it. I couldn't overcome the complacency. . . . They went to the dog races at night or dashed around the countryside."[8] Relaxing the rules did not stoke motivation—the second helping of cake was not as enticing. A year earlier, many of the players were worried about proving themselves. Now they were successful, battle tested, and cocksure. Sawyer's attempts to counteract that attitude relied on hardline discipline as one might use in a classroom.

The previous summer, when the Phillies seemed on the verge of running away with the National League pennant, Edgar Williams had profiled Eddie Sawyer for the *Philadelphia Inquirer*. He wrote of Sawyer treating his players as individuals and rarely, if ever, raising his voice. He never called them out for mistakes and spoke about the need to relate to them.

"I learned from teaching that you get more out of young men if you're sort of a pal to them," he explained. "I try to find interests in common with the boys. When the boys know you have ideas outside of baseball that coincide with theirs, they work harder."[9]

That would have been news to a number of his players, who would likely say that Sawyer rarely spoke to them at all. There was no question he knew each of their strengths and weaknesses, and some took Sawyer's silence as confidence in them. Others regarded it at as indifference. Ed Sanicki had hit 3 home runs and a double in his seventeen Major League at bats. He returned for a brief stint at the beginning of the 1951 season, only to be sent down again to never return, and he was puzzled by his fate.

Four decades later Sanicki recalled, "Ed Sawyer was a quiet manager. Ed Sawyer never said, 'Boo.' He'd never give you any advice. I'm not bitter towards him. . . . I'd just like to face him and say, 'Why? Why didn't you let me be at bat fifty times?' Just ask him, you know, 'Skip, what the hell happened?'"[10]

BUILDING ON THE accomplishments of 1950 was to prove difficult for several reasons. Foremost was the unavailability of Curt Simmons. Then Del Ennis strained his back during an exhibition game, and it hampered him the entire season. As a result, his offensive production dropped by nearly half—and fan disenchantment aimed in his direction more than doubled.[11] Andy Seminick was not fully recovered from his ankle injury. Bob Miller's back still troubled him—and would forever so.

Nevertheless, the team opened the 1951 season winning six of its first nine games, a much better start than in 1950. The last of those contests was a Robin Roberts shutout of Brooklyn before a crowd of more than thirty thousand at Shibe Park. Del Ennis and Dick Sisler roared out of the gate, pushing the .400 mark in early May, while Ashburn, Hamner, and Jones were all playing solid baseball. The win tied the Phillies for the league lead with St. Louis, as Sawyer stuck to his 1950 lineup.[12]

But the reason for the uneasiness Eddie Sawyer felt in spring training began manifesting itself as the season got underway. Eddie Waitkus was struggling to keep his batting average above .200. Mike Goliat was struggling to stay above .100. Andy Seminick was carted off on a stretcher after being beaned by Max Lanier of the Cardinals, costing him a week and a half, and after his return his batting average dropped one hundred points.[13] The pitching was inconsistent.

By mid-May the Phillies had fallen to last place—albeit only four games out of first—following a ghastly 18–9 loss to Chicago, in which the Cubs scored all but one of their runs in the first four innings. Rookie pitcher Leo Cristante took the mound for Philadelphia and failed to record an out in his first Major League start—it would be four years before he was given another. Cristante, who had recorded an 18–5 mark for Wilmington in 1950, plus 4 wins for the Blue Rocks in the Governor's Cup Series, was strafed by the first four batters of the game, who collectively raked three doubles and a single. The rookie was pulled in favor of Bob Miller, who fared little better.[14]

Sawyer and Carpenter began making roster moves. Utility man Tommy Brown was purchased from Brooklyn in early June, the Phillies selling outfielder Dick Whitman to the Dodgers farm club at Saint Paul to make room.[15] Brown, whom Robin Roberts had retired for the final out to clinch the 1950 pennant, broke in with Brooklyn in 1944 at age sixteen and remains the youngest player to homer in a Major League game. But he never found a regular position with the Dodgers. He hit 10 home runs in a little more than a half season for the Phillies, including a grand slam against Pittsburgh on June 21 that moved Philadelphia into fourth place.[16]

Brown noticed big differences between his old and new clubhouses. "Eddie Sawyer was more like a father [figure]," he said. "I think he relied on his coaches more than himself." The atmosphere in the locker room was different as well, with much less energy than had been the case in 1950. Brown noticed. "It was a quiet clubhouse. No 'rah-rahs' or anything like that. It [didn't have] the closeness of the Dodgers."[17] The "peppery" attitude Sawyer had bragged about a year earlier was gone.

THE SAME MONTH they acquired Brown, the Phillies sent Mike Goliat to the Minors and signed another bonus baby, Ted Kazanski, a seventeen-year-old high school shortstop out of St. Ladislaus High School in Detroit. Bidding for the youngster started at around $50,000 and increased from there. Interest intensified as high school graduation approached—Kazanski could not help but notice the number of teams scouting him, said to number at least a dozen. He complained, "They've been bothering my father quite a bit."[18]

Bob Carpenter flew to Michigan to personally sign Kazanski to a bonus said to be around $80,000—enough to outbid the hometown Detroit Tigers and higher than the team's previous record amount paid to Curt Simmons. The signing took place at 3:00 a.m. in the Kazanski home, only hours after graduation exercises were complete.[19] Eddie Krajnik immediately proclaimed Kazanski "the finest baseball player signed out of Detroit in the last 10 years."[20] That was a bold statement for a Phillies scout to make, considering that both Stan Lopata and Bob Miller had been signed out of the Motor City.

Four months earlier, Bob Carpenter had shelled out a reported $50,000 for college football and baseball star Ben Tompkins, who had been a third baseman for the University of Texas baseball team, which won back-to-back College World Series. He was also the Longhorns' starting quarterback in 1950, leading Texas to a 9-2 record and contention for the National Championship.[21] Tompkins had a draft deferral as long as he was in college, which of course ended when he signed with the Phillies. Two weeks later he entered military service and served two years.[22]

Meanwhile, fellow bonus baby Tom Casagrande seemed a solid investment that summer. The impressive two-way athlete was assigned to Wilmington, as Robin Roberts and Curt Simmons had been, reflecting the high regard in which the Phillies held him. Casagrande played first base and the outfield when not pitching but was proving more successful on the mound. He celebrated the Fourth of July with a one-hitter against Sunbury, allowing only a one-out first inning single, for his 7th win in 9 decisions.[23] On July 11 he was matched against Bob Miller and the Phillies in an exhibition game and limited the defending National League champions to 2 hits in six innings. More than five thousand people witnessed the game at Wilmington, with the Phillies featuring a lineup that included Eddie Waitkus, Willie Jones, Granny Hamner, Del Ennis, and Richie Ashburn.[24]

A week later against York, Casagrande pitched no-hit ball for ten innings, striking out 11 while walking only 1 in regulation. At one point he retired twenty-three straight hitters. His no-hit effort ended when he gave up a lead-off double in the eleventh. After a walk and a fielder's choice loaded the bases, Casagrande recorded his thirteenth strikeout but then allowed a single that resulted in defeat.[25]

As July gave way to August, Casagrande was at it again, picking up his 10th win of the season with a seven-inning no-hitter against Harrisburg. The red-headed left-hander allowed 3 walks while striking out 7.[26] He followed that by defeating Lancaster, 3–1, striking out 11 and driving in 2 of Wilmington's runs with a single.[27] On August 30 he earned wins in both ends of a doubleheader, tossing a three-hitter in the seven inning opener and two innings of relief in the nightcap, after starting the game in right field.[28] And, on September 13, Casagrande pitched the clincher of the Governor's Cup, defeating Sunbury, 11–3, to complete a four-game sweep of the Interstate League playoff series.[29]

Casagrande experienced mixed success with the bat, hitting 4 home runs with a .238 batting average in eighty-five games and an excellent .367 on base percentage. He excelled as a pitcher, compiling a record of 14-7, plus 3 wins in the playoffs. His earned run average was an impressive 2.48, and he allowed just over 6 hits per nine innings.

Meanwhile, Ted Kazanski completed his first season as a pro, playing in Terre Haute. Bob Carpenter trekked to Indiana in July to witness the young shortstop in action.[30] At that point it was obvious that Kazanski's glove, deemed to be outstanding, was far ahead of his bat—his batting average was below .200, and he had recorded only 4 extra-base hits in his first 129 at bats.[31] The week of Carpenter's visit, Kazanski stroked 10 hits in 29 at bats, raising his average to .215 and driving in 7 runs in a like number of games.[32] And that's basically the level he maintained, finishing with an average of .216 in eighty-eight games. While he had not set the world afire, it was a respectable, even encouraging, debut for a seventeen-year-old playing in Class B. New York Giants scout Tom Sheehan called Kazanski one of the best young infielders in the Minor Leagues.[33]

IN LATE JULY, with rumors swirling about dissension in the ranks, Eddie Sawyer dusted off his edicts of August 1949 and again cracked the whip. He banned card playing, employed a rigid curfew both at home and on the road, and declared that a new season had begun.[34] The team seemed to respond, winning seven of eight games, including an exhilarating doubleheader sweep of Boston, capped by Dick Sisler's fifteenth inning walk-off single in the nightcap off Warren Spahn. Russ Meyer and Johnny Sain began the game pitching ten innings of shutout ball against each other, with Ken Heintzelman and Spahn dueling after that.[35]

On August 11 Robin Roberts shut out the New York Giants at the Polo Grounds for his 16th win of the season. Eddie Sawyer continued sticking to his Whiz Kids lineup with the exception of second base, where Putsy Caballero—who hit his first and only Major League home run that day—was stationed in place of Mike Goliat. The win moved the Phillies within a game of second-place New York, albeit fourteen games behind Brooklyn. The Giants had returned home to face the Phillies after being swept in a three-game series by the Dodgers at Ebbets Field, and second place seemed Philadelphia's for the taking. Stan Baumgartner wrote that the Giants seemed apathetic, observing, "Leo Durocher's men walked back and forth from the field as if they had finished the season in Brooklyn Thursday night. They had no pep, no life and for the most part swung their bats as if they were merely trying to prevent striking out."[36] It seemed no one would catch the Dodgers in 1951, especially the Giants.

The fates of the Phillies and Giants quickly careened in opposite directions. New York revived its pennant hopes with a sixteen-game winning streak after the loss to Roberts, six of those at Philadelphia's expense. Conversely, after Roberts threw his shutout, Eddie Sawyer's men dropped eight straight. Rumors flew.

The Phillies were said to be dissatisfied with Jim Konstanty, who was trying to throw the ball past hitters rather than relying on his ability to mix a variety of off-speed pitches. Phillies coaches were reportedly casting blame on Andy Skinner. Coach Benny Bengough had reportedly become so angry with Konstanty that he scoffed, "I could catch that guy barehanded." Although Bob Carpenter issued strong denials, it was reported that Konstanty was on the trading block.[37]

Philadelphia sank to fifth place by Labor Day, twenty games behind Brooklyn. After hitting leadoff all season, in September Eddie Waitkus was dropped to sixth and then seventh in the batting order. Mike Goliat was recalled from Baltimore and then waived to the St. Louis Browns.[38] There was no more talk about repeating.

The Phillies did play a role in the outcome of the 1951 pennant race, for the third-consecutive season ending the year by playing vitally important games against Brooklyn, which had seen its thirteen-game lead over the New York Giants melt away during the season's final weeks.[39] After splitting the first two games of the series marking the end of the regular season, the Dodgers and Giants were tied for first, and the Phillies were playing Brooklyn with the National League pennant hanging in the balance.

Philadelphia jumped out to a 6–1 lead behind Bubba Church, but the Dodgers fought back, keeping an eye on the scoreboard as New York took on the Boston Braves. A Dodgers win coupled with a Giants loss would clinch the pennant for Brooklyn. An opposite pair of results would clinch for the Giants. Matching outcomes would force a best-of-three playoff.

As Carl Erskine warmed up for the bottom of the seventh, the metal panels on the scoreboard clicked into place, breaking the news that New York had defeated Boston, 3–2.

Jolted by the realization that a loss would end their season, the Dodgers tied the game in the eighth inning with a three-run rally, keyed by Rube Walker's two-run double and Carl Furillo's single. The game moved into extra innings, tied 8–8, with Don Newcombe and Robin Roberts facing each other in relief.

After neither team scored in the tenth, Andy Pafko made a great running catch in the eleventh to save extra bases, and possibly the game, on Andy Seminick's liner with a runner on first. In the twelfth, the Phillies loaded the bases with one out. After Del Ennis struck out, Eddie Waitkus hit a line shot near second base. Jackie Robinson threw himself at the ball and snagged it no more than two inches off the ground. He then rolled over, and the ball trickled toward the bag as the umpire ruled the ball as having been caught for the third out. Robinson, the wind knocked out of him, remained on the ground for a couple of minutes, gathering his senses. The Phillies felt Robinson had trapped the ball, but that opinion did not matter.

Newcombe weakened in the thirteenth inning, walking two batters after retiring the first two. He was replaced by Bud Podbielan, who retired Eddie Pellagrini on a routine fly ball to end Philadelphia's threat.

Jackie Robinson, the hero of the twelfth inning, then became the hero of the fourteenth with a home run off Robin Roberts into the left-field seats, giving Brooklyn a 9–8 lead. Bud Podbielan retired the Phillies in the bottom of the fourteenth, concluding another epic battle between the teams, this one taking four-and-a-half hours to play and years off the lives of those with a rooting interest.[40]

The joy in Flatbush was temporary. With the dramatic win, the Dodgers finished the regular season tied with New York, forcing a playoff with the Giants that resulted in a lifetime supply of heartbreak for Brooklyn baseball fans.[41]

THE 1951 PHILLIES ended the year in fifth place, with an extremely disappointing 73-81 record. Philadelphia was 24-29 in one-run games, versus a 30-16 record in 1950. After breaking even with Brooklyn in 1950, the Phillies dropped 15 of 22 to the Dodgers in 1951.

Jim Konstanty had not been anywhere near the force as during his MVP season, declining from a record of 16-7 with 22 saves and an earned run average of 2.66 to a mark of 4-11 with only 9 saves and a 4.05 ERA. Andy Seminick's batting average fell to .227. Putsy Caballero batted .186 in eighty-four games as Mike Goliat's replacement. Del Ennis hit just 15 home runs, only 2 after August 2. Eddie Waitkus's batting average dropped twenty-seven points, and his defensive performance fell off as well. Dick Sisler, while hitting a solid .287, went from 83 runs batted in to only 52.

Financially, it was a down year as well. Attendance declined by 280,000, and the Phillies lost $250,000. The club-owned farm teams struggled financially, adding to the strain on the parent club. Wilmington's attendance was one-third what it had been four years earlier. Terre Haute was down 40 percent over the same period, even with a pennant-winning team. Bradford's attendance had dropped nearly two-thirds. Overall attendance for Minor League baseball had declined by 33 percent over the previous two years.[42] None of this was helping the Phillies' bottom line.

After collectively turning a small profit in 1947, when Minor League baseball was in the midst of boom times, Phillies farm teams had lost money every year. By 1951 the red ink totaled $250,000. More than $300,000 was spent supporting Wilmington in 1950 and 1951. Utica had already been shuttered after that franchise was propped up with nearly $90,000 in 1950.[43]

Bob Carpenter put the Class D Bradford farm club up for sale. Joe Reardon announced the Phillies were hoping to find someone to purchase the team "at a price around $5,000 or $6,000," but likely failed to generate enthusiasm among potential buyers by revealing $130,000 had been pumped into the franchise since its acquisition seven years earlier.[44] The team's operating loss exceeded $90,000 during that time frame, with attendance during the 1950 and 1951 seasons running at roughly 50 percent of what it had been before the Phillies purchase.[45] At one point, Bob Carpenter had built a farm system that included ownership of five Minor League franchises. Now only Terre Haute and Wilmington remained under direct control, and the latter had drawn only two-thirds the number of ticketholders that had signed pledges meant to address Carpenter's threat to move the franchise.[46]

ON OCTOBER 30, 1951, a beaming Eddie Sawyer signed a three-year contract to manage the Philadelphia Phillies, the longest such agreement in team history. Bob Carpenter was determined to send a message, giving Sawyer the time-honored, and historically foreboding, vote of confidence.

Carpenter was direct, stating, "I signed him for three years, to show my confidence in his ability as a manager and to put to end all rumors that have been circulating since midseason."[47]

Sawyer then publicly put the Phillies on notice, with only Richie Ashburn and Robin Roberts granted safe haven. He declared Andy Seminick as "very bad" in 1951, dismissed Bubba Church's 15 wins, calling him a "spot pitcher," and announced the Phillies were open to trading Del Ennis. "As a whole . . . our club was spoiled," said Sawyer. "Some of the players got too much money; others believed the fancy things they read about themselves in the papers. They were still living in the honeymoon atmosphere of the World Series. They bought new cars and new homes, and rested on their laurels.

"Next year it will be different. They will have to get down to earth—or go down to Baltimore [the Phils' farm affiliate]. I believe a lot of them will be cut in salary, but that is [Bob Carpenter's] business, not mine."[48]

Bent on fostering competition as he had in 1949 and 1950, Sawyer announced his intention to invite several prospects to training camp in 1952. Among those deemed worthy of a spring look-see were Minor League out-fielders Danny Schell and Jim Command, pitchers Jack Sanford and Jake Schmitt, and Ted Kazanski.[49] All but Schmitt would eventually appear in the Majors, although only Sanford would do so with any real success. None of them played for the Phillies that year.

Sawyer followed through with his plan to reinstitute the bans he felt had served the club well in 1950 and that had been revived during the last two months of 1951. There was to be no card playing, swimming, joyriding, or late hours. And no wives—including his own—during training camp or on road trips.[50] He also made good on his promise to shake up the team, trading Andy Seminick and Dick Sisler to Cincinnati. Second baseman Connie Ryan, who it was hoped would finally plug the hole in the middle of the Phillies infield, was acquired in the deal, along with catcher Smoky Burgess and pitcher Howie Fox.[51] In late March Ken Johnson was sold to the Detroit Tigers.[52] Camaraderie was shattered. Del Ennis said, "Everybody was gripin'."[53]

Sawyer was certain the return of Curt Simmons was the answer in 1952, but it was not yet clear when he would be discharged. Rumors swirled during training camp placing his return anywhere from April to June. "If I could tell about Simmons, I could tell you about our pennant chances," said Sawyer. "We have heard Curt might get out by June 15. If he does, he probably would need about three weeks to get ready. That would make him available by July 4."[54]

Jim Konstanty was determined to get back on track, admitting that he had changed his tactics from his MVP season. After reviewing film with Andy Skinner he realized, "Somehow, I'd got myself all out of balance. Trying to throw hard."[55] Referring to his previous success, Konstanty admitted, "I think I 'experimented' myself out of it. Now I want to experiment myself back into it."[56]

The Phillies' manager asked Bob Carpenter to address Eddie Waitkus's "clowning" during exhibition games.[57] This was about the same time Waitkus learned that Ruth Ann Steinhagen was to be released from Kankakee State Hospital—she was freed a couple of weeks into the season, which understandably caused major concern on the ballplayer's part. Wanting the matter over with, Waitkus decided against pressing charges now that his assailant had been declared sane.[58]

Sawyer resorted to an old tactic to motivate Waitkus, declaring newly acquired Nippy Jones as the man to beat for the first base job.[59] The former Cardinals first baseman, acquired during the winter in the Rule 5 draft, had not been the same since undergoing disc surgery on his neck after the 1949 season. Jones ultimately appeared in only eight games for the Phillies, spending most of the year in the Minors, while Waitkus played in 146 games, rebounding with a season statistically similar to his 1950 campaign.[60]

During training camp, Sawyer levied his first fine as Phillies manager, docking Willie Jones $200 for "conduct detrimental to the welfare of the ball club." Conventional wisdom was that Jones had violated curfew.[61]

"Players came and went as they pleased last year and a few of them thought they could get away with it this year," said an obviously annoyed Sawyer. "They're not going to get away with it, now or at any other time during the season, especially when we're on the road and living in hotels."[62]

Sawyer also punished Steve Ridzik for missing curfew, ordering him to pitch batting practice the next day until he told him to stop.[63] Ridzik responded late in spring training with a nine-inning complete-game no-hitter in Savannah against the St. Louis Cardinals.[64]

One encouraging development that spring was the physical condition of Del Ennis, who was determined to rebound from a poor season caused in part by a strained muscle in his back. He reported in excellent shape, arriving early to Clearwater some ten pounds lighter than he had the previous spring. Ennis explained, "You've got to do something when you have a year like I did."[65]

Near the end of camp, Curt Simmons received word he would be discharged by early April.[66] The Phillies were nearly as ecstatic about the news as their pitcher. Simmons was photographed warming up at Shibe Park prior to the City Series opener against the Athletics, and the team celebrated his imminent return with a convincing 6–0 win.[67]

As Opening Day approached, Eddie Sawyer rewarded Granny Hamner for the example he set, naming him team captain, the first time in his career Sawyer had ever designated a player as such.[68] On the other hand, Bubba Church landed in Sawyer's doghouse for being out of shape during training camp, a year after staging a brief holdout. Sawyer pitched him only twice before shipping him to Cincinnati near the end of May.[69] The transaction was painful for Church. "It was like being outcast from your family," he said.[70]

Ernie Harwell penned a nationally syndicated series, profiling each Major League manager for the coming season and defined Sawyer as "a well upholstered, balding baseball manager." He also labeled Sawyer "one of the best handlers of men in baseball."[71]

BOB CARPENTER'S TWO newest bonus babies continued their progression through the organization in 1952. Eighteen-year-old Ted Kazanski spent most of spring training with the Baltimore Orioles of the AAA International League.[72] He was impressive enough to open the season in Baltimore, and he hit a game-winning sacrifice fly in his second game, against Toronto, before adding back-to-back two-hit games later in the week against Rochester.[73] At the end of April, after hitting a respectable .257 in twelve games but making an uncharacteristic 5 errors, Kazanski was sent to Class-A Schenectady, a not totally unexpected development with the Phillies wary of rushing the teenage prospect.[74]

Tom Casagrande also opened the year with Baltimore but jumped the team during the first week of the season, complaining about not having been signed to a Phillies contract.[75] Following a tense telephone conversation with Bob Carpenter, during which Casagrande was reportedly told no additional money was forthcoming, he returned to the Orioles.[76]

After making a start against Montreal and suffering through a pounding of 8 hits and 7 runs in three and one-third innings, Casagrande was also sent to Schenectady, where he spent the rest of season.[77] Soon after his arrival, he posed for a photo with fellow bonus babies Ted Kazanski and Stan Hollmig, who were now his teammates. The caption noted that the three were said to collectively represent a Phillies investment of $165,000.[78]

DEL ENNIS STARTED 1952 showing he meant to make up for 1951. In the second game of the season, he exhibited his renewed physical fitness, chasing a Willie Mays fly ball deep into the gap at the Polo Grounds. Stumbling as he went to make the catch, he reached out and speared the ball bare-handed for a dramatic out.[79] Ennis also hit a tenth-inning walk-off triple in the first game of a doubleheader against the Braves, one of only two wins the Phillies collected in their first eight contests.[80] He closed out April with 7 runs batted in over three games and then homered twice on May 6 to back Robin Roberts' two-hit shutout of Pittsburgh.[81]

Curt Simmons made his first Major League appearance in eighteen months on April 29, a complete-game victory over the Chicago Cubs at Wrigley Field.[82] After being knocked out of the box in Cincinnati, he was given extra rest and made a triumphant return to Shibe Park, throwing back-to-back shutouts—the first a two-hitter against the Cubs, highlighted by fanning 12, including striking out the side in the ninth.[83] Again given extra rest, Simmons followed that with a three-hit shutout against woeful Pittsburgh—which entered the game with a 5-27 record—aiding his cause with a three-run inside-the-park home run, the only round-tripper he ever hit in the Major Leagues. The victory moved the Phillies within a game of the .500 mark, and Simmons moved into the regular rotation.[84]

Simmons continued to pitch well, picking up as if he had never left. Yet, even with Simmons's comeback, and what would develop into a historic season from Robin Roberts, Eddie Sawyer's disciplinarian strategy to motivate his team did not produce results in the standings. At the end of May the Phillies had a record of 17-20 and sat in fifth place.

Sawyer held a clubhouse meeting prior to a doubleheader against Pittsburgh. After scolding his players, he announced a shake-up of the coaching staff, naming Ken Silvestri as a player-coach and designating Cy Perkins as liaison to the players regarding any complaints they had.[85] The players continued grousing, and Bob Carpenter met with the team during a road trip in St. Louis, around the same time Sawyer, possibly feeling some pressure from the owner regarding the team's performance, revoked Granny Hamner's captaincy. "I feel the team would be better off if I handled all the duties," he explained.[86] At that point, Simmons and Roberts had a combined record of 11-4, while the rest of the pitching staff had won 7 and lost 19. Rumors surfaced that the Boston Braves wanted Hamner and were willing to part with Warren Spahn but that Sawyer was reluctant to surrender an everyday player for a pitcher.[87]

At the end of the road trip, during which Philadelphia dropped ten of twelve, Carpenter complained, "You look at the Phillies today, and they remind you of a fighter flat on his back in the ring. You don't know whether he's going to get up!"[88]

On June 27, only minutes after Curt Simmons had thrown a three-hit shutout against the Giants to "improve" fifth-place Philadelphia's record to 28-35, Bob Carpenter called reporters to his office for a press conference. He announced the resignation of Sawyer and the hiring of Steve O'Neill, a veteran of three previous managerial assignments who was nearly two decades older than the man he was replacing.[89]

Sawyer, who Carpenter said would remain with the organization on special assignment to review the farm systems of other teams, then joined the press conference and told reporters, "I resigned for the best interests of the club. We felt the team should have done better and we just had to do something about it. Perhaps I will be of more value in my new job."[90]

At that point, Robin Roberts was not particularly upset to see Sawyer go. "When Bob Carpenter fired Eddie . . . and replaced him with Steve O'Neill, I was pretty noncommittal about the whole thing. We were not playing very well for the second consecutive season and it was fairly obvious that Eddie was not getting along particularly well with Carpenter, so it was not much of a surprise to me when it happened."[91]

Richie Ashburn had a different take: "Sawyer was a hands-off manager for the most part. . . . I think Robin in the beginning would have liked to have seen more reaction out of Eddie Sawyer. Well, Eddie Sawyer didn't miss anything. If he thought something ought to be talked about he would talk about it. He didn't bother the people that played hard. He never said a word to those guys because he didn't think he had to."[92]

Eddie Sawyer's new contract had been for three seasons. He lasted less than three months. It was a rough ending for yet another Phillies manager and doubly painful in this case because of the success Sawyer had so recently enjoyed. He had been an outstanding manager with a reputation for getting the most from his roster. But in the end, he had, as they say, "lost the clubhouse," while being equally lost in how to get it back. Eddie Sawyer had discovered it much more complicated to manage men than it had been to manage boys.

13

From Contender to Afterthought

AS 1952 THREATENED to become a lost season, a bright spot for the Phillies organization was hosting the nineteenth Major League All-Star Game at Shibe Park on July 8. Theirs was the only franchise never to have hosted the star-studded exhibition—Bob Carpenter had stepped aside so the 1951 edition could be played in Detroit to coincide with that city's 250th anniversary celebration.[1] But Philadelphia's delayed turn was impacted by inclement weather, which forced cancellation of both batting and infield practice.[2]

Curt Simmons, who had won 7 games to that point, 4 by shutout, was named starting pitcher by National League manager Leo Durocher. He pitched the first three innings, allowing only one hit—a Dom DiMaggio double—while striking out three.[3] Philadelphia baseball fans were afforded an additional rooting interest when Bobby Shantz of the Athletics struck out the side in the bottom of the fifth for the American League, at which point the game was called due to rain and poor field conditions, entered into the books as a 3–2 National League victory.[4]

The Phillies continued to be well-represented at All-Star Games during the first half of the 1950s, having boasted four All-Stars in 1951—with Richie Ashburn, Del Ennis, and Robin Roberts in the starting lineup—and the same number in 1953.[5] The team landed three representatives in 1952, 1954, and 1955. Roberts, in the midst of six straight years pitching at least 300 innings, served as the National League's All-Star Game starting pitcher five times between 1950 and 1955. The only year he did not start, Curt Simmons did. And Simmons did so again in 1957, stretching the Phillies run of All-Star Game starting pitchers to seven in eight years.[6] Even when not winning, the Whiz Kids remained popular.

Following Eddie Sawyer's resignation, the Phillies played extremely well for Steve O'Neill, an easy-going veteran who had won the World Series both as a player, with Cleveland in 1920, and as a manager, with Detroit in 1945. O'Neill's most recent engagement had been with the American League Boston Red Sox, which finished third in 1951. O'Neill was well-respected and had never suffered a losing season during his eleven years in the dugout while guiding the fortunes of ballplayers representing Cleveland, Detroit, and Boston. To Bob Carpenter's delight, Philadelphia won 59 and lost only 32 after O'Neill was hired, rallying to finish in fourth place.

Robin Roberts played a major role in Philadelphia's second-half surge with an incredible season, winning 28 games—ten more than any other National League pitcher that year, and the most in the Senior Circuit since Dizzy Dean captured the same number in 1935. Roberts tossed complete-game wins in fifteen of his final sixteen starts in 1952, including a seventeen-inning marathon to defeat Boston. Another plus for the Phillies was the performance of Curt Simmons. Despite missing spring training, the left-hander won 14 games and led the Major Leagues with 6 shutouts.

The team's success down the stretch raised expectations for the coming year, which were reinforced when the team began the 1953 season with a 9-2 record. The twenty-six-year-old Roberts, gunning for his fourth-consecutive 20-win season, roared out of the gate along with Simmons, rekindling memories of the magical Whiz Kids. By late June, Roberts had a record of 12-4 with a 2.16 earned run average; he ultimately completed his first 20 starts. Going back to the previous August, he strung together 28 consecutive complete games—according to the National Baseball Hall of Fame, it remains the longest such streak since 1920, the end of the Dead Ball Era.[7] Roberts reached the 20-win mark on August 12, a week earlier than he had in 1952.

Embarking on his sixth Major League campaign despite being only twenty-four years of age, Curt Simmons was, if anything, better than Roberts at the beginning of 1953, winning 6 of his first 7 decisions with a 1.42 ERA. His sixth victory was likely the best performance of his career, a one-hitter against the Milwaukee Braves. After yielding a single to Bill Bruton on the first pitch of the game, Simmons did not allow another baserunner, retiring twenty-seven straight, ten by strikeout.[8] The win moved the Phillies ahead of the Braves and into first place with a record of 16-7, but they played only slightly better than break-even the rest of the way.

Simmons was sidelined for a month after injuring himself while mowing his lawn, running over and cutting the toes of his left foot.[9] He quipped, "Fortunately, I had my old Army boots on. I lost about half-an-inch of my big toe, but it truly didn't bother me that much."[10] Despite the injury, Simmons won 16 games. Robin Roberts won 23, his fourth straight 20-win season. Granny Hamner, switching to second base midyear, was outstanding and drove in 92 runs, second on the team only to Del Ennis, who plated 125 runners. Richie Ashburn hit .330.

Even with those solid Whiz Kid performances, the Phillies did not win, or come close to doing so, in 1953, their 83-71 record leaving them twenty-two games behind pennant-winning Brooklyn. What's more, by the end of the season Steve O'Neill was confronting player dissension.

Eddie Waitkus had been upset all year, beginning with Philadelphia's trade for Earl Torgeson. The Boston first baseman was acquired in a deal for Russ Meyer, with Meyer subsequently shipped by the Braves to Brooklyn.[11] The arrival of Torgeson reduced Waitkus' role to that of pinch-hitter for the first two months of 1953. After temporarily reclaiming his starting role in late June when Torgeson injured his ankle, Waitkus played well, his batting average peaking near .350 before settling in the .290s.[12] But by mid-September he was back on the bench and not only unhappy but also drinking heavily—Carol Waitkus felt her husband was using alcohol to self-medicate.[13]

A rumor surfaced that Waitkus was going to be traded to the Chicago Cubs for shortstop Roy Smalley, an announcement that had to have given him pause, considering Ruth Ann Steinhagen's freedom.[14] Waitkus had previously confided to Russ Meyer that he feared for his safety and was aware that during Steinhagen's time under psychiatric care she had sworn to kill the first baseman if he ever married.[15]

Two days after the Cubs rumor was published, Waitkus jumped the club and headed home, claiming his father had suffered a heart attack. But there were serious questions about the severity of his father's illness. Bob Carpenter phoned Waitkus, and the two carried out a heated exchange, concluding with the Phillies owner suspending the popular first baseman without pay, effective the day he left the team.[16]

At the same time Waitkus was being suspended, Jim Konstanty went public with a complaint. The thirty-six-year-old had been productive in 1953—if somewhat inconsistent. By the end of August he had won 14 games while being utilized as both a starter and reliever. But once the pennant was out of reach, Steve O'Neill stopped using him—Konstanty took the mound only five times in September, pitching a total of five and two-thirds innings.

The veteran right-hander vented to reporters. "I went to Steve about it and he gave me two or three answers. I told him I thought I should have worked more; that my arm was okay. He told me that even if a fellow had a rubber arm he wouldn't work him too often and that he felt he should give others a chance. With the club fighting for third and extra money that seems like a strange answer.

"So I said to him, 'I guess I'm not your kind of pitcher then. So I will be happy to be traded.'"

Konstanty claimed O'Neill's response was, "We'll trade you if we can but we aren't going to give you away."[17]

Both discontented players reported for spring training the next March. Attempting to make amends, Waitkus admitted being wrong in leaving the team and wrote a letter of apology to Carpenter. It did not help.[18] Despite his incredible popularity among Phillies fans, Waitkus was sold to the Baltimore Orioles—the former St. Louis Browns beginning their first season in a new locale—for $40,000. That same day, Baltimore's other first baseman, Dick Kryhoski, suffered a broken wrist. Waitkus, who admitted "sitting on the bench last season drove me crazy," was handed the Orioles starting job by default.[19]

Konstanty survived spring training but was also on his way out. In late August 1954, he was sold to the New York Yankees for $20,000. A day earlier he had confided to Stan Baumgartner that his days with the Phillies were over. He told the reporter, "I hope some club thinks enough of me to give me a chance."[20]

THE PHILLIES FARM SYSTEM hit a lull in the early 1950s—no major contributors were uncovered during the entire first half of the decade. The new crop of bonus babies did not pan out as hoped. On top of that, owners alarmed by rapidly escalating payments to teenage novices revived the bonus rule with a new twist—any player signed to a bonus greater than $4,000 had to be placed immediately on the Major League roster and remain there for two years. Then they became eligible for assignment to the Minor Leagues, although only for one year, at which point the player had to return to the parent club or be subject to waivers.[21]

That did not deter Bob Carpenter from opening his wallet, or attempting to. The Phillies were said to be among the finalists to land high school first baseman Frank Leja, who was reportedly seeking $90,000 to sign.[22] He ended up with the New York Yankees.

Ben Tompkins, the $50,000 bonus baby of 1951, returned from two years military service to play infield at Terre Haute in 1953, where he hit .316 with 15 home runs. But he was less successful against higher competition and never reached the Majors during a playing career that ended after the 1959 season. He later became an attorney in Texas and an official in the National Football League, serving two decades as a back judge and working two Super Bowls.

The Phillies did close a high-profile deal. Subject to the new bonus rule, they signed eighteen-year-old pitcher Tom Qualters out of McKeesport High School, near Pittsburgh, to an amount said to exceed $40,000, which he asked to have spread out over eight years. That led some to speculate that the price tag may have been as much as $80,000.[23] Qualters ultimately became a prime example of the damage the bonus rule too often inflicted on young players. He appeared in only one regular season game for the Phillies in two years, pitching exactly one-third of an inning. Outside of spring training or the odd exhibition, Qualters remained rooted to the bench, while his teammates branded him with the unflattering nickname "Moneybags." As his two-year stint in baseball purgatory neared its end in June 1955, Qualters eagerly awaited his next assignment by the Phillies. "I don't know where they're going to send me, and I don't care," he said. "I just want to pitch in games—somewhere—anywhere."[24]

Following a stint in the minors, Qualters pitched for the Phillies and Chicago White Sox in 1957 and 1958 but did not record a decision either year. By the time he was twenty-seven, his baseball career was over, and he began a long stint as an enforcement officer for the Pennsylvania Fish and Boat Commission and as its southwest regional manager.

Meanwhile, Tom Casagrande won 27 games over two seasons with Schenectady, but it seemed that the Phillies never had the same regard for him following his Baltimore walkout. After spending 1954 spring training with Philadelphia, Casagrande was sent on option to the Boston Red Sox Triple A affiliate in Louisville.[25] After winning 6 of 8 decisions for the Colonels and then starting the 1955 season with Syracuse, Casagrande was again optioned to Louisville.[26] The Colonels had him fill in at first base following a rough stretch on the mound, and he slammed a pair of home runs, generating debate as to his future.

A pained Casagrande protested, "I'd rather pitch. . . . I entered professional baseball with two strikes on me." He explained, "I was the big bonus kid. . . . That was a big enough burden to carry. On top of that, they called me the 'new Babe Ruth.' . . . It was a horrible experience and too much pressure for a kid. I began making a lot of errors. They got on me more.

"Then my hitting began to suffer. I got down on myself. I had taken all I could from the fans. . . . I really took a beating. I'd rather pitch."[27]

Casagrande pitched mostly relief in 1955, with little success, while hitting .333 in a limited offensive role. He was billed as "the pinch-hitting pitcher." Assigned again to Louisville in 1956, he pitched relief and also played outfield and first base but struggled in all areas.[28] After a brief stint with Tulsa in 1957, Casagrande was out of organized baseball, pitching for a semipro team in Connecticut and operating a sporting-goods store.[29]

Even though he never played in the Majors, Tom Casagrande did receive a Major League baseball card, in the 1955 Topps set, one of three players depicted that year who never reached the big leagues.[30] Casagrande eventually settled in Guilford, Connecticut, and worked as a conductor for Amtrak, where he was employed for thirty years. He passed away in 2016.[31]

The team's most expensive bonus baby, Ted Kazanski, continued rising through the ranks. After starting the 1953 season in the International League, the nineteen-year-old was recalled by Philadelphia in late June. Eager to see a return on their unprecedented investment, Steve O'Neill benched Connie Ryan and moved Granny Hamner to second base, installing Kazanski—who was already being billed as a great defensive player—at shortstop.[32]

The Phillies were in fourth place at the time, and Kazanski made a spectacular debut, driving in 4 runs with a single and a pair of doubles in a 13–2 rout of the Chicago Cubs at Wrigley Field. He participated in two double plays and made a nice running catch in short center field.[33] Dizzy Dean, broadcasting the game, was impressed and compared Kazanski to Marty Marion.[34]

Interest was intense as Kazanski arrived in Philadelphia on June 29 for the City Series benefit game versus the Athletics. The Phillies expected a big crowd, with Tom Qualters pitching and Kazanski playing shortstop. The event was preceded by a two-hour show featuring singer Teresa Brewer and various skill contests for youngsters, including the opportunity to swing a bat against Robin Roberts and Bobby Shantz.[35]

Qualters was hit hard by the Athletics, but Kazanski played well, collecting 2 hits.[36] He made his official home debut on July 3 against the New York Giants; by that point, his offense was coming back to earth. After hitting .321 with 7 runs batted in during his first six games, Kazanski collected 1 hit in his next 21 at bats, and his average fell to the low .200s. He played off and on with the Phillies through the 1958 season, and another six years in the Minors after that. But he appeared in his last Major League game at age twenty-four and retired with a lifetime batting average of .217.

SIX YEARS AFTER the death of Herb Pennock, Bob Carpenter, perhaps weary of constant battles with his players, relinquished day-to-day command of the Phillies, naming Roy Hamey as the team's first general manager since The Squire. Hamey had risen through the ranks in the Minor Leagues, primarily in the Yankees organization, before being hired as general manager of the Pittsburgh Pirates in 1947. He remained there until Branch Rickey took his place following Rickey's departure from Brooklyn in October 1950. At that point, Hamey returned to the Yankees, where he served as the top assistant to general manager George Weiss.

None too pleased with the roster he had inherited, Hamey vowed to make changes. While continuing to shell out large bonuses to high school players, hoping to land the next Roberts or Simmons, the Phillies had ignored the cheapest route to acquiring already developed talent. Hamey ordered the team's scouts to scour the Negro Leagues—much of which had already been picked clean by other teams.[37] At that point the Phillies were the only National League franchise never to have had a Black player on its Major League roster.

A month into his tenure, Hamey weathered the team's first controversy— one he had not instigated. It involved Granny Hamner, who contacted police after he saw a car that had tailgated him parked outside his house. Police arrested the man, a private detective hired by Bob Carpenter to follow Phillies players in their off-hours.[38] Carpenter apologized, claiming that the investigator had followed the wrong player. Stan Lopata was most puzzled by the fact that the Phillies owner was having his players tailed in Philadelphia versus on the road. "Then," noted Lopata, "he got a detective that was supposed to be following Willie Jones, and he followed Granny Hamner."[39] Hamner remained skeptical about the misidentification.

THE PHILLIES DID NOT win, or contend, in 1954. Or 1955. Or 1956. Steve O'Neill was not the answer. Neither was Terry Moore. Or Mayo Smith.

Robin Roberts was widely considered the best right-hander in the National League, if not in all of baseball. He was in his prime, throwing a pair of one-hitters within two weeks in early 1954.[40] Two years later Roberts made the cover of *Time* magazine, depicted in a stylistic painting produced from two weeks of posing for artist Henry Koerner. The feature article crowned him the game's best pitcher.[41] Unfortunately, Roberts' string of consecutive 20-win campaigns ended at six when he lost on the last day of the 1956 season to end the year with a 19-18 record.[42] Instead of extending his record of success, Roberts led the National League in losses. But he remained a formidable pitcher.

Richie Ashburn had won a pair of batting titles and regularly hit .330 or better while setting defensive records in center field that remain intact.[43] Del Ennis drove in 100 or more runs four straight years. Granny Hamner and Willie Jones were one of the best left-side infield combinations in baseball. But the Philadelphia Phillies were unable to recapture the magic of their pennant-winning season. It was the Brooklyn Dodgers that won pennants and became famously remembered as "The Boys of Summer" during the 1950s. The Phillies became known as ordinary at best—or more often as an afterthought.

Jackie Mayo remembered Bob Carpenter telling him, "You don't want to go anywhere. We're going to have a *looong* time when we have a great team."[44] Looking back, Robin Roberts had trouble comprehending the suddenness at which the magic had disappeared, sighing, "I mean, you couldn't believe how we'd gone from a real organized group that was making it work to all of a sudden we were just ordinary again. It was a real disappointment."[45]

Phillies players were often quizzed about the team's failure to contend post-1950. In March 1955, *Sport* magazine carried an article by Ed Linn in which he provided an autopsy of sorts on the Whiz Kids. He asked several players, anonymously, their opinion about what had happened. Under that cloak of anonymity, one player insisted, "The trouble was that we had a bunch of young kids from small towns, and everything came too quick and went to their heads. Sawyer was a good manager, but he was too nice a guy to handle them the way they should have been handled." The player added, "I figured I was on a real contender for five years, and instead we dropped right out of it. It has been the biggest disappointment of my life."[46]

Ed Linn quoted Eddie Sawyer as saying the team had won too early. But another player, who had been traded away, labeled the Whiz Kids moniker as so much hype, pointing to the number of veterans on the team. Arguing that Sawyer had developed most of the young talent on the roster, the player added, "Then he took a chance on a 32-year-old relief pitcher, made an outfielder out of Sisler, squeezed that one good year out of a half-a-dozen guys, and stole a pennant. He had imagination, that Sawyer. How they let him get out of baseball, I'll never know."[47]

SEEKING A STRONGER hand after employing a series of players' managers, Bob Carpenter sacked Steve O'Neill following the 1954 All-Star Game, with the team's record at 40-37. The timing of the dismissal left intact, barely, O'Neill's unblemished mark as a Major League manager without a losing season. Phillies scout and former St. Louis Cardinals outfielder Terry Moore became the new Phillies skipper, said to be hired on an interim basis.

Several weeks later, Moore held a meeting and told the players that he had let them think he was an interim manager in order to see who would go all out—and who would not—if they thought he was a placeholder. Moore then announced a series of fines should curfew be violated.

After Moore went public with the message he had delivered to the players, Granny Hamner exploded, branding Moore's stunt ridiculous. With the surveillance incident undoubtedly fresh in his mind, Hamner barked, "One of these days, the Philadelphia front office will grow up and stop treating us like high school kids."[48]

Robin Roberts, serving as the team's player representative, issued a statement on behalf of the other players, indicating that Hamner's comments were his own and did not reflect the opinions of his teammates. There was conjecture that Roberts had been pressured to issue the statement.[49]

A Phillies tradition, rivals at odds shaking hands for the benefit of photographers—this time featuring Moore and Hamner—was published. It was declared that Hamner had apologized, and Moore announced the rescinding of a fine he had imposed on the shortstop.[50]

But Roy Hamey punctured the bubble of manufactured harmony, grumbling, "I have reports that some of our players have remarked, 'We got rid of Sawyer and O'Neill and now we'll get rid of this guy.'"[51]

The attempt to heal the rift between Moore and the players failed. Whether, as Roy Hamey had alleged, they schemed to get rid of managers no longer mattered. Terry Moore had lost their respect and could not recover it. Ultimately, his tenure was indeed temporary.[52] And more changes were coming.

In November 1954 Joe Reardon resigned after eleven years in charge of the team's Minor League system.[53] Cy Perkins was let go a couple of weeks later, a move that distressed Robin Roberts so much that he called on Bob Carpenter personally and offered to pay Perkins's salary out of his own pocket. The gesture was declined.[54]

WHILE THE PHILLIES were experiencing a mild case of chaos, the Macks were out of money. With Connie Sr. frail of body and mind, Earle Mack and his brother Roy feuded while vainly trying to hold on. There was much back and forth after the 1954 season, the uncertainty increasingly irritating the other American League owners, who thought a deal had been struck with Chicago businessman Arnold Johnson, who planned to move the franchise to Kansas City, as it was clear if the team remained in the Macks' control it was headed for bankruptcy before reaching 1955.

Then came some serious last-minute drama involving a potential rescue by a group of Philadelphia investors who obtained the signatures of Connie, Earle, and Roy on a deal to keep the team where it was. But Roy was convinced by Arnold Johnson to secretly sabotage the deal at a special meeting of American League owners, leaving his father and brother no choice but to sell to Johnson, vice chairman of the nation's largest vending-machine company, Automatic Canteen. Ironically, Roy had been the holdout among the three when Johnson made his original offer.

Arnold Johnson had begun looking into the purchase during the summer, remarking that he saw "nothing wrong that a few million dollars won't cure." He assumed $800,000 in debt, spent $1,200,000 to retire the stadium mortgage, and paid $1,504,000 for stock in the franchise, with $604,000 going to Connie Mack and $450,000 each to Roy and Earle.[55]

The Mack brothers were both offered three-year contracts with no specified responsibilities. Connie Sr. was named honorary president—the ninety-two-year-old attended 1955 Opening Day in Kansas City to mark its return to Major League Baseball.[56] Incredibly, as a rookie with the Washington Nationals in 1886, Mack had played two games against the Kansas City Cowboys during their only season as members of the National League.[57]

As part of the deal, Johnson obtained title to the ballpark in Philadelphia, which he needed to sell to pay for his acquisition of the Athletics. Even had that not been the case, Johnson had no intention of simply handing over the stadium to Bob Carpenter so the Phillies owner could have what had previously been a two-team baseball market all to himself for nothing. Johnson had recently purchased Yankee Stadium and Blues Stadium in Kansas City and had no interest in expanding his portfolio of athletic venues. In fact, he was forced to sell "The House That Ruth Built" to gain approval from the American League to purchase the A's. He threatened to leave the Phillies without a stadium in which to play if they failed to take the facility off his hands.

So, on the day Joe Reardon resigned, Bob Carpenter, who was much more interested in Jack Kelly's plan for a new fifty-thousand-seat ballpark in Philadelphia, reluctantly agreed to buy Shibe Park, which had been renamed Connie Mack Stadium in early 1953. He complained, "We need the ballpark like we need a hole in the head. But we can't do anything else but buy from Arnold Johnson if we are to remain in Philadelphia, and we intend to do that."[58] Carpenter noted that prior to the stadium purchase the Phillies had been paying minimal rent—ten cents per ticket sold—and reiterated that he supported an effort to build a new ballpark and had no plans to alter or refurbish the existing one, although later in the decade he did make some renovations. Despite being saddled with an aging facility he did not want, Carpenter made peace with his circumstance. When time came to move the Athletics property, Carpenter forbade anyone touching Connie Mack's office and encouraged the living legend to continue using it, which he did until his death in early 1956.[59]

THE LACK OF EFFORT to integrate the Phillies even as National League rivals scooped up star after star from the Negro Leagues is often laid at the feet of Bob Carpenter. In 1952 the Phillies finally signed their first Black player, veteran Negro Leaguer Eugene Jones, who was past his thirtieth birthday. Jones spent the year with Granby of the Provincial League, joined there midyear by outfielder Alphonso Gerard, a thirty-three-year-old Negro League veteran, who was released at the end of the season.[60] Jones was released the next January.[61] Ted Washington, a teenage shortstop for the Philadelphia Stars, managed by the legendary Oscar Charleston, was signed in September 1952, shortly after starting in the Negro East-West All-Star Game.[62] But he was drafted into the military during training camp in 1953, was injured while in the service, and never played in the Phillies organization.[63]

Even the lowly Athletics had integrated before they departed for Kansas City, with former Homestead Grays pitcher Bob Trice making his debut in September 1953.[64] In the off-season, the A's acquired Vic Power from the Yankees in a trade and brought in Hilldale legend Judy Johnson to mentor Power and Trice during training camp.[65] Power played 127 games as a first baseman–outfielder for the Philadelphia Athletics in 1954, despite missing a week and a half after he was beaned by Tom Qualters during the annual midseason benefit game between the Phillies and A's.[66] Power was an All-Star during the team's first two seasons in Kansas City.

The same year Trice and Power played for the Athletics, the Phillies were rumored to be purchasing Pancho Herrera and Hank Mason from the Kansas City Monarchs. The two *were* signed and played for Schenectady in 1955 but remained far from the Major Leagues for some time.[67]

Those scattered instances aside, the relationship between the Phillies and Black ballplayers during the early to mid-1950s was essentially nonexistent. By the middle of the decade the team was one of only three without a Black player on its Major League roster—the others being the Detroit Tigers and the Boston Red Sox.

The team's reputation became an obstacle to signing Black talent. Scout Chuck Ward said that in the summer of 1954 he lost out on signing first baseman Al Griggs after the prospect was warned by two players, "The Phillies do not want Negroes on their team."[68]

After Ted Washington's military induction, the Phillies did not have another Black player in their farm system until 1955, with Herrera and Mason joined by eighteen-year-old Chuck Randall, the first nonprofessional Black player signed by the Phillies, and Nate Dickerson, a nineteen-year-old first baseman assigned to Pulaski of the Appalachian League. Randall was discovered at Glassboro High School in New Jersey by Jocko Collins and upon signing posed for a photograph with Collins and Bob Carpenter.[69] He was assigned to Bradford in the PONY League in June and hit .351 in seventy-eight games. But he was again assigned to Class D the next year.[70] Dickerson hit .311 with 12 home runs in seventy-five games and was likewise returned to Class D in 1956, as a teammate of Randall in Mattoon, Illinois, in the Midwest League. By the end of that season, nine Black players were under contract to the Phillies, most at the lowest rungs of the Minor Leagues.[71]

Randall hit .301 for Mattoon, with 19 home runs despite missing a month after injuring his ankle on a stolen-base attempt.[72] When he was assigned to Class D for a third year, Randall approached the Phillies and asked why. He said he was told, "We know you can do it, but it's just not the time."[73] In 2024 the Phillies unveiled an exhibit called "Pioneers in Pinstripes," honoring their early black Minor League players. Randall participated and generously said that he was not sure whether the response to his question had to do with his race or his age.

Meanwhile, the Phillies continued signing bonus babies—notably all of whom were white—with little to show for their money and effort. In August 1955 the Phillies beat out fourteen other Major League teams to sign six-foot-three, eighteen-year-old outfielder–first baseman Fred Van Dusen, who had been named New York's High School Player of the Year. Hall of Famer Al Simmons called the youngster "the best young prospect I've ever seen."[74] Van Dusen and his father did not want to commit to a bonus contract that would force the youngster to sit in Philadelphia for two years, so they signed for a lesser amount in exchange for the teenager spending September with the Phillies before being sent to the Minor Leagues in 1956. Van Dusen had only one plate appearance, in which he was hit by a pitch.[75] He won the Carolina League MVP Award in 1957 but never again appeared in the Majors.

A month after signing Van Dusen, the Phillies handed a $40,000 bonus to twenty-year-old University of Texas catcher Mack Burk.[76] Reporting to the Phillies in 1956, he had two Major League at bats while appearing in fifteen games that year, all but two of them as a pinch runner. Burk caught only one Major League inning in his career, and his only Major League hit came as a pinch hitter for Curt Simmons in a game against Cincinnati.[77]

Seven years after the incident involving Granny Hamner and Malcolm Poindexter, and nearly a decade after the Phillies dreadful treatment of Jackie Robinson, the *Philadelphia Tribune* ran yet another article about the absence of Black players on the Phillies and pointed specifically to the Poindexter episode as a factor in its continued criticism of the team.[78]

Still, nothing happened. The local chapter of the NAACP decried not only the lack of Black players on the Phillies roster but also the lack of Black employees in *any* capacity.[79] Considering the substantial history of Black baseball in and around Philadelphia, it was disheartening to that community, numbering a half million, which largely boycotted the team.

Bob Carpenter finally responded with a letter to Charles Shorter, executive director of the Philadelphia branch of the NAACP. He maintained that the Phillies were not in the least prejudiced, noting the Black players in the farm system. He insisted, "The only reason why the Phillies do not have Don Newcombe, Hank Aaron, and Bill Bruton is because they can't be bought." He pointed to Black concession and maintenance employees, as well as scout William Yancey and new part-time talent hunter Tom Dixon.[80]

The Phillies finally listed a Black player on their Major League roster in 1957, when shortstop John Kennedy, a gifted athlete considered to have great promise despite not playing baseball until after high school, was invited to spring training.[81]

The arrival of Kennedy especially excited Black fans. But it was difficult for him to truly feel part of the team. During training camp, he was forced to live in a private home away from his teammates and eat at segregated restaurants. He played well but was in the lineup only sporadically during spring training, appearing in fifteen of the team's thirty-two exhibition games, three of those as a pinch runner. Kennedy's reputation was that of bat over glove, but he made only 1 error, against Cincinnati on March 28.[82] After that he had only 5 at bats in the team's final thirteen exhibition games. Kennedy batted .343 with 12 hits in 35 at bats, was involved in turning 7 double plays, and carried a solid .979 fielding average. But the Phillies played Bobby Morgan and Roy Smalley as much or more than Kennedy. Then on April 5, Philadelphia traded for shortstop Chico Fernández, sending five players and cash to Brooklyn for the Cuban, who was installed as the starting shortstop.[83] Claude Harrison Jr. wrote in the *Philadelphia Tribune* of Kennedy's solid play and his disappointment in the trade for Fernández. "What more can the Phils ask?" he said.[84]

Despite this, Harrison praised the Phillies for finally making the move that had been awaited so long. He wrote, "After nearly a decade of campaigning by the Negro Press, the Philadelphia Phillies of the National

League has signed two Negro ballplayers, John Kennedy and Chico Fernandez. And thousands of Negroes throughout Philadelphia are happy because the Phillies have finally seen the light."[85]

Scout Bill Yancey had categorized the highly competitive Kennedy as "can't miss," but the infielder played in only five regular season games for the Phillies, batting twice without a hit before being sent to the Minors, never to return.[86] His replacement was another Black player, thirty-three-year-old utility man Chuck Harmon, acquired from the Pittsburgh Pirates.[87] When asked if he been given a fair chance with the Phillies, Kennedy shrugged and said, "I don't know."[88]

By the summer of 1957, the number of Black players in the Phillies system had risen to twenty-two, including Chico Fernández, John Kennedy, and Chuck Harmon.[89]

THE MAN WHO had the distinction of managing the first Black Phillies players, and of course the rest of the team, Mayo Smith, succeeded Terry Moore at the start of 1955.[90] That season began ominously, with Curt Simmons only able to throw two innings during training camp due to arm problems. Then Richie Ashburn and Del Ennis collided while chasing a Mickey Mantle fly ball during an exhibition game in Wilmington.[91] The collision cost Ashburn most of the first two weeks of the 1955 season, ending his 730 consecutive games played streak, while Ennis suffered a hairline fracture of his fibula and began the year wearing a makeshift Frank Wiechec cast that allowed him to play despite the injury.[92]

Smith and the Phillies endured a thirteen-game losing streak early in his first season, and a ten-game slide at almost the exact same point of his second year. But the team showed promise in Smith's third campaign, actually reaching first place in July 1957 for two days before settling back into fifth. It was a year that saw the Phillies farm system finally produce. Pitcher Jack Sanford, who was one day older than ten-year veteran Curt Simmons, was a National League All-Star and the circuit's Rookie of the Year in 1957, winning 19 games and finally overcoming his reputation for possessing a fiery temper, which Russ Meyer could only dream of doing. Dick Farrell, nicknamed "Turk," also had a great rookie season as the team's closer, winning 10 games and saving an equal number. First baseman Ed Bouchee finished second to Sanford for National League Rookie of the Year, and captured the

Regular Rookie Player of the Year honor from *The Sporting News*.[93] Another rookie, outfielder Harry Anderson, hit 17 home runs. Ted Kazanski had his best season, with a .265 batting average in 185 at bats as a utility man.

Some old faces also contributed. Bob Miller made a comeback as a relief pitcher, saving 6 games and winning 2 with an earned run average of 2.69. And the Phillies reacquired Ron Northey, their best player of the war years. The thirty-seven-year-old was signed the morning of July 30 after his release by the Chicago White Sox and that night slugged an eighth-inning, two-run pinch-hit home run against Cincinnati as the Phillies improved to a record of 56-44.[94]

That proved the team's high mark of the season. The Phillies faded in August and finished fifth with a 77-77 mark. Looking back on a promising year that slipped away during the summer, it was team's young guard that carried the load while the remaining Whiz Kids, finally receiving another opportunity to contend, failed to deliver. Injuries caught up to Granny Hamner and Willie Jones, who hit .227 and .218, respectively. Robin Roberts lost a shocking 22 games while winning only 10—Mayo Smith said that Roberts needed to come up with another pitch and called him "confused and bewildered."[95] Richie Ashburn failed to hit .300 for only the second time since 1949.[96] With reinforcements finally arriving, the old guard was in danger of becoming the "Wheeze Kids."

HAVING THE CITY to themselves, Phillies attendance increased each of the first three years following the departure of the Athletics, reaching more than 1.1 million in 1957, third best in the National League and the team's highest since 1950. Despite the slump at the end of Mayo Smith's third campaign, the future seemed bright. Sanford had arrived as a solid starter. Twenty-seven-year-old Ray Semproch seemed ready for the Majors after having been in the farm system since 1951. Twenty-two-year-old Don Cardwell was yet another promising arm that could be added to stalwarts Roberts, who it was assumed would bounce back, and Simmons, who had recovered from arm problems to start the 1957 All-Star Game. And the Phillies added to their offense in the off-season by acquiring outfielder Wally Post from Cincinnati for pitcher Harvey Haddix.[97]

But Ed Bouchee's sophomore season was sidetracked by his shocking arrest in Spokane, Washington, in January 1958, for indecent exposure involving young girls.[98] He pled guilty to two counts and was sentenced to probation on the condition he undergo psychiatric care.[99] Bouchee worked out with the Phillies between treatments beginning in early June but was not cleared to play by Commissioner Frick until July.[100]

The Phillies played well at times in 1958—on July 10 they were in fourth place, only three games out of first. Ten days later they had slipped to sixth, and Mayo Smith was fired. The man replacing him was a surprise. After spending much of the decade trying to fill Eddie Sawyer's spot, Bob Carpenter circled back to his pennant-winning manager in an effort to return to the glory days. Of course, outgoing manager Smith posed for a photo with his successor.[101]

BEGINNING HIS SECOND tenure as Phillies manager, Eddie Sawyer inherited a team with some recognizable faces. Stan Lopata was still around and had developed into a two-time All-Star after changing his hitting approach at the suggestion of roommate Johnny Wyrostek.[102] Roberts and Simmons and Ashburn and Jones and Hamner and Bob Miller also remained. Since 1950, the Phillies had gone through less turnover than any other National League team.[103]

One player extremely happy to see Sawyer was Robin Roberts, who had been indifferent regarding the manager's first departure. "As I looked back on that time later on," said Roberts, "it was obvious that Eddie was a great manager to play for."[104]

Despite their relative stability, the Whiz Kids had been slowly disassembled over the previous couple of years. Eddie Waitkus was cut by the Orioles in July 1955 and returned to the Phillies, where he finished the season, hitting .280 in thirty-three games.[105] He was released at year's end and at age thirty-six decided to retire.[106] Andy Seminick, who was also brought back by the Phillies during the 1955 season, retired and became a coach.[107]

Del Ennis, the hometown boy who for some reason had become an incessant target of the boo birds at Connie Mack Stadium, was dealt to St. Louis in November 1956 for outfielder Rip Repulski and infielder Bobby Morgan. Earlier that year, Ennis had hit his 244th career home run, breaking the team record held by his boyhood idol, Chuck Klein.[108]

"Surely, it was a surprise," remarked Ennis upon hearing about the trade. "But that's baseball. You have to expect changes in baseball, I guess."[109]

Within a month of Sawyer taking over, the Phillies had fallen to last place, where they finished the season, even while leading the league in batting average. Robin Roberts, Willie Jones, and Richie Ashburn all had bounce-back years. Ashburn won his second batting title with a .350 average despite going hitless in 28 at bats in early July. Roberts won 17 games. Harry Anderson hit 23 home runs and batted .301. Veteran Dave Philley set a Major League record with 8-consecutive pinch hits.

But Granny Hamner played in only thirty-five games, a knee injury ending his season in late May—a big blow, as he was hitting .301.[110] Stan Lopata suffered a dislocated thumb on a play at home plate and saw his home runs and RBI drop by half compared to 1957.[111] Wally Post, recovering from off-season hernia surgery, hit only 12 home runs. Curt Simmons again had arm problems and won 7 while losing 14. Bob Miller's ERA ballooned to 11.69. Jack Sanford won only 10 games. Ted Kazanski hit .228. And the Phillies led the league in runners left on base.

During the off-season, the Phillies traded Jack Sanford to San Francisco for Rubén Gómez and catcher Valmy Thomas—Sanford would win 80 games over the next five years for the Giants, while Gomez won 3 for the Phillies.[112] Eddie Sawyer continued making moves as training camp got underway in 1959, the first resulting in the sale of Bob Miller to the St. Louis Cardinals.[113] Late in spring training Stan Lopata was sent to the Milwaukee Braves in a six-player deal that also ended Ted Kazanski's time in Philadelphia.[114] Granny Hamner, who had been racked by injuries that led him to contemplate becoming a pitcher, was traded to Cleveland in mid-May. Three weeks later, Willie Jones was sent to the same team.[115]

Despite all the changes, the 1959 season proved no better than 1958. John Quinn, coming off two consecutive pennants with the Milwaukee Braves, replaced Roy Hamey as general manager, but the team slipped into last place on May 16 during a nine-game losing streak and, excepting two days, remained there for the rest of the year.[116] Harry Anderson's batting average dropped more than sixty points. Curt Simmons missed almost the entire season with an elbow injury, Robin Roberts had another off year, and the team's woes at second base continued with rookie George "Sparky" Anderson hitting only .218 in 152 games as the starter.[117] Anderson eventually made the Hall of Fame, but as a manager, not as a player. The team's final record was 64-90. They also brought up the rear of the National League in attendance. The Phillies had begun the decade at the top of the heap and ended it at the bottom.

14

I Gave It All I Had

BY 1960, THERE were few active Whiz Kids left. Del Ennis had just retired after splitting a half season with the Cincinnati Reds and Chicago White Sox. Russ Meyer, Bob Miller, Bubba Church, and Andy Seminick had hung up their spikes, as had Eddie Waitkus and Jim Konstanty. Dick Sisler had taken a job managing in the Pacific Coast League. Granny Hamner was in the Minors as a player-coach and attempting to become a full-time pitcher. Mike Goliat was in the International League, as he had been since 1952. Stan Lopata was barely hanging on with the Milwaukee Braves. Willie Jones was doing likewise in Cincinnati.

On January 11, 1960, Richie Ashburn was traded to the Chicago Cubs for Alvin Dark, John Buzhardt, and Jim Woods. Ashburn's leaving the Phillies after twelve seasons was front-page news in Philadelphia and, besides Eddie Sawyer, left only Robin Roberts and Curt Simmons among the Whiz Kids in Philadelphia as the 1960 season began.[1]

Roberts and Simmons were roommates, the two having long been close friends despite being complete opposites in so many ways. One was a righty, the other a lefty. One had a smooth pitching motion, the other's was jarring, full of twists and turns. One was a college graduate, the other signed a baseball contract out of high school. One was a city boy, the other from a small town. One was outgoing, the other introverted.

And they had divergent philosophies about life. Simmons tended toward pessimism, although Roberts said it would be more accurate to label his friend "a realist." Considering himself a "lucky unlucky guy," Simmons thought his roommate "an over boarder," conveying a sometimesoveroptimistic outlook on life.[2] A decade after their greatest triumph, the two were struggling to keep the Phillies, and themselves, relevant.

Following back-to-back last-place finishes, spring training in 1960 had its stressful moments for Eddie Sawyer. He fined Jim Owens, Joe Koppe, and Bobby Gene Smith $100 each for their involvement in a bar fight in Clearwater. Bob Carpenter docked Owens an additional $500 because of his past reputation for extracurricular altercations. The pitcher responded by threatening to quit before reconsidering.[3] A week after completing a three-game exhibition series against the Chicago White Sox in Puerto Rico, Sawyer expressed optimism regarding the coming season before making an ill-advised remark about infielder Ted Lepcio, a holdout until mid-March, calling him "one of the worst-looking major league ball players I've ever seen."[4] That quip did nothing to enhance the manager's standing in the clubhouse.

Sawyer made it to Opening Day, a 9–4 loss in Cincinnati during which Robin Roberts was unable to hold onto an early 4–0 lead.[5] Then Sawyer tabbed Curt Simmons—outstanding during spring training with a 1.97 earned run average in thirty-two innings after missing most of 1959 while recovering from elbow surgery—to pitch the home opener.[6] However, prior to the game Sawyer abruptly resigned, revealing that the thought of doing so had been on his mind and declaring, "I wouldn't ever want to be a major league manager again." Bob Carpenter insisted he had attempted to persuade Sawyer to reconsider, saying of the manager's decision, "It certainly came as a shock to me."[7]

When pressed further about his sudden departure, the story goes that Sawyer wisecracked, "I am forty-nine years old and want to live to be fifty."[8] He was replaced by Gene Mauch, although Phillies coach Andy Cohen handled the home opener because Mauch was in Minneapolis, where he had been managing the American Association Millers. Simmons took the mound as scheduled but failed to survive the second inning, although the Phillies rallied to win the game in ten innings, 5–4.[9] Mauch arrived and gave the soon-to-be thirty-one-year-old Simmons one more start, at Pittsburgh, during which the left-hander was lifted in the first inning with the bases loaded and two runs having scored without his retiring a batter.[10] After making a couple of relief appearances, Simmons was unceremoniously cut from the team, his career record with the Phillies standing at 115-110.[11]

According to Simmons, it was Roberts who inadvertently broke the news of his release, expressing shock and sympathy while mistakenly thinking Simmons already knew.[12] (For his part, Roberts stated in his autobiography that Gene Mauch came to their hotel room and delivered the news to Simmons in person.)[13] The two pitchers had partnered in Phillies success and were now being separated in the wake of Phillies failure.

Simmons was not totally shocked, telling Frank Dolson, "As soon as Sawyer [resigned] I was out as far as the Phillies were concerned. If Sawyer had stayed, I would have pitched. When he left I knew they were gonna get rid of me."[14] He also betrayed a trace of indignation, saying, "Sure, I thought the Phillies would trade me, but release me—no."[15]

Robin Roberts was the last Whiz Kid standing.

AFTER CURT SIMMONS DEPARTED, Robin Roberts struggled through another season and a half with the Phillies, player and team locked in a downward spiral. Roberts had won 61 games while suffering 71 defeats between 1956 and 1959, twice leading the National League in losses and setting a record for home runs allowed in a season in 1956 with 46, breaking the record of 41 that he had set the year before.[16] He could still thread the needle, but his fastball was not as consistent as it had once been. This is not to imply that period of his career was devoid of highlights. On May 13, 1958, he defeated the Milwaukee Braves, 5–2, for his 191st victory in a Phillies uniform, surpassing Grover Cleveland Alexander's previous team record.[17] A couple of months later, the thirty-one-year-old fired a three-hitter against the Chicago Cubs for the 200th win of his career, the only blemish on his day resulting from a Dale Long solo home run. Afterward Roberts said, "Sure, I felt this game was something extra, but I wasn't as nervous as I thought I would be."[18]

Roberts began the 1960 season with a 1-7 record, and self-doubt crept in. Warming up before a game at Connie Mack Stadium, he heard the familiar voice of Cy Perkins. The old coach, who had also mentored Lefty Grove and Mickey Cochrane, reassured Roberts. "You're throwing good," he told him. "I was worried about you, but you are all right. Some people don't understand what a good delivery you have. Just keep pitching."[19]

Roberts regained his confidence and ended the year with a 12-16 mark. He followed that with perhaps the best spring training of his career, beginning the exhibition schedule pitching twenty-four scoreless innings, a streak that ended when Pittsburgh's Dick Stuart hit a home run off him.[20] But success in March did not translate to the regular season. On June 5, 1961,

Roberts pitched a complete-game victory against the San Francisco Giants, his 234th win for the Phillies, but only his first of the season.[21] For the second straight year Roberts was saddled with a record of 1-7 in early June. He later spent a month on the injured list after hurting his knee sliding into second base and upon his return was rarely used. He ended the year with that lone victory over San Francisco, against 10 losses.

If the 1961 season had been a disaster for Robin Roberts, it had been likewise for the Phillies. After beginning the year with a mediocre 6-9 start, the team spun into a ten-game slide. There were a pair of seven-game losing streaks in June and early July. After splitting a doubleheader on July 28, taking the nightcap to end a five-game losing streak, the Phillies did not win again until August 20, losing twenty-three straight games—the most in the Major Leagues since 1899. The Phillies dropped eight one-run games during the unprecedented streak, and scored 3 runs or fewer eighteen times.

The nightmare ended the same way it had begun, in the nightcap of a doubleheader with John Buzhardt earning the win. Warren Spahn captured the first game for Milwaukee, the 302nd win of his Major League career. Keyed by Buzhardt's successful squeeze bunt on a pitch aimed at his head, the Phillies scored 4 runs in the eighth inning of the second game and held on to win, 7–4. An enthusiastic crowd greeted the players at the airport on their return to Philadelphia, where a relieved Gene Mauch remarked, "It's been a long, long time" and joked, "Now that I think of it, I should have tried getting seven runs more often. I guess I just never thought of that."[22]

When asked later about the experience, Mauch said, "I'll never be able to describe it. I doubt if anyone can describe it for me. But, as you can imagine, it was awful."[23]

Despite the win, the Phillies remained nineteen-and-a-half games behind *seventh* place. The team eventually compiled an abysmal 47-107 record, their fourth consecutive last-place finish. It was a result reminiscent of the Baker Bowl days.

Roberts did not particularly relish his two seasons under the caustic Gene Mauch, who at times attempted humor at the expense of his players, something the competitive Roberts didn't always take well to. Mauch also employed signs that catcher Clay Dalrymple joked would be more at home in a CIA code book. Dalrymple remembered Roberts telling him, "I don't want any part of that. Use my signs. One's a fast ball, two's a curve ball, three's a slider, four's a change. . . . Pitching is NOT that complicated."[24]

It was reported that Mauch and general manager John Quinn thought Roberts unable or unwilling to adjust his approach, stubbornly relying almost exclusively on his fastball instead of adapting to the toll taken on his arm by age and workload.[25] At one point Mauch made a derisive postgame comment, saying about Roberts, "He threw like Dolly Madison."[26] Recently retired Stan Lopata was asked his opinion about the game's greatest pitchers and praised Roberts while marveling at Warren Spahn expanding his repertoire in anticipation of losing his hard stuff. Of Roberts, he said, "He still thinks he has the fastball. He can be pretty bull-headed."[27]

Outside of a cameo appearance in 1966 by Steve Ridzik, the final time a Whiz Kid played a regular-season game in a Phillies uniform came on September 28, 1961, when Robin Roberts pitched four innings against the Los Angeles Dodgers, allowing 5 runs, all unearned.[28] Afterward he told reporters, "Physically, I am better than I have been in years, but I'm pressing, trying too hard. I need to feel wanted, and I don't feel that way here anymore." He then succinctly summed up his situation: "I think it would be better for everyone if I left the Phillies."[29]

A few days after making public his request to be traded, Roberts was sold to the New York Yankees for $25,000, acquired by Roy Hamey, the former Phillies general manager who was now running the Bronx Bombers.[30] The purchase of Roberts by the Yankees was possible only after his passing through waivers, and after the Houston Colt .45s and New York Mets declined to select him in the expansion draft due to the price tag to acquire him and his comparatively high salary. Bob Carpenter declared his hope that the transaction would allow Roberts to play for a contender and participate in a World Series. For his part, Roberts insisted, "I think I can still pitch, and I'm glad to have the opportunity to pitch for the Yankees."[31] An era had ended.

Roberts faced his old team in an exhibition game that spring. Afterward, the Phillies retired his number, 36, in a private, informal "ceremony."[32] He struggled with New York and, while granted a momentary reprieve and placed on the Opening Day roster, was released by the Yankees shortly after the 1962 season began without appearing in a game.[33] Once again Cy Perkins was in contact, this time by phone, exhorting the thirty-five-year-old pitcher.

"Don't let them run you out of the game," Morgan pleaded. "You'll be pitching shutouts when you're 40. I'm telling you, kid, don't you dare quit. There's no way you can't keep pitching."[34]

Stan Lopata also called, offering to catch Roberts and give him an honest evaluation. Following the session, Lopata noted Roberts was open to making adjustments and said, "He still looked good to me. His curveball was real sharp. He obviously is changing speeds a lot and that's helped him."[35]

Roberts did not quit. After trying out first with Baltimore and then with Cincinnati, where he impressed Reds manager Fred Hutchinson but failed to reach agreement on salary, Roberts signed with the Orioles.[36] He pitched two perfect innings of relief in his debut for Baltimore on May 21, and then joined the starting rotation.[37] Roberts's first win for Baltimore was a 5–2 decision against the Yankees.[38] He added three more wins in a row, the last two complete games. The key, according to Roberts, was throwing a straight change-up off his fastball rather than adding an entirely new pitch—in the past he had attempted developing a separate change-up: "But instead of throwing the hitters off stride, I threw myself off." Of his new approach, he said, "Once I started throwing it, my easy fastball motion came back."

He also addressed the reports of his stubbornness about changing speeds. "I think it was more a lack of understanding on my part. I was forcing my pitching, trying too hard."[39]

Roberts ended the season with a solid 10-9 record and a 2.78 earned run average, kicking off a three-and-a-half-year stint with Baltimore, where he helped mentor a staff of talented young arms, including Steve Barber, Milt Pappas, Chuck Estrada, Wally Bunker, and Dave McNally. They were collectively dubbed "The Baby Birds."

WHEN THE PHILLIES let Curt Simmons go in May 1960, he still had 78 wins in his left arm. Old teammate Solly Hemus, managing the St. Louis Cardinals, had been impressed by Simmons during spring training and signed him on his thirty-first birthday.[40] The left-hander spent a month in the Cardinals bullpen before getting a start. Simmons's first win of the year—his first in nearly two years—was a 1–0 triumph against the Phillies at Connie Mack Stadium in which he pitched eight and two-thirds innings.[41] He later fired a five-hit shutout against his old team.[42] Simmons won 7 games in 1960, 4 of them at the expense of the Phillies, pitching into the ninth inning each time.

Simmons became a dependable member of the Cardinals staff, winning 9 and 10 games the next two years. Compared with when he broke in more than a decade earlier, Simmons was thicker, but fit. He still had his crew cut, and his windup and delivery remained full of motion that made it hard for batters to pick up the ball out of his hand. And he was healthy again. In 1963, his fourth season with St. Louis, Simmons crafted one of the best seasons of his career, winning 15 games, including 6 by shutout. St. Louis finished second to the Los Angeles Dodgers, rallying to close the gap after trailing by six games on August 31. Simmons was a major factor in the surge, firing 3 consecutive shutouts in September. The Cardinals surprised themselves, moving into contention and threatening to catapult Stan Musial—playing his final season—into his first World Series in seventeen years. But the Dodgers completed a three-game sweep of the Cardinals, including a contest in which Simmons allowed 3 runs in eight innings of a 4–0 loss to Sandy Koufax.[43] St. Louis lost 8 of its last 10 and finished second.

THE PHILLIES FINALLY had a Black star in 1964, $70,000 bonus baby Dick Allen, dubbed "Richie" by the press, and a manager, the fiery Gene Mauch, with staying power.[44] The team had rebounded quickly from the debacle of 1961, with winning records in both 1962 and 1963. General Manager John Quinn completed a number of deals that brought in young talent, including Tony Taylor, Johnny Callison, Tony González, and Cookie Rojas to go with homegrown players Allen, Chris Short, Art Mahaffey, Rick Wise, and Alex Johnson. Quinn added Jim Bunning in a trade prior to the 1964 season, and the Phillies were serious contenders.

Like the Whiz Kids, these Phillies had a large lead in late September—in this case six-and-half games with twelve to play. It appeared insurmountable. It wasn't. They lost their advantage in just seven days.

Like their 1950 counterparts, the Phillies had made a big run in August and then suffered injuries and ran out of pitching—Gene Mauch having real confidence only in Chris Short and Jim Bunning—the latter having in June pitched the Major League's first regular-season perfect game in forty-two years. Unlike their 1950 counterparts, these Phillies did not win the pennant.

The man responsible for extending the Phillies losing streak to ten games that September, essentially eliminating them from what had seemed a sure pennant, was Curt Simmons, pitching for the St. Louis Cardinals. On September 30, 1964, Simmons went eight innings—carrying a no-hitter until two out in the seventh—once again defeating his former employer and moving his current team into first place with three games left.[45] Although he claimed to have no greater desire to beat the Phillies than anyone else, during his first five years with the Cardinals it seemed that Simmons repeatedly gained a measure of revenge by repeatedly beating Philadelphia—at the end of the 1964 season his career record against them stood at 16-2.[46]

Ironically, two pitchers Mauch and the Phillies had unceremoniously dumped, Roberts and Simmons, won 31 games between them that year, with Simmons capturing 4 straight victories in the season's final month and Roberts winning his final two starts of the year.

The Phillies had collapsed in almost the same manner as they had fourteen years earlier, only this time there was no Dick Sisler to bail them out on the season's last day. He was busy serving as manager of the Cincinnati Reds, who tied the Phillies for second place, one game behind St. Louis.[47] A week before Simmons's win, Sisler had managed the Reds to a crushing 1-0 defeat of Philadelphia, a game made infamous in Phillies lore for Chico Ruiz scoring the game's only run on a steal of home.[48]

Like Roberts, the optimist, Simmons the pessimist had made adjustments to his arsenal, becoming a control pitcher of sorts. He followed up his great 1963 campaign by winning a career-high 18 games while walking only 49 batters in 244 innings, playing a major role in the Cardinals winning the 1964 National League pennant. Fourteen years after being forced into the role of spectator, Curt Simmons was finally to pitch in a World Series against the New York Yankees.

Simmons drove in the Cardinals' only run of the third game of the 1964 World Series while earning a no-decision, a game in which he allowed only 4 hits and 1 run in eight innings while retiring seventeen Yankees on ground balls. He was walking down the runway to the clubhouse when he heard the roar of the crowd, reacting to Mickey Mantle's game-winning walk-off home run for the Yankees on the first pitch from reliever Barney Schultz.[49] Simmons's second start resulted in a loss in Game Six.[50] But the Cardinals won the seventh game behind Bob Gibson, finally making Curt Simmons a member of a world champion, one for which he had been a major contributor. Simmons was grateful for the opportunity, insisting, "The 1964 pennant here was the thrill of my life, especially because I got to pitch in the World Series. I wouldn't have appreciated the '50 Series as much because I was younger then."[51]

ROBIN ROBERTS WON 27 games during the 1963 and 1964 seasons for Baltimore, capturing 8 of his last 12 decisions in 1963, and 9 of his last 13 the next year, when the Orioles led the American League during much of August and September before finishing a close third. In 1965 the thirty-eight-year-old Roberts was assigned a nineteen-year-old rookie roommate named Jim Palmer, whose Major League debut came in relief of the veteran, one bonus baby future Hall of Famer relieving another.[52] Roberts regularly treated Palmer and Dave McNally to dinner, where the three talked about pitching. Palmer remembered the advice Roberts gave him: "You don't need much of a breaking ball if you know where your fast ball is going."[53]

Roberts lasted only two innings in his 1965 debut, but followed that with four consecutive complete-game wins. Then he dropped seven in a row and fell out of the rotation. Shortly after the All-Star break, Roberts asked for his release so he could start for another team and add to his 276 career wins.[54]

In early August Roberts signed with the Houston Astros, which three years earlier had passed on him in the expansion draft. He threw shutouts in his first two starts, one of them against Gene Mauch and the Phillies before a crowd of thirty-one thousand, and allowed only 2 runs in his first twenty-seven innings with Houston.[55] When Roberts blanked the Phillies, after having been turned down by general manager John Quinn before signing with the Astros, the headline in the *Philadelphia Daily News* trumpeted, "Old 'Dolly Madison' Roberts Ices Phillies' Cream-Puff Batters, 8–0."[56]

He ended the 1965 season with a 10-9 combined record with Baltimore and Houston, and a 2.78 earned run average, the same exact marks he had recorded in 1962.[57]

Shortly after the season ended Roberts underwent elbow surgery to remove bone chips, the first time he had ever gone under the knife.[58] He recovered in time to serve as Houston's 1966 Opening Day starter, his thirteenth such assignment, breaking a National League record held—of course—by Grover Cleveland Alexander.[59]

During the off-season, Roberts was appointed to a search committee, tasked with recommending a new executive director for the Major League Baseball Players Association. Roberts, who had been the National League's lead player representative from 1955 through 1959, succeeding Ralph Kiner after he was traded to the American League, was well respected by players around the Majors and was handed the assignment even though he was no longer an active rep.[60] The committee eventually settled on Marvin Miller, whom Roberts backed strongly as the best man for the role, and the players voted to approve the recommendation. The owners were much less pleased about the hiring of Miller—whether that impacted what remained of Roberts's career is open to speculation.[61]

Roberts began the 1966 season by dropping his first three starts—despite pitching well in two of them—then won 3 in a row, including a shutout of the Chicago Cubs in which he struck out 9.[62] But his elbow remained balky despite the surgical procedure, and he fell out of the rotation in June. The Astros released him on July 4.[63]

With Cy Perkins having passed away three years earlier, Roberts sought another individual for an opinion as to whether he should continue his career: Ken Silvestri, who was coaching for the Atlanta Braves. After a bull-pen session Silvestri told Roberts, "You throw better than seven of the guys on our staff." Roberts replied, "Hawk, you're not kidding me?" Silvestri replied, "No I'm not, don't you give up."[64]

A week later Roberts signed as player–pitching coach for the Chicago Cubs, the team he had rooted for as a kid, mimicking the players as radio broadcasts echoed from the kitchen window.[65] The Cubs, managed by Leo Durocher, were headed for a last place 103-loss season and in the midst of overhauling their roster. Undoubtedly, Cubs general manager John Holland remembered the veteran right-hander's shutout of his team earlier in the season and saw Roberts as a mentor to a young staff, as he had been in Baltimore.

Roberts pitched a complete-game win in his debut for Chicago, defeating Pittsburgh, 5–4, and followed that with an eleven-inning performance in a no-decision against Cincinnati and eight solid innings, striking out 6 and allowing only 2 runs, in a loss to St. Louis. But he failed to last longer than five innings in his next six starts and, in a familiar and recurring theme, was dropped from the rotation.

But while he was with the Cubs he mentored a young right-hander whom Chicago had acquired in April from the Phillies. Ferguson Jenkins would call Roberts an idol and frequently mentioned him as an influence when interviewed about his career. Jenkins would go on to forge a career strikingly similar to that of Roberts.[66]

Robin Roberts's last Major League win, the 286th of his career, was earned with two shutout innings of relief against Atlanta on August 29, making him the only pitcher to have ever defeated the Boston, Milwaukee, *and* Atlanta Braves.[67] His final Major league appearance came on September 3, one inning of relief against the Pittsburgh Pirates. After surrendering a three-run home run to Willie Stargell—the 505th Roberts had allowed in his career to extend a Major League record that stood until 2010—he settled down and retired Gene Alley on a double play grounder.[68] He was released at season's end and shortly thereafter was hospitalized for a bleeding ulcer.[69]

Despite having gone from Opening Day starter to being out of a job while pitching for two of baseball's worst teams, Roberts was not quite ready to quit. He worked out as usual with Curt Simmons over the winter and, feeling his arm was strong enough to continue, wrote to seven teams asking for an opportunity.[70]

After receiving no replies, Roberts called Bob Carpenter and signed a contract to pitch for Philadelphia's Eastern League affiliate in Reading, Pennsylvania. "If Robbie proves he can pitch with Reading," said Carpenter, "either we or some other club will give him a chance to pitch in the majors."[71]

Wearing a jersey with the familiar Phillies logo stitched across the chest and an unfamiliar No. 9 on his back, Roberts made his bow with Reading.[72] As he hung his jacket on a hook in the visiting clubhouse at Williamsport, Roberts explained to columnist Frank Dolson why he was continuing his career. "The people who criticize, they don't understand. Most of them don't know I had an arm operation. They don't know how well I'm throwing."[73] Roberts gave himself a June 15 deadline to receive a Major League offer.

Roberts pitched well in his debut, striking out 9 and walking only 1 batter in a 1–0 loss to the Williamsport Mets. Jerry Johnson, a converted third baseman who was only four years old when Roberts first broke in as a professional, allowed just 6 hits in beating a future Hall of Famer.[74]

It was definitely a different atmosphere in the Eastern League. Dallas Green, who was Roberts's roommate as well as a player-coach for Reading, was boarding the team bus one day when he caught sight of several men high on scaffolds, cleaning the side of a hotel building. Choosing that as a moment of motivation, he yelled, "All you pitchers look up. That might be you someday. Pitch like hell."[75]

The old Whiz Kid was effective for Reading, winning 5 and losing 3, with seven complete games and a 2.48 earned run average. He threw back-to-back shutouts in May, but in June had to exit back-to-back starts in the third and second innings because of pulled leg muscles.[76] Around the same time, thirty-two-year-old Dallas Green was recalled to the Phillies. Green told Frank Dolson that Roberts was discouraged when no scouts came to see him pitch. "I think he's proved his point," Green said. "Now it's up to baseball."[77]

Extending his self-imposed deadline three days because of his pair of aborted starts, Robin Roberts boarded the Reading team bus for one final road trip. During a rest stop he approached thirty-one-year-old outfielder Howie Bedell, who had been playing professionally for more than a decade. Bedell, who in 1962 spent a half season with the Milwaukee Braves, was the defending Eastern League batting champion and had been acquired by Reading just before the season started in a trade for Hank Aaron's brother-in-law.[78]

Roberts asked, "Howie, how do you do this? Not only *how* do you do this, *why* do you do this?"

Bedell told Roberts, "I do it because I love it."

Roberts replied, "I don't get it. This is a hard ride to have to make."[79]

Roberts struck out 7 in seven innings in his final game for Reading, a no-decision against Williamsport on June 18, and departed before his teammates realized he had left. When they entered the clubhouse after the game, Roberts's uniform was hanging on the wall, and he was nowhere to be found.[80]

At the time, Roberts declared to reporters, "I'm in good shape now and we'll see what happens. . . . I've satisfied myself that my arm is sound again." He announced that he was ready to return to the Majors and was going home to await a call from a Major League team.[81] On the drive home, Roberts said he added up his 9 wins in Wilmington in 1948, his 5 with Reading, and his Major League total and realized that he had won exactly 300 games, just as Cy Perkins had predicted.[82]

He visited the Phillies clubhouse and told reporters, "I went to Reading to get in shape, and I got in shape. I know there aren't too many 40-year-old pitchers looking for jobs. I think I can pitch two or three years, not just this year."[83]

A couple of weeks later Roberts was in town to take part in a television interview with his old friend Richie Ashburn and asked Gene Mauch if he could work out a bit. He threw batting practice to several Phillies backups, with Ashburn serving as his catcher. Mauch made little effort to feign interest, claiming, "I was so danged busy here that I didn't get a chance to see how it looked."[84]

The decision of whether to retire, for someone with the supercompetitive nature of Roberts, was no doubt difficult. While he waited, Roberts did some sports reports for WPEN radio and pitched a game for Maje McDonnell's All-Stars, which included some retired Phillies and A's players.[85] But the market was light for forty-year-old pitchers, and no call ever came.

In August Roberts finally accepted that his career was over, telling Al Cartwright of the *Wilmington Evening Journal*, "It just didn't work out." While listing several options he had for a postcareer life, he admitted, "I'm left in a little bit of a vacuum. I don't know what to do."[86]

Years later, Howie Bedell ran into Roberts at an event and asked him why he had departed the Reading locker room so quickly. "Howie," said Roberts, "I gave it all I had, and I had nothing left. And I didn't want to stay in the clubhouse and see people."[87]

CURT SIMMONS WAS NOT as effective in 1965, his record falling to 9-15. He began the 1966 season in St. Louis but was sold on waivers to the Chicago Cubs in June, a couple of weeks before being joined there by Robin Roberts, who became his pitching coach, as well as reunited teammate.[88] Simmons made his Cubs debut by throwing a five-hit shutout to defeat the New York Mets.[89] But as is often the lot of veterans nearing the end of their careers, within a year Simmons was again on the move, a thirty-eight-year-old left-hander sold in August 1967 to the California Angels.[90] Managed by Bill Rigney, the Angels had taken up residence in last place on June 8 but surged to within a game and a half of first on July 22, thanks to a 34-12 streak. At that point they lost five straight, falling six games back, and sought the addition of a veteran lefty like Simmons to provide a spark for the stretch run.

Once again Simmons made a brilliant debut with a new team, allowing 10 hits while shutting out the New York Yankees on August 9 for a 7–0 win. He also had 2 hits in 3 at bats, including a run-scoring double. "This was one of the biggest," Simmons said with a wide grin after the game. "Naturally I was concerned because I haven't pitched very much. I was concerned about my control and I got a little tired . . . but I'm very happy with the results."[91] Simmons's win ignited a four-game winning streak that again moved the Angels within a game and a half of first. But that was followed by seven-game losing streak from which they could not recover, preventing them from meaningful participation in one of the most frenetic pennant races in baseball history, four teams entering the final weekend fighting for the 1967 American League pennant, with the "Impossible Dream" Boston Red Sox ultimately emerging triumphant.

Simmons went 2-1 with a 2.60 earned run average in fourteen appearances for the Angels. He worked out of the bullpen in September and was effective, picking up a win with two perfect innings of relief against the Yankees, and a three-inning save against Minnesota. During the month he allowed only 1 earned run in twelve innings over eight relief appearances. His final Major League assignment came on the dramatic last day of the season, twenty years and three days after his big league debut against the Giants. He was brought in against Detroit to relieve Rickey Clark with two out in the second inning and the Angels trailing, 3-1. Simmons got Dick Tracewski to hit a lazy fly ball, stranding a runner at third. He was pinch-hit for by Jay Johnstone, having retired the only batter he faced. The Angels rallied to win the game, eliminating the Tigers and clinching the pennant for Boston.[92]

Both Robin Roberts and Curt Simmons had admirably battled the lengthening shadows that increasingly encroached upon their careers, but in the end the "realist" had an easier time letting go than did the "over boarder."

Simmons was released by the Angels in October in order for them to reserve younger players on the forty-man roster.[93] He reacted by assuming the role of general manager at the Limekiln Golf Course, a Montgomery County concern in which he and Robin Roberts had partnered, along with several others.[94] Within a month of his final game, Simmons was happily running the mowers at Limekiln—presumably avoiding his toes.[95] He and Roberts eventually bought out their partners and owned the entire operation.

Not only was Simmons the last Whiz Kid to play in a Major League game, outlasting Robin Roberts and Steve Ridzik, who made their final appearances in 1966, but he was also the last of the Wilmington Blue Rocks, along with Jack Sanford and Barney Schultz, whose careers had also come to an end with the conclusion of the 1967 season.

Contacted that December at Limekiln, Simmons betrayed no emotion in confirming his retirement. "I don't want to be a hanger-on," he said. "It was a good life while it lasted."[96]

15

Ghosts of Greatness Past

THE FIRST WHIZ KIDS reunion was held in June 1963. Cosponsored by the Phillies and the Atlantic Refining Company (ARCO), the event drew twenty-five of the players.[1] Several gathered at the Warwick, site of the team's victory party in 1950, after being honored with a parade through the center of the city. Nearly all of them had retired as players, so they caught up, enjoyed a luncheon, and posed for a group photo. Among those pictured were Eddie Waitkus, Del Ennis, Andy Seminick, Curt Simmons (starting pitcher that day for the St. Louis Cardinals), Mike Goliat, Richie Ashburn, Dick Sisler, Granny Hamner, and Eddie Sawyer.[2]

Bob Carpenter was among those addressing the players at the luncheon. He told them, "Seeing all of you back again has been a privilege and a rare tribute. It was a great year for all of us." He concluded with a joke many took as carrying an undercurrent of truth: "You gave me my first pennant and my first ulcer as well. Thank you."[3]

More than thirty-five thousand fans were on hand at Connie Mack Stadium despite it being a Wednesday, attending a three-inning old-timer's exhibition preceding the regular-season game between the Phillies and Cardinals. As the players struggled into uniforms, Bob Miller wisecracked, "Nothing's changed. Everybody's a little fatter, that's all."[4]

It was the Whiz Kids versus the "Is Kids," the latter consisting of current Phillies players and coaches. Fans were amped as Byrum Saam introduced Putsy Caballero, Ken Heintzelman, Bob Miller, Bubba Church, Dick Whitman, Jimmy Bloodworth, Jackie Mayo, Bill Nicholson, Ken Silvestri, and Stan Lopata. Then the Whiz Kids starters were greeted as they took their positions, with Russ Meyer taking the mound—Curt Simmons and Robin

Roberts being unavailable for duty, remaining very much active Major League pitchers. Meyer evoked belly laughs from the crowd by flinging the rosin bag high up into the air, recalling the time he had done so in anger over yet another umpire's call, only to have it land on his head.

Robin Roberts tossed a couple of warm-up pitches and later pinch-hit. Dick Sisler brought a roar from the crowd with a double off the scoreboard. Andy Seminick smacked a home run off Phillies pitching coach Al Widmar for the only run the Whiz Kids tallied. The best entrance by far was that of Jim Konstanty. When the time came to call for a relief pitcher, a helicopter landed behind third base and Konstanty emerged, trudging to the mound as he had so many times for the team in red pinstripes.

The Is Kids team won, 3–1. The players sat in the clubhouse afterward, Del Ennis crushing a beer can in his hands while everyone traded stories about their amazing run in 1950.[5]

SIX YEARS LATER, the Phillies honored their All-Time greatest players, voted by fans as part of Major League Baseball's centennial celebration. The Whiz Kids were well represented, both on the team and in person. Richie Ashburn and Del Ennis were named to the team's outfield, Granny Hamner got the nod at shortstop, Andy Seminick was the catcher, Robin Roberts was the right-handed pitcher, and Eddie Waitkus was declared the team's greatest first baseman. Willie Jones, unable to attend the ceremony, was honored as the team's third baseman—Mike Schmidt's Major League debut remained more than three years away.[6] Roberts was selected the all-time greatest Phillie, edging Grover Cleveland Alexander, Chuck Klein, Richie Ashburn, and Dick Allen.[7]

For Eddie Waitkus the event was a hiatus from his troubles, as he reminisced with a large gathering of teammates for what turned out to be the last time. It had been a major struggle since the shooting two decades earlier, alcohol and depression tightening its unremitting grip on the retired first baseman. Waitkus and his wife separated, he suffered a nervous breakdown, and after a few years working for a trucking company and on the sales floor of a department store, he was often unemployed, outside of each June when he coached kids at the Ted Williams baseball camp, where he assumed the role Jack Burns had played for him and his childhood buddies so many years before. He served as the camp's hitting instructor and loved it, experiencing nearly complete rejuvenation each year—nearly. But at the end of each summer, Waitkus retreated to his rented room in Cambridge, fighting off depression but never seeking help despite confessing to his son, "I'm a sad clown, happy on the outside, making people laugh. But inside I'm crying."[8]

On September 16, 1972, the same day Mike Schmidt hit his first career home run and three years after being honored as the all-time greatest Phillies first baseman, Eddie Waitkus died of esophageal cancer that had spread to his lungs.[9] He was the first of the Whiz Kids players to pass, only fifty-three years old. However, between his harrowing military service and the encounter with Ruth Ann Steinhagen, Waitkus seemed three decades older than the age listed on his death certificate.

His assailant outlived him by forty years, her day-to-day existence cloaked in anonymity. Never again did she comment on the incident that destroyed two people. She lived with her parents and sister and then alone after they had all passed, ultimately succumbing to injuries suffered in a fall at her home in December 2012, her death unnoticed by the press until three months after it occurred.[10]

ON OCTOBER 1, 1970, the Phillies played their final game at Connie Mack Stadium, closing the venue that for sixty-two seasons had hosted Philadelphia baseball, including thirty-three for the Phillies. Bob Carpenter and Connie Mack Jr. were on hand. So was Claude Passeau, who in 1938 was the first winning pitcher for the Phillies at what was then called Shibe Park. Nearly thirty-two thousand fans came to say goodbye—and haul the stadium away piece by piece. A ceremony had been planned with prizes for fans, and a helicopter was to transport home plate to the new Phillies headquarters, Veterans Stadium. Those on hand had other plans.

By the eighth inning fans were boldly dashing onto the field, one purloining a ball from the pitcher's mound. Another grabbed outfielder Ron Stone's arm as he chased a single. When rookie Oscar Gamble lined a walkoff single to give the Phillies a 2–1 win over the Montreal Expos, manager Frank Lucchesi rushed out to congratulate him. Refusing Lucchesi's handshake, Gamble screamed, "Run man, run like hell. We'll be happy later."[11]

As the game ended, fans began tearing out the seats around them, some carrying off entire rows. Others sprinted onto the field and ripped apart the playing surface. One man carted away a toilet.[12] He hauled it to Charley Quinn's Deep Right Field Café, a landmark saloon located on the other side of the outfield wall. Displaying his trophy he shouted, "Quinn, Connie Mack used this!"[13]

It had been decided beforehand that police should not use a heavy hand, so as to avoid tactics that risked inflaming the situation. Perched above the bedlam, Richie Ashburn witnessed the carnage from the press box and was aghast, remarking, "These people are crazy." Then he caught a glimpse of his sons ripping out a stadium chair. "Believe it or not," he laughed while recounting the story, "I still have that seat."[14]

ON AUGUST 16, 1975, the Whiz Kids gathered at Veterans Stadium to celebrate the twenty-fifth anniversary of the last Phillies pennant. Three years earlier, Bob Carpenter, who by that time had spent half of his life in charge of the Phillies, turned over the reins to his thirty-two-year-old son, Robert R. M. Carpenter III, known as Ruly. After nearly three decades in charge, Carpenter assured everyone, "I'll still be around and I'll be up to see a lot of ball games."[15]

The former team president was on hand as each Whiz Kid was presented a ring commemorating the 1950 pennant.[16] Forty thousand were in attendance, paying tribute to the city's greatest living sports heroes. Instead of a helicopter, Jim Konstanty arrived aboard a fire engine. This time both Robin Roberts and Curt Simmons pitched against a team of 1950 All-Stars.[17] Most of the players were on hand, the largest gathering they would have from that point, as age and illness began taking an inevitable toll. Eddie Waitkus was already gone, and Jim Konstanty would be within a year, his remains tended to in Oneonta by his longtime undertaker friend, Andy Skinner.[18] The tee-totaling bullpen ace succumbed to liver cancer.

After finishing nine votes shy that year, anticipation grew that Robin Roberts would be inducted into the Baseball Hall of Fame in 1976. And he was, named on forty-six ballots more than the minimum necessary for induction. At a press conference in New York he joked, "I said a lot of bad things about you gentlemen [last year] but I take it all back."[19]

In early August, Roberts joined fellow inductees Bob Lemon, Fred Lindstrom, and Cal Hubbard for the ceremony. Eddie Sawyer and Curt Simmons were on hand, as was Roberts's elementary school principal, Clarence Lindsay, and his high school teammate Bob Cain. Roberts joked that the

Hall of Fame had denied one of his requests. "I asked Kenny Smith [director of the Hall] if he didn't think it would be appropriate if I were to invite every man who hit a home run off me. He said Cooperstown isn't big enough."[20]

ON JULY 25, 1980, Mike Schmidt homered twice against the Atlanta Braves, giving him 261 career round-trippers to break the team record of 259, held by Del Ennis since 1956.[21] Less than three months later, on October 14, 1980, there arrived an even bigger Phillies milestone. Seventy-year-old Eddie Sawyer was on hand, standing at his field-level seat at Veterans Stadium, wearing a jacket and tie and a Phillies cap while holding a baseball in his right hand. Catcher Bob Boone waited on the field as Sawyer gently tossed him the ball. The two then shook hands, and Boone handed the baseball back to Sawyer, a souvenir for throwing out the first pitch of the Opening Game of the 1980 World Series between the Phillies and the Kansas City Royals.[22] It was the first time the city of Philadelphia had been the site of a Fall Classic game since the Whiz Kids of 1950—and only the third World Series in franchise history.

Sawyer had watched the Phillies clinch the National League pennant at his Valley Forge home two days before, when they won the League Championship Series against Houston. A lot had changed since the Phillies last captured a flag—in 1950 there were sixteen Major League teams; now there were twenty-six, with two divisions in each league. Philadelphia, St. Louis, and Boston had only one Major League team instead of two, and the Phillies played on artificial turf in a multipurpose stadium they shared with the Philadelphia Eagles of the National Football League. Their World Series opponent had not even existed prior to the retirement of every Whiz Kid as a player.

The Phillies went on to defeat the Royals in six games, the final game still ranking by some measures as the most watched World Series game in television history, with a 40.0 rating and nearly fifty-five million viewers.[23] It also featured two of baseball's most enduring images: Pete Rose being Johnny-on-the-spot, snagging a foul pop-up that had bounced out of catcher Bob Boone's glove, the miraculous moment followed a few minutes later by reliever Tug McGraw—who had saved the Phillies first World Series game victory in sixty-five years in the opener—thrusting his arms high into the air after striking out Willie Wilson to end the Series. The Phillies had finally won their first world championship, ninety-seven years after the team was founded.

Richie Ashburn was a Phillies broadcaster and burst with pride at the team's accomplishment. "I enjoyed this year's pennant for selfish reasons," he said. "I'm tired of hearing about the so-called Philadelphia jinx and the collapse of the '50 and '64 Phillies. The '80 Phillies have destroyed some ghosts that have haunted us in Philadelphia all too long."[24]

A year later, Ruly Carpenter, distressed by free agency and escalating player salaries, sold the Phillies to a group led by team vice president Bill Giles, ending nearly four decades of franchise ownership by the Carpenter family. The sale price topped $30 million, the highest ever paid for a Major League baseball team to that point, and quite a return on the $400,000 paid for the team thirty-eight years earlier. In an echo to the days of Horace Fogel, one of Giles's partners was Taft Broadcasting of Cincinnati.[25]

By this point the Phillies were becoming an ongoing success, even with the inevitable ups and downs in the standings. They regularly drew in excess of two million fans per year and carried one of baseball's highest payrolls. Modern fans could be excused for failing to comprehend the long years of futility that had preceded the current era. The Phillies had once been a franchise players avoided. Dick Allen could not wait to escape, and Curt Flood refused to come. Then Steve Carlton had a legendary season, winning 27 games for a bad team in 1972. Mike Schmidt arrived late that same year and became the greatest third baseman in baseball history. Pete Rose signed as a free-agent to play for the Phillies. Philadelphia increasingly became a desired destination for players. In 1993 the Phillies drew more than three million spectators and appeared in their third World Series in Veterans Stadium. Fifteen years later, they won another World Series.

AFTER RICHIE ASHBURN was traded to the Chicago Cubs and spent two years with them, he played one final season with the expansion New York Mets, hitting .306. Ashburn was the Mets representative on the 1962 National League All-Star team, making him one of a select few to have been an All-Star in both his first and last seasons in the Majors. He singled in his final Major League at bat—and in a manner befitting a legendarily bad ball club was subsequently retired on a triple play.[26]

Upon ending his playing career, Ashburn was hired as a broadcaster for Phillies games, a job he held for the rest of his life. His entertaining stories kept the 1950 Phillies at the forefront, even as he became an eternally beloved Philadelphia sports institution. In 1995 Richie Ashburn was the second Whiz Kid inducted into the Hall of Fame, recognized by the Veterans Committee for his prodigious defensive statistics reflecting his ability as one of the game's great center fielders, in addition to his lifetime .308 batting average. Ashburn's ninety-year-old mother was able to share the moment with him.[27] "I'll tell you, I was so surprised," said Genevieve "Toots" Ashburn, "that I ended up crying about it, but I don't know why."[28]

The march of time had taken its toll—Ashburn was no longer young, and he made his living with his wit and voice rather than his bat and glove. The house where he grew up in Tilden was the site of a ballfield. "Home plate is where our house used to be," he said.[29]

But what had not changed was the love of the Philadelphia fan base for the Whiz Kids. A wave of Phillies red enveloped Cooperstown that summer, as Ashburn joined Mike Schmidt for the induction ceremony, two greats from different eras entering the Hall of Fame together.[30]

Ashburn was overcome by emotion at one point during his speech, pausing to admonish himself to "hang on" as he began mentioning the passing of his father, twin sister, and daughter. After recognizing those that had influenced his career and introducing his mother, Ashburn criticized the current state of the game—the battles between players and owners that had led to a strike in 1994, and the lack of a commissioner—and asked if the game had a death wish.

"I hope baseball is paying attention" he said, addressing the audience. "You're not here because they're having fireworks. You're not here because they're giving away something."

For Ashburn it was, always, because of the game that fans came to the ballpark. He later half apologetically said to *Philadelphia Inquirer* sports columnist Bill Lyon about his speech, "You wing it a little bit and you hope you get through it."[31] He had, and a second Whiz Kid was in the Hall.

Two years later, nearing the end of his thirty-fifth season behind the microphone, Richie Ashburn succumbed to a heart attack in a New York hotel room. The news unleashed an immediate sense of loss. "Whitey" was gone, and no one could truly replace him. Fans under forty years of age could not remember listening to a Phillies game without his voice being part of it.

Ashburn's death was front-page news in Philadelphia, where it was dutifully reported that after retiring to his room following a 13–4 Phillies win over the Mets at Shea Stadium, he called the team's traveling secretary, complaining of feeling ill. By the time the Phillies trainer arrived, Ashburn was gone.[32]

Philadelphia sports fans were distraught, as was his mother, reached at her home in Tilden, which Ashburn always visited at the end of the season. She said, "It's hard for me to even realize it's happened. I was just so looking forward to having him home."[33]

THE LAST FORMAL REUNION of the Whiz Kids came in July 2000, marking the team's fiftieth anniversary. By this point the reunions served as side events at the stadium rather than the focal point. Participation was dwindling—ten of the seventeen living players and coach Maje McDonnell joined in festivities held prior to a game between the Phillies and the Baltimore Orioles. Eddie Sawyer had passed away in September 1997, two weeks after Richie Ashburn's death.[34] In the interim so had Russ Meyer, Milo Candini, and Dick Sisler. The remaining players were happy to gather once more. Andy Seminick said of the reunions, "It makes me feel young again." Robin Roberts lamented the inevitable and unyielding march of time, remarking, "So many guys aren't here, but we have only good memories of that year." Roberts said he still followed the game but admitted that most of the time spent by the Whiz Kids involved catching up and reminiscing. "There's only so many hours and so many stories you can tell," he said. "We've got to use up the old stories."[35]

WHAT MADE THE "Whiz Kids" different, memorable, and—for a brief time—successful? It is difficult if not impossible to accurately measure the impact of things that did not happen. For instance, what if Roy Hamey had leapfrogged his plan to scour the Negro Leagues for players into planting the team's flag in the Caribbean? No one will ever know.

Among the things that did happen, Bob Carpenter's willingness to embrace the unconventional—outside of the obvious point made earlier about Black players—while at the same time charting his own course and sticking to it, served the franchise well for the first half-dozen years. Carpenter hired Eddie Sawyer and let him take a risk on a relief pitcher in his thirties, whose fastball could not break a pane of glass, and make him the backbone of the pitching staff, using him in a way no relief pitcher had ever been. Their best defensive player was a first baseman with no power, they had another first baseman playing left field, and a second baseman and third baseman learning their positions in the Major Leagues. Their pitching ace threw almost nothing but fastballs, and their center fielder's arm was more or less average. But the Phillies managed to look past that and recognize the talent and commitment both possessed to eventually land them in the Hall of Fame.

The Phillies of that era were in some ways ahead of their time, with a trainer who believed in the most advanced methods and coaches who were not just lifelong buddies of the manager but teachers who taught, working for a former college professor. They established schools for recruiting and developing talent, to instruct in the Phillies method of playing baseball. They tried things, and it worked.

And then it didn't. The Phillies continually attempted to re-create what had worked in 1950, instead of recognizing the shift in the baseball landscape that began on April 15, 1947, and adapting their plan to that reality. Dynasties develop through foresight, opportunity, resources, and luck. Injuries inevitably took their toll. Players reverted to their norms after career years. Opponents took them more seriously. The Phillies were lucky that in 1944 they finally had an owner with sufficient capital—and patience—for the team to undertake a massive overhaul of the franchise and the way it went about developing talent.

But they lost too much money chasing maybes in the 1950s, while passing on a pipeline of finished talent provided by the Negro Leagues. Some argued that prejudice blinded the franchise. In the 1940s Bob Carpenter and the Phillies gambled on amateur talent and won. In the 1950s they gambled and lost, at a time when the downside was much greater, with the game as a whole entering a transition period that was less stable financially.

THE WHIZ KIDS are part of baseball history. As with all athletes, when remembered they remain in the mind's eye as they were—young, funny, heroic. And always young.

Bubba Church looked back and said that he did not really appreciate the era in which he played until about thirty years later. "We competed, we wanted to win. But we respected each other."[36]

Stan Lopata marveled at the continued popularity of the team long after his playing days and said, "It's tough to explain, but wherever you go, from Detroit to Portland to Philadelphia, they know the Whiz Kids."[37] Despite their lacking a World Series title, the players were always treated as heroes, especially in Philadelphia. But as Lopata observed, their fan base stretched even further. Legendary college basketball coach Bobby Knight was an unabashed fan of the Whiz Kids, proud that he could name every member of the starting lineup, including second baseman Mike Goliat.[38]

Many of the Whiz Kids were close. Putsy Caballero had roomed with Richie Ashburn in the Minor Leagues, and they became fast friends. Caballero followed through on a promise to name his first son after Ashburn.[39] After his playing days, Caballero moved back to New Orleans and was involved in his father-in-law's pest-control business, where his coworkers included trumpeter Al Hirt and clarinetist Pete Fountain.[40] He survived Hurricane Katrina, but water filled his home during the disaster, and he lost all of his baseball mementoes.

Bob Carpenter died in 1990 of cancer at age seventy-four. He was noted for taking over the team at a young age, being thrilled when the Phillies finally won a World Series in 1980, and having the Whiz Kids be his "biggest thrill."[41]

It was said that football was his favorite sport, that he was a regular guy, and that he could be a tough negotiator who was not a fan of agents or the players' union. "Look, if a player comes in to me and we sit and talk, and he's had a good year, he's going to get whatever he wants from me," he said. "But if he comes in with a sharp-shooting lawyer, I'm going to dig up every negative thing I can about that player."[42]

Del Ennis said of Carpenter, "He was the best owner I ever played for." Eddie Sawyer called him "tender-hearted" and said, "When he fired me in 1952, I think it was tougher on him than it was on me."[43] Dick Sisler told a story of sneaking in after curfew during training camp and running into Carpenter. Certain he was in trouble, Sisler was surprised when the owner called him over and said, "Don't be in such a hurry. Come on over here and have a beer." Sisler said, "That's the kind of guy he was."[44]

Robin Roberts ultimately tackled his postbaseball career with the same competitive nature he brought to the diamond, first spending a decade with an investment firm while continuing his morning sports show on WPEN. He became friends with author James Michener and stayed in touch with the game he had once dominated. In 1976 Roberts was offered the position of head baseball coach at the University of South Florida and helped establish a strong program there, including a still school-best record of 45-13 in 1982—a team that included his son, Jimmy, who was All-Sun Belt Conference. Roberts sent four players to the big leagues: Chris Welsh, Tony Fossas, Tim Hulett, and Scott Hemond. He also authored a pair of books, one about the magical 1950 season, with contributions from many of his teammates, and an autobiography—both assisted by baseball historian C. Paul Rogers.

Roberts's wife, Mary, the love of his life, passed away following a stroke in 2005, and Robin's final five years were tough for him. When he died in 2010, fans stopped to salute his statue located outside Citizens Bank Park, the Phillies home beginning in 2004.[45] Roberts's death left six living Whiz Kids plus coach Maje McDonnell for the sixty-year anniversary of the team's pennant. Simmons was the youngest at eighty.[46]

Aging, as they say, is not for the faint of heart. It is hard—doubly so for those whose athletic ability is such a part of their identity. Time marched on, as did Curt Simmons. He spent many years managing Limekiln, with his family and that of Robin Roberts actively involved in its operation. One of the frequent visitors to the club was Bobby Shantz, who lived five miles from Simmons and the course, in Ambler, Pennsylvania.

Shantz and Simmons had pitched in the same ballpark in Philadelphia at the same time for different teams, but they went back even further to a game played in Egypt in October 1947. Shantz appeared with a semipro team from Souderton, while Simmons, a week after his epic Major League debut against the New York Giants, took the mound for Egypt. Shantz beat Simmons, 4–1, striking out 14 batters, although Simmons did hit a double and scored the only run off Shantz.[47] That performance helped catapult Bobby Shantz to a long Major League career that included an American League MVP Award in 1952. But that was in the past, as the two joked about their shared experiences.

Simmons's teammates passed as the years rolled on, each invariably noted first and foremost in their obituary notice for being a Whiz Kid. Many of the fans who remembered them were passing on as well. For Simmons there would be annual celebrations in Egypt, questions from curious reporters, and anniversary recaps of the 1950 season. Inevitably, the time that lapsed between these observances lengthened.

In November 2011 Simmons was inducted into the Philadelphia Sports Hall of Fame—among the other honorees were Biz Mackey, Jimmy Dykes, and Moses Malone.[48] At the banquet, held at the Sheraton Society Hill in Philadelphia, Simmons deflected most questions, saying, "I'm glad they remembered me, but I don't usually go to these kinds of things."[49]

In June 2012, on the sixty-fifth anniversary of his pitching against the Phillies there, the ballfield in Egypt was named in honor of Curt Simmons. It was a bittersweet event, Simmons's wife, Dot, having passed three months before after several years of bad health.[50] It was a beautiful day as Simmons was paraded down Main Street in a convertible, tossing candy to kids as he passed. Dallas Green and the Phillie Phanatic were among those on hand for the event. One fan in his twenties said, "It's like Christmas and everyone's birthday rolled into one. We have a lot of pride for Egypt."[51]

In 2016, at age eighty-six and having undergone three hip replacements, Simmons grew melancholy. "Once in a while, some old guy will come up and say something about the 'Whiz Kids.' But not very often anymore. A lot of the fans who remember us have died or moved away."[52]

As their teammates passed, Bob Miller and Curt Simmons remained in touch, calling each other regularly as the last two living Whiz Kids. Limekiln Country Club closed in December 2019, sold to developers to make way for senior housing. Simmons, who lived next to the course, was especially saddened by its demise, watching his former haven slowly reclaimed by nature while awaiting bulldozers. It seemed a metaphor for what was happening to him and his teammates. "I don't like to sit out there anymore," he told Frank Fitzpatrick, a reporter for the *Philadelphia Inquirer*.[53]

In 2020 Miller was interviewed for a retrospective *Philadelphia Daily News* article about the Whiz Kids, seventy years after their greatest accomplishment. He reflected wistfully, remarking, "I remember the wonderful guys I played with. I just wish they were still around and I could go have a Coke with Russ Meyer and some of the guys. We really had a great, great something. . . . I don't know what the hell you'd call it. It was a winning attitude. It was beautiful."[54]

Simmons became the last of the Whiz Kids at the death of Miller in November 2020 at the age of ninety-four. His time as head baseball coach at the University of Detroit, where he won 896 games, was lauded. "Coach Miller was a larger-than-life person to generations of Titan baseball players," said his successor, Chris Czarnik.[55] But above all else, in his final profile Bob Miller was remembered as a Whiz Kid, always and forever.

They continued celebrating Curt Simmons Day in Egypt, and Simmons continued appearing as long as he was able, an honor he enjoyed up to his death on December 13, 2022.[56] The Whiz Kids were no more.

And yet, at the same time they still *were*. Bound by a common accomplishment, a common experience, a common bond, a bond shared in a different way, and through a different experience, by the fans who had rooted for them—fans who had long suffered and starved for something to celebrate. There came a time when many of the team's players were no longer remembered individually, but the whole of them was never forgotten. When introduced by name and having been a Whiz Kid, faces would light up with the unmistakable delight of recognition.

Although they had not achieved all they had wanted to in October 1950, often lamenting the aftermath of winning the pennant, along with the team's failure to again reach the World Series, these men had experienced a moment with the sports world focused on them. They reached the pinnacle of their profession and earned a permanent place in baseball history. Many of their fans were now gone but had passed down their memories to the next generation, which found a way to make those memories their own. In a city where sports fandom takes on an almost religious caste, the players arguably became among its saints—even if some had a bit of sinner in them.

The Whiz Kids had achieved this immortality of sorts thanks to three big moments that happened only minutes apart, the lack of any of which would have relegated the team to a mere asterisk and a painful memory: a throw from the outfield, a swing of the bat, and a fierce competitor bearing down on an opponent from the rubber at Ebbets Field with two out in the bottom of the tenth on an October afternoon in 1950.

These singular successes were buttressed by hundreds of successes *and* failures during year—and the successes and failures during the long history of an often-frustrating franchise. Players and fans alike had floated within a built-up reservoir of desire for a winner. When the dam burst, it released decades of frustration feeding a crescendo that made the 1950 Philadelphia Phillies the Whiz Kids.

Always and forever.

NOTES

I. A HISTORY OF PHILADELPHIA BASEBALL

1. *United States Gazette*, March 28, 1826, 2.
2. *Philadelphia Public Ledger*, May 14, 1838, 1.
3. *Philadelphia Public Ledger*, October 11, 1859, 1.
4. Nemec, *Major League Baseball Profiles*, 1:373.
5. *Brooklyn Union*, June 16, 1865, 1. Reach had been courted by the Athletics—in 1864 they had "borrowed" him from the Eckfords for several games—and he even umpired at least one of their contests, a practice the *Brooklyn Daily Eagle* condemned as ruining competition. In all likelihood, the Athletics were paying him for his trouble. Reach is often called baseball's first professional player, but other players had previously been paid, including Jim Creighton and several of the Athletics. *Brooklyn Daily Eagle*, June 23, 1864, 2; *Brooklyn Daily Eagle*, August 2, 1864, 2; and Seymour and Seymour Mills, *Baseball: The Early Years*, 47–48.
6. *New York Times*, October 31, 1865, 5; *Philadelphia Inquirer*, October 31, 1865, 4; and *Philadelphia Inquirer*, November 7, 1865, 4.
7. *Philadelphia Evening Telegraph*, October 2, 1866, 4; and *Philadelphia Inquirer*, October 2, 1866, 4.
8. *Brooklyn Daily Eagle*, October 16, 1866, 2.
9. *Harper's Weekly*, November 3, 1866, 697, illustration.
10. *Philadelphia Inquirer*, October 16, 1866, 1.
11. *Philadelphia Inquirer*, October 23, 1866, 4.
12. Jeff Laing, "Philadelphia—October 1866." The article quotes research published by Eric Miklich in *The Base Ball Player's Chronicle*.
13. *Philadelphia Inquirer*, October 11, 1871, 2.
14. *Philadelphia Inquirer*, December 12, 1867, 3; Seymour and Seymour Mills, *Baseball: The Early Years*, 42; and "The Pythian Base Ball Club: Political Activism on the Diamond," Villanova University, accessed December 10, 2023, https://exhibits.library.villanova.edu/institute-colored-youth/community-moments/philadelphia-pythians.
15. *Philadelphia Inquirer*, September 4, 1869, 2. The newspaper included a complete play-by-play of the game.

16. *Pittsburgh Daily Post*, September 7, 1869, 2.
17. *London Daily News*, August 11, 1874, 2. The Athletics and Boston Red Stockings were abroad for seven weeks, with Boston winning ten of the sixteen games. Pitcher Dick McBride broke his thumb in the final exhibition, played in Dublin. When the teams returned to Philadelphia on September 9, large crowds were on hand to greet them, along with a fireworks display. *Philadelphia Inquirer*, September 10, 1874, 2.
18. *London Observer*, August 9, 1874, 5. The *Observer* deemed baseball a "modified, or rather a developed, Rounders."
19. *Philadelphia Inquirer*, May 27, 1875, 3. Two months later, Joe Borden, pitching under the pseudonym Joe Josephs, pitched a no-hitter for the Philadelphia Pearls (also called the "Phillies"—see later note) against Chicago, the only no-hitter ever pitched in the National Association. Borden was also the winning pitcher in the first game in National League history. *Philadelphia Inquirer*, July 29, 1875, 2; and Westcott, "Joe Borden."
20. *Philadelphia Inquirer*, July 4, 1876, 3.
21. *Philadelphia Inquirer*, December 8, 1876, 1; *1877 Constitution and Playing Rules of the National League of Professional Baseball Clubs*, 41–45; and Warrington, "Entering the National League."
22. *Philadelphia Times*, September 29, 1883, 2. Large crowds had gathered around the *Times* offices and at the ballpark, receiving word of the game relayed by telegraph. For more on the team, see Hofmann and Nowlin, *1883 Philadelphia Athletics*.
23. *Philadelphia Times*, October 2, 1883, 1. A committee met the team's train at Harrisburg and escorted the players to Philadelphia, with a stop in Lancaster. More than one hundred police officers and two hundred fifty railroad representatives were assigned to Broad Street Station to maintain order for the team's arrival in Philadelphia.
24. *Philadelphia Inquirer*, March 29, 1901, 6; *Philadelphia Inquirer*, February 25, 1909, 10; and Warrington, "Entering the National League," 76–77. Farrelly and Walsh owned 100 of the 150 shares issued at one hundred dollars each. Reach and Pratt each owned twenty shares, and Rogers ten. The partnership was registered on November 1, 1882, under the name Philadelphia Ball Club Limited, for a term of twenty years. Also see Warrington, "Philadelphia in 1882 League Alliance."
25. The nickname *Phillies* was used as early as 1875, in connection with one of the National Association teams, also called the Pearls, or Whites, as opposed to the better-known and more successful Philadelphia Athletics of the same league. Philadelphia briefly had an Eastern League entry in 1881 that was occasionally called Phillies before it moved to Baltimore. When Philadelphia joined the reborn League Alliance for 1882, the team was sometimes called Phillies during the season. Nicknames were informal in those years, usually created by newspapers for their coverage. *Philadelphia Times*, May 17, 1875, 4; *Philadelphia*

Times, May 20, 1875, 4; *Philadelphia Times*, June 25, 1875, 1; *Philadelphia Times*,
June 28, 1875, 4; *Philadelphia Times*, August 19, 1875, 4; *Philadelphia Times*,
August 20, 1875, 4; *Philadelphia Inquirer*, June 25, 1881, 2; *Philadelphia Inquirer*,
April 14, 1882, 2; and *Philadelphia Inquirer*, April 3, 1883, 8.

26. *Philadelphia Times*, December 7, 1882, 3. The woman, Sarah McLaughlin, "gave
birth" (likely miscarried) a couple of days after taking ill. She told her mother
that she became sick after Henderson gave her a bottle of liquid. Although
arrested after a coroner's inquest, there is no record that Henderson was found
guilty or served jail time.

27. *Baltimore Sun*, May 28, 1883, 5. It is assumed that since Henderson took up
employment with a team in another state, his legal issues were resolved one
way or another.

28. *Philadelphia Inquirer*, May 2, 1887, 3.

29. *Philadelphia Inquirer*, August 31, 1885, 3.

30. *Philadelphia Inquirer*, February 8, 1925, 26. Shettsline, originally an office boy
for John I. Rogers, was with the Phillies almost from the beginning in various capacities, including ticket taker. He became business manager and then
interim field manager in June 1898, replacing George Stallings. When the team
played well, Shettsline remained in the dugout, picking up third-place finishes
in 1899 and 1900 and second place in 1901. But after the team lost several players to the American League and fell to seventh in 1902, Shettsline returned
to his role as business manager. He was named president in 1905, but in 1909
moved back to business manager, remaining in the position until he was let
go in November 1926 and replaced by Gerald Nugent. *Philadelphia Inquirer*,
June 19, 1898, 12; *Philadelphia Inquirer*, November 19, 1926, 24; and *Philadelphia
Inquirer*, February 23, 1933, 16.

31. *Philadelphia Inquirer*, April 30, 1888, 8; and *Philadelphia Times*, April 30, 1888, 1.
Among those present when Ferguson died were team trainer Tom Taylor and
teammates Jack Clements and Sid Farrar. Ferguson's passing came less than a
year after the death of his infant daughter. *Philadelphia Times*, June 10, 1887, 1.

32. *Philadelphia Inquirer*, April 12, 1888, 3.

33. *Philadelphia Inquirer*, April 17, 1888, 3.

34. *Philadelphia Inquirer*, May 1, 1888, 8. For more about Ferguson's career, see
Nemec, *Major League Baseball Profiles*, 2:292–93; and Hofmann, "Charlie
Ferguson." The Phillies staged a benefit game four days later against a popular
local team, the Riverton Ball Club, raising $150 for Ferguson's widow. *Philadel-
phia Inquirer*, May 5, 1888, 3.

35. Surprisingly, the team's leading hitter was not Hamilton, Thompson, or
Delahanty—it was switch-hitting fourth outfielder "Tuck" Turner, a one-time
amateur teammate of Wee Willie Keeler, who hit .418 in 347 official at bats.

36. *Philadelphia Inquirer*, August 7, 1894, 1; and *Philadelphia Inquirer*, August 12,
1894, 24. Fires were a problem around the league that year—the previous day,
a blaze had claimed the grandstand of the Chicago ballpark during a game,

and Boston had lost its ballpark to flames just shy of three months before that. *Chicago Tribune*, August 6, 1894, 1, 2; and *Boston Globe*, May 16, 1894, 1.

37. *Philadelphia Inquirer*, April 16, 1895, 6. The innovation was known as the Compton System. It cost ten, fifteen, or twenty-five cents to "see" the game, although those receiving a certificate at a home game received a discount. After interest flagged, the venture moved to a new venue, the Winter Circus, for a few days, after which the experiment was discontinued. *Philadelphia Inquirer*, June 21, 1895, 5; *Philadelphia Inquirer*, June 23, 1895, 16; and *Philadelphia Inquirer*, July 26, 1895, 5.

38. *Philadelphia Inquirer*, April 19, 1895, 6.

39. *Philadelphia Inquirer*, November 14, 1895, 5; and *Philadelphia Inquirer*, August 2, 1896, 8. That season, the Phillies uniquely employed left-handers at both catcher—Jack Clements—and shortstop—Bill Hulen.

40. *Washington Times*, October 21, 1901, 6. Like Lajoie the year before, Delahanty led the American League in batting average in 1902. The next summer, he perished in the Niagara River under mysterious circumstances, his body recovered at the base of Horseshoe Falls. For more about Delahanty's death, see Sowell, *July 2, 1903*.

41. *Philadelphia Inquirer*, September 18, 1900, 10; and *Cincinnati Enquirer*, September 18, 1900, 4. Numerous and inaccurate accounts place this sordid chapter at the feet of George Stallings, who managed the Phillies in 1897 and 1898 and had a reputation for such hijinks, but this incident unfolded under William Shettsline's watch. A week later, the Brooklyn Superbas were hosting the Phillies and complained that Murphy was stationed in an apartment across the street, continuing his use of opera glasses to steal signs and signal them to his teammates. Apparently, the Phillies were in league with the Pittsburgh Pirates in cheating—both knew about the other and agreed to a truce when they played in exchange for not revealing the scheme. A year earlier, former Phillies pitcher Bill Magee charged that Murphy regularly used opera glasses and sat in Shettsline's office located under the center-field bleachers, signaling batters by adjusting a window shade. *Brooklyn Daily Eagle*, September 27, 1900, 14; Dittmar, "Shocking Discovery," 52–53, 65; and *Sporting Life*, October 21, 1899, 10.

42. *Philadelphia Inquirer*, March 1, 1903, 14. Reach and Rogers retained ownership of the stadium. *Philadelphia Inquirer*, November 27, 1909, 1.

43. *Philadelphia Inquirer*, June 11, 1903, 10; and Rogers, "Napoleon Lajoie, Breach of Contract," 340. Lajoie was prevented from playing in Philadelphia, and when the Phillies obtained another injunction in 1902, the Athletics released him, and he signed with Cleveland, where he continued as a major star. The team was eventually nicknamed "Naps" in his honor. Until the lawsuit was dropped, whenever Cleveland played in Philadelphia, Lajoie would stay in Atlantic City until the series ended.

44. *Philadelphia Inquirer*, August 9, 1903, 1, 2, 10; and *Philadelphia Inquirer*, August 10, 1903, 1, 2. Not enough ambulances were available to ferry the injured to

the hospital, so other vehicles were commandeered. The balcony was utilized as a walkway and located on the outside of the ballpark, held in place by joists at the top—most of which were rotted—with no bracing underneath. The balconies and bleachers had never been properly inspected. The Phillies were idle for eleven days, then played fifteen games at the home field of the Athletics, Columbia Park, before their ballpark was cleared for the return of spectators. One of the jurors at the inquest was the builder of the 1887 ballpark that burned down. For an excellent discussion of the ballpark's history and this tragic incident, see Warrington, "Baseball's Deadliest Disaster"; and Morton, "Coroner's Jury and Bankruptcy." Six years earlier, one hundred feet of railing along the left-field bleachers gave way during a bicycle race, sending 150 spectators tumbling ten feet. Nine people were transported to the hospital. *Philadelphia Inquirer*, June 27, 1897, 1.

45. *Philadelphia Inquirer*, February 25, 1909, 10; and *Philadelphia Inquirer*, February 26, 1909, 6.
46. *Philadelphia Inquirer*, June 29, 1909, 1, 2.
47. *Philadelphia Inquirer*, November 27, 1909, 10.
48. *Cincinnati Enquirer*, November 27, 1909, 8.
49. *Philadelphia Inquirer*, November 27, 1909, 1, 10; and *Philadelphia Inquirer*, December 26, 1909, 10.
50. *Philadelphia Inquirer*, December 31, 1909, 1, 10. Rogers expressed regret at not being able to retain ownership of the grounds, declaring it an excellent real estate investment that would be worth a half million dollars within a decade.
51. *Philadelphia Inquirer*, October 1, 1936, 22; and *Philadelphia Inquirer*, June 26, 1938, 39.
52. Lane, "Horace Fogel," 25.
53. *Chicago Tribune*, July 30, 1910, 7.
54. *Philadelphia Inquirer*, September 14, 1910, 10; and *Syracuse Post-Standard*, January 19, 1911, 14.
55. *Philadelphia Inquirer*, August 17, 1911, 10.
56. Cravath was drafted by the Pittsburgh Pirates a couple of weeks later but had already signed with the Phillies. The National Commission awarded Cravath to Philadelphia. *Philadelphia Inquirer*, September 2, 1911, 10; *Pittsburgh Press*, September 3, 1911, 5; and *Pittsburgh Post-Gazette*, September 30, 1911, 10.
57. *Atlanta Constitution*, August 18, 1912, 12B.
58. *Philadelphia Inquirer*, June 16, 1912, sporting section, 3.
59. *Philadelphia Inquirer*, November 27, 1912, 1, 10; and *Philadelphia Inquirer*, November 28, 1912, 1, 8.
60. *Philadelphia Inquirer*, December 15, 1912, 18; and Lane, "Horace Fogel," 32.
61. *Philadelphia Inquirer*, January 1, 1913, 10.
62. *Philadelphia Inquirer*, January 16, 1913, 1, 10.
63. *Philadelphia Inquirer*, August 15, 1913, 10; and *Philadelphia Inquirer*, October 21, 1913, 12.

64. *Philadelphia Inquirer*, April 11, 1914, 12. Although the Phillies won the case, the judge's ruling also called baseball's reserve clause into question and instigated an expansion of the Federal League player raids. Weeghman v. Killefer.

65. *Cincinnati Enquirer*, February 12, 1915, 8.

66. *Portland Morning Oregonian*, December 15, 1914; and *Portland Morning Oregonian*, March 15, 1915.

67. *Philadelphia Inquirer*, October 9, 1915, 1, 11. Woodrow Wilson attended the second game of the World Series, alongside his fiancée of three days, Edith Galt, making him the first sitting president to attend the Fall Classic. *Philadelphia Inquirer*, October 10, 1915, 1, 11.

68. Baker, "Alexander as Player and Man," 54–56.

69. *Philadelphia Evening Public Ledger*, December 12, 1917, 14.

70. *Philadelphia Inquirer*, December 12, 1917, 16.

71. *Philadelphia Inquirer*, December 12, 1917, 16. Prendergast won 13 games in his first season with Philadelphia and then never won another Major League game. Dillhoefer was traded to the St. Louis Cardinals in 1919 and became a favorite of manager Branch Rickey but contracted typhoid while on his honeymoon in January 1922 and died a few weeks later at age twenty-eight. *St. Louis Post-Dispatch*, February 23, 1922, 1.

72. *Philadelphia Inquirer*, December 30, 1917, 12.

73. National army enlistment and assignment card, 2845730, for Grover Cleveland Alexander. National Archives, *Baseball: National Pastime*. Alexander enlisted on April 29, 1918, after pitching three games for the Cubs, winning two.

74. *Philadelphia Inquirer*, May 15, 1927, 1, 6.

75. After O'Doul hit .398 and .383, he was traded to Brooklyn for two pitchers: Jumbo Elliott, who had one good season for the Phillies, in 1931, and Clise Dudley, who did not. *Philadelphia Inquirer*, October 15, 1930, 19.

76. *Philadelphia Inquirer*, December 5, 1930, 18.

77. *Philadelphia Inquirer*, December 5, 1930, 18.

78. *Philadelphia Inquirer*, November 8, 1932, 20.

79. *Philadelphia Inquirer*, November 8, 1933, 1. The vote to repeal the ordinance and replace it with one allowing Sunday baseball passed overwhelmingly, by a more than eight-to-one margin for repeal and five to one for the replacement.

80. William and Laura Baker are interred in Brooklyn's Green-Wood Cemetery. Laura Baker's death date comes from the cemetery's records.

81. Rogers and Nowlin, *Whiz Kids Take Pennant*, 7. In 1950 Edgar Williams wrote that this incident came after a Cubs-Phillies doubleheader at the Baker Bowl and the fan had written in black paint "Because They Stink." *Philadelphia Inquirer Baseball Guide*, April 17, 1950, 5.

82. Davids, "Baker Bowl."

83. *Chicago Tribune*, June 3, 1937, 24.

84. *Philadelphia Inquirer*, June 26, 1938, sports section, 5.

85. *Philadelphia Inquirer*, July 1, 1938, 23.
86. *Philadelphia Inquirer*, November 12, 1940.
87. *Philadelphia Inquirer*, November 13, 1942, 35.
88. Salisbury, "If Anyone Should Have Been a Phillie." The article quotes from Campanella's autobiography, *It's Good to Be Alive*, which places the event in 1945. However, the involvement of Lobert and Nugent in the story would date its occurrence to 1942.
89. *Philadelphia Inquirer*, December 13, 1942, 37, 41.
90. *Philadelphia Inquirer*, February 10, 1943, 31, 32.
91. Veeck met briefly with Nugent during the 1942 World Series, but evidence points to the increased embellishment of his version of events over the years. When having opportunities in both Cleveland and St. Louis to do what he claimed he had wanted to do in Philadelphia, he failed to do so. For a pair of excellent discussions regarding Veeck's story, see "A Baseball Myth Exploded: Bill Veeck and the 1943 Sale of the Phillies," published in *The National Pastime*, volume 18, by the Society of American Baseball Research (SABR) in 1998, and "The Veracity of Veeck" in the *Baseball Research Journal*, published in the fall of 2013, also by SABR.
92. *Philadelphia Inquirer*, February 21, 1943, 45.

2. THE FIRST WHIZ KIDS

1. *Philadelphia Inquirer*, February 21, 1943, S-1, S-4.
2. *Philadelphia Inquirer*, February 21, 1943, S-4.
3. *New York Daily News*, October 11, 1941, 29. Harmon signed to play only one game, due to radio broadcasting duties he had in Detroit.
4. *Brooklyn Citizen*, September 2, 1942, 8.
5. *Philadelphia Inquirer*, February 20, 1943, 21; *Philadelphia Inquirer*, February 22, 1943, 22; *Philadelphia Inquirer*, February 23, 1943, 27; and *Philadelphia Inquirer*, February 25, 1943, 24.
6. *San Francisco Examiner*, February 26, 1943, 18.
7. *Harrisburg Telegraph*, March 19, 1943, 17.
8. *Harrisburg Telegraph*, March 25, 1943, 23.
9. *Lebanon (PA) Daily News*, March 25, 1943, 12.
10. *Harrisburg Telegraph*, March 9, 1943, 13.
11. *Philadelphia Inquirer*, January 23, 1943, 19.
12. *Philadelphia Inquirer*, March 18, 1943, 21.
13. *Philadelphia Inquirer*, April 17, 1943, 22.
14. *Philadelphia Inquirer*, April 7, 1943, 10.
15. *Philadelphia Inquirer*, March 25, 1943, 28.
16. *Cleveland Plain Dealer*, March 31, 1943, 16; and *Harrisburg Telegraph*, March 31, 1943, 16.
17. *Philadelphia Inquirer*, March 10, 1943, 32.

18. *Philadelphia Inquirer*, September 7, 1943, 24. For Dahlgren's side of the story and insistence that his career was forever damaged by gossip about marijuana use, see *Rumor in Town*, written by Dahlgren's grandson, Matt.

19. *Philadelphia Inquirer*, April 28, 1943, 30.

20. *Philadelphia Inquirer*, April 30, 1943, 30.

21. *Philadelphia Inquirer*, May 19, 1943, 34; and *Philadelphia Inquirer*, May 24, 1943, 22.

22. *Philadelphia Inquirer*, June 2, 1943, 32.

23. *Philadelphia Inquirer*, June 26, 1943, 16.

24. *Philadelphia Inquirer*, July 4, 1943, 11; and *Philadelphia Inquirer*, July 13, 1943, 20.

25. *Philadelphia Inquirer*, July 28, 1943, 28; and *Philadelphia Inquirer*, July 31, 1943, 16.

26. *Philadelphia Inquirer*, July 28, 1943, 28, 29.

27. *Philadelphia Inquirer*, July 29, 1943, 24, 25. Earl Whitehill was also fired.

28. *Philadelphia Inquirer*, July 31, 1943, 16.

29. *Philadelphia Inquirer*, August 2, 1943, 20.

30. *Philadelphia Inquirer*, August 2, 1943, 20, 21.

31. *Philadelphia Inquirer*, August 3, 1943, 22.

32. *Philadelphia Inquirer*, December 4, 1943, 14.

33. *Philadelphia Inquirer*, November 24, 1943, 24.

34. *Philadelphia Inquirer*, May 3, 1943, 24.

35. *Knoxville News-Sentinel*, September 12, 1943, b-1; and *Philadelphia Inquirer*, September 13, 1943, 21.

36. *Philadelphia Inquirer*, September 16, 1943, 30.

37. *Philadelphia Inquirer*, November 24, 1943, 24.

38. *Philadelphia Inquirer*, November 24, 1943, 24, 25.

39. *Philadelphia Inquirer*, December 4, 1943, 14.

40. *Philadelphia Inquirer*, November 24, 1943, 24, 25. Robert Carpenter Sr. had purchased two thousand shares, roughly a ten percent stake, in the Phillies two months earlier.

41. Cox became founder, co-owner, and vice president of the Brooklyn Football Dodgers in 1946. There, he ran afoul of star quarterback Glenn Dobbs, the league's MVP, who openly complained to *Tulsa World* sports editor B. A. Bridgewater about Cox's meddling and trying to tell him how to play. *Tulsa Daily World*, December 3, 1947, 20.

42. *New York Times*, March 30, 1989, b8.

43. *Philadelphia Inquirer*, November 22, 1972, 8. Bob Carpenter remembered securing a three-day pass so he could sign papers to take over the team.

44. *The Sporting News*, December 16, 1943, 5.

45. Taxiera, *Unique Look at Big League Baseball*, 267.

46. *Spalding's Official Football Guide*, 1937, 72, 147; *Spalding's Official Football Guide*, 1938, 78, 147; *Wilmington News Journal*, October 30, 1937, 12; and *Wilmington News Journal*, November 11, 1937, 34.

47. *Wilmington News Journal*, June 20, 1938, 10.
48. *Wilmington Morning News*, January 16, 1940, 1.
49. *The Sporting News*, December 2, 1943, 4.
50. *Philadelphia Inquirer*, December 3, 1943, 30.
51. *Philadelphia Inquirer*, March 19, 1944, 27.
52. *Philadelphia Inquirer*, November 25, 1943, 24.
53. *Philadelphia Inquirer*, December 1, 1943, 32.
54. *Philadelphia Inquirer*, December 2, 1943, 26.
55. *Philadelphia Inquirer*, December 7, 1943, 28.
56. *Philadelphia Inquirer*, December 21, 1943, 20.
57. *Wilmington News Journal*, December 8, 1943, 18.
58. *Bradford Evening Star*, February 15, 1944, 7.
59. *Philadelphia Inquirer*, January 25, 1944, 20.
60. *Philadelphia Inquirer*, March 5, 1944, 2-s.
61. *Philadelphia Inquirer*, March 9, 1944, 22.
62. *The Sporting News*, March 16, 1944, 10.
63. Associated Press, *Scranton Times Tribune*, May 30, 1944, 10. Eddie Sawyer, who had just taken over as manager at Utica, said he had suggested the name Blue Sox for the team. Roberts and Rogers, *Whiz Kids and 1950 Pennant*, 31.
64. Associated Press, *Washington Evening Star*, May 30, 1944, A-9.
65. *Philadelphia Inquirer*, August 2, 1944, 21.
66. *Philadelphia Inquirer*, October 2, 1944, 17, 18.
67. *Philadelphia Inquirer*, January 28, 1945, s-1; and *Philadelphia Inquirer*, January 30, 1945, 16.
68. *Richmond News Leader*, July 7, 1944, 16.
69. *The Sporting News*, March 8, 1945, 5.
70. *Philadelphia Inquirer*, September 15, 1944, 24.
71. *Philadelphia Inquirer*, September 10, 1944, 21; *The Sporting News*, September 21, 1944, 13; and Rogers and Nowlin, *Whiz Kids Take Pennant*, 45.
72. *Philadelphia Inquirer*, September 16, 1944, 13.
73. *Richmond News Leader*, September 20, 1944, 20.
74. *Richmond News Leader*, October 20, 1944, 20.
75. *Nebraska State Journal*, February 4, 1945, 2-B.
76. *Tilden Citizen*, April 11, 1946, 8; and *Tilden Citizen*, April 25, 1946, 1. Bob Ashburn was injured in a car accident in California while serving in the military.
77. *The Sporting News*, March 31, 1948, 7.
78. *Lincoln Star*, July 22, 1943, 8.
79. *Lincoln Star*, June 25, 1944, 1-B.
80. *Lincoln Journal Star*, August 4, 1944, 10.
81. *New York Daily News*, August 8, 1944, 30; and *Brooklyn Daily Eagle*, August 8, 1944, 10.
82. *The Sporting News*, March 31, 1948; and *Chicago Tribune*, April 30, 1960, 34.
83. *The Sporting News*, March 31, 1948, 7.

84. *Philadelphia Inquirer*, May 6, 1945, s-1.
85. Rogers and Nowlin, *Whiz Kids Take Pennant*, 77.
86. *Philadelphia Inquirer*, May 14, 1945, 17.
87. Brown, "Hamner of Whiz Kids," 60.
88. In addition to Barrett, the other 20-game losers were Eppa Rixey in 1917 and 1920, George Smith in 1921, Jack Scott in 1927, Bucky Walters *and* Joe Bowman in 1936, Hugh Mulcahy in 1938 and 1940, Rube Melton in 1942, and Ken Raffensberger in 1944.
89. Foxx's best pitching performance came against Cincinnati in the nightcap of an August 19 doubleheader. He allowed only 1 hit in the first six innings, mixing a fastball with some off-speed pitches before weakening in the seventh. Anton Karl came in to save the 4–2 win for Foxx. *Philadelphia Inquirer*, August 20, 1945, 14.
90. *Philadelphia Inquirer*, June 30, 1945, 14. Chapman hit .314 in 51 at bats for the Phillies.
91. *Philadelphia Inquirer*, September 5, 1942, 25. Jocko Collins had signed Ennis after he hit 2 home runs and a double against a pitcher Jocko had come to scout. *The Sporting News*, June 19, 1946, 9.
92. Klein's four-home-run game was in Pittsburgh, not Philadelphia.
93. *Philadelphia Inquirer*, April 14, 1946, s2.
94. *Philadelphia Inquirer*, May 6, 1946, 22.
95. *St. Louis Post-Dispatch*, June 9, 1946, pt. 3, 1.
96. Ennis, interview by C. Paul Rogers.
97. *The Sporting News*, June 19, 1946, 9.
98. *The Sporting News*, November 27, 1946, 2.
99. *Philadelphia Inquirer*, December 11, 1946, 30.
100. *Philadelphia Inquirer*, December 6, 1946, 34.
101. *St. Louis Post-Dispatch*, December 8, 1946, section 5, 1.
102. *Philadelphia Inquirer*, May 4, 1947, s1, s2.
103. Thornley, "Howie Schultz."
104. *Philadelphia Inquirer*, April 1, 1997, f7.
105. *Philadelphia Inquirer*, April 1, 1997, f7. Harold Parrott, in his book *The Lords of Baseball*, claimed he heard Pennock make the call, but Keith Craig, who wrote a 2016 biography of Pennock, found no corroboration for the story and indicated in an interview that some sources identified the caller as Bob Carpenter. Steven Hoffman, "New Biography Looks at the Life and Career of the Squire of Kennett Square," *Chester County Press* (pa), July 5, 2016, https://www.chestercounty.com/2016/07/05/116281/new-biography-looks-at-the-life-and-career-of-the-squire-of-kennett-square.
106. *Philadelphia Inquirer*, May 10, 1947, 14.

3. SIGNING UP 479 WINS

1. Tomasic took up pro baseball after the war, in 1946 when he was twenty-eight. He struck out 238 batters in 165 innings for Kingston in Class D and followed

that up in 1947 at Class B with 18 wins and 278 strikeouts for Trenton. Tomasic spent the next three years at Jersey City, the top farm club of the Giants, and made two appearances for New York in 1949, resulting in a loss and an ERA of 18.00 as a thirty-one-year-old rookie. After his drubbing with the Giants, Tomasic disgustedly remarked, "Same old story. You win in the minors, but get your brains beat out up here." Tomasic did pitch against Simmons once, in the Interstate League, but his one-inning relief appearance did not make it into the official records due to rain that caused the game's ending to revert to the prior inning. *Wilmington Morning News*, July 8, 1947, 17; and *New York Daily News*, January 12, 1950, 70.

2. *Allentown Morning Call*, June 30, 1981, 25.
3. *Philadelphia Inquirer*, July 4, 1944, 14.
4. *Philadelphia Inquirer*, August 6, 1945, 14.
5. *Philadelphia Inquirer*, August 7, 1945, 20.
6. *Allentown Morning Call*, August 9, 1945, 11.
7. *Philadelphia Inquirer*, August 12, 1945, S1, S3. The award committee consisted of Cy Morgan, Herb Pennock, and Ben Chapman of the Phillies and Chief Bender and Ira Thomas, representing the Athletics.
8. *Brooklyn Daily Eagle*, August 29, 1945, 17, 18. Simmons also singled in a run in the fourth inning.
9. *Allentown Morning Call*, August 30, 1945, 13.
10. Brown, "Bonus Baby," 62.
11. *Allentown Morning Call*, September 1, 1945, 10.
12. *Allentown Morning Call*, September 2, 1945, 10.
13. *Allentown Morning Call*, May 11, 1946, 13.
14. *Allentown Morning Call*, August 31, 1946, 9; *Allentown Morning Call*, September 4, 1946, 13; and *Allentown Morning Call*, September 6, 1946, 19.
15. *Allentown Morning Call*, April 9, 1947, 14.
16. *Allentown Morning Call*, April 23, 1947, 13.
17. *Allentown Morning Call*, April 30, 1947, 18.
18. *Allentown Morning Call*, May 17, 1947, 10.
19. *Allentown Morning Call*, June 3, 2012, A3.
20. *Allentown Morning Call*, June 3, 1947, 16. Although the thirty-seven-year-old Rowe was a pitcher, he was also an excellent hitter, belting 2 home runs with a .278 batting average in 1947.
21. *Wilmington Morning News*, June 17, 1947, 1, 17.
22. *Wilmington Morning News*, June 17, 1947, 1, 17. Also see Rogers, "The Day Phillies Went to Egypt."
23. *Allentown Morning Call*, June 17, 1947, 16.
24. *Allentown Morning Call*, June 17, 1947, 16.
25. *Philadelphia Inquirer*, June 17, 1947, 25.
26. *Wilmington Morning News*, June 21, 1947, 15.
27. *Wilmington News Journal*, June 21, 1947, 11.

28. *Allentown Morning Call*, June 3, 2012, A3.
29. *Wilmington News Journal*, August 11, 1947, 14.
30. *Wilmington News Journal*, August 15, 1947, 8.
31. *Wilmington Morning News*, July 17, 1947, 8.
32. *Wilmington Morning News*, August 21, 1947, 24.
33. *Wilmington Morning News*, July 23, 1947, 18.
34. *Wilmington News Journal*, July 25, 1947, 12.
35. *Wilmington Morning News*, March 23, 1948, 24.
36. *Philadelphia Inquirer*, September 26, 1947, 35.
37. *Philadelphia Inquirer*, September 29, 1947, 25.
38. *Philadelphia Inquirer*, September 29, 1947, 25, 26.
39. *Wilmington News Journal*, October 28, 1947, 22.
40. Rogers and Nowlin, *Whiz Kids Take Pennant*, 140; and Brown, "Mr. Roberts," 59.
41. Roberts and Rogers, *My Life in Baseball*, 9.
42. *Illinois State Journal*, April 1, 1934, 3; *Illinois State Journal*, April 7, 1935, 9; and *Illinois State Journal*, March 29, 1936, 5. East Pleasant Hill Elementary School closed in the late 1950s, with a portion of the property eventually sold to make way for a freeway interchange.
43. Brown, "Mr. Roberts," 59.
44. *Time*, May 28, 1956.
45. *Illinois State Journal*, September 22, 1937, 1; and Roberts and Rogers, *My Life in Baseball*, 2–3. The accused, Andrew Skrelevicus, shot a couple during an argument and ditched the weapon in a pasture. Skrelevicus admitted ownership and was convicted.
46. Brown, "Mr. Roberts," 59.
47. Roberts and Rogers, *My Life in Baseball*, 3.
48. *Illinois State Journal*, September 4, 1937, 10. In his autobiography, Roberts places his meeting Bob Feller in 1936, but Joe DiMaggio had been the guest speaker that year. His meeting with Feller happened in 1937. Grover Cleveland Alexander, who was living in Springfield temporarily (see later note), was also at the game and spoke briefly.
49. Roberts and Rogers, *Whiz Kids and 1950 Pennant*, 68.
50. *Illinois State Journal*, June 15, 1969, 1. The occasion of the interview was in honor of Roberts being named the greatest player in Philadelphia Phillies history, narrowly edging out Alexander for the honor, as part of the celebration of professional baseball's centennial in 1969. Roberts remembered Alexander's speech occurring when he was in eighth grade in 1940. Actually, it happened in 1937 when Roberts was ten years old. East Pleasant Hill principal Clarence Lindsay invited the pitching legend to speak to the school's athletes. Alexander's remarks were not quite as brief as Roberts remembers—he also related several baseball stories but no doubt added the admonition about alcohol, since he was attempting to quit drinking at that time and also was attempting to get back into baseball. By 1940 Alexander was working as a ticket taker at a

race track in Cleveland, again headed down a destructive path that led to his death a decade later at age sixty-three. *Illinois State Journal*, May 21, 1937, 22; and *Cleveland Plain Dealer*, July 13, 1940, 15.

51. *Illinois State Journal*, November 15, 1942, 7.
52. *Illinois State Journal*, April 15, 1942, 8; and Brown, "Mr. Roberts," 60. No details were published about the death of Robin's brother Thomas other than he had been accidentally shot.
53. *Illinois State Journal-Register*, February 14, 1975, 19.
54. Roberts and Rogers, *My Life in Baseball*, 11–12. A former big league pitcher and Minor League manager, Essick was the Yankees West Coast scout and was credited with signing several Yankees stars, including Joe DiMaggio and Lefty Gomez.
55. *Lansing State Journal*, March 6, 1945, 9.
56. Newcombe, "Roberts Is Phillies Stopper," 57.
57. *Lansing State Journal*, May 27, 1946, 11.
58. *Montpelier Evening Argus*, August 26, 1946, 7. It was a seven-inning nightcap of a doubleheader, and since Robin's team was the visitor, he only pitched six innings for his no-hitter.
59. Newcombe, "Roberts Is Phillies Stopper," 57.
60. *Boy's Life*, September 1951, 39; and Roberts and Rogers, *My Life in Baseball*, 22–23.
61. *Detroit Free Press*, December 14, 1947, 26.
62. *Lansing State Journal*, October 22, 1947, 20. Roberts had originally been scouted by Jack Rossiter for the Phillies, and Ward got involved after it became clear Roberts was a great prospect during his second summer in Vermont. Meanwhile, Detroit Tigers scout Wish Egan, who covered the Big Ten for the local big league franchise, passed on him. Brown, "Mr. Roberts," 59.
63. *Wilmington News Journal*, April 23, 1948, 20.
64. Rogers and Nowlin, *Whiz Kids Take Pennant*, 143.
65. Rogers and Nowlin, *Whiz Kids Take Pennant*, 143.
66. *Wilmington News Journal*, April 15, 1948, 40; and *Wilmington News Journal*, April 16, 1948, 20.
67. *Wilmington News Journal*, April 23, 1948, 20.
68. *Wilmington Morning News*, April 30, 1948, 1, 39; and *Wilmington News Journal*, April 30, 1948, 20.
69. *Wilmington Morning News*, May 5, 1948, 26.
70. Roberts and Rogers, *My Life in Baseball*, 35.
71. McDonnell, interview by C. Paul Rogers.
72. Newcombe, "Roberts Is Phillies Stopper," 56.
73. Rogers and Nowlin, *Whiz Kids Take Pennant*, 144.
74. *The Sporting News*, May 26, 1948, 7.
75. *Wilmington News Journal*, May 28, 1948, 20.
76. *Wilmington News Journal*, June 7, 1948, 18.
77. *Wilmington News Journal*, June 18, 1948, 18.

4. MOVING ON WITHOUT THE SQUIRE

1. The five champions included Utica in the Eastern League, Salina in the West-
ern Association (which lost in the playoffs), Schenectady in the Canadian-
American League, Vandergrift in the Middle Atlantic, and Wilmington, which
finished second in the Interstate League but then took the championship in
the playoffs behind Curt Simmons.

2. When Church was originally signed, Ben Chapman convinced him to say he
was a year younger than his actual age of twenty-two. Chapman also wanted
Church to be an everyday player, while Herb Pennock liked his curveball and
wanted him to pitch full-time. Rogers and Nowlin, *Whiz Kids Take Pennant*, 55,
56.

3. Among the interesting prospects who failed to make it were Tommy Lasorda,
who spent 1948 with Schenectady, and Lon Simmons, who pitched briefly
for Terre Haute in 1946. Simmons later became a sportscaster for the San
Francisco Giants and Oakland Athletics and also for the San Francisco 49ers,
receiving the Ford C. Frick Award in 2004. Neil Johnston was a six-foot-eight
pitcher for three seasons in Terre Haute and Wilmington, before joining the
Philadelphia Warriors of the National Basketball Association. A six-time All-
Star and three-time scoring champion, he was inducted into the Basketball
Hall of Fame in 1990. Career Minor Leaguer Lee Riley signed with the Phillies
in 1944. In all, he spent twenty-two years in the Minors, retiring after the 1949
season at age forty-two with 248 career home runs. He also played four games
for the Phillies, with 1 hit in 12 at bats. His son, Hall of Fame NBA coach Pat
Riley, was born in 1945, while Lee Riley was playing in the Phillies organization. Bert Convy was signed out of North Hollywood High School and played
outfield for two years in the low Minors during the 1951 and 1952 seasons. He
later became a well-known actor and game-show host.

4. *Philadelphia Inquirer*, February 15, 1946, 28. Bessie Largent worked with her
husband Ray as a scouting team for the Chicago White Sox during the 1920s
and 1930s. They signed, among others, Hall of Famer Luke Appling. But
Houghton was the first solo female scout. She had played baseball most of
her life, joining the female semiprofessional Philadelphia Bobbies at age ten,
and three years later touring with the team in Japan for a month. She also had
played on a barnstorming team that traveled through the South taking on
men's teams. She remained with the organization through the 1950 season,
reportedly signing more than a dozen players for the Phillies, although none
made the Major Leagues. Among those she signed were infielder Chuck Wat-
son and pitcher Ed Zeidler, who won 16 games for Bradford in 1949 before he
was drafted and shipped to Korea, losing three years. Edith Houghton lived to
age one hundred. *Philadelphia Daily News*, February 12, 2013, 54; and *Somerset
(PA) Daily American*, July 9, 1949, 4.

5. *Philadelphia Inquirer, Everybody's Weekly*, July 18, 1948, 6.

6. *Philadelphia Inquirer*, January 13, 1948, 26.

7. *Philadelphia Inquirer*, January 25, 1948, s-3.

8. *Philadelphia Inquirer*, January 31, 1948, 1, 18.

9. *Philadelphia Inquirer*, January 31, 1948, 18.

10. *Philadelphia Inquirer*, February 2, 1948, 20. Saam began his career with the Athletics and added the Phillies to his duties when they made Shibe Park their home. Both teams began broadcasting their road games in 1950, so Saam could no longer do both, and chose the Athletics. After Arnold Johnson moved the A's to Kansas City, Saam returned to the Phillies and remained with them until his retirement in 1975. He also announced for the Philadelphia Eagles of the NFL and the Philadelphia Warriors of the NBA.

11. *Philadelphia Inquirer*, February 2, 1948, 28.

12. *Philadelphia Inquirer*, February 6, 1948, 32.

13. *Philadelphia Inquirer*, January 31, 1948, 18.

14. *Philadelphia Inquirer*, February 6, 1948, 32.

15. *Philadelphia Inquirer*, February 13, 1948, 38. Krausse was to work with pitchers at Bradford, Carbondale, Dover, Portland, Schenectady, and Vandergrift. Earnshaw was to work with pitchers assigned to Utica and Toronto.

16. *Philadelphia Inquirer*, February 6, 1948, 32.

17. *Philadelphia Inquirer*, February 28, 1948, 16. Pie Traynor was selected along with Pennock.

18. *Philadelphia Inquirer*, February 11, 1948, 28.

19. *Philadelphia Inquirer*, April 8, 1948, 28.

20. Sisler, interview by Brent Kelley.

21. *Philadelphia Inquirer*, April 22, 1948, 26; and *Philadelphia Inquirer*, April 23, 1948, 41.

22. *Philadelphia Inquirer*, August 4, 1948, 30. Baseball Reference lists the Verban transaction as a waiver deal to the Cubs, but press accounts denied that, stating the sale was in excess of the waiver price.

23. *Philadelphia Daily News*, April 4, 1988, BB-17.

24. *Atlanta Journal Constitution*, April 22, 1948, 12. There were four missed third strikes by the catcher. Three batters were thrown out at first base, but a fourth reached base safely. Radcliffe allowed one hit and walked two batters. Two more batters reached base on errors. Montgomery, "Georgia's 1948 Phenoms."

25. *Atlanta Journal Constitution*, May 16, 1948, 2D.

26. *Atlanta Journal Constitution*, June 2, 1948, 17.

27. *Atlanta Journal Constitution*, June 4, 1948, 11.

28. *Wilmington Morning News*, July 17, 1948, 10.

29. *Cordele (GA) News*, obituary, November 21, 2019.

30. *Wilmington Morning News*, July 17, 1948, 10; and *Philadelphia Inquirer*, September 29, 1948, 41.

31. *Toronto Star*, September 7, 1949, 18.

32. Radcliffe's misfortune was a lack of control and constantly being placed at too high a Minor League level compared with his experience. The Yankees first assigned him in 1950 to AAA Kansas City, before dropping him to Single A Binghamton, where he went 9-8. Assigned to Kansas City again in 1951, he was dropped to AA Texas League and eventually drifted down to Class C by 1953, compiling a 13-13 record for Natchez of the Cotton States League. Lack of control proved his undoing during a career that ended in 1954.

33. *Cincinnati Enquirer*, May 10, 1948, 18. If you want to be entertained, watch Andy Varipapa's trick shots on YouTube sometime.

34. *Philadelphia Inquirer*, June 19, 1948, 18.

35. *Philadelphia Inquirer*, June 24, 1948, 32. Danny Murtaugh had 18 in 1941. Ashburn's final total of 32 steals was the highest by a Phillie since Hans Lobert's 41 in 1913.

36. *St. Louis Post-Dispatch*, July 14, 1948, 4C. The final score was 5-2 in favor of the American League.

37. *Philadelphia Inquirer*, July 17, 1948, 1, 14.

38. *Philadelphia Inquirer*, July 17, 1948, 15.

39. *Philadelphia Inquirer*, July 27, 1948, 26.

40. McDonnell, interview.

41. *Philadelphia Inquirer*, July 28, 1948, 32.

42. *The Inquirer World Series Guide*, October 4, 1950, 10.

43. *Philadelphia Inquirer*, August 29, 1948, s-1, s-6; and *The Sporting News*, September 8, 1948, 12. Harry Walker replaced Ashburn in the lineup for the rest of the season.

44. *Philadelphia Inquirer*, September 15, 1948, 43.

45. Baumgartner, "Willie Is No Puddinhead," 91–92.

46. Roberts and Rogers, *Whiz Kids and 1950 Pennant*, 62.

47. *Philadelphia Inquirer*, September 15, 1948, 43.

48. *Boston Globe*, June 28, 1946, 12.

49. *Brooklyn Daily Eagle*, October 4, 1948, 13.

50. *Philadelphia Inquirer*, October 3, 1948, 2-s.

51. *Philadelphia Inquirer*, March 1, 1949, 30; and *Philadelphia Inquirer*, March 7, 1949, 26.

52. The Phillies drew 767,429 in 1948, the second straight year attendance had declined by 140,000, after peaking at more than 1,000,000 in 1946.

53. *Philadelphia Inquirer*, October 5, 1948, 34.

54. *Philadelphia Inquirer*, October 11, 1948, 26.

55. *Philadelphia Inquirer*, December 15, 1948, 47.

56. *Philadelphia Inquirer*, March 6, 1949, 2s.

57. *Tampa Tribune*, March 18, 1949, 19.

58. *Philadelphia Inquirer*, March 17, 1949, 30.

59. *Philadelphia Inquirer*, March 9, 1949, 39, 40.

60. *Philadelphia Inquirer*, March 12, 1949, 19.

61. *Philadelphia Inquirer*, March 16, 1949, 41.
62. *Philadelphia Inquirer*, April 27, 1949, 37.
63. McDonnell, interview.
64. *Philadelphia Inquirer*, June 3, 1949, 45.
65. *Philadelphia Inquirer*, June 8, 1949, 41.

5. I'M UNPREDICTABLE

1. Bob Brumby, "Can Eddie Waitkus Come Back?," 83; and *Boston Globe*, June 15, 1949, 7.
2. Theodore, *Baseball's Natural*, 23.
3. *Boston Globe*, June 16, 1937, 22.
4. *Boston Globe*, June 16, 1937, 23.
5. *Boston Globe*, December 22, 1938, 21.
6. Clark played in the Minors from 1899 through 1910 and was a successful baseball coach at Occidental College in Los Angeles, capturing five titles with a winning percentage of .791.
7. *Lewiston (ME) Daily Sun*, August 9, 1937, 13; *Portland (ME) Evening Express*, August 16, 1937, 16; and *Portland (ME) Press Herald*, August 17, 1937, 9. Lisbon Falls won its first game, against the Leyden Colorado Miners, 9–8, and upset Arkansas City, 6–2, in its second game. It lost to the eventual champion, Eason Oilers of Enid, Oklahoma, in the third game, 15–6. *Wichita Eagle*, August 19, 1937, 1, 8.
8. *Boston Globe*, December 22, 1938, 21.
9. *Boston Globe*, December 22, 1938, 9.
10. *Tulsa World*, July 14, 1940, sports section, 1; and *Chicago Tribune*, April 16, 1941, 25, 26.
11. *Chicago Tribune*, June 24, 1946, 25. In 1977 Bump Wills and Toby Harrah hit back-to-back inside-the-park home runs against the New York Yankees.
12. Theodore, *Baseball's Natural*, 36–37.
13. *Chicago Tribune*, December 15, 1948, pt. 4, 1, 2.
14. *Philadelphia Inquirer*, December 15, 1948, 47.
15. Theodore, *Baseball's Natural*, 69.
16. *Philadelphia Inquirer*, June 8, 1949, 41.
17. *Philadelphia Inquirer*, June 10, 1949, 46.
18. *Chicago Sun-Times*, June 16, 1949, 19.
19. *Philadelphia Inquirer*, June 15, 1949, 43; and *Chicago Tribune*, June 15, 1949, pt. 3, 1.
20. *Chicago Tribune*, June 18, 1949, 1.
21. *Philadelphia Inquirer*, June 16, 1949, 3; and *Chicago Sun-Times*, June 16, 1949, 4. The full text of the note read as follows:

    Mr. Waitkus, It's extremely important that I see you as soon as possible. We're not acquainted, but I have something of importance to speak to you about. I think it would be to your advantage to let me explain it to you. As I'm leaving the hotel the day after tomorrow, I'd appreciate it greatly if you would see me as soon as possible.

My name is Ruth Ann Burns, and I'm in Room 1297A. I realize this is a bit out of the ordinary, but as I said, it's rather important. Please come soon. I won't take up much of your time, I promise.

22. *Philadelphia Inquirer*, June 16, 1949, 3; and *Chicago Sun-Times*, June 16, 1949, 4.
23. *Chicago Sun-Times*, June 16, 1949, 4. This was included in Miss Steinhagen's signed statement to police.
24. *Chicago Sun-Times*, June 16, 1949, 4.
25. *Chicago Sun-Times*, June 16, 1949, 4.
26. *Philadelphia Inquirer*, June 16, 1949, 3.
27. *Philadelphia Inquirer*, June 16, 1949, 1, 3.
28. *Philadelphia Inquirer*, June 15, 1949, 1.
29. Theodore, *Baseball's Natural*, 13.
30. McDonnell, interview.
31. *Chicago Tribune*, June 17, 1949, 1.
32. *Chicago Sun-Times*, June 16, 1949, 19.
33. *Chicago Tribune*, June 24, 1949, 7.
34. *Chicago Tribune*, June 17, 1949, 1.
35. *Chicago Tribune*, July 1, 1949, 1, 42.
36. *Chicago Tribune*, July 2, 1949, pt. 2, 2; and *Chicago Tribune*, July 3, 1949, pt. 2, 3.
37. *Chicago Tribune*, July 8, 1949, pt. 3, 4.
38. *Chicago Tribune*, July 8, 1949, pt. 3, 4.
39. *Philadelphia Inquirer*, July 10, 1949, 1; and *Chicago Tribune*, July 10, 1949, pt. 2, 4.
40. *Philadelphia Inquirer*, July 18, 1949, 1, 3.
41. Also see Rob Edelman's article in the 2013 edition of the SABR's *National Pastime*, "Eddie Waitkus and 'The Natural.'"
42. *Philadelphia Inquirer*, July 21, 1949, 30.
43. *Rochester Democrat and Chronicle*, July 21, 1949, 28.
44. *Philadelphia Inquirer*, July 30, 1949, 15.
45. *Tilden Citizen*, June 17, 1948, 1.
46. Roberts and Rogers, *Whiz Kids and 1950 Pennant*, 179.
47. Ennis, interview.
48. *Philadelphia Inquirer*, May 26, 1948, 45; and *Philadelphia Inquirer*, June 6, 1948, 2s.
49. *Philadelphia Inquirer*, August 6, 1949, 16.
50. Brown, "Hamner of Whiz Kids," 60.
51. *Philadelphia Inquirer*, August 6, 1949, 15; and *Philadelphia Inquirer*, August 7, 1949, S4.
52. *Philadelphia Inquirer*, August 6, 1949, 15.
53. *Philadelphia Inquirer*, July 30, 1949, 15; and *Philadelphia Inquirer*, August 13, 1949, 15.
54. Baumgartner, "Brains Behind Phillies," 92.

55. *Philadelphia Inquirer*, August 9, 1949, 30.
56. Baumgartner, "Brains Behind Phillies," 92.
57. *Philadelphia Inquirer*, August 7, 1949, s1.
58. *Philadelphia Inquirer*, August 8, 1949, 23, 24.
59. Ennis, interview.
60. *Philadelphia Inquirer*, August 17, 1949, 34.
61. Roberts and Rogers, *Whiz Kids and 1950 Pennant*, 185.
62. *Philadelphia Inquirer*, August 17, 1949, 32.
63. *Philadelphia Inquirer*, July 1, 1913, 1, 12. For more on this incident and the riot that occurred later in the season, see Warrington, "Great Philadelphia Ballpark Riot."
64. *Philadelphia Inquirer*, August 22, 1949, 1.
65. *Philadelphia Inquirer*, August 22, 1949, 24.
66. *Philadelphia Inquirer*, August 15, 1949, 17.
67. *Philadelphia Inquirer*, August 20, 1949, 14.
68. *Philadelphia Inquirer*, September 5, 1949, 17.
69. *Philadelphia Inquirer*, September 9, 1949, 47.
70. *Philadelphia Tribune*, October 4, 1949, 1. The photographer, Malcolm Poindexter, claimed that Hamner had used racial slurs, not directed at him, but that he reacted to. After Hamner shoved the five-foot-two, 114-pound Poindexter to the ground, the cameraman was escorted off the premises by police. Three years later Hugh Brown published an article about Hamner in *Sport* magazine and recounted the incident, relating that Poindexter was snapping photos and Hamner became angry, grabbing the photographer roughly and breaking a glass plate. Brown did not say what Hamner had reportedly yelled but did say that the shortstop "was accused of acting toward the Negro photographer in the manner of a Southern klansman," an accusation Hamner vehemently denied. Having read the *Sport* article, Poindexter noted that Hamner's attitude had changed following his interactions with Jackie Robinson and Roy Campanella at the 1952 All-Star Game but challenged the version of events that had Hamner becoming angry at photos being taken of the Phillies in the dugout, reiterating that he had taken offense at racially charged language Hamner had used and had called him on it. Brown, "Hamner of Whiz Kids," 60–61; *Philadelphia Tribune*, August 26, 1952, 11; and *Philadelphia Daily News*, May 8, 1981, 58.
71. *Philadelphia Inquirer*, September 29, 1949, 32; and *Pittsburgh Post-Gazette*, September 15, 1949, 21.
72. *Philadelphia Inquirer*, October 18, 1949, 37. The players also awarded half shares to Putsy Caballero, Jocko Thompson, Mike Goliat, and longtime clubhouse man Russell "Unk" Henry, who had been with the team since the early 1920s.
73. *Philadelphia Inquirer*, October 3, 1949, 27, 30.
74. *Philadelphia Inquirer*, September 7, 1949, 43.
75. *Philadelphia Inquirer*, November 8, 1949, 33.

76. *Wilmington Journal-Evening News*, June 11, 1949, 1; and *Philadelphia Inquirer*, June 12, 1949, 18, 34.
77. Philadelphia National League Club General Ledger.
78. Roberts and Rogers, *Whiz Kids and 1950 Pennant*, 193.

6. I'M GLAD TO BE!

1. *The Sporting News*, December 28, 1949, 1, 2.
2. *Philadelphia Inquirer Magazine*, March 19, 1950, 11.
3. *Philadelphia Inquirer Magazine*, March 19, 1950, 11.
4. Philadelphia National League Club General Ledger. Terre Haute and Bradford had nearly broken even, but Utica lost nearly $70,000 and Wilmington more than $27,000.
5. Although double of that in the prewar years, Major League attendance would continue to decline until the late 1950s.
6. *Philadelphia Inquirer*, November 8, 1949, 33.
7. *Philadelphia Inquirer*, December 9, 1949, 45.
8. *Miami Herald*, December 3, 1949, 14-A.
9. *The Sporting News*, November 23, 1949, 26.
10. Theodore, *Baseball's Natural*, 49.
11. *Philadelphia Inquirer*, March 16, 1950, 32.
12. Theodore, *Baseball's Natural*, 58.
13. *Philadelphia Inquirer Magazine*, November 5, 1950, 20; and *Philadelphia Inquirer*, March 11, 1956, S3.
14. Brumby, "Can Eddie Waitkus Come Back?," 83.
15. *St. Petersburg Times*, January 17, 1950, 19.
16. *St. Petersburg Times*, December 14, 1949, 28.
17. Theodore, *Baseball's Natural*, 57.
18. *St. Petersburg Times*, January 30, 1950, 10.
19. *Philadelphia Inquirer*, January 10, 1950, 30.
20. *The Sporting News*, January 18, 1950, 13.
21. *Miami News*, March 5, 1950, 3-D.
22. *Philadelphia Inquirer*, April 17, 1950, 34. Some Florida newspapers used the term sporadically during spring training, including the *Orlando Sentinel* as early as March 12. *Orlando Sentinel*, March 12, 1950, 14.
23. Roberts and Rogers, *Whiz Kids and 1950 Pennant*, 218.
24. *Philadelphia Inquirer*, February 19, 1950, 4S.
25. *The Sporting News*, February 8, 1950, 12.
26. *Philadelphia Inquirer*, February 20, 1950, 26.
27. *Philadelphia Inquirer*, March 23, 1950, 33.
28. Rogers and Nowlin, *Whiz Kids Take Pennant*, 101.
29. Williams, "Comeback Jim Konstanty," 24.
30. Williams, "Comeback Jim Konstanty," 24.
31. Roberts and Rogers, *Whiz Kids and 1950 Pennant*, 277.

32. Duncan, "Jim Konstanty, All-Time Fireman," 18.

33. John Horne, in discussion with the author, April 9, 2024. Horne, who serves as the coordinator of rights & reproductions at the National Baseball Hall of Fame, hosted a program at the hall that marked the fiftieth anniversary of the Whiz Kids. Jim Konstanty's family attended, accompanied by Andy Skinner, and Konstanty's daughter told this story.

34. *Philadelphia Inquirer*, November 18, 1949, 57.

35. *Philadelphia Inquirer*, September 30, 1949, 47.

36. *San Diego Union*, December 8, 1949, B-3.

37. *Philadelphia Inquirer*, February 25, 1950, 15. Davis's army discharge was not to become official until June 3.

38. *Philadelphia Inquirer*, March 9, 1950, 30; and *Los Angeles Times*, March 23, 1950, pt. 4, 1. It was said at least eight Major League baseball teams had made offers to Davis, including one of $50,000. Branch Rickey reportedly had offered Davis $40,000 to play for the Dodgers, although he refused to confirm that. *Los Angeles Times*, January 22, 1950, pt. II, 8; and *The Sporting News*, November 2, 1949, 9.

39. *The Sporting News*, February 1, 1950, 9; *The Sporting News*, February 15, 1950, 12; and *Philadelphia Inquirer*, February 4, 1950, 13.

40. *Philadelphia Inquirer*, February 27, 1950, 29; and Philadelphia National League Club General Ledger. Meyer received an advance of $1,500 on November 1 and another on December 16 of $750.

41. *Philadelphia Inquirer*, March 4, 1950, 13.

42. *Philadelphia Inquirer*, February 18, 1950, 18.

43. *Philadelphia Inquirer*, March 15, 1950, 49.

44. *Wilmington News Journal*, March 15, 1950, 28.

45. *Philadelphia Inquirer*, March 16, 1950, 32. Seminick and Carpenter split the difference, the catcher signing for $12,500.

46. *Philadelphia Inquirer*, March 6, 1950, 25.

47. *Philadelphia Inquirer*, February 9, 1950, 31.

48. *Philadelphia Inquirer*, August 29, 1948, S1.

49. *Wilmington News Journal*, March 13, 1950, 20.

50. *Philadelphia Inquirer*, February 3, 1950, 39. Bob Carpenter took out insurance policies on the pair—a $500,000 policy on Sawyer and $100,000 on Borowy.

51. *The Sporting News*, February 15, 1950, 12.

52. *Philadelphia Inquirer*, February 1, 1950, 36.

53. *Philadelphia Inquirer*, February 3, 1950, 39.

54. *Philadelphia Inquirer*, March 10, 1950, 48.

55. *Philadelphia Inquirer*, April 17, 1950, 23.

56. *Philadelphia Inquirer*, January 22, 1950, S5.

57. *Philadelphia Inquirer*, March 15, 1950, 47; and Ed Sanicki, in discussion with the author, 1991. The Phillies gave Sanicki a bonus of $2,000.

58. Baumgartner, "Phillies Gamble on Youth," 77.

59. Baumgartner, "Brains Behind Phillies," 93.
60. *The Sporting News*, February 15, 1950, 12; and *Tilden Citizen*, November 10, 1949, 1.
61. Newcombe, "Making of Richie Ashburn," 76.
62. *Philadelphia Inquirer*, September 3, 1950, 4s.
63. *Philadelphia Inquirer*, March 6, 1950, 25.
64. Baumgartner, "Like Sisler, Like Son," 87.
65. Baumgartner, "Like Sisler, Like Son," 44.
66. *Tampa Daily Times*, March 28, 1950, 10.
67. *Philadelphia Inquirer*, October 2, 1949, s3.
68. Brown, "Bonus Baby," 62.
69. *Philadelphia Inquirer*, March 17, 1950, 47.
70. *Philadelphia Inquirer*, March 23, 1950, 33.
71. Rogers and Nowlin, *Whiz Kids Take Pennant*, 122.
72. *Philadelphia Inquirer*, March 23, 1950, 33.
73. *Wilmington News Journal*, March 14, 1950, 19.
74. Rogers and Nowlin, *Whiz Kids Take Pennant*, 143.
75. *Philadelphia Inquirer*, March 12, 1950, s-1, s-5.
76. *Philadelphia Inquirer*, March 16, 1950, 32.
77. *Philadelphia Inquirer*, April 11, 1950, 35.
78. *Philadelphia Inquirer*, March 16, 1950, 32, 33.
79. *Tampa Morning Tribune*, March 17, 1950, d-1, and *Tampa Morning Tribune*, March 19, 1950, d-1, d-4.
80. *Philadelphia Inquirer*, April 15, 1950, 17.
81. *Philadelphia Inquirer*, April 4, 1950, 35.
82. *Philadelphia Inquirer*, April 6, 1950, 35.
83. *Philadelphia Inquirer*, March 17, 1950, 47.
84. *Philadelphia Inquirer*, March 29, 1950, 47; and *St. Louis Post-Dispatch*, April 4, 1950, 4c. Miller had been working out with the Cardinals once it became clear he was no longer in Sawyer's plans.
85. *Philadelphia Inquirer*, April 3, 1950, 28.
86. *Philadelphia Inquirer*, February 22, 1950, 42; and *Wilmington News Journal*, March 9, 1950, 40.
87. *Philadelphia Inquirer*, April 9, 1950, 2s.
88. *Philadelphia Inquirer*, March 22, 1950, 49.
89. *Philadelphia Inquirer*, March 26, 1950, 2-s.
90. *Philadelphia Inquirer*, March 27, 1950, 25.
91. *Philadelphia Inquirer*, March 28, 1950, 31.
92. *Philadelphia Inquirer*, March 23, 1950, 33, 35.
93. *Miami Herald*, March 22, 1950, 3-d.
94. *Philadelphia Inquirer*, October 25, 1950, 43.
95. *Philadelphia Inquirer*, April 13, 1950, 36.
96. *Philadelphia Inquirer*, April 21, 1950, 57.

97. *Miami Herald*, March 31, 1950, 2-B.
98. *Philadelphia Inquirer*, April 11, 1950, 35. Bicknell spent two years in military service and never made it back to the Majors, finally retiring in 1957.
99. *Philadelphia Inquirer*, April 15, 1950, 16.
100. *Philadelphia Inquirer*, February 9, 1950, 31.
101. *Philadelphia Inquirer*, April 16, 1950, 1S, 2S.
102. *Philadelphia Inquirer*, April 17, 1950, 31, 34.
103. *Philadelphia Inquirer*, April 16, 1950, 2S. The Athletics were rated fifth-best in American League, with odds of ten to one to win the pennant.

7. YOU GUYS WANT TO WIN

1. The Dodgers won seven pennants (1947, 1949, 1952, 1953, 1955, 1956, and 1959), the Braves three (1948, 1957, and 1958), and the Giants two (1951 and 1954). A similar domination occurred in the American League between 1947 and 1958, with only the Yankees and Indians winning pennants—the Yankees capturing all but two, in 1948 and 1954. After the White Sox won the 1959 pennant, the Yankees reeled off five more pennants in a row. Between 1949 and 1964, only one season, 1959, featured a World Series that was not played at least partially in New York.
2. *Philadelphia Inquirer*, April 18, 1950, 34.
3. Philadelphia National League Club General Ledger, account 52–2, sheet 1.
4. *Philadelphia Inquirer*, April 18, 1950, 34.
5. *1951 Official Baseball Guide*, 51.
6. *Philadelphia Inquirer*, April 11, 1950, 35.
7. *Philadelphia Inquirer*, April 19, 1950, 1, 47; and *Daily News* (New York), April 19, 1950, 88, 94. Lawrence won a Tony Award in 1962 as musical director for *How to Succeed in Business Without Really Trying*. He also scored the films *Network* and *The French Connection*. He eventually won nine Emmy Awards for his work as a musical director in television.
8. *Brooklyn Daily Eagle*, April 18, 1950, 23.
9. *Brooklyn Daily Eagle*, April 19, 1950, 21.
10. *Daily News* (New York), April 19, 1950, 88.
11. *Philadelphia Inquirer*, April 19, 1950, 1, 47. The previous franchise best was 27,203 for the 1947 opener.
12. Peary, *We Played the Game*, 119.
13. Paxton, "Whiz Kids," 78. Frank O'Rourke was a popular and prolific author of sports fiction in the late 1940s and early 1950s.
14. Paxton, "Whiz Kids," 79.
15. Brown, "Hamner of Whiz Kids," 23.
16. *Philadelphia Inquirer*, April 19, 1950, 47, 48.
17. *Philadelphia Inquirer*, April 20, 1950, 32.
18. *Philadelphia Inquirer*, April 21, 1950, 53.
19. *Philadelphia Inquirer*, May 2, 1950, 34. With a runner on third and two out in the third inning, Earl Torgeson dragged a bunt that Eddie Waitkus fielded

and threw to Meyer covering first. Thinking he had retired the batter, Meyer instead learned that Barlick ruled Torgeson safe, allowing a run to score. Meyer waved at Barlick in disgust, at which point Barlick ejected him. This enraged Meyer, who went after Barlick while Hamner and Waitkus attempted to restrain him. At the argument's conclusion, Meyer flipped a baseball, which hit Barlick in the leg, and then bumped him with his chest, leading to the fine and suspension. *Philadelphia Inquirer*, May 1, 1950, 29.

20. *Philadelphia Inquirer*, May 15, 1950, 29, 30.
21. *Boston Globe*, April 22, 1950, 1, 4.
22. *Boston Globe*, April 23, 1950, 46.
23. *Philadelphia Inquirer*, April 23, 1950, S1, S2.
24. *Boston Globe*, April 23, 1950, 46.
25. *Brooklyn Daily Eagle*, April 27, 1950, 25.
26. *Philadelphia Inquirer*, April 27, 1950, 31. Reese's ball was hit deep enough that the Phillies had no play at the plate, so they let it fall safely. The protest was denied, National League president Ford Frick ruling that it was within the umpire's power to use his judgment to call interference. *Philadelphia Inquirer*, May 3, 1950, 47.
27. *Philadelphia Inquirer*, April 30, 1950, S1, S4.
28. Roberts and Rogers, *Whiz Kids and 1950 Pennant*, 220–21.
29. Roberts and Rogers, *Whiz Kids and 1950 Pennant*, 221. The batter who hit the line drive was Earl Torgeson.
30. *Philadelphia Inquirer*, April 30, 1950, S5.
31. *Philadelphia Tribune*, April 22, 1950, 10.
32. Church, interview by Rick Bradley.
33. *Philadelphia Inquirer*, April 21, 1950, 19. Rosenthal had been a passenger in a car with several other members of his high school band when the vehicle was involved in a head-on collision. The eighteen-year-old driver of the car Rosenthal was in had earlier collided with a pair of parked cars, causing the other passengers to plead with him to let them out. The driver was eventually sentenced to jail after pleading no contest to one count of involuntary manslaughter. *Philadelphia Inquirer*, October 18, 1950, 53.
34. *Philadelphia Inquirer*, April 29, 1950, 13.
35. *Philadelphia Inquirer*, April 29, 1950, 17.
36. *Philadelphia Inquirer*, May 5, 1950, 1, 26.
37. *Philadelphia Inquirer*, June 27, 1950, 27.
38. *Philadelphia Inquirer*, April 28, 1950, 52.
39. *Rochester Democrat and Chronicle*, July 11, 1950, 24.
40. *Philadelphia Inquirer*, April 30, 1950, 4S.
41. *Philadelphia Inquirer*, May 4, 1950, 37. Jim Konstanty relieved Johnson with no one out and two men on base, picking up a save.
42. *Rochester Democrat and Chronicle*, July 11, 1950, 24.
43. Brumby, "Can Eddie Waitkus Come Back?," 23.

44. *Philadelphia Daily News*, December 14, 2022, A34.

45. *Philadelphia Inquirer*, May 10, 1950, 61.

46. *Philadelphia Inquirer*, May 12, 1950, 49.

47. *Philadelphia Inquirer*, May 12, 1950, 49.

48. *Philadelphia Inquirer*, May 12, 1950, 49.

49. *Philadelphia Inquirer*, May 11, 1950, 34. The Cincinnati press reported it as a straight waiver deal. *Cincinnati Enquirer*, May 11, 1950, 32.

50. *Philadelphia Inquirer*, May 18, 1950, 34.

51. *Philadelphia Inquirer*, May 18, 1950, 34.

52. *Philadelphia Inquirer*, May 22, 1950, 28. Richie Ashburn and Granny Hamner reached base via a single and a walk when Waitkus came to the plate against Al Brazle. Waitkus struck out on a full count. Ashburn, who had taken off for third on the pitch, was caught in a rundown and tagged out by Marty Marion, who then saw Hamner wandering between first and second. He threw to Stan Musial, playing first base, who tagged Hamner for the third out.

53. *Philadelphia Inquirer*, May 25, 1950, 36. Ennis pulled the muscle while running to first base on a grounder to short.

54. *Philadelphia Inquirer*, June 12, 1950, 24, 26.

55. *Philadelphia Inquirer*, July 1, 1950, 1, 15. Bloodworth had also been the hero of a City Series exhibition against the A's four days earlier, hitting a home run in the seventh inning and a two-run double in the eighth. He was crowned the game's Most Valuable Player and awarded a television set. *Philadelphia Inquirer*, June 27, 1950, 33.

56. Church, interview.

57. *Philadelphia Inquirer*, June 13, 1950, 34.

58. *Philadelphia Inquirer*, June 16, 1950, 41.

59. *Philadelphia Inquirer*, June 21, 1950, 42.

60. Brown, "Terrible Tempered Russ Meyer," 86.

61. *Rochester Democrat and Chronicle*, July 11, 1950, 24.

62. *Philadelphia Inquirer*, June 23, 1950, 41.

63. *Philadelphia Inquirer*, June 28, 1950, 42.

64. Roberts and Rogers, *Whiz Kids and 1950 Pennant*, 228.

65. *Philadelphia Inquirer*, July 2, 1950, 29.

66. Roberts and Rogers, *Whiz Kids and 1950 Pennant*, 230.

67. *Philadelphia Inquirer*, July 5, 1950, 49.

68. Rogers and Nowlin, *Whiz Kids Take Pennant*, 334.

69. Roberts and Rogers, *Whiz Kids and 1950 Pennant*, 144.

70. Duncan, "Jim Konstanty, All-Time Fireman," 93. Robin Roberts told John Horne of the Baseball Hall of Fame that he also asked Andy Skinner for advice on occasion. Horne, discussion.

71. *Philadelphia Inquirer*, July 3, 1950, 17; and *Philadelphia Inquirer*, July 9, 1950, S1.

72. *Philadelphia Inquirer*, July 9, 1950, S1.

73. Roberts and Rogers, *Whiz Kids and 1950 Pennant*, 228.

74. *Philadelphia Inquirer*, July 10, 1950, 23. Contemporary box scores do not list this as a double play.
75. *Philadelphia Inquirer*, July 11, 1950, 21. Columnist Frank Brookhouser reported that the Athletics were seeking a Black player to boost the gate in 1951 and had already scouted a local high school pitcher.

8. DON'T SAY I AM PREDICTING

1. The Phillies had three All-Star representatives in 1940, 1946, and 1947.
2. *Philadelphia Inquirer*. July 9, 1949, 14. Southworth posed with Heintzelman and Roberts for a photo on Friday night before the first game of the series and attempted to explain his decision, but that only seemed to inflame both Phillies players and fans. Obviously struggling through both personal and personnel issues, a month later Southworth took a leave of absence from the Braves for the rest of the season, because of "ill-health." *Boston Globe*, August 17, 1949, 1, 20.
3. *Philadelphia Inquirer*, July 11, 1950, 25.
4. *Philadelphia Inquirer*, July 12, 1950, 37.
5. *Chicago Tribune*, July 12, 1950, pt. 3, 1, 4, 8.
6. *Philadelphia Inquirer*, July 12, 1950, 37.
7. *Rochester Democrat and Chronicle*, July 11, 1950, 24.
8. *Rochester Democrat and Chronicle*, July 11, 1950, 24.
9. *Toronto Star*, July 12, 1950, 16.
10. *Toronto Star*, July 11, 1950, 12. The Dodgers, Cubs, Tigers, and Red Sox had all achieved very slight gains in attendance.
11. *1951 Official Baseball Guide*, 111.
12. *Philadelphia Inquirer*, July 15, 1950, 1, 13.
13. *Philadelphia Inquirer*, July 16, 1950, s-1.
14. *Philadelphia Inquirer*, July 17, 1950, 1, 21, 22.
15. *Philadelphia Inquirer*, July 19, 1950, 1, 38.
16. *Philadelphia Inquirer*, July 19, 1950, 38, 40.
17. Roberts and Rogers, *Whiz Kids and 1950 Pennant*, 233.
18. *Philadelphia Inquirer*, July 22, 1950, 13.
19. *Philadelphia Inquirer*, July 24, 1950, 22.
20. *Philadelphia Inquirer*, July 25, 1950, 1, 28.
21. *Philadelphia Inquirer*, July 26, 1950, 1, 32.
22. Rogers and Nowlin, *Whiz Kids Take Pennant*, 286.
23. *Philadelphia Inquirer*, July 26, 1950, 1, 32.
24. Roberts and Rogers, *Whiz Kids and 1950 Pennant*, 237.
25. Associated Press, *Indianapolis News*, July 26, 1950, 15.
26. *Scranton Times Tribune*, July 26, 1950, 40.
27. *Philadelphia Inquirer*, July 27, 1950, 1, 28. Meyer claimed that when Cubs hitter Hank Sauer shifted around in the batter's box he had thought time out had been called, and that was why he had stopped his wind-up. Angered at the

resulting balk call, Meyer charged umpire Lon Warneke, chest-bumping him before giving him a hard shove, bringing the ejection.

28. *Philadelphia Inquirer*, July 27, 1950, 28.
29. *Philadelphia Inquirer*, July 31, 1950, 20. The Zeisers and their friends had started the club in 1947 in response to what they felt was harsh treatment of Seminick by Phillies fans. The team agreed to recognize the club after the catcher gave his approval. The girls published a regular newsletter, provided gifts to Phillies wives when they gave birth, and sent magazines and newspapers to shut-ins. They had also held a day in Seminick's honor in 1949, only a month after Ruth Ann Steinhagen's attack on Eddie Waitkus. The Zeisers had no such obsession with Seminick, who became a great friend of the family. Seminick often went hunting with their father. The sisters regularly babysat for Seminick's young son and helped other clubs form in honor of other Phillies. The club remained active until Seminick's death in 2004. Anne Zeiser died on New Year's Eve 2005. Betty died in December 2014. Rogers and Nowlin, *Whiz Kids Take Pennant*, 332; *Philadelphia Inquirer*, July 15, 1949, 34; *Philadelphia Inquirer*, March 27, 1992, D-1; *Philadelphia Inquirer*, December 5, 2014, B-7; *Philadelphia Daily News*, March 5, 2004, 134; and *Philadelphia Daily News*, January 4, 2006, 18.
30. *Philadelphia Inquirer*, July 31, 1950, 1, 19, 20.
31. *Philadelphia Inquirer*, July 20, 1950, 30. The *Inquirer* claimed the A's received $100,000 in return for Dillinger, while the *1951 Baseball Guide* reported that the Athletics received only $35,000. In his biography of Connie Mack, Norman Macht pegged the payment at $50,000. *1951 Baseball Guide*, 12; and Macht, *Grand Old Man*, 465.
32. *Philadelphia Inquirer*, December 14, 1949, 49.
33. *Philadelphia Inquirer*, June 9, 1950, 1, 49; and Macht, *Grand Old Man*, 460–63.
34. Warrington, "Departure without Dignity."
35. *Philadelphia Inquirer*, July 31, 1950, 29, 31.
36. *1951 Baseball Guide*, 97.
37. *Philadelphia Inquirer*, August 29, 1950, 26, 27; and Macht, *Grand Old Man*, 513–14.
38. *Philadelphia Inquirer*, August 29, 1950, 27.
39. *Ft. Myers News-Press*, February 29, 1952, 1; *Ft. Myers News-Press*, June 6, 1952, 1; *Ft. Myers News-Press*, December 22, 1952, 1; and Macht, *Grand Old Man*, 509.
40. *Philadelphia Inquirer*, September 3, 1950, S1.
41. *Philadelphia Inquirer*, August 8, 1950, 1, 28, 29; and Roberts and Rogers, *Whiz Kids and 1950 Pennant*, 246.
42. *Philadelphia Inquirer*, August 12, 1950, 1, 14.
43. *Philadelphia Inquirer*, August 13, 1950, 4S.
44. *Boston Globe*, August 10, 1950, 20. Although irritated, Elliott said that Stanky moving into his sightline had nothing to do with his striking out.
45. *Philadelphia Inquirer*, August 13, 1950, 4S.
46. Roberts and Rogers, *Whiz Kids and 1950 Pennant*, 248–49.

47. *Philadelphia Inquirer*, August 13, 1950, 6s.
48. *Philadelphia Inquirer*, August 13, 1950, 1s, 4s.
49. *Philadelphia Inquirer*, August 13, 1950, 1s.
50. Ennis, interview.
51. *1951 Baseball Guide*, 53.
52. Rogers and Nowlin, *Whiz Kids Take Pennant*, 332.
53. *Philadelphia Inquirer*, August 17, 1950, 1, 30.
54. *Philadelphia Inquirer*, August 26, 1950, 1, 13.
55. *Philadelphia Inquirer*, August 31, 1950, 1, 28.

9. FIGHTIN' PHILS FIGHT THEMSELVES

1. *Philadelphia Inquirer*, September 1, 1950, 36.
2. *Philadelphia Inquirer*, September 4, 1950, 1, 4.
3. *Toronto Star*, July 19, 1950, 13; and *Toronto Star*, September 12, 1950, 10.
4. *Philadelphia Inquirer*, July 8, 1949, 34; and *Philadelphia Inquirer*, September 2, 1950, 14.
5. Roberts and Rogers, *Whiz Kids and 1950 Pennant*, 286. During the 1950 season, Ashburn and his wife shared an apartment in Philadelphia with Mike Goliat and Goliat's wife. *Tilden Citizen*, October 12, 1950, 1.
6. *Philadelphia Inquirer*, September 10, 1950, 1-s, 6-s.
7. Brown, "Terrible-Tempered Russ Meyer," 85.
8. *Chicago Tribune*, July 21, 1947, 29. Meyer returned to pitch one inning in relief near the end of September.
9. Brown, "Terrible-Tempered Russ Meyer," 85.
10. *Philadelphia Inquirer*, September 9, 1950, 1, 13.
11. *Philadelphia Tribune*, September 9, 1950, 1; *Philadelphia Tribune*, September 30, 1950, 1; and Poindexter, Jr. v. Hamner.
12. *Philadelphia Tribune*, September 30, 1950, 1; and Poindexter, Jr. v. Hamner. Thirty years later, Poindexter said the settlement amount came to $350. He also said that the incident led to his career as a reporter. *Philadelphia Daily News*, May 8, 1981, 58.
13. *Philadelphia Tribune*, August 26, 1952, 11.
14. *Philadelphia Inquirer*, September 11, 1950, 1, 27.
15. *Philadelphia Inquirer*, May 16, 1952, 40. Mayo's only official Major League home run, in 1952, glanced off the same Shibe Park light pole that his lost home run in 1950 had. His first and only official big league homer came at the expense of Cincinnati's Ewell Blackwell.
16. *Brooklyn Daily Eagle*, September 12, 1950, 13.
17. Church, interview.
18. Ennis, interview.
19. Roberts and Rogers, *Whiz Kids and 1950 Pennant*, 289–90; and Rogers and Nowlin, *Whiz Kids Take Pennant*, 58.
20. *Philadelphia Inquirer*, September 16, 1950, 16.

21. *Philadelphia Inquirer*, September 16, 1950, 1, 15.
22. *Philadelphia Inquirer*, September 16, 1950, 15, 16.
23. *Philadelphia Inquirer*, September 17, 1950, 1s, 4s.
24. *Philadelphia Inquirer*, September 17, 1950, 1s.
25. Roberts and Rogers, *Whiz Kids and 1950 Pennant*, 228.
26. *Philadelphia Inquirer*, September 19, 1950, 35.
27. *Philadelphia Inquirer*, September 5, 1950, 38.
28. *Philadelphia Inquirer*, September 18, 1950, 1, 28.
29. *Philadelphia Inquirer*, September 19, 1950, 35.
30. *Philadelphia Inquirer*, September 20, 1950, 1, 32.
31. *Philadelphia Inquirer*, September 20, 1950, 40. Hiller revealed that an opponent had told him that he had a "tell" when throwing a forkball. Against the Phillies, he made a correction and threw a shutout.
32. *Philadelphia Inquirer*, September 21, 1950, 31.
33. *Philadelphia Inquirer*, September 24, 1950, s-1.
34. *Philadelphia Inquirer*, September 25, 1950, 28; and Rogers and Nowlin, *Whiz Kids Take Pennant*, 58.
35. *Brooklyn Daily Eagle*, September 25, 1950, 12.
36. *Philadelphia Inquirer*, September 26, 1950, 47.
37. *Philadelphia Inquirer*, September 27, 1950, 41.
38. *Philadelphia Inquirer*, September 28, 1950, 32, 34.
39. Rogers and Nowlin, *Whiz Kids Take Pennant*, 162.
40. Roberts and Rogers, *Whiz Kids and 1950 Pennant*, 302.
41. *Philadelphia Inquirer Magazine*, November 5, 1950, 20.
42. McDonnell, interview.
43. *Philadelphia Inquirer*, September 29, 1950, 1, 47.
44. *Philadelphia Inquirer*, October 1, 1950, 8s.
45. *Philadelphia Inquirer*, September 29, 1950, 1, 47, 53.
46. *Philadelphia Inquirer*, October 1, 1950, 8s.
47. *Philadelphia Inquirer*, September 29, 1950, 47.
48. *Brooklyn Daily Eagle*, September 30, 1950, 6.
49. *Philadelphia Inquirer*, September 30, 1950, 15.
50. Brown, "Terrible-Tempered Russ Meyer," 44, 45. Meyer attended the Braves game with Eddie Waitkus and Maje McDonnell. Meyer later insisted that he and the others had asked the photographer to stop taking photos so they could focus on the game. "So this sob," said Meyer, "stuck his camera right in front of me and I popped him." Roberts and Rogers, *Whiz Kids and 1950 Pennant*, 307.
51. *Philadelphia Inquirer*, October 1, 1950, s1.
52. *Brooklyn Daily Eagle*, September 29, 1950, 19.
53. Roberts and Rogers, *Whiz Kids and 1950 Pennant*, 309.
54. *New York Times*, October 1, 1950, 160.
55. *Philadelphia Inquirer*, October 1, 1950, 1-s, 8-s; and *Brooklyn Daily Eagle*, October 1, 1950, 1, 26, 27.

56. *Philadelphia Inquirer*, October 1, 1950, 8-s.
57. *Brooklyn Daily Eagle*, October 1, 1950, 1.
58. Roberts and Rogers, *Whiz Kids and 1950 Pennant*, 313.

10. SISLER, HEMINGWAY, THE YANKEES

1. *Brooklyn Daily Eagle*, October 25, 1950, 21; and McCue, *Mover & Shaker*, 74–83.
2. *Brooklyn Daily Eagle*, November 7, 1950, 12.
3. *Philadelphia Inquirer*, October 1, 1950, s1.
4. *Brooklyn Daily Eagle*, October 1, 1950, 27.
5. McDonnell, interview.
6. *Pensacola News*, September 30, 1964, 1B. Jimmy Bloodworth related this story during an interview conducted when the Phillies collapsed during the National League pennant race in 1964.
7. Roberts and Rogers, *My Life in Baseball*, 84. In his autobiography, and during an interview at the Whiz Kids fiftieth reunion, Roberts claimed he did not know he was pitching until an hour before the game started, when Eddie Sawyer tossed him a baseball and told him, "Good luck." However, the newspaper that morning named Roberts as the starting pitcher that day and declared that he was all that stood between the Phillies and the most colossal collapse of a pennant aspirant in the history of the National League. *Philadelphia Inquirer*, October 1, 1950, 1s.
8. *Philadelphia Inquirer*, October 3, 1950, 37.
9. *Philadelphia Inquirer*, October 2, 1950, 32. Columnist Tommy Holmes said that a ball landing on that ledge against the screen had happened only once before. *Brooklyn Daily Eagle*, October 2, 1950, 12.
10. Roberts and Rogers, *Whiz Kids and 1950 Pennant*, 314.
11. *Philadelphia Inquirer*, October 2, 1950, 36.
12. *Brooklyn Daily Eagle*, October 2, 1950, 12. Cal Abrams maintained that Robin Roberts missed a sign for a pick-off play at second base, which brought Ashburn rushing in to back up a throw that never came. Abrams said Stock did not realize that until after already waving him around third. Abrams, interview by SABR.
13. Roberts and Rogers, *Whiz Kids and 1950 Pennant*, 315.
14. Lopata, interview by Rick Bradley; and Roberts and Rogers, *Whiz Kids and 1950 Pennant*, 316.
15. Newcombe, "Making of Richie Ashburn," 76.
16. Ennis, interview.
17. Roberts and Rogers, *Whiz Kids and 1950 Pennant*, 319.
18. *Philadelphia Daily News*, September 27, 1990, s14.
19. *Brooklyn Daily Eagle*, October 2, 1950, 12.
20. *Philadelphia Inquirer*, October 2, 1950, 1.
21. Roberts and Rogers, *Whiz Kids and 1950 Pennant*, 335.
22. *Brooklyn Daily Eagle*, October 2, 1950, 12. *Death in the Afternoon* is Hemingway's nonfiction exploration of Spanish bullfighting, published in 1932.

23. *Brooklyn Daily Eagle*, October 2, 1950, 1, 3.
24. *Brooklyn Daily Eagle*, October 2, 1950, 12.
25. *Philadelphia Inquirer*, October 2, 1950, 32.
26. *Brooklyn Daily Eagle*, October 2, 1950, 12.
27. McDonnell, interview.
28. *Philadelphia Inquirer*, October 2, 1950, 36.
29. Roberts and Rogers, *My Life in Baseball*, 89. Burt Shotton, Pee Wee Reese, Gil Hodges, and Duke Snider also visited the Phillies clubhouse to offer congratulations. *Philadelphia Inquirer*, October 2, 1950, 36.
30. *Philadelphia Inquirer*, October 2, 1950, 1, 12.
31. *Philadelphia Inquirer*, October 2, 1950, 12.
32. *Philadelphia Inquirer*, October 2, 1950, 3.
33. *Philadelphia Inquirer*, October 2, 1950, 32.
34. *Brooklyn Daily Eagle*, November 28, 1950, 1, 16.
35. *Pittsburgh Post-Gazette*, January 12, 1951, 18.
36. *St. Louis Post-Dispatch*, February 7, 1946, 1-E. Sisler was such a sensation in Cuba that he was offered a $12,000 contract with Jorge Pasquel's outlaw baseball league in Mexico, which he turned down. *St. Louis Post-Dispatch*, February 15, 1946, 8C.
37. Hemingway, *Old Man and the Sea*, 21–22.
38. *Daily News* (New York), October 5, 1950, 80.
39. Roberts and Rogers, *Whiz Kids and 1950 Pennant*, 339–40.
40. Duncan, "Jim Konstanty, All-Time Fireman," 93.
41. *Philadelphia Inquirer*, October 4, 1950, 53.
42. *Daily News* (New York), October 4, 1950, 51.
43. Sisler pinch-hit twice in 1946 for the St. Louis Cardinals, grounding out twice. Whitman, playing for the Brooklyn Dodgers, was struck out by Allie Reynolds to end Game Four of the 1949 World Series. In addition, Ken Silvestri had been a member of the Yankees when they appeared in the 1941 World Series, but he did not play in any of the games.
44. *Philadelphia Inquirer*, October 5, 1950, 33.
45. *Philadelphia Inquirer*, October 5, 1950, 33. Both right- and left-handed batters hit .202 against Konstanty in 1950, but the slugging average of left-handers was only .290 versus a .330 mark managed by right-handers.
46. *Philadelphia Inquirer*, October 5, 1950, 1, 33, 36.
47. *Philadelphia Inquirer*, October 6, 1950, 45.
48. *Daily News* (New York), October 6, 1950, 83.
49. *Philadelphia Inquirer*, October 6, 1950, 1, 45.
50. *Philadelphia Inquirer*, October 6, 1950, 1, 4s.
51. *Daily News* (New York), October 6, 1950, 83.
52. *Philadelphia Inquirer*, October 6, 1950, 45.
53. *Daily News* (New York), October 7, 1950, 28.
54. *Daily News* (New York), October 7, 1950, 33.

55. *Philadelphia Inquirer*, October 7, 1950, 1, 13, 14; and *Daily News* (New York), October 7, 1950, 28.
56. *1951 Baseball Guide*, 115; and Brown, "Hamner of Whiz Kids," 61.
57. *Philadelphia Inquirer*, October 7, 1950, 13.
58. *Philadelphia Inquirer*, October 7, 1950, 14.
59. Taxiera, *Unique Look at Big League Baseball*, 267.
60. The film, titled *The Winning Team* and starring Doris Day and Ronald Reagan, was released in 1952.
61. Sher, "Ups and Downs of Old Pete," 50.
62. *Howard County (NE) Herald*, November 8, 1950, 1, 8.
63. Ford had a career Minor League record of 51-20 when the Yankees promoted him. He still holds the record with 10 World Series wins and the most consecutive scoreless innings pitched in World Series play with thirty-three.
64. *Daily News* (New York), October 8, 1950, 94.
65. *Philadelphia Inquirer*, October 8, 1950, S-1.
66. *Philadelphia Inquirer*, October 8, 1950, S-4.
67. *Philadelphia Inquirer*, October 8, 1950, S-4.
68. *Philadelphia Inquirer*, October 7, 1950, 14.

11. THEY'LL WIN THE PENNANT

1. *Philadelphia Inquirer*, October 9, 1950, 1; and *The Sporting News*, October 18, 1950, 7. The Yankees, with a much larger seating capacity, had to refund more than $350,000 for just one game. The Phillies refund was $100,000 less for two games.
2. *Philadelphia Inquirer*, October 9, 1950, 27.
3. *Philadelphia Inquirer*, October 19, 1950, 1, 33.
4. Pappas, "Team Profits and Selected Payrolls."
5. *Philadelphia Inquirer*, October 19, 1950, 33.
6. The Phillies topped the Athletics in attendance in 1901, Mack's first season, from 1915 through 1920—excepting 1918—in 1943, and again in 1946, when they became the first Philadelphia team to top one million paid admissions.
7. Baumgartner, "Brains Behind Phillies," 16.
8. Philadelphia National League Baseball Club General Ledger.
9. Philadelphia National League Baseball Club General Ledger.
10. *Philadelphia Inquirer*, July 3, 1956, 19.
11. *Philadelphia Inquirer*, October 9, 1950, 27. Radio and television revenue for the 1950 World Series totaled $975,000, while ticket sales brought in $953,669. The owners ultimately voted to deposit the disputed television receipts into the player's pension fund. *Philadelphia Inquirer*, November 17, 1950, 53.
12. Philadelphia National League Baseball Club General Ledger.
13. *1951 Baseball Guide*, 115.
14. Philadelphia National League Baseball Club General Ledger.
15. *Charlotte News and Observer*, October 10, 1950, 2-B. J. W. Jones signed with Shreveport originally and was optioned by the Sports to Kilgore. He never

made it to the Major Leagues but played ten years in the Minors, for the most part in the Texas League with Shreveport. Sporting News Player Contract Card for J. W. Jones.

16. *Tilden Citizen*, October 12, 1950, 1.
17. *Tilden Citizen*, October 19, 1950, 1.
18. *Tilden Citizen*, November 9, 1950, 1, 4.
19. *Richmond Times-Dispatch*, October 10, 1950, 17.
20. *Richmond Times-Dispatch*, October 26, 1950, 20; and *The Sporting News*, December 6, 1950, 19.
21. *Elizabethton Star*, November 10, 1950, 1, 10.
22. *The Sporting News*, October 18, 1950, 6. There was initial concern that if Seminick's ankle did not heal properly, a screw might have to be inserted.
23. *Philadelphia Inquirer*, November 3, 1950, 43.
24. *Boston Globe*, October 28, 1950, 4. Waitkus married Carol Webel in Albany a year later. Bill Nicholson served as his best man. *Binghamton (NY) Sunday Press*, November 18, 1951, 13-A.
25. Theodore, *Baseball's Natural*, 85.
26. *Philadelphia Inquirer*, November 10, 1950, 49.
27. *Philadelphia Inquirer*, November 3, 1950, 43.
28. *Philadelphia Inquirer*, November 17, 1950, 55.
29. *Philadelphia Inquirer*, August 31, 1977, 8-D. McTear served as a sort of on-call physician for the Phillies from 1948 to 1957, while maintaining his private practice. He also served in the same role during the 1950s for La Salle College. His specialties were as an internist and cardiologist, and he later served as director of medical services at St. Mary's and St. Joseph's Hospitals in Philadelphia.
30. *Philadelphia Inquirer*, October 26, 1950, 34.
31. *The Sporting News*, April 11, 1951, 10.
32. Rogers and Nowlin, *Whiz Kids Take Pennant*, 238.
33. Roberts and Rogers, *Whiz Kids and 1950 Pennant*, 111.
34. *Philadelphia Inquirer*, December 10, 1950, 4S.
35. *Philadelphia Inquirer Magazine*, November 5, 1950, 20.
36. Paxton, "Whiz Kids," 47; and *The Sporting News*, June 22, 1963, 13.
37. *St. Louis Post-Dispatch*, November 4, 1950, 7.
38. *St. Louis Post-Dispatch*, November 26, 1950, 6-I.
39. *Allentown Morning Call*, February 1, 1951, 26.
40. *Franklin (PA) News Herald*, March 22, 1951, 14.
41. *Pittsburgh Press*, November 12, 1951, 19.
42. *Philadelphia Inquirer*, October 26, 1950, 34.
43. *Illinois State Journal*, December 19, 1950, 20.
44. *Illinois State Journal*, December 18, 1950, 14.
45. *Philadelphia Inquirer*, November 3, 1950, 43.
46. *Philadelphia Inquirer*, October 10, 1950, 40.
47. *1951 Baseball Guide*, 107; and *The Sporting News*, November 8, 1950, 2.

48. Del Ennis finished fourth, Granny Hamner sixth, and Robin Roberts seventh in the balloting. Since then, no relief pitcher has won a Most Valuable Player Award in the National League. Rollie Fingers with Milwaukee in 1981, Willie Hernandez with Detroit in 1984, and Dennis Eckersley with Oakland in 1992 captured the honor in the American League. There was no Cy Young Award in 1950, the honor being inaugurated in 1956 after Young's death.
49. *Philadelphia Inquirer*, November 9, 1950, 33.
50. *Oneonta Star*, November 7, 1950, 8.
51. *The Sporting News*, November 8, 1950, 2.
52. *Philadelphia Inquirer*, January 2, 1951, 24.
53. *Philadelphia Inquirer*, January 10, 1951, 35.
54. *The Sporting News*, November 1, 1950, 5. The other rookies named were pitcher Whitey Ford; catcher Mickey Grasso, Washington; first baseman Joe Adcock, Cincinnati; second baseman Roy Hartsfield, Boston Braves; third baseman Danny O'Connell, Pittsburgh; shortstop Chico Carrasquel, Chicago White Sox; outfielders Bill Howerton, St. Louis Cardinals; Sam Jethroe, Boston Braves; and Irv Noren, Washington; and utilityman Don Lenhart, St. Louis Browns.
55. *The Sporting News*, November 15, 1950, 6.
56. *Philadelphia Inquirer*, November 9, 1950, 33.
57. *Philadelphia Inquirer*, October 12, 1950, 34. The other teams trying to sign Casagrande were said to be the Yankees, Red Sox, Cubs, Pirates, Reds, Indians, and Tigers.
58. *The Sporting News*, October 11, 1950, 1.
59. *The Sporting News*, October 11, 1950, 10. As concerned as Carpenter said he was about these prospects, he got the names wrong for two of the three. Thornton "Knipper" was Thornton Kipper, and he called Stan Palys "Charley Payls," getting both his first and last name wrong. All three played for the Phillies during the 1950s.
60. *The Sporting News*, November 22, 1950, 16.
61. *Brooklyn Daily Eagle*, October 14, 1950, 6; Philadelphia National League Club General Ledger, account 52–2, sheet 1.
62. *Philadelphia Inquirer*, November 17, 1950, 53.
63. *The Sporting News*, November 22, 1950, 16.
64. *1951 Baseball Guide*, 151–52; and *Philadelphia Inquirer*, December 13, 1950, 53. Part of the argument against the high school rule was the disadvantage baseball experienced when competing with college football for top athletes. There remained sentiment for limits, but the current rule was to continue until December 31, 1951, while a committee formulated alternative regulations. *Philadelphia Inquirer*, December 8, 1950, 61.
65. Rogers and Nowlin, *Whiz Kids Take Pennant*, 147.
66. *Philadelphia Inquirer*, December 15, 1950, 61.
67. *Philadelphia Inquirer*, December 9, 1950, 15; and Philadelphia National League Baseball Club General Ledger.

68. *Wilmington Morning News*, November 17, 1950, 54.
69. *Philadelphia Inquirer*, December 22, 1950, 36, 40.

12. WILL THEY WANT THEIR SECOND?

 1. *Philadelphia Inquirer Magazine*, February 4, 1951, 10.
 2. *The Sporting News*, December 13, 1950, 21; and *Philadelphia Inquirer Magazine*, February 4, 1951, 10.
 3. *Philadelphia Inquirer Magazine*, February 4, 1951, 10.
 4. *St. Petersburg Times*, February 16, 1951, 23.
 5. *Philadelphia Inquirer*, January 5, 1951, 33.
 6. *Philadelphia Inquirer*, January 13, 1951, 13.
 7. *Philadelphia Inquirer*, February 26, 1951, 23. Church had to cover his hotel bill until he settled his contract negotiations.
 8. Baumgartner, "Will Phillies Sweat Their Way Back?," 72.
 9. *Philadelphia Inquirer Magazine*, August 20, 1950, 10.
10. Snelling, *Glimpse of Fame*, 19.
11. Silverman, "Del Ennis Puzzle," 46.
12. *Philadelphia Inquirer*, April 27, 1951, 51.
13. *Philadelphia Inquirer*, May 4, 1951, 37.
14. *Philadelphia Inquirer*, May 19, 1951, 14, 16.
15. *Philadelphia Inquirer*, June 8, 1951, 46.
16. *Philadelphia Inquirer*, June 22, 1951, 37.
17. Brown, interview by Al Quimby.
18. *Detroit Free Press*, June 6, 1951, 22.
19. *Detroit Free Press*, June 12, 1951, 18. Some sources claim Kazanski received a total of $100,000. He was paid in four annual installments of $20,000, with the first issued on January 3, 1952. Since it seems unlikely he received no money until seven months after signing, it is possible he was given $20,000 up front and the remainder in four installments. However, nothing to that effect appears in the Phillies ledger for that time period. Philadelphia National League Club General Ledger, account 52–2, sheet 1; and *Baltimore Sun*, March 18, 1952, 17.
20. *Philadelphia Inquirer*, June 12, 1951, 33.
21. *Philadelphia Inquirer*, February 1, 1951, 28, 30.
22. *Philadelphia Inquirer*, February 13, 1951, 32.
23. *Wilmington Morning News*, July 5, 1951, 17.
24. *Wilmington Morning News*, July 12, 1951, 30. Eddie Waitkus and Tommy Brown got the only Phillies hits off Casagrande.
25. *Wilmington Morning News*, July 19, 1951, 32.
26. *Wilmington Morning News*, August 21, 1951, 20.
27. *Wilmington Morning News*, August 25, 1951, 12.
28. *Wilmington Morning News*, August 31, 1951, 34.
29. *Wilmington Morning News*, September 14, 1951, 50.

30. *Terre Haute Tribune*, July 12, 1951, 20. Among those accompanying Carpenter were Joe Reardon, Eddie Collins Jr., and Johnny Nee.
31. *Terre Haute Tribune*, July 19, 1951, 20.
32. *Terre Haute Tribune*, July 26, 1951, 21.
33. *Philadelphia Inquirer*, December 9, 1951, s3.
34. *Philadelphia Inquirer*, August 2, 1951, 23.
35. *Philadelphia Inquirer*, August 8, 1951, 36, 38.
36. *Philadelphia Inquirer*, August 12, 1951, 1s, 2s.
37. *Philadelphia Inquirer*, August 25, 1951, 13.
38. *Philadelphia Inquirer*, September 8, 1951, 13; and *Philadelphia Inquirer*, September 13, 1951, 32.
39. New York went on a historic run at the end of the 1951 season. After their sixteen-game winning streak, the Giants split four games, and then won eight of ten. After losing two, they ended the regular season with twelve wins in thirteen games. They had a record of 37-7 between August 12 and September 30.
40. *Philadelphia Inquirer*, October 1, 1951, 1, 13, 23, 24.
41. The New York Giants defeated Brooklyn in the best-of-three playoff in dramatic fashion, thanks to Bobby Thomson and the famous "Miracle of Coogan's Bluff."
42. Subcommittee on Study of Monopoly Power, *Organized Baseball*, 107.
43. Philadelphia National League Club General Ledger. The Phillies transferred $103,000 to Utica's books in 1950 and also set up a loss reserve of $152,000 before deciding to shut down the franchise.
44. *Philadelphia Inquirer*, October 31, 1951, 47.
45. Philadelphia National League Club General Ledger.
46. *1952 Baseball Guide*, 275. Wilmington's paid attendance in 1951 was 43,135.
47. *Philadelphia Inquirer*, October 31, 1951, 1.
48. *Philadelphia Inquirer*, October 31, 1951, 1, 47. Sawyer's remark about players buying new cars and new homes was interesting in light of the fact that shortly after that statement, in April 1952, the Phillies lent Robin Roberts $11,300 to help him purchase a home. The total amount of the purchase was $28,700, with a bank loan covering the remainder. Roberts repaid the Phillies by the end of the season. Philadelphia National League Club General Ledger.
49. *Philadelphia Inquirer*, December 9, 1951, s3.
50. *Philadelphia Inquirer*, January 12, 1952, 13; and *Philadelphia Inquirer Magazine*, February 17, 1952, 10.
51. *Philadelphia Inquirer*, December 11, 1951, 1, 49. The Phillies also sent infielder Eddie Pellagrini and pitcher Niles Jordan to Cincinnati.
52. *Philadelphia Inquirer*, March 22, 1952, 14.
53. Ennis, interview.
54. *St. Petersburg Times*, March 26, 1952, 26.
55. *Philadelphia Inquirer*, March 20, 1952, 28.
56. *Philadelphia Inquirer*, January 31 1952, 25.

57. *Philadelphia Inquirer*, March 19, 1952, 45.
58. *Philadelphia Inquirer*, April 18, 1952, 10. Steinhagen told reporters that she planned to return to the hospital and work as an occupational therapist. That, of course, did not happen.
59. *St. Petersburg Times*, March 7, 1952, 37.
60. Jones was sent to Baltimore, where he struggled for most of the season. The Orioles, which had purchased his contract, gave permission for Jones to seek a deal with another team. That resulted in his being sold to the Sacramento Solons of the Pacific Coast League prior to the 1953 season. *Sacramento Bee*, February 5, 1953, 24.
61. *St. Petersburg Times*, March 28, 1952, 34.
62. *St. Petersburg Times*, March 28, 1952, 34.
63. Rogers and Nowlin, *Whiz Kids Take Pennant*, 134, 135.
64. *Philadelphia Inquirer*, April 5, 1952, 17. Ridzik's is one of only three recognized spring training complete-game no-hitters against a Major League team— the others being Pittsburgh's Cy Blanton against Cleveland in 1939 and the Cardinals Murry Dickson against the Yankees in 1948. His was one of three no-hitters that spring, the other two being combined efforts thrown by Jim Hearn and Monty Kennedy of the New York Giants and Warren Spahn and Ernie Johnson of the Boston Braves. "Spring Training No-Hitters," Nonohitters .com, March 30, 2016, https://www.nonohitters.com/spring-training-no -hitters/.
65. *St. Petersburg Times*, March 1, 1952, 15.
66. *Philadelphia Inquirer*, March 28, 1952, 45.
67. *Philadelphia Inquirer*, April 13, 1952, s1, s2.
68. *Philadelphia Inquirer*, March 19, 1952, 45.
69. *Philadelphia Inquirer*. May 24, 1952, 15. The Phillies acquired outfielder Johnny Wyrostek, who had previously played for the Phillies in 1946–47, and pitcher Kent Peterson in the deal.
70. Church, interview.
71. *St. Petersburg Times*, March 29, 1952, 12.
72. *Baltimore Sun*, March 15, 1952, 11.
73. *Baltimore Sun*, April 18, 1952, 21; *Baltimore Sun*, April 20, 1952, 4D; and *Baltimore Sun*, April 21, 1952, 15.
74. *Baltimore Sun*, April 30, 1952, 19.
75. *Baltimore Sun*, April 18, 1952, 21.
76. *Baltimore Sun*, April 20, 1952, 4D.
77. *Baltimore Sun*, May 1, 1952, 21.
78. *Schenectady Gazette*, May 6, 1952, 20. The breakdown was $100,000 for Kazanski, $40,000 for Casagrande, and $25,000 for Hollmig.
79. *Daily News* (New York), April 18, 1952, 70. Ennis had made a similar bare-handed catch against Jackie Robinson during a game in 1950. Roberts and Rogers, *Whiz Kids and 1950 Pennant*, 241.

80. *Philadelphia Inquirer*, April 21, 1952, 23, 24. Unfortunately, Ennis made an eighth-inning throwing error in the nightcap, shortly after a minor collision in the outfield with second baseman Connie Ryan, which allowed 2 runs to score. The Phillies lost the game, 2–1.

81. *Philadelphia Inquirer*, May 7, 1952, 53, 55.

82. *Philadelphia Inquirer*, April 30, 1952, 45, 47.

83. *Philadelphia Inquirer*, May 14, 1952, 1, 49.

84. *Philadelphia Inquirer*, May 23, 1952, 37. Curt Simmons's home run came in the sixth inning off Pittsburgh's Red Munger. Pirates center fielder Bob Del Greco raced in to catch Simmons's line drive but misjudged it. As Del Greco realized the ball was going to go over his head, he reached up with his bare hand but managed only to deflect it. By the time the outfielder tracked down the ball, Simmons had scored on what was ruled a three-run home run.

85. *Philadelphia Inquirer*, June 2, 1952, 25.

86. *Philadelphia Inquirer*, June 8, 1952, s1, s2.

87. *Philadelphia Inquirer*, June 10, 1952, 30. Spahn was thirty-one years old and had been a 20-game winner four times in the previous five years. After an off-year in 1952, he won 20 or more games nine of the next eleven years, including 23 wins in 1963 at age forty-two.

88. *Philadelphia Inquirer*, June 13, 1952, 41.

89. *Philadelphia Inquirer*, June 28, 1952, 1, 13.

90. *Philadelphia Inquirer*, June 28, 1952, 1, 13. Carpenter denied that Sawyer would serve as general manager, and he confirmed that the remaining two years of Sawyer's contract would be honored.

91. Roberts and Rogers, *Whiz Kids and 1950 Pennant*, 139.

92. Roberts and Rogers, *Whiz Kids and 1950 Pennant*, 139.

13. FROM CONTENDER TO AFTERTHOUGHT

1. *Detroit Free Press*, December 8, 1950, 38; and *Detroit Free Press*, December 12, 1950, 22. It was not the first All-Star Game played at Shibe Park. The Athletics hosted the event in 1943.

2. *Philadelphia Inquirer*, July 9, 1952, 45.

3. *Philadelphia Inquirer*, July 9, 1952, 1, 43, 45.

4. An old-timer's game was played twenty years later as an opportunity to complete the shortened All Star Game. The game was "resumed" in the sixth inning with the National League leading, 3–2. Bobby Shantz picked up where he had left off for the American League and was torched for 5 runs. The National League "won" 8–3. *Philadelphia Inquirer*, August 20, 1972, 1-D, 14-D.

5. Willie Jones was the fourth Phillies All-Star in 1951, and Granny Hamner was the fourth representative in 1953.

6. Bob Friend of the Pittsburgh Pirates started the 1956 All-Star Game for the National League. Roberts shares with Lefty Gomez and Don Drysdale the record for most All-Star starts by a pitcher with five.

7. Cady Lowery, "Robin Roberts Notches 28th Straight Complete Game," National Baseball Hall of Fame, retrieved December 23, 2023, https:// baseballhall.org/discover/inside-pitch/robin-roberts-28-consecutive -complete-game.

8. *Philadelphia Inquirer*, May 17, 1953, 1s, 6s.

9. *Philadelphia Inquirer*, June 5, 1953, 41.

10. *Philadelphia Daily News*, December 14, 2022, 34.

11. *Philadelphia Inquirer*, February 17, 1953, 29. Meyer, who won 13 games and had a career best in innings pitched for the Phillies in 1952, pitched well for the Dodgers in 1953 and 1954 and won a World Series ring with them in 1955.

12. *Philadelphia Inquirer*, June 29, 1953, 20.

13. Theodore, *Baseball's Natural*, 102.

14. *Philadelphia Inquirer*, September 18, 1953, 47.

15. Theodore, *Baseball's Natural*, 89–90.

16. *Philadelphia Inquirer*, September 27, 1953, 2s; and *Philadelphia Inquirer*, September 28, 1953, 27.

17. *Philadelphia Inquirer*, September 27, 1953, s2.

18. *Philadelphia Inquirer*, January 15, 1954, 31.

19. *Philadelphia Inquirer*, March 17, 1954, 42. Waitkus played in ninety-five games for Baltimore and batted .283.

20. *Philadelphia Inquirer*, August 23, 1954, 1, 16.

21. Pollock, "He Got $52,000," 91; and *1953 Baseball Guide*, 97.

22. *Philadelphia Inquirer*, September 27, 1953, 2s.

23. *Philadelphia Inquirer*, June 17, 1953, 45; and *Philadelphia Inquirer*, June 20, 1953, 16. Qualters had thrown four no-hitters in high school and struck out 439 batters in 237 innings in his three years on the varsity team. For more on Qualters's unfortunate career, see Stephen D. Boren's article, "Tom Qualters' Amazing 1954 Season for the Philadelphia Phillies," in sabr's *National Pastime*, 2013.

24. Pollock, "He Got $52,000," 91.

25. *Louisville Courier-Journal*, April 24, 1954, 19.

26. *Louisville Courier-Journal*, May 10, 1955, section 2, 9.

27. *Louisville Courier-Journal*, June 2, 1955, section 2, 10.

28. *Louisville Courier-Journal*, April 24, 1956, section 2, 5.

29. *Meriden Journal*, July 11, 1957, 4.

30. The other two with Topps cards were long-time Minor Leaguers Lou Ortiz and Jack Parks.

31. *New Haven Register*, November 24, 2016.

32. *Philadelphia Inquirer*, June 23, 1953, 30.

33. *Philadelphia Inquirer*, June 26, 1953, 37.

34. *Philadelphia Inquirer*, June 26, 1953, 41.

35. *Philadelphia Inquirer*, June 29, 1953, 20.

36. *Philadelphia Inquirer*, June 30, 1953, 33, 35.

37. *Philadelphia Inquirer*, April 17, 1954, 1, 16; and Linn, "Tragedy of Phillies," 74. The Pittsburgh Pirates, Cincinnati Reds, and St. Louis Cardinals all integrated at the beginning of the 1954 season.

38. *Philadelphia Inquirer*, May 21, 1954, 1, 33, 34. The detective was eventually given a suspended sentence for a firearm found in his vehicle. According to Hamner, the gun was only licensed for use in Delaware. *Philadelphia Inquirer*, November 20, 1954, 13; and *Philadelphia Daily News*, April 5, 1972, 51.

39. Lopata, interview.

40. Roberts one-hit the Milwaukee Braves on April 29, allowing only a third-inning lead-off double to Del Crandall, and then one-hit Cincinnati, surrendering a home run to Bobby Adams leading off the game and then retiring twenty-seven batters in a row. *Philadelphia Inquirer*, April 30, 1954, 1, 37; and *Philadelphia Inquirer*, May 14, 1954, 1, 37.

41. *Time*, May 28, 1956.

42. *Philadelphia Inquirer*, October 1, 1956, 23. Roberts lost to the New York Giants, 8–3, after leading, 2–1, after four innings and trailing only 4–2 going into the eighth inning. Rookie first baseman Bill White hit 2 home runs, and pitcher Al Worthington added a three-run shot.

43. Ashburn set records with nine seasons recording more than 400 putouts, four of them with 500 or more. Only Tris Speaker and Willie Mays recorded more career putouts as a center fielder.

44. *Philadelphia Daily News*, March 26, 2010, 89.

45. *Philadelphia Daily News*, March 26, 2010, 89.

46. Linn, "Tragedy of the Phillies," 70.

47. Linn, "Tragedy of the Phillies," 70.

48. Linn, "Tragedy of the Phillies," 74; and *Philadelphia Inquirer*, August 26, 1954, 22.

49. Linn, "Tragedy of the Phillies," 75.

50. *Philadelphia Inquirer*, August 26, 1954, 1, 22.

51. *Philadelphia Inquirer*, August 26, 1954, 1.

52. *Philadelphia Inquirer*, October 15, 1954, 1, 35.

53. *Philadelphia Inquirer*, November 9, 1954, 26.

54. *Philadelphia Inquirer*, November 25, 1954, 47; and Rogers and Nowlin, *Whiz Kids Take Pennant*, 143.

55. *Time*, August 16, 1954, 37; and *Philadelphia Inquirer*, November 9, 1954, 26.

56. *Philadelphia Inquirer*, November 9, 1954, 26; and *Kansas City Star*, April 13, 1955, 42. Mack returned in July for a reunion of A's greats, arriving at the airport wearing a big smile, a straw hat, and a bolo tie, photographed while leaning on Jimmie Foxx. *Kansas City Times*, July 20, 1955; and Macht, *Grand Old Man*, 574. Also see Robert Warrington's article in the 2010 Fall *SABR* Baseball Research Journal, "Departure without Dignity."

57. *Kansas City Journal*, October 8, 1886, 2; and *Kansas City Journal*, October 10, 1886, 2.

58. *Philadelphia Inquirer*, November 9, 1954, 26. It was reported that Carpenter paid $1.6 million to Johnson for the stadium.
59. Kuklick, *To Everything a Season*, 126; and Macht, *Grand Old Man*, 528–70.
60. *Philadelphia Tribune*, September 20, 1952, 12. Jones won 7 and lost 9 for Granby. A former Negro Leaguer and U.S. Virgin Islands native, Alphonso Gerard hit .303 for Granby and Three Rivers—his Sporting News Contract Card indicates he was with Granby from July 28 to September 5. His contract card also shows him as a scout for the San Francisco Giants from 1964 to 1973. The Provincial League often operated independently in Canada and was historically a haven for Black and Latino ballplayers. For more on Alphonso Gerard, see his SABR biography by Rory Costello.
61. Sporting News Contract Card for Cecil Eugene Jones. Jones's contract card classifies him as English, while a contemporary article in the *Philadelphia Tribune* identifies him as Black and Baseball Reference identifies him as an ex-Negro League pitcher. *Philadelphia Tribune*, July 29, 1952, 11.
62. *Philadelphia Tribune*, September 20, 1952, 10, 12; and Beer, *Oscar Charleston*, 310.
63. *Philadelphia Tribune*, April 11, 1953, 10; and Kenny Ayres, "Pioneer in Pinstripes: The Ted Washington Story," January 31, 2024, https://beyondthebell.mlblogs .com/pioneer-in-pinstripes-45c2a01c1b4a.
64. *Philadelphia Inquirer*, September 14, 1953, 29, 31. Trice eventually won 9 and lost 9 during the 1953 and 1954 seasons for the Athletics.
65. *Philadelphia Inquirer*, February 4, 1954, 22; *Philadelphia Inquirer*, December 17, 1953, 29; and *Philadelphia Tribune*, December 19, 1953, 1, 3.
66. *Philadelphia Inquirer*, June 29, 1954, 26, 29. Power was hit above the right temple and knocked unconscious. Carried from the field, he was revived in the clubhouse and was taken to the hospital for overnight observation.
67. *Philadelphia Tribune*, October 5, 1954, 1, 2. Both Herrera and Mason eventually played for the Phillies—Herrera in 1958 and 1960–1961, and Mason in 1958 and 1960. Mason appeared in four games for the Phillies, with no decisions and a 10.13 earned run average. Herrera hit 31 home runs and batted .271 in three hundred Major League games and hit 274 home runs in the Minor Leagues during a career that lasted into the 1970s.
68. *Pittsburgh Courier*, July 3, 1954, 25.
69. Philadelphia Phillies, "Pioneer in Pinstripes—Chuck Randall," video, 5:16, February 10, 2023, https://www.youtube.com/watch?v=eBJ_iJlTpIE. This is a short documentary profiling Randall.
70. *Philadelphia Tribune*, September 20, 1955, 12. Randall remained in the Phillies farm system through 1958, but outside of a handful of games never rose above Class B. *Philadelphia Tribune*, February 14, 1956, 10.
71. *Philadelphia Tribune*, October 6, 1956, 7. The nine included Charles Field, a catcher just signed out of Oakland, California; James Stewart; Herrera; Mason; Randall; Dickerson; Ed Logan, who hit .385 as a teammate of Nickerson and

Randall in Mattoon in 1956; D. D. Vaughn; and William Hill. Only Herrera and Mason reached the Majors.

72. *Mattoon (IL) Journal Gazette*, May 9, 1956, 5; and *Mattoon (IL) Journal Gazette*, May 22, 1956, 9.

73. *Philadelphia Inquirer*, February 11, 2024, C1, C7.

74. *Philadelphia Inquirer*, August 21, 1955, S3.

75. *Philadelphia Inquirer*, September 12, 1955, 21. Van Dusen was hit by Humberto Robinson in the nightcap of a doubleheader against the Milwaukee Braves.

76. *Philadelphia Inquirer*, September 25, 1955, 2S.

77. *Philadelphia Inquirer*, June 6, 1956, 38.

78. *Philadelphia Tribune*, July 28, 1956, 7.

79. *Philadelphia Tribune*, June 26, 1956, 1, 2.

80. *Philadelphia Tribune*, July 3, 1956, 1, 2.

81. *Philadelphia Tribune*, March 2, 1957, 6. Kennedy was the first Black player signed by the Phillies who reached the Majors. Chico Fernández became the first Black player for the Phillies in a Major League game and was the team's starting shortstop in both 1957 and 1958.

82. *Philadelphia Inquirer*, March 29, 1957, 35.

83. *Philadelphia Inquirer*, April 6, 1957, 18.

84. *Philadelphia Tribune*, April 13, 1957, 13.

85. *Philadelphia Tribune*, April 16, 1957, 1.

86. *Philadelphia Tribune*, April 9, 1957, 13.

87. *Philadelphia Inquirer*, May 12, 1957, 2S. Harmon was reported to be thirty-one at the time of his acquisition.

88. *Philadelphia Tribune*, June 15, 1957, 13.

89. *Philadelphia Tribune*, June 4, 1957, 11.

90. *Philadelphia Inquirer*, October 15, 1954, 1, 35.

91. *Wilmington Morning News*, April 9, 1955, 1, 24.

92. *Philadelphia Inquirer*, April 10, 1955, S1; *Philadelphia Inquirer*, April 12, 1955, 27; and *Philadelphia Inquirer*, July 10, 1955, S3.

93. *The Sporting News*, November 13, 1957, 10. At the time, *The Sporting News* had a practice of separate awards for rookie pitchers and position players.

94. *Philadelphia Inquirer*, July 31, 1957, 28, 30. Northey's home run enabled him to tie the Major League record of 9 career pinch-hit round-trippers. "That was a record I've been after a long time. It felt good, real good," he said. That mark has since been shattered—Matt Stairs currently holds the record with 23. As of 2024 Northey still shares with Willie McCovey and Rich Reese the Major League record of 3 career pinch-hit grand slams.

95. Reichler, "Price of Stubbornness," 89.

96. One other legendary story from 1957 has Richie Ashburn hitting a foul ball that broke the nose of a woman named Alice Roth, whose husband was a Philadelphia newspaper sports editor. Supposedly as Mrs. Roth was being carried away by stretcher, Ashburn hit another foul that struck her in the leg. The

tale has been repeated innumerable times over the years, and the Roth family has told their side of the story through grandson Preston Roth, who is said to have been present at the incident. Hunter Doyle, "Richie Ashburn's Foul Balls Live on in the Roth Family," Phillies Nation, last updated December 26, 2022, https://www.philliesnation.com/2022/12/richie-ashburns-fouls-balls-live-on-in-roth-family/.

97. *Philadelphia Inquirer*, December 7, 1957, 21.
98. *Spokesman-Review*, January 18, 1958, 1; and *Spokesman-Review*, February 6, 1958, 12. For more than a month the community of Spokane had been beleaguered by reports of a man in a station wagon luring young girls into his car. When some schoolgirls managed to record a license plate number, it was traced back to Bouchee, who confessed to five incidents involving girls ages six to eighteen. He exposed himself to them and showed them pornographic material. He was charged with two counts that occurred on New Year's Eve 1957, involving girls aged six and ten.
99. *Spokesman-Review*, February 21, 1958, 1; and *Spokesman-Review*, March 7, 1958, 10.
100. *Philadelphia Inquirer*, June 17, 1958, 12; *Philadelphia Inquirer*, June 25, 1958, 12; and *Philadelphia Inquirer*, July 2, 1958, 13, 15. In his ruling, the judge said of Bouchee that his "problem is more medical than legal."
101. *Philadelphia Inquirer*, July 23, 1958, 1, 36.
102. Lopata, interview. Wyrostek had seen Rogers Hornsby on television and relayed some of the legend's general advice, telling Lopata he should just concentrate on making contact. Lopata started working on that, while changing his batting stance to one similar to that of an old Minor League teammate, Wally Novak. It worked, as Lopata averaged 24 home runs over the 1955–1957 seasons, after having hit only 35 over his first seven years in the big leagues. It has often been stated that Hornsby offered his advice directly, but Lopata denied that ever happened.
103. The Phillies had seven players on their roster in 1958 that had been on the team in 1950. The Dodgers had five, and no other National League team had more than one.
104. Roberts and Rogers, *Whiz Kids and 1950 Pennant*, 140.
105. *Philadelphia Inquirer*, July 30, 1955, 16.
106. *Philadelphia Inquirer*, October 6, 1955, 26; and Theodore, *Baseball's Natural*, 109–10.
107. *Philadelphia Inquirer*, October 13, 1956, 18. Seminick was activated in September 1957 and played in eight games.
108. *Philadelphia Inquirer*, June 20, 1956, 36, 37. Ennis's home run came off Johnny Klippstein of the Cardinals. It was the game-winner, capping a four-run eighth inning of a 4–2 Phillies win.
109. *Philadelphia Inquirer*, November 21, 1956, 26.
110. *Philadelphia Inquirer*, May 30, 1958, 20.

111. *Philadelphia Inquirer*, July 14, 1958, 22.
112. *Philadelphia Inquirer*, December 4, 1958, 46.
113. *Philadelphia Inquirer*, February 5, 1959, 38.
114. *Philadelphia Inquirer*, April 1, 1959, 38.
115. *Philadelphia Inquirer*, May 17, 1959, S1; and *Philadelphia Inquirer*, June 6, 1959, 19.
116. *Philadelphia Inquirer*, January 14, 1959, 34, 38. Quinn was also given the title of vice president.
117. The Phillies had traded veteran outfielder Rip Repulski and a pair of Minor League pitchers, Jim Golden and Gene Snyder, to the Los Angeles Dodgers for Anderson, whose reputation was that of a great defensive second baseman and as an "Eddie Stanky type . . . a take-charge guy," according to Roy Hamey. Anderson's year with the Phillies was his only stint in the Major Leagues. *Philadelphia Inquirer*, December 24, 1958, 18.

14. I GAVE IT ALL I HAD

1. *Philadelphia Inquirer*, January 12, 1960, 1, 24.
2. McHugh, "Lucky Unlucky Guy," 76.
3. *St. Petersburg Times*, March 31, 1960, C-1.
4. *Philadelphia Inquirer*, April 15, 1960, 22; and *St. Petersburg Times*, March 16, 1960, 3-C.
5. *Philadelphia Inquirer*, April 13, 1960, 42, 45.
6. *Philadelphia Inquirer*, April 14, 1960, 38.
7. *Philadelphia Inquirer*, April 15, 1960, 1, 22, 23.
8. Roberts and Rogers, *My Life in Baseball*, 171
9. *Philadelphia Inquirer*, April 15, 1960, 1, 22, 23.
10. *Philadelphia Inquirer*, April 22, 1960, 30.
11. *Philadelphia Inquirer*, May 13, 1960, 37.
12. McHugh, "Lucky Unlucky Guy," 76.
13. Roberts and Rogers, *My Life in Baseball*, 171.
14. *Philadelphia Inquirer*, June 26, 1960, 5-S.
15. *St. Louis Post-Dispatch*, June 24, 1966, 5B.
16. Taxiera, *Unique Look at Big League Baseball*, 295. Roberts's single-season record stood until 1986, when Minnesota's Bert Blyleven surrendered 50 home runs.
17. *Philadelphia Inquirer*, May 14, 1958, 44, 45.
18. *Philadelphia Inquirer*, August 2, 1958, 14.
19. Roberts and Rogers, *My Life in Baseball*, 172. In his autobiography, Roberts claimed that was the last time he ever saw Cy Perkins. But the coach was present at the 1963 Whiz Kids reunion, four months before his death. Richie Ashburn introduced both men at the luncheon. *Philadelphia Inquirer*, June 6, 1963, 39; and *Philadelphia Inquirer*, October 3, 1963, 43.
20. *Philadelphia Daily News*, April 4, 1961, 71; and *Philadelphia Inquirer*, April 8, 1961, 19. Stuart hit his home run with two out in the first. Roberts entered with game not having allowed a run in twenty-three and one-third innings.

21. *Philadelphia Inquirer*, June 6, 1961, 36, 40.
22. *Philadelphia Inquirer*, August 21, 1961, 24, 34.
23. Burick, "What It Feels Like," 49.
24. *Philadelphia Inquirer*, August 8, 1976, E1.
25. Merchant, "Pitcher Who Lives in Past," 80.
26. Merchant, "Pitcher Who Lives in Past," 62.
27. *Lancaster New Era*, July 28, 1961, 15.
28. *Philadelphia Inquirer*, September 29, 1961, 38. Ridzik, who pitched one game for the 1950 Phillies, was reacquired at the end of his career and pitched in two games for the 1966 Phillies.
29. *Philadelphia Inquirer*, October 12, 1961, 44.
30. *Philadelphia Inquirer*, October 17, 1961, 1, 34.
31. *Philadelphia Inquirer*, October 17, 1961, 1.
32. *Philadelphia Inquirer*, March 22, 1962, 37; and *St. Petersburg Times*, March 22, 1962, 2-C. The retirement of Roberts's number was held at the Causeway Inn in Tampa after the game, which Roberts won despite allowing 4 runs in three innings.
33. *Baltimore Sun*, April 26, 1962, 38. Roberts made five exhibition appearances for the Yankees, allowing 15 hits and 8 runs in eleven innings. He had been originally signed as insurance in case the Yankees lost pitchers Bill Stafford and Roland Sheldon to military service. When they were not called, Roberts was let go. *Baltimore Sun*, May 22, 1962, 23.
34. Roberts and Rogers, *My Life in Baseball*, 181.
35. *Bristol (PA) Daily Courier*, September 20, 1962, 29.
36. *Baltimore Sun*, May 12, 1962, 15, 18; and *Cincinnati Enquirer*, May 17, 1962, 41. After Roberts worked out, Hutchinson—a former star pitcher himself—said, "Can't tell too much watching a guy throw on the sidelines, but he appeared loose and threw fairly hard."
37. *Baltimore Sun*, May 22, 1962, 17, 22.
38. *Baltimore Sun*, June 12, 1962, 17. Roberts almost ignited an all-out brawl between the Orioles and the Yankees. Rookie first baseman Boog Powell was beaned his second time up, carried from the field on a stretcher. Roberts felt it intentional and in the bottom of the inning fired a pitch over the head of New York's first batter, Roger Maris. Roberts and Rogers, *My Life in Baseball*, 183.
39. *The Sporting News*, December 1, 1962, 34.
40. *St. Louis Post-Dispatch*, May 20, 1960, 4C.
41. *Philadelphia Inquirer*, June 26, 1960, 1-S.
42. *Philadelphia Inquirer*, August 10, 1960, 38.
43. *St. Louis Post-Dispatch*, September 18, 1963, 4C. The win gave Koufax a record of 24-5 on the year. It was the second time Simmons had lost to Koufax in 1963, plus a no-decision in which he pitched thirteen innings while allowing only 7 hits and 1 run. *St. Louis Post-Dispatch*, August 22, 1963, 1E.

44. Allen was signed by Phillies scout John Ogden because Allen's mother thought him the most trustworthy among the talent hunters who had approached them. *Philadelphia Inquirer*, June 12, 1960, 2s; and *Wilkes-Barre Record*, March 25, 1964, 4.
45. *Philadelphia Inquirer*, October 1, 1964, 1, 34, 36. Dick Allen ended Simmons's no-hit bid with a line shot back through the box. Simmons joked, "I was just glad it didn't hit me."
46. *St. Louis Post-Dispatch*, October 1, 1964, 4D. After the game, he was asked how long he would keep pitching. He joked, "As long as it can keep me from going to work." Simmons's final career mark against the Phillies was 19-6.
47. Sisler had taken over on an interim basis for Fred Hutchinson, who had terminal cancer.
48. *Philadelphia Inquirer*, September 22, 1964, 1, 36. Allen Lewis wrote after Ruiz's steal cut Philadelphia's lead to five-and-a-half games, "If the Phillies should lose the National League pennant—and there's no real cause for alarm as yet—it might be correct to say the flag will have been stolen from them." After the Phillies collapse, the incident became known in Philadelphia as "The Curse of Chico Ruiz."
49. *St. Louis Post-Dispatch*, October 11, 1964, 1B. Simmons battled Jim Bouton to a 1–1 tie at Yankee Stadium when he was lifted for a pinch hitter in the top of the ninth. Mantle's home run set a new World Series career home run record, moving him past Babe Ruth.
50. *St. Louis Post-Dispatch*, October 15, 1964, 1A, 1E. Simmons allowed 7 hits and 3 runs in six and one-third innings. The Cardinals lost the game, 8–3.
51. *St. Louis Post-Dispatch*, June 22, 1966, 4C.
52. *Baltimore Sun*, April 18, 1965, A-1, A-2; and Roberts and Rogers, *My Life in Baseball*, 195.
53. *Philadelphia Inquirer*, August 8, 1976, E1.
54. *Baltimore Sun*, July 28, 1965, 17, 18.
55. *Houston Chronicle*, August 6, 1965, section 6, 1, 2; and Houston Chronicle, August 10, 1965, section2, 1, 2.
56. *Philadelphia Daily News*, August 10, 1965, 57.
57. Roberts made ten starts for Houston, winning 5 games and losing 2 with a 1.89 ERA.
58. *Houston Post*, October 20, 1965, section 4, 3.
59. *Houston Post*, April 13, 1966, section 4, 1. As of 2025 Tom Seaver holds the Major League record for Opening Day starting pitcher assignments with sixteen, fourteen of them in the National League. Steve Carlton shares the NL record with Seaver, all fourteen of his Opening Day starts coming for the Phillies.
60. The others on the search committee were Jim Bunning, Harvey Kuenn, and Bob Friend.
61. Roberts and Rogers, *My Life in Baseball*, 219–22; and Haupert, "Marvin Miller and Birth of MLBPA." Roberts later expressed some disappointment in Miller's

combative negotiations posture. While he still supported Miller, Roberts said, "I do wish that Marvin had been a little more temperate and had displayed more reverence for the game of baseball and the place it has in this country." Roberts and Rogers, *My Life in Baseball*, 225.

62. *Houston Post*, May 5, 1966, section 4, 1, 7.

63. *Houston Post*, July 5, 1966, section 4, 1.

64. Roberts and Rogers, *My Life in Baseball*, 205–6; and Milton Richman, United Press International, *Jersey City Journal*, May 2, 1967, 27.

65. *Chicago Tribune*, July 14, 1966, section 3, 2.

66. Like Roberts, Jenkins was a superior control pitcher who surrendered a lot of home runs. Like Roberts, he strung together six straight 20-win seasons and completed a high number of his starts. He ended his career with 284 wins, two fewer than Roberts, with both lasting nineteen Major League seasons.

67. *Chicago Tribune*, August 30, 1966, section 3, 1, 2. Roberts pitched the thirteenth and fourteenth innings against Atlanta.

68. *Chicago Tribune*, September 4, 1966, section 2, 2. Jamie Moyer passed Roberts in 2010. He retired in 2012, having allowed 522 home runs in his career.

69. *Chicago Tribune*, October 4, 1966; *The Sporting News*, October 8, 1966, 50; and Roberts and Rogers, *My Life in Baseball*, 211.

70. *The Sporting News*, May 20, 1967.

71. *Philadelphia Inquirer*, April 8, 1967, 23.

72. *The Sporting News*, May 13, 1967, 5.

73. *Philadelphia Inquirer*, April 27, 1967, 34, 48.

74. *Williamsport Sun-Gazette*, April 26, 1967, 40. Johnson eventually pitched ten years in the Major Leagues.

75. *The Sporting News*, May 13, 1967, 5.

76. *Hanover (PA) Evening Sun*, June 8, 1967; and *Reading Eagle*, June 14, 1967, 58.

77. *Philadelphia Inquirer*, June 19, 1967, 28.

78. *The Sporting News*, May 6, 1967, 35. Bedell, who had a forty-three-game hitting streak for Louisville in the American Association in 1961, hit .196 in fifty-eight games for the Braves in 1962. He made a brief return to the Major Leagues in 1968 as a pinch hitter for the Phillies, collecting 1 hit in 7 at bats. His only run batted in came on a sacrifice fly that ended Don Drysdale's then record scoreless innings streak at fifty-eight and two-thirds. Bedell was acquired by Reading in a Minor League trade for infielder Bob Lucas. Lucas's sister was married to Hank Aaron. His brother, Bill Lucas, became the first Black general manager in Major League history, with the Atlanta Braves. *Philadelphia Inquirer*, June 3, 1968, 35; and *Philadelphia Inquirer*, June 10, 1968, 34.

79. Howie Bedell, "Final Bow: Robin Roberts Pitches One Last Time for Reading," interview by Reading Fightin' Phils, video, 3:43, June 28, 2016, https://www.youtube.com/watch?v=14p4-w20nqM.

80. Bedell, "Final Bow."

81. *Reading Eagle*, June 18, 1967, 49; and *York Gazette and Daily*, June 19, 1967, 15.
82. Roberts and Rogers, *My Life in Baseball*, 213.
83. *Philadelphia Daily News*, June 23, 1967, 52.
84. *Philadelphia Daily News*, July 6, 1967, 63.
85. *Philadelphia Daily News*, August 9, 1967, 50.
86. *Wilmington Evening Journal*, August 18, 1967, 25.
87. Bedell, "Final Bow."
88. *Chicago Tribune*, June 23, 1966, section 3, 4.
89. *Chicago Tribune*, June 27, 1966, section 3, 1, 2.
90. *Chicago Tribune*, August 7, 1967, section 3, 2.
91. *Anaheim Bulletin*, August 10, 1967, C1.
92. *Anaheim Bulletin*, October 2, 1967, C1, C2. The Minnesota Twins and Chicago White Sox also entered the final weekend with a chance to win the pennant.
93. *Anaheim Bulletin*, October 3, 1967, C2. The Angels also released Bill "Moose" Skowron.
94. *Allentown Morning Call*, December 13, 1967, 47.
95. *The Sporting News*, November 11, 1967, 36.
96. *Philadelphia Daily News*, December 13, 1967, 50.

15. GHOSTS OF GREATNESS PAST

1. Of the twenty-seven invitees, only Ken Johnson and Blix Donnelly did not attend. Johnson was always disappointed in his career and felt he had not been of much help to the Phillies in 1950, even though they needed all 4 of his wins to capture the pennant. He never attended any of the reunions. C. Paul Roberts, email message to author, June 1, 2024. All four coaches, Benny Bengough, Cy Perkins, Maje McDonnell, and Dusty Cooke, were on hand.
2. *Philadelphia Inquirer*, June 6, 1963, 37, 39.
3. *The Sporting News*, June 22, 1963, 13.
4. *Philadelphia Daily News*, June 6, 1963, 61.
5. *Philadelphia Daily News*, June 6, 1963, 65.
6. *Philadelphia Daily News*, August 6, 1969, 54, 56. Others honored were Chris Short as left-handed pitcher, Cookie Rojas at second base, and the late Chuck Klein as the third outfielder.
7. *Philadelphia Daily News*, June 12, 1969, 64.
8. Theodore, *Baseball's Natural*, 120.
9. *Boston Globe*, September 17, 1972, 84; and Theodore, *Baseball's Natural*, 132.
10. *Chicago Tribune*, March 15, 2013, 1, 7.
11. *Philadelphia Daily News*, October 2, 1970, 3.
12. *Philadelphia Inquirer*, October 2, 1970, 1.
13. *Philadelphia Daily News*, October 2, 1970, 3, 4.
14. Richie Ashburn, "Last Game At Connie Mack Stadium Part 2," interview, Sports Gaming Channel, video, 9:53, May 21, 2020, https://www.youtube.com/watch?v=BRCv3-musa8. The stadium was finally demolished in 1976.

15. *Philadelphia Inquirer*, November 22, 1972, 1, 8. Bob Carpenter retained his position as chairman of the board.

16. *Philadelphia Daily News*, August 15, 1975, 68.

17. *Philadelphia Inquirer*, August 17, 1975, 1C, 5C.

18. *Buffalo News*, June 12, 1976, 8.

19. *Philadelphia Inquirer*, January 23, 1976, 1-D.

20. *Philadelphia Inquirer*, August 10, 1976, 2-C.

21. *Philadelphia Inquirer*, July 26, 1980, 1-C.

22. *Philadelphia Inquirer*, October 15, 1980, 4-C; and *Philadelphia Daily News*, October 15, 1980, 4.

23. The other most-watched game in World Series history was the seventh game of the 1986 World Series between the New York Mets and Boston Red Sox, which had more than fifty-five million viewers. The sixth game of the Phillies-Royals series had the highest rating—percentage of homes with televisions that tuned in—of any game in World Series history.

24. *Philadelphia Bulletin*, October 14, 1980.

25. *Philadelphia Inquirer*, October 30, 1981, 1A, 2A, 9C.

26. *Chicago Tribune*, October 1, 1962, F2. At his Hall of Fame induction, Ashburn said that after his last game, which saw the Mets end their first season with a record of 40-120, Casey Stengel addressed the team, saying, "I don't want anyone to feel bad about this. Fellas, this has been a team effort. No one or two people could have done this."

27. *Philadelphia Inquirer*, March 8, 1995, D1.

28. *Philadelphia Inquirer*, July 9, 1995, C2.

29. *Philadelphia Inquirer*, July 9, 1995, C2.

30. Ashburn ended his Phillies career with 2,217 hits, three more than Ed Delahanty. Thirty years later, shortly before he retired, Mike Schmidt hit a double on April 20, 1989, for his 2,218th hit with the Phillies, breaking Ashburn's team record. *Philadelphia Inquirer*, April 21, 1989, D1.

31. *Philadelphia Inquirer*, July 31, 1995, C1, C6.

32. *Philadelphia Inquirer*, September 10, 1997, A1.

33. *Philadelphia Inquirer*, September 10, 1997, A1, A16.

34. *Philadelphia Inquirer*, September 23, 1997, B4.

35. *Philadelphia Inquirer*, July 9, 2000, C9. Present for the 2000 reunion were Putsy Caballero, Bubba Church, Stan Lopata, Jackie Mayo, Maje McDonnell, Bob Miller, Steve Ridzik, Robin Roberts, Andy Seminick, Curt Simmons, and Paul Stuffel.

36. Church, interview.

37. *Philadelphia Daily News*, September 27, 1990, S13.

38. Rogers and Nowlin, *Whiz Kids Take Pennant*, 7.

39. *Philadelphia Daily News*, July 26, 1995, H-22.

40. *Philadelphia Daily News*, April 7, 1986, BB-6; and Roberts and Rogers, *Whiz Kids and 1950 Pennant*, 350.

41. *Philadelphia Inquirer*, July 11, 1990, A1, A4.
42. *Philadelphia Inquirer*, July 11, 1990, A4.
43. *Philadelphia Inquirer*, July 11, 1990, A4.
44. *Philadelphia Daily News*, July 11, 1990, 72.
45. *Philadelphia Daily News*, May 7, 2010, 1.
46. *Philadelphia Daily News*, May 7, 2010, 104. The others were Stan Lopata, Jackie Mayo, Putsy Caballero, Bob Miller, and Paul Stuffel.
47. *Allentown Morning Call*, October 6, 1947, 12.
48. *Philadelphia Inquirer*, November 11, 2011, C07.
49. *Allentown Morning Call*, November 11, 2011, C1, C5.
50. *Allentown Morning Call*, May 31, 2012, C1, C2.
51. *Allentown Morning Call*, June 3, 2012, A1, A3.
52. *Philadelphia Inquirer and Daily News*, April 4, 2016, P22.
53. *Allentown Morning Call*, September 1, 2020, C1.
54. *Philadelphia Daily News*, March 26, 2010, 89.
55. *Detroit Free Press*, November 29, 2020, C7.
56. *Allentown Morning Call*, December 14, 2022, A1.

BIBLIOGRAPHY

ARCHIVES

Baseball Reference.com
Bettman Archive (via Getty Images)
C. Paul Rogers
Chicago Sun-Times Collection, Chicago History Museum
Gannett Archive
Genealogybank.com
Library of Congress: Prints and Photographs Division
Michigan State University Athletic Department
National Baseball Hall of Fame, Cooperstown, New York
New York Daily News Photo Archive (via Getty Images)
New York Public Library: The Miriam and Ira D. Wallach Division of Art, Prints and
    Photographs
Newspapers.com
Paper of Record
ProQuest
Retrosheet
Robert Warrington
SABR Oral History Collection
Society for American Baseball Research, Biography Project
Sporting News Player Contract Cards (via LA84 Foundation)
Temple University Libraries, SCRC, Philadelphia, Pennsylvania

BOOKS

Achorn, Edward. *The Summer of Beer and Whiskey*. New York: Public Affairs, 2013.
Beer, Jeremy. *Oscar Charleston: The Life and Legend of Baseball's Greatest Forgotten
    Player*. Lincoln: University of Nebraska Press, 2019.
Block, David. *Baseball Before We Knew It: A Search for the Roots of the Game*. Lincoln:
    University of Nebraska Press, 2005.
Craig, Keith. *Herb Pennock: Baseball's Faultless Pitcher*. Lanham MD: Rowman &
    Littlefield Publishers, 2016.

Dahlgren, Matt. *Rumor in Town: A Grandson's Promise to Right a Wrong*. California: Woodlyn Lane, 2007.

Gershman, Michael. *Diamonds: The Evolution of the Ballpark*. Boston: Houghton Mifflin, 1993.

Hemingway, Ernest. *The Old Man and the Sea*. New York: Charles Scribner and Sons, 2003. First published 1952 by Charles Scribner and Sons.

Hofmann, Paul, and Bill Nowlin, eds. *The 1883 Philadelphia Athletics: American Association Champions*. Phoenix: Society for American Baseball Research, 2022.

Kuklick, Bruce. *To Everything a Season*. Princeton NJ: Princeton University Press, 1991.

Macht, Norman. *The Grand Old Man of Baseball: Connie Mack in His Final Years, 1932–1956*. Lincoln: University of Nebraska Press, 2014.

Marmer, Mel, and Bill Nowlin, eds. *The Year of the Blue Snow: The 1964 Philadelphia Phillies*. Phoenix: Society for American Baseball Research, 2013.

McCue, Andy. *Mover & Shaker: Walter O'Malley, the Dodgers, & Baseball's Westward Expansion*. Lincoln: University of Nebraska Press, 2014.

——. *Stumbling around the Bases: The American League's Mismanagement in the Expansion Eras*. Lincoln: University of Nebraska Press, 2022.

National Archives. *Baseball: The National Pastime in the National Archives*. Washington DC: National Archives, 2016. https://www.archives.gov/publications/ebooks/baseball.html.

Nemec, David, ed. *Major League Baseball Profiles, 1871–1900*. Vol. 1, *The Ballplayers Who Built the Game*. Lincoln NE: Bison Books, 2011.

——, ed. *Major League Baseball Profiles, 1871–1900*. Vol. 2, *The Hall of Famers and Memorable Personalities Who Shaped the Game*. Lincoln NE: Bison Books, 2011.

Parrott, Harold. *The Lords of Baseball: A Wry Look at a Side of the Game the Fan Seldom Sees*. 2nd ed. Atlanta: Longstreet Press, 2002.

Peary, Danny. *We Played the Game*. New York: Black Dog and Leventhal Publishers, 1994.

Roberts, Robin, and C. Paul Rogers. *My Life in Baseball*. Chicago: Triumph Books, 2003.

——. *The Whiz Kids and the 1950 Pennant*. Philadelphia: Temple University Press, 1996.

Rogers, C. Paul, and Bill Nowlin, eds. *The Whiz Kids Take the Pennant: The 1950 Philadelphia Phillies*. Phoenix: Society For American Baseball Research, 2018.

Seymour, Harold, and Dorothy Seymour Mills. *Baseball: The Early Years*. New York: Oxford University Press, 1960.

——. *Baseball: The Golden Years*. New York: Oxford University Press, 1971.

Snelling, Dennis. *A Glimpse of Fame*. Jefferson NC: McFarland, 1993.

Sowell, Mike. *July 2, 1903: The Mysterious Death of Big Ed Delahanty*. New York: Macmillan, 1992.

Taxiera, Joe. *A Unique Look at Big League Baseball*. Self-published, April 2011.

Theodore, John. *Baseball's Natural*. Lincoln: University of Nebraska Press, 2006.

Westcott, Rich, and Frank Bilovsky. *The Phillies Encyclopedia*. 3rd ed. Philadelphia: Temple University Press, 2004.

Wiggins, Robert Peyton. *The Federal League of Base Ball Clubs: The History of an Outlaw Major League, 1914–1915*. Jefferson NC: McFarland, 2009.

ARTICLES

Baker, William. "Alexander as a Player and a Man." *Baseball Magazine*, January 1916.

Baumgartner, Stan. "The Brains Behind the Phillies." *Sport*, January 1951.

——. "Like Sisler, Like Son." *Sport*, October 1950.

——. "Phillies Gamble on Youth." *Sport*, June 1950.

——. "Will the Phillies Sweat Their Way Back?" *Sport*, April 1952.

——. "Willie Is No Puddinhead." *Sport*, August 1950.

Breen, Matt. "South Jerseyan among 'Pioneers in Pinstripes.'" *Philadelphia Inquirer*, February 11, 2024.

Brown, Hugh. "The Bonus Baby Who Made Good." *Sport*, October 1952.

——. "Hamner of the Whiz Kids." *Sport*, September 1952.

——. "Mr. Roberts—the Story of a Winner." *Sport*, August 1956.

——. "The Terrible-Tempered Russ Meyer." *Sport*, December 1952.

Brumby, Bob. "Can Eddie Waitkus Come Back?" *Sport*, April 1950.

Burick, Sy. "What It Feels Like to Lose 23 in a Row." *Baseball Digest*, March 1962.

Davids, L. Robert. "Baker Bowl." *SABR Research Journal*, 1982.

Dittmar, Joe. "A Shocking Discovery." *SABR Baseball Research Journal*, 1991.

Duncan, Andy. "Jim Konstanty, the All-Time Fireman." *Sport*, May 1951.

Edelman, Rob. "Eddie Waitkus and 'The Natural': What Is Assumption? What Is Fact?" *SABR National Pastime*, 2013. https://sabr.org/journal/article/eddie -waitkus-and-the-natural-what-is-assumption-what-is-fact/.

Haupert, Michael. "Marvin Miller and the Birth of the MLBPA." *SABR Baseball Research Journal*, Spring 2017. https://sabr.org/journal/article/marvin-miller-and -the-birth-of-the-mlbpa/.

Hofmann, Paul. "Charlie Ferguson." SABR Biography Project, n.d. https://sabr.org /bioproj/person/Charlie-Ferguson/.

Laing, Jeff. "Philadelphia—October 1866: The Center of the Baseball Universe." *SABR National Pastime*, 2013. https://sabr.org/the-national-pastime-archives/ #toggle-id-1.

Lane, F. C. "Horace Fogel, the Man Who Is Trying to Wreck Baseball." *Baseball Magazine*, June 1913.

Linn, Ed. "The Tragedy of the Phillies." *Sport*, March 1955.

McHugh, Roy. "A Lucky Unlucky Guy." *Sport*, February 1964.

Merchant, Larry. "Pitcher Who Lives in the Past." *Sport*, May 1962.

Montgomery, Wynn. "Georgia's 1948 Phenoms and the Bonus Rule." *Baseball Research Journal*, Summer 2010.

Morton, Ed. "Coroner's Jury and Bankruptcy: Aftermath of the 1903 Ball Park Horror." *Connie Mack–Dick Allen Chapter* (blog). Philadelphia Chapter of the Society for American Baseball Research, April 25, 2021. https://phillysabr.com/2021/04/25/coroners-jury-and-bankruptcy-aftermath-of-the-1903-ball-park-horror/.

Newcombe, Jack. "The Making of Richie Ashburn." *Sport*, September 1951.

———. "Roberts Is the Phillies Stopper." *Sport*, June 1952.

Paxton, Harry. "The Whiz Kids." *Sport*, June 1964.

Pollock, Ed. "He Got $52,000 for Pitching One Inning." *Baseball Digest*, July 1955.

Reichler, Joe. "The Price of Stubbornness for Robin Roberts." *Sport*, February 1958.

Rogers, C. Paul. "The Day the Phillies Went to Egypt." *SABR Baseball Research Journal*, Fall 2010. https://sabr.org/journal/article/the-day-the-phillies-went-to-egypt/.

———. "Napoleon Lajoie, Breach of Contract and the Great Baseball War." *SMU Law Review* 55, no. 1 (January 2002): 323–45. https://scholar.smu.edu/cgi/viewcontent.cgi?article=1934&context=smulr.

Salisbury, Jim. "If Anyone Should Have Been a Phillie, It Was Hall of Famer Roy Campanella." NBC Sports Philadelphia, last updated May 16, 2020. https://www.nbcsportsphiladelphia.com/mlb/if-anyone-should-have-been-a-phillie-it-was-hall-of-famer-roy-campanella/399729/.

Seamon, Richard. "The Whole Story of Pitching." *Time*, May 28, 1956.

Sher, Jack. "The Ups and Downs of Old Pete." *Sport*, April 1950.

Silverman, Al. "The Del Ennis Puzzle." *Sport*, August 1952.

Thornley, Stew. "Howie Schultz." Society for American Baseball Research, SABR Biography Project, n.d. https://sabr.org/bioproj/person/howie-schultz/.

Warrington, Robert D. "Baseball's Deadliest Disaster: Black Saturday in Philadelphia." *National Pastime*, 2013.

———. "Departure without Dignity: The Athletics Leave Philadelphia." *SABR Baseball Research Journal*, Fall 2020. https://sabr.org/journal/article/departure-without-dignity-the-athletics-leave-philadelphia/.

———. "Entering the National League: The Phillies' Bumpy Journey." *SABR Baseball Research Journal*, Fall 2022. https://sabr.org/journal/article/entering-the-national-league-the-phillies-bumpy-journey/.

———. "The Great Philadelphia Ballpark Riot." *National Pastime*, 2013.

———. "Philadelphia in the 1882 League Alliance." *SABR Baseball Research Journal*, Fall 2019. https://sabr.org/journal/article/philadelphia-in-the-1882-league-alliance/.

Westcott, Rich. "Joe Borden: The First No-Hit Pitcher and National League Winner." *National Pastime*, 2003. https://sabr.org/the-national-pastime-archives/#toggle-id-1.

Williams, Edgar. "Comeback Jim Konstanty." *Baseball Digest*, September 1955.

Woolley, Edward Mott. "The Business of Baseball." *McClure's Magazine*, July 1912.

INTERVIEWS

Abrams, Cal. SABR Oral History Collection, n.d.

Brown, Tommy. Interview by Al Quimby. SABR Oral History Collection, October 10, 1994.

Church, Bubba. Interview by Rick Bradley. SABR Oral History Collection, December 5, 1995.

Ennis, Del. Interview by C. Paul Rogers. Audio, August 8, 1993. C. Paul Rogers collection.

Lopata, Stan. Interview by Rick Bradley. SABR Oral History Collection, March 22, 1994.

McDonnell, Maje. Interview by C. Paul Rogers. Audio, August 9, 1993. C. Paul Rogers collection.

Sisler, Dick. Interview by Brent Kelley. SABR Oral History Collection, June 29, 1992.

GUIDES

1877 Constitution and Playing Rules of the National League of Professional Baseball Clubs.

Spalding's Official Football Guide, 1937.

1943 Baseball Guide and Record Book. A. S. Barnes.

1944 Baseball Guide and Record Book. A. S. Barnes.

1951 Official Baseball Guide and Record Book.

1952 Official Baseball Guide and Record Book.

1953 Official Baseball Guide and Record Book.

OTHER DOCUMENTS

Malcolm Poindexter, Jr. v. Granville Hamner, file 1139. E.D. Penn (1950).

Pappas, Doug. "Team Profits and Selected Payrolls." SABR Business of Baseball Committee.

Philadelphia National League Club General Ledger and Accounts Payable. November 1, 1949, to October 31, 1952. In the author's collection.

Subcommittee on Study of Monopoly Power of the Committee on the Judiciary, *Organized Baseball.* 82nd Cong. (May 27, 1952). https://search.law.villanova.edu /Record/232386.

Weegham v. Killefer. 215 F. 168 (W.D. Mich. 1914).

INDEX

Aaron, Henry, 97, 186, 262n78
Abrams, Cal, 126, 131–32, 133, 134, 248n12
Adams, Bobby, 258n40
Adams, Buster, 21, 27, 36
Adcock, Joe, 252n54
Albright, Joe, 37
Alexander, Babe, 62, 72, 97, 156
Alexander, Grover Cleveland, 11, 12, 14, 199, 224n73; health of, 144; playing record of, 12–13, 193; relationship of, with William Baker, 13; speaks in Springfield, 42, 144, 230n48, 230n50; trade of, to Chicago Cubs 13–14; and World Series (1950), 143–44;
All-Star Game, Major League (1950), 102, 103–4
Allen, Dick, 197, 210, 264n44, 264n45
Allen, Johnny, 17, 19
Alley, Gene, 201
Anderson, George "Sparky," 190, 262n117
Anderson, Harry, 188, 190
Anson, Adrian "Cap," 4
Appling, Luke, 232n4
Ashburn, Bob, 28, 227n76
Ashburn, Donna, 28
Ashburn, Genevieve, 68, 211, 212
Ashburn, Neil, 28, 68
Ashburn, Richie, 79, 87, 108, 151, 187, 202, 243n52, 246n5; and Alice Roth foul ball incident, 260n96; All-Star

Game, 53, 173, 210; attitude of, 29, 55, 58, 71–72, 81, 83, 86; broadcast career of, 207, 210, 211; death of, 211; defensive play of, 83, 92, 101, 131, 180, 258n43; in Esquire Game, 29; on firing of Eddie Sawyer, 172; and Hall of Fame, 211, 267n26, 267n30; illegal signings of, 28, 29; and New York Mets, 210; offense of, 53, 55, 87, 94, 107, 189, 190; and pennant-clinching game vs. Dodgers, 131–32, 248n12; retirement of 210–11, 267n26; scouts and, 29; and Spring Training (1950) vs. Ed Sanicki, 82–84, 85–86, 87; trade of, to Chicago Cubs, 191; and Whiz Kids Reunion, 262n19; and World Series (1950), 139, 141, 143, 148
Athletics (American Association), 5, 7, 220n22, 220n23
Athletics (National Association), 4, 5, 220n17
Athletics (National League), 5
Athletics (Original), 2, 3, 219n5
Atlantics (Brooklyn), 2, 3

Bacharach Giants, 14
Bacon, Walter, 50
Bagby, Jim, Sr., 85
Baker Bowl, abandonment by Phillies 16; collapse of stands 14; condition of 15; and 1915 World Series 12
Baker, Del, 80